Remote Places, Public Spaces

The Story of Creative Works with Ten Small Communities

Edited by

Davide Fassi and
Annalinda De Rosa,
Politecnico di Milano, Milan

Inge Eller,
Cité du design – ESADSE,
Saint-Étienne

Michael Dumiak

Human Cities

Birkhäuser
Basel

Introduction

Davide Fassi,
Annalinda De Rosa,
Inge Eller,
and Michael Dumiak

In the 21st century, cities face rapid urbanisation, economic and cultural globalisation, and environmental crises. During these last few decades, cities have forgotten citizens' crucial needs in their race for progress, development, and inter-city competition to attract investments. They have forgotten that they are made for people, not cars. Urbanisation gained ground and changed landscapes and how people live, work, and spend their leisure time. However, the COVID-19 pandemic has increased interest in rural areas in many European countries. The concept of working has changed a great deal, as new technologies can be accessed everywhere. It has suddenly become easier for people to be digital nomads while living in prime residential areas, which are less accessible but allow people to live affordably and reconnect with nature. The Human Cities/SMOTIES project was designed before the pandemic and started just after the first lockdown. SMOTIES highlighted the creativity of small and remote European places.

The Human Cities concept is universal, and for us it began taking shape in 2006 as a platform for interdisciplinary exchange to examine the liveability of public spaces by using participatory design to feed into processes and innovation. Four main projects have been undertaken over the years, involving different partners and topics, but with a common denominator: designing public spaces with people in mind. This has helped to consolidate the approach and created opportunities for several cities to implement innovative artistic and design projects, develop network-building capacity, and diffuse cultural values.

The platform started with its Celebrating Public Space project (2008-2010), funded by the European Union's Culture programme. The project examined how design theory and practice could conceptualise and generate viable solutions to establish unprecedented forms of community and public spaces in cities. The inaugural Human Cities Festival, Celebrating Public Space, held in May 2010 in Brussels, was an international symposium that featured an exhibition called Places to Be, which presented the outcomes of various activities carried out in cities as part of the project and issued an international call for ideas. This effort led to subsequent projects, underpinned by a robust theoretical framework to enhance people's active engagement.

The Reclaiming Public Space project (2010-2012) focused on grassroots initiatives of non-institutional actors such as citizens, artists, and associations. These initiatives aimed to shift the configuration and ownership of public spaces. These creative, human-centred endeavours, contributing to diverse forms of urban investment, sought to harmonise two facets of the public space concept: the political – as a forum for exchange and participation – and the tangible – as an inclusive space. The Human Cities Festival's Reclaiming Public Space took place in Brussels in March 2012, accompanied by a symposium known as the Civil Society Reclaims Public Space: Cross Perspectives Based on Research. This initiative aimed to promote active engagement and participation among people through a human-centred and participatory design approach, exploring and experimenting with the desire to reclaim public spaces.

Challenging the City Scale (2014-2018) was an interdisciplinary project co-funded by the European Union's Creative Europe Programme. That initiative transformed contemporary cities, mainly focusing on how residents reinvent urban spaces through various experiments. The project engaged with diverse locales, such as vacant spaces, shops, public squares, parks, and streets in towns and cities. Since it aimed to work with inhabitants to improve their urban living environment, its research and activities relied on the contribution of other disciplines: architecture and urban planning, social sciences (sociology, economics), arts (theatre, street art, performance), education (formal and informal), and technology (modelling, makers' hubs). The lessons fed into the project's approach based on experiments, research, and practice. We concluded that public space was clearly no longer a field exclusive to specialists. Rather, in many European cities, it is subject to debate among citizens. In such debates, designers and architects often act as empathic mediators. Over four years, the project has seen countless activities and outputs: an investigation, co-creative sessions, experiments, international workshops and conferences, master classes, exhibitions, digital catalogues, videos, a website, publications, and a book, *Challenging the City Scale: Journeys in People-Centred Design*.

When applying for the Creative Europe funding in 2019, the partners decided to add a new challenge to the network to get out of what became a comfort zone, namely the urban context, and apply the expertise, approach and methodologies developed throughout the years to small and remote places. The project SMOTIES: Creative Works with Small and Remote Places (2020-2024) was carried out in ten small and remote European places that are depopulated, relationally remote depositories of material and immaterial culture at risk of not being sufficiently valued, consolidated, and handed down, and can therefore be lost. The goal is to allow these places to benefit from the cultural and creative works developed in public spaces by the ten project partners, known as nodes of creativity, through a shared methodology (based on design thinking and future studies). The four-year activities engage local communities to build its audience, facilitate out-of-country travel among creative professionals, develop master classes and educational training, and evaluate the project's impact to create a long-term legacy in the places involved.

The ten nodes of creativity (partners) include public institutions, design centres, creative agencies, national associations, and research centres located in ten European cities: Milan, London, Reykjavik, Tallinn, Ljubljana, Funchal, Saint-Étienne, Graz, Cieszyn, and Ermoupoli. They were chosen because of their particularity of position, cultural uniqueness, development potential, and consolidated role in their creative sector. They are not "small and remote places" but leading players in their national context as interlocutors, activators, and supporters of creative works to be anchored in public spaces in a selected small and remote place in their country.

SMOTIES deals with issues linked to the complex situation of far-flung places in Europe: small and remote places and inner areas suffer from "relational remoteness" because there is little knowledge-exchange impact regarding socio-economic, creative, and political innovation. Remoteness is not necessarily defined by geographical location – since mobility, in principle, transcends space – but by poor connections. Some urban settlements have experienced a population decline in recent years in areas far from and close to acknowledged centres, i.e. city suburbs.

The outcomes of this project aim to create a legacy for the places where they are based, and to address future development in terms of participatory and relational place-based potentials, supporting more systemic and just social innovation. Over the past four years, therefore, SMOTIES developed a toolbox, including a method to frame the design of public spaces in small and remote places and a publication with 50 best practices from Europe. This publication sums up the outcomes of more than 60 meetings with locals, 30 training sessions and master classes, 30 prototyping studios to test the results in the field, and 60 travelling talks which, in addition to a website and social media, disseminated the project to others.

The book's three parts will explore the approaches, engagement, outputs and legacy of SMOTIES.

Part 1 gathers ten stories taken from a variety of narrative perspectives and at different points in SMOTIES project development: some were close to finishing, others recalibrating, still others were closer to the beginning. Taken together they are meant to illuminate the many aspects of collaborative design pursued by the partners in the SMOTIES initiative. These voices from the territories are presented from the point of view of a design and culture reporter and editor who, during a year-long journey through ten European countries, visited all the small and remote villages chosen by project partners. The stories draw on interviews with residents and members of associations active in these areas; these sketches are an effort to understand what makes these places so vivid and unique and reflect what brings them together.

Part 2 is devoted to the experience and cooperation among partners and local stakeholders. They shared, compared, analysed and developed various methods and tools. Through conversations with the players involved, this section examines how these areas have been approached, with their strengths and challenges, how the residents and associations were engaged in this creative process, how different tools and instruments were implemented, succeeding in bringing out new ideas for reinventing public space, imagining solutions for the inhabitants with the inhabitants of these areas far from the big cities.

Part 3 uses an academic approach to analyse the work completed over the four-year project. The researchers' final scientific reflections on the research topics include a study on power relations in participatory design practices, participatory purposes, the social impact of design in remote areas, a reflection on case studies around the world, methods for prototyping public space, and design-driven processes of ethnographic research in territories.

These threads (concepts) underlie SMOTIES to stimulate experts, researchers, creative people, policymakers in the future beyond SMOTIES.

Celebrating Public Space (2008-2010)

Partners involved in this initiative led by Institut supérieur d'Architecture de la Communauté française de Belgique La Cambre [BE], Pro Materia [BE], The Lighthouse [UK], Politecnico di Milano [IT], Urban Planning Institute volunteered geography as a driver of the Republic of Slovenia [SI], with the expertise of Culture Lab [BE] and in collaboration with Cité du design – ESADSE, Saint-Étienne [FR].

Reclaiming Public Space (2010-2012)

Partners involved in the project led by ULB-Faculté d'Architecture La Cambre-Horta [BE], Pro Materia [BE], Cité du design – ESADSE, Saint-Étienne [FR], Politecnico di Milano [IT], Urban Planning Institute of the Republic of Slovenia [SI], Strategic Design Scenarios [BE], Time Circus [BE], and Clear Village [UK].

Challenging the City Scale (2014-2018)

Partners involved in the project led by Cité du design – ESADSE, Saint-Étienne [FR], Politecnico di Milano [IT], Urban Planning Institute of the Republic of Slovenia [SI], Clear Village [UK], Zamek Cieszyn [PL], Association Design Week Belgrade [RS], Pro Materia [BE], Aalto University [FI], FH Joanneum, University of Applied Sciences [AT], Estonian Association of Designers [EE], Bilbao-Bizkaia Design & Creativity Council – BEAZ [ES], and with expertise of Culture Lab [BE].

SMOTIES: Creative Works with Small and Remote Places (2020-2024)

Partners involved in the project led by Politecnico di Milano [IT], Zamek Cieszyn [PL], FH Joanneum, University of Applied Sciences [AT], Urban Planning Institute of the Republic of Slovenia [SI], Clear Village [UK], Cité du design – ESADSE, Saint-Étienne [FR], Estonian Association of Designers [EE], University of the Aegean [GR], Universidade da Madeira [PT], Alternance slf [IS].

Part 1.

Edited by Michael Dumiak

Village Voices

Paths of Desire

Michael Dumiak

The first conceit in the late Douglas Adams' satirical sci-fi romp *The Hitchhiker's Guide to the Galaxy* involves the protagonist lying down in front of a bulldozer about to destroy his house in order to pave a bypass road.

The twist is that the hero is being unreasonable here because everything had been done by the book. Public viewing of the work order had been made available, more or less, with no objections having been raised, though of course our hero, Arthur Dent, had been spectacularly unaware of the proceedings. The even bigger picture is that the Vogon aliens are moments away from destroying the Earth in the same way, for the same reasons: the planning had been planned, and the Earth needed to be reshaped in the name of progress.

It may be a stretch (but not a complete stretch) to say this is one kind of experience the public has with the creation of public space. We are busy going about our actual lives and then the space around us changes, and we don't know why; and we might have had some input had we the wherewithal, or had we understood earlier. The bus stop is either there, and not here; or here, and not there; or it is not at all there. We either don't know why, or accept it because it has always been so.

For the past four years – and that means through the awful heights of the COVID-19 pandemic, an experience that profoundly disoriented daily life – designers, small nonprofits, artists, academics, architects, students, and residents engaged with one another to concentrate on the wants, needs, and expectations for making use of public spaces in a set of small and remote places across the European continent.

A central goal of SMOTIES is to transform remote places into more liveable spaces by involving local residents in the development of cultural and creative activities. SMOTIES is a play on "cities" and "small and remote places". But SMOTIES are not cities at all: one village featured here has 23 residents. Another may have fewer than that, depending on time of year.

These are the sorts of places that designers, architects, civic administrations – and culture creators – tend to overlook. Or frame as places to fret over, and to treat as politically troubling. Or to leave. Being humble, and finding ways to engage a remote place on its own terms and over a long time, is often left out of this perspective.

Each of the places described in the coming pages are absolutely specific: each has unique circumstances, history, language, culture, dynamics, and shape. They are places of their own time and space. Seen together, though, they project a rich picture of the accelerating forces impacting contemporary rural living. This may be in small or picayune ways. But small ways are the stuff of daily lived experiences.

Sometimes they reveal different facets of the same challenge. In Oberzeiring, Austria, there is the issue of the small paved-over village square, and what to do about the bus that pulls through it; and in the French countryside near Saint-Étienne, the issue is how to influence and change mobility methods when the car is used for everything, even driving children 300 metres down the road.

What you're about to read, presented in three parts, are three ways of understanding and exploring what designers and residents, together, might imagine, why they might want to do so, and how.

The first part tells stories of these initiatives as they are in action: that is, operating in their local context. The second part reflects the perspective of the designers and what they've observed and learned. The final piece is a survey of peer-reviewed academic reports or investigations by designers presenting some of the findings they gathered over the course of the SMOTIES initiative.

What kind of public spaces do we have in remote areas? How can they be created cooperatively? How can they be created with the participation of not only local residents, but also people who work in the cultural sector? The stories these pages tell are meant to show the possibilities when designers – of all varieties – either actively choose or get an opportunity to work in rural settings, in small and remote places.

As we start off, a small shopfront on a street corner in a Welsh village is falling apart on the inside. A community outreach person for a Welsh power utility, village residents, and SMOTIES partners come together to restore and reopen it as a gallery. But it is not just a place to show and sell things. One summer weekend, there's a local conservationist and peat expert showing samples in the room. Up the hill from the village, it turns out, work is ongoing to improve conditions for healthy peat – fields of organic soil that may wind up as a carbon sink, absorbing and trapping greenhouse gases. On another weekend, a local archaeologist engages people coming through the door with ancient finds.

The gallery aspires to be a point of connection for local culture. This corner space is also a nice point from which to continue building connections.

It's not clear right now if this is sustainable. Will it be there five years from now? It could depend wholly on the property owner. But applying art and design creatively to programming in response to local expressions of wants and needs can help to make a stronger case for it. Applying a rigorous practice of visualising what this could look like from the beginning, as through windows on the future, can boost the chances of success. This is what the SMOTIES partner network did along the way with its project development. That does not mean certainty, but it does increase the likelihood of really reaching people where they live. This is a pressing need.

In rural France six percent of people go to work on foot; two percent by bicycle; two percent by public transport. Ninety percent go by car. As SMOTIES partners talked with residents in the rural Dorlay River Valley, mobility came up again and again as a vital concern.

The partners organised an event and found expression of this in designing shoelaces (Dorlay was once a textile centre). They are a graphic representation of the state of transport as it now stands.

This doesn't solve the mobility issue, but it is a marker for local residents to reflect (and reflect upon) what is a vexing, volatile, and sometimes caricatured everyday need, one that can prompt eruptions in protest. Climate change is an anxiety in the countryside, too. Highly visible standard-bearers of rural economies and rural culture – farmers – are under intense pressure, as European capitals were reminded through 2023 and 2024 when protesters in tractors and trucks turned up and blockaded roads in angry thousands.

In fact an array of seemingly urban themes are very much seen in small and remote places: the changing climate, mobility and ageing, housing concerns, income inequality, and gentrification. The spaces are different; so is the context.

But all of the small and remote places in this publication have been thoroughly upended by shocks to their local economies and services. It could be the slate quarry that's gone, or the textile mills, or the paper factory, or the transport routes. The schools have shut. The local shops have been gone for years. And all are in places of natural beauty.

Picking up where it left off previous to the COVID-19 pandemic, the rapid evolution of remote working is also wreaking change. Technology is a rushing current in remote places: if it is possible to make a money-spinner out of overnight rents for rooms booked online, it changes things. Tourism changes things. Nobody wants to be just a scenic backdrop and service provider for holidaymakers. But it is unclear what incentives can compete with it.

One goal of SMOTIES is to reach a place where it's possible to be creative, together. This comes in many guises and not just in making objects. SMOTIES partners strove to be creative in finding ways to engage residents as well as in the experiments and cultural actions they took. This could be delightful. Contrasting. Challenging. Distinctive. Thought-provoking.

Each SMOTIES effort evolved through steps. First was to find promising locations that met a specific set of circumstances to be considered remote. As the project developed, partners would meet and engage with residents, organise specific kinds of events together (gathering to talk and tell stories in specific sites, making maps with local narratives, creating together). One team went so far as to put on a cake-baking competition to draw out residents.

There's an expression in Costa Rica (and probably elsewhere) that to be a village you only need four things: a school, a bar, a football pitch, and a church. It's lighthearted – but there's something to it. One thing that developed in the SMOTIES work is that often a church became a principal element for connecting communities. Not always. It is an institution that can be viewed with scepticism in some quarters. But it very often still carries weight. And has community space.

The SMOTIES work involves civics – mayors and planning commissions – and it meant having to negotiate among well-intentioned but competing interests and finding knowledgeable, compelling, and dedicated voices.

The stories that people know and tell can enhance (or obscure) the identity of a place. In the Italian Piedmont, the Politecnico di Milano used audio narrative to light up hidden landscapes freighted with meaning, recording little stories or moments tied to everyday locations the residents would offer. Exploring oral history helped some of the SMOTIES partners connect with residents and understand the present. Developing those stories can be effective if listened to. The Bobrek housing estate in Poland, for instance, was built over what once was a village that was then repurposed – somewhat similar to Arthur Dent's house in *Hitchhiker's Guide*. There are people on the estate who know about this, and it might have something to do with their sceptical attitude towards development.

There's a concept in design, especially in landscape design, described as the 'path of desire'. This is the informal path worn into grass that people take instead of the wayfinding that planners mean for them to. It might be a better outcome if, in collaborating with pedestrians, a path of desire and a planned path were made to be similar or the same. But this is often easier said than done.

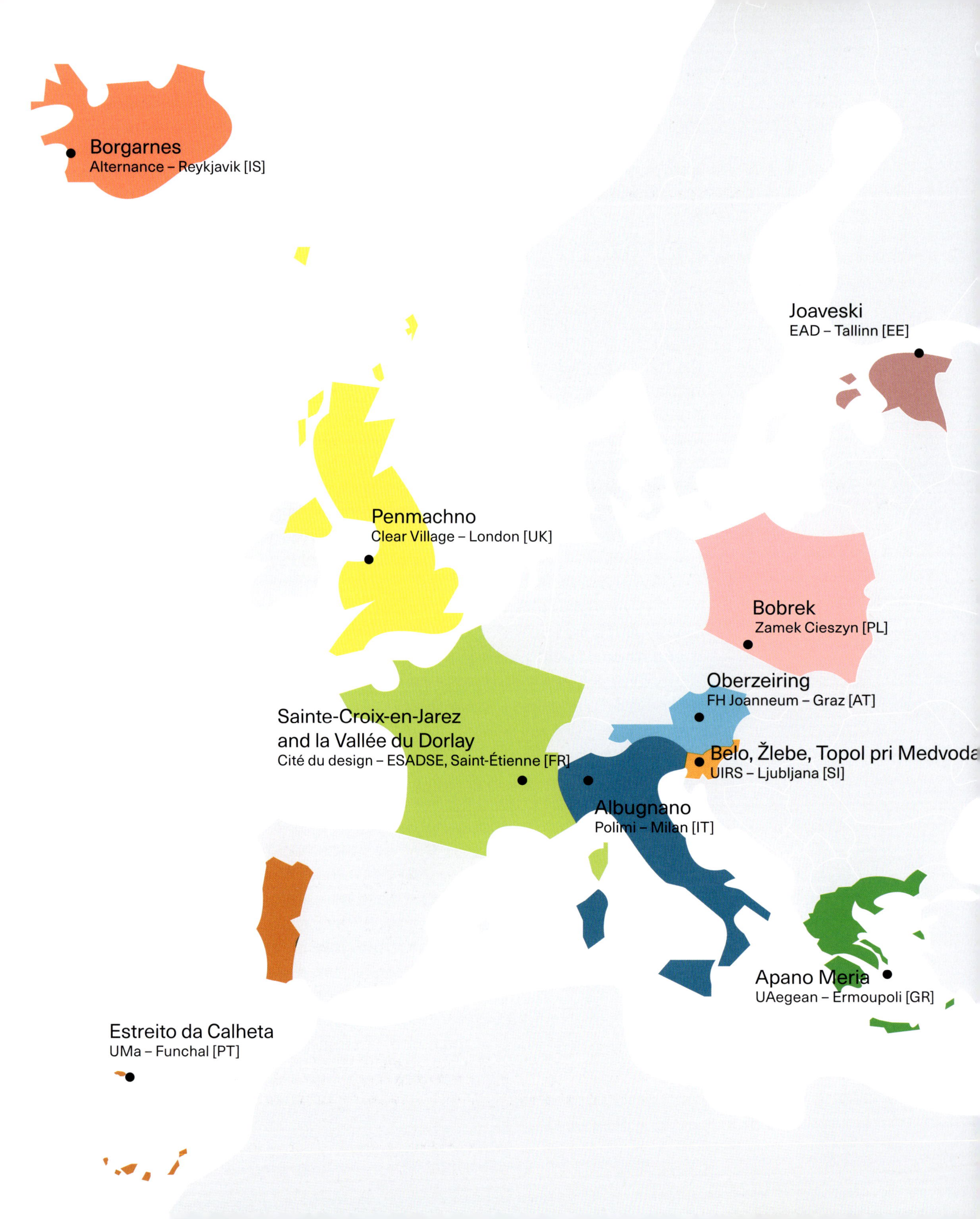

Borgarnes
Alternance – Reykjavik [IS]
Joaveski
EAD – Tallinn [EE]
Penmachno
Clear Village – London [UK]
Bobrek
Zamek Cieszyn [PL]
Oberzeiring
FH Joanneum – Graz [AT]
Sainte-Croix-en-Jarez
and la Vallée du Dorlay
Cité du design – ESADSE, Saint-Étienne [FR]
Belo, Žlebe, Topol pri Medvoda
UIRS – Ljubljana [SI]
Albugnano
Polimi – Milan [IT]
Apano Meria
UAegean – Ermoupoli [GR]
Estreito da Calheta
UMa – Funchal [PT]

“O holl bentrefi Cymru
Y gorau gennyf i
Yw pentref bach Penmachno
Ar lan y ddisglair li”

“Of all of Wales’s places
My favourite is by far
Penmachno by the river
That flows and shines like stars”
Short poem in Welsh,
attributed to Gwynfor Griffiths
of Penmachno

Clear Village Trustee Limited, London [UK]

Location:
Penmachno, Wales

Penmachno is a village on the edge of rugged moorland in a river valley of great natural beauty. It was once home to workers in the large slate quarries that shuttered in the early 1960s. The valley is the birthplace of the modern Welsh written language; it is a tourist destination for hikers and adventure seekers and, as major cities like London and Birmingham become unaffordable, is even becoming a commuter base.

SMOTIES Partner: Clear Village Trustee Limited, London

Clear Village is a small nonprofit cultural agency based in London, United Kingdom, led by the futurist Thomas Ermacora. It last worked with the Human Cities initiative in London, where the group helped organise the 'Maker Mile', a loose (and temporary) network connecting traditional and new maker enterprises in the East End. Clear Village uses art, craft, and design as tools to empower and connect communities.

Penmachno

Key involvement in project

Clear Village:
Kristin Luke, artist, Penmachno resident; Josie King, designer and design researcher; Frank van Hasselt, chief executive; Rhodri Owen, artist, furniture maker, resident, Ysbyty Ifan.

Sian Rhun, Hwb Penmachno; Mark Gahan, Rural Futures.

What they set out to do

By working with a local steering group, to build programmes of activities and exhibitions in a renovated village space and link these to a new community hub currently in development; to create a venue for creative locals celebrating and promoting their products.

What the project accomplished

Helped map the cultural history of the valley, drawing on oral narratives and interviews; set up creative workshops for all age groups; brought art, books and discussion over the rural roads to communities in a Vauxhall van; instigated the launch of Oriel Machno, a small cultural space on Penmachno's primary street corner; set up a digital fabrication suite in a new community centre.

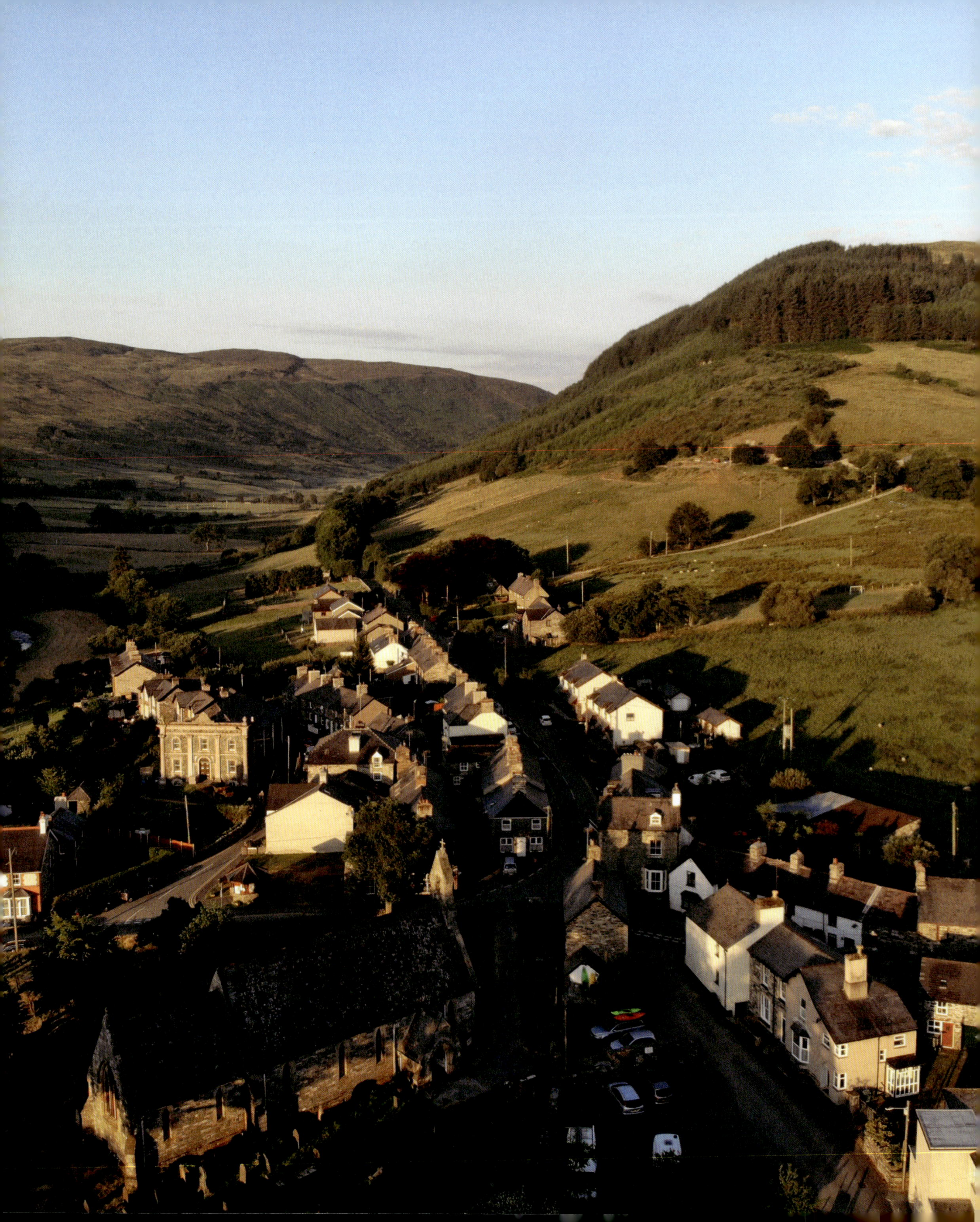

Lifting Stones

Sian Rhun's father is a lifelong builder. When she takes her children down one of the roads in the village of Penmachno, in northern Wales, she points and tells them: "Ah! Your grandad's built this." Rhun makes the point that the houses he worked on are all stone builds.

She puts perfect lamb roast on the dinner table, a spontaneous and cosy invitation on a summer night. The lamb came from up the hill; it's a place in view from Sian's kitchen. Her kids, shy, mischievous, laughing, dig in. They speak Welsh. They knew that lamb by name.

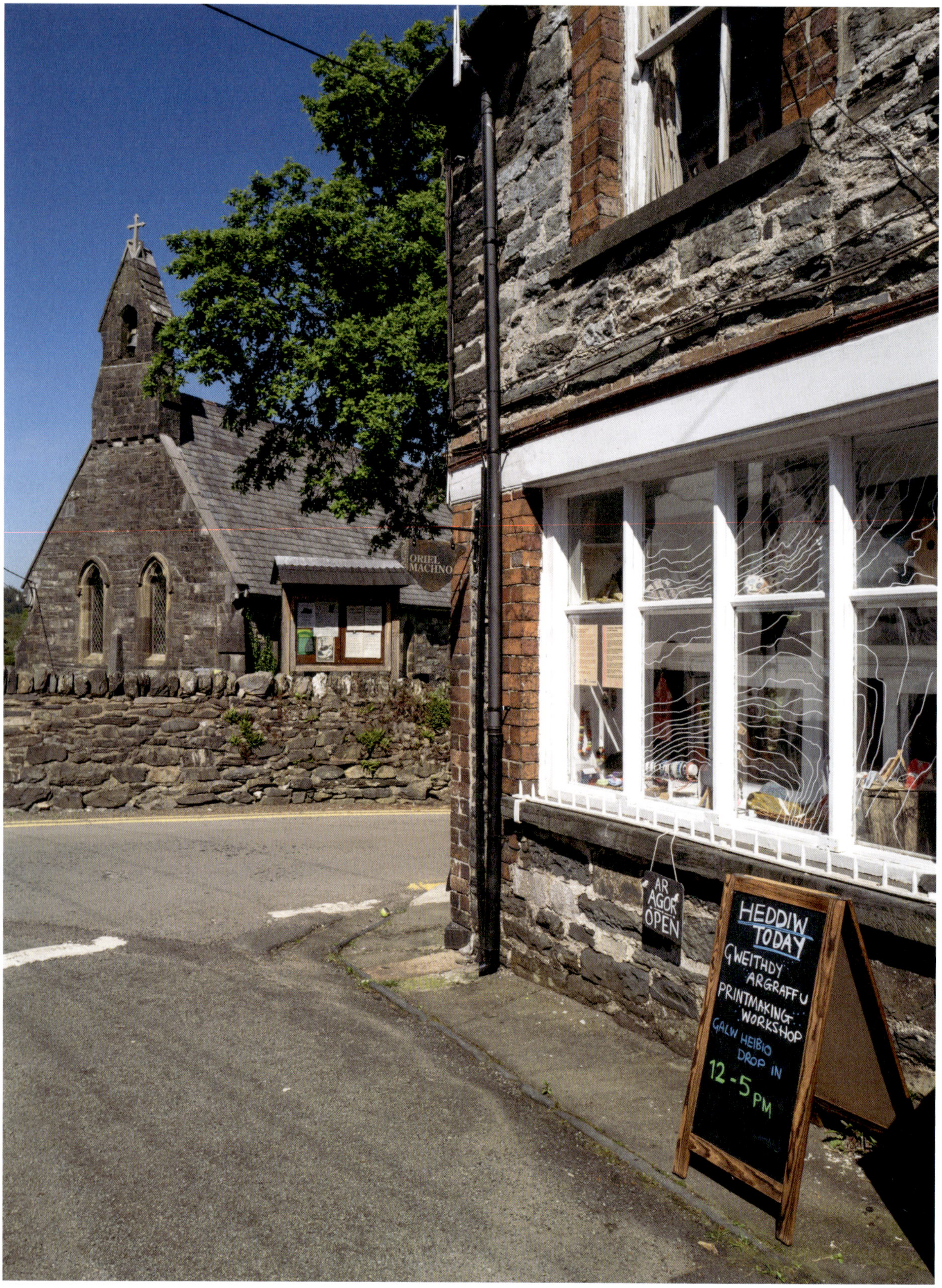

P.20: Village of Penmachno, North Wales. © Wikipedia / Allatseanow

Left: Oriel Machno, corner of High Street and Llewelyn, Penmachno, Wales. © Mark McNulty

This may seem farm-to-table and throwback, rustic, charming, and, in many ways, it is (Rhun and her family are extremely charming). But Penmachno is not a postcard, and its future, as is the future of so many similarly small and remote places around Europe, is up in the air.

Signs are there, directions uncertain. After years without, the tiny village now has a shop: on the shelves are staples, wine, fruit and veg, and it is run cheerfully and well by a closeknit South Asian family. There's a pub quiz on next door. The owner of The Eagles cooks on weekend evenings. On this evening, a Dutchman and his two teen sons are staying up in the bunkhouse above, ready for a few days' hiking.

But for some time it's been hard for young people to stay here for long.

One day in 2018 a note got pinned to the hexagonal gazebo across from the stone wall of the slate cemetery, launching a village survey. It came from a brightly named effort – Rural Futures – run by a local power utility and funded via the National Lottery. It reached Kristin Luke, an American fine artist, recently arrived resident, and a member of Clear Village, a London cultural nonprofit. And that is what eventually led to the window displays in the now newly renovated one-room corner space down the road from the gazebo: Oriel Machno, which in Welsh means Machno Gallery, after the river that runs under the bridge to Sian Rhun's house.

It is not an art gallery, though there is art there.

On a summer day, Oriel Machno's picture window shelves show contemporary knits, jewellery from the valley; graphics and drawings on postcards from local printmakers. Next week, this room will be filled with samples of water-logged peat brought down from the high blanket bogs stretching out vast on the other side of the moorland above the village. In previous weeks Penmachno residents gathered here to share mementos: images of country-fair games and kids dressed as Rubik's Cubes or sporting polyester scarves from the '80s ska-pop sensation Madness.

Until recently the building that now houses Oriel Machno was crumbling inside, a place for dust motes and a cast-off analogue film enlarger sitting abandoned. It was bereft as the closed-down quarry on the other end of the valley that used to employ so many here, putting food on the table with work that was durable but otherwise clanky, dusty, cold, long, and hard.

Luke and her Clear Village colleagues got involved in bringing Oriel Machno to being because the village had reached a point where it was asking what happens next.

The pinned gazebo note from Rural Futures came courtesy of community organiser Mark Gahan of Severn Wye Energy.

Gahan canvassed the area even as the COVID-19 pandemic wore on, month after month. The idea was to engage with rural residents in tackling rural economic and social issues and build more stable and sustainable living environments – to repair and keep the rural social fabric viable and intact (and, presumably, to keep Severn energy flowing). Gahan dropped mailers into home letterboxes.

The surveys asked villagers what they wanted to see, today and in decades to come; Luke spotted him working in ad hoc conditions in the tumbledown abandoned photoprint space on Llewelyn Street. Gahan's efforts drew a crowd in social halls and rundown spaces through the valley, and varying responses: curiosity, apathy, enthusiasm.

Some embraced the idea of rural futures. Others were sceptical about the financial grant sources and wondered if the proposals would contribute to the displacement of longtime residents. In doing so they raised a current concern expressed many times to SMOTIES team members: this is, often, a rural echo of urban anxiety over gentrification.

Gahan's questions touch directly on the fault lines and sore nerves running through rural and isolated communities, where, at least in the UK, disquiet lingers over federalism, and land, and Brexit, and history, and scarce housing, and rural hollowing-out. The nerves

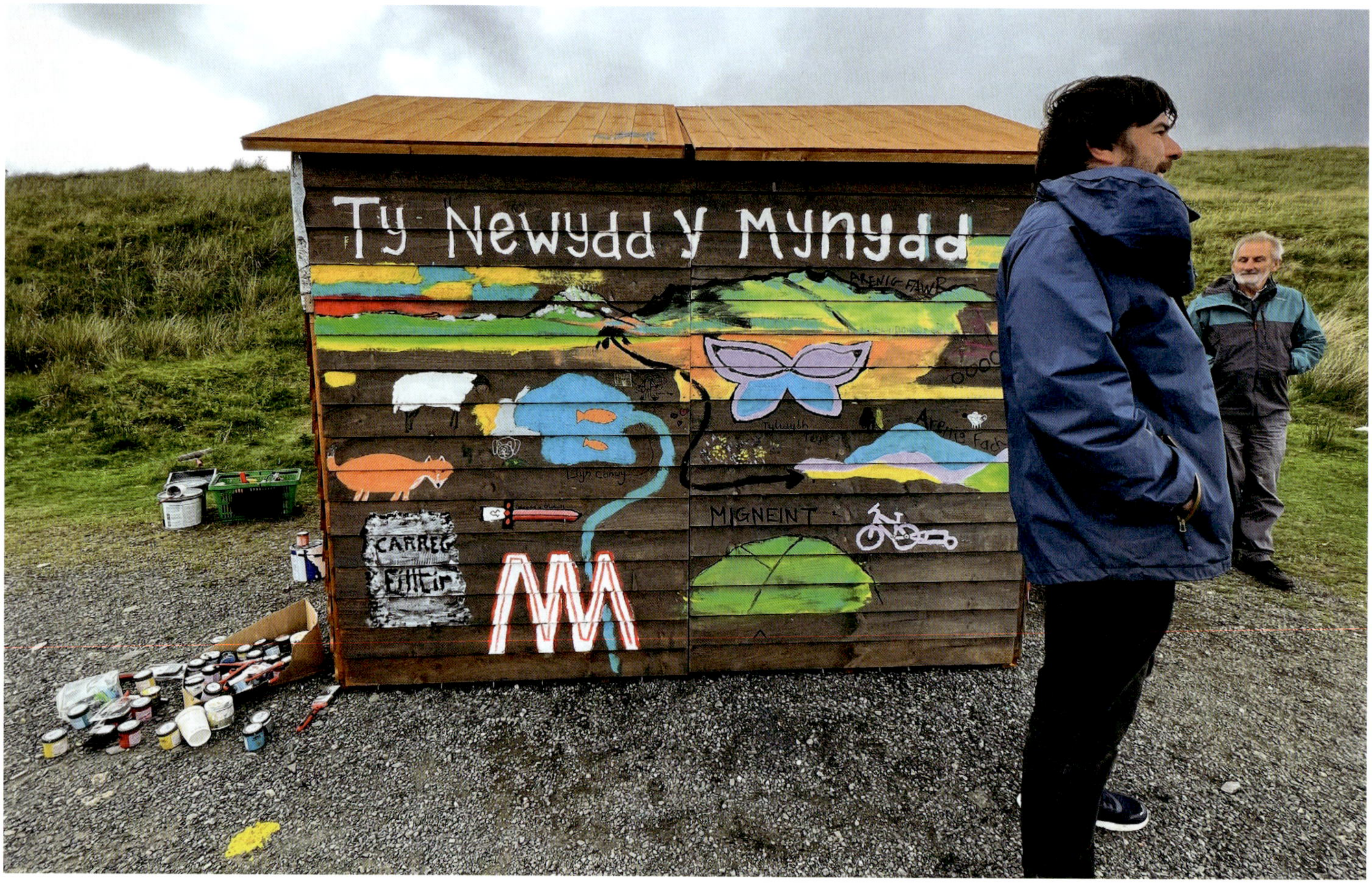

fan out more broadly – touching what it is to make a place, how it will be viable for those who live there, and in the end who will be able to live there.

How do intentions take shape, where are they coming from, who controls them, and how are they given a voice?

Kristin Luke came up to Gahan after a Rural Futures meeting in an old Penmachno schoolhouse, at that point a building in need of new uses and top-to-bottom renovation. She asked him about the room he had been working in on the corner road. That's how she got to know Lindsey and Peter Haveland, who own the space that would become Oriel Machno. It's the Havelands who ran the enlarger.

Luke and Sian Rhun (the farm-to-table cook) organised volunteer labour and sweat equity to clean up and repair the store space; for that, the Havelands traded five years' open play for Oriel Machno at cost.

The threads run further: Rhun, whose family tree has been firmly rooted in the Machno valley for generations, worked with Gahan for grants to start renovating the former schoolhouse.

In April 2024 the now-renovated schoolhouse opened as the Penmachno *hwb*, a community centre with a small studio space for workshops and craft and more broadly as a common space. "The thing that comes up again and again is a gym," Rhun says. "It wouldn't be my first choice to put there, but you have to listen to what everyone else wants. It'll get people out of the house and socialising, and to be active." It has already been used for private parties, a youth club, a home schooling group, and craft events. There are plans in the pipeline to book a few pop-up catering evenings. Bingo could be in the picture. "Bingo is a surprising hit. People love bingo."

Left: Prints on the mountain: Rhodri Owen stands by an installation invoking Welsh texts and myth on the high road between Penmachno and Ysbyty Ifan, a nearby village.

Owen helped organise the core team of dedicated local volunteers that keep Oriel Machno open to the public. Most of the volunteers contribute their crafts to stock the window displays. © Michael Dumiak

Right: Community mapping workshop working with the Risograph, Capel Garmon. © Kristin Luke

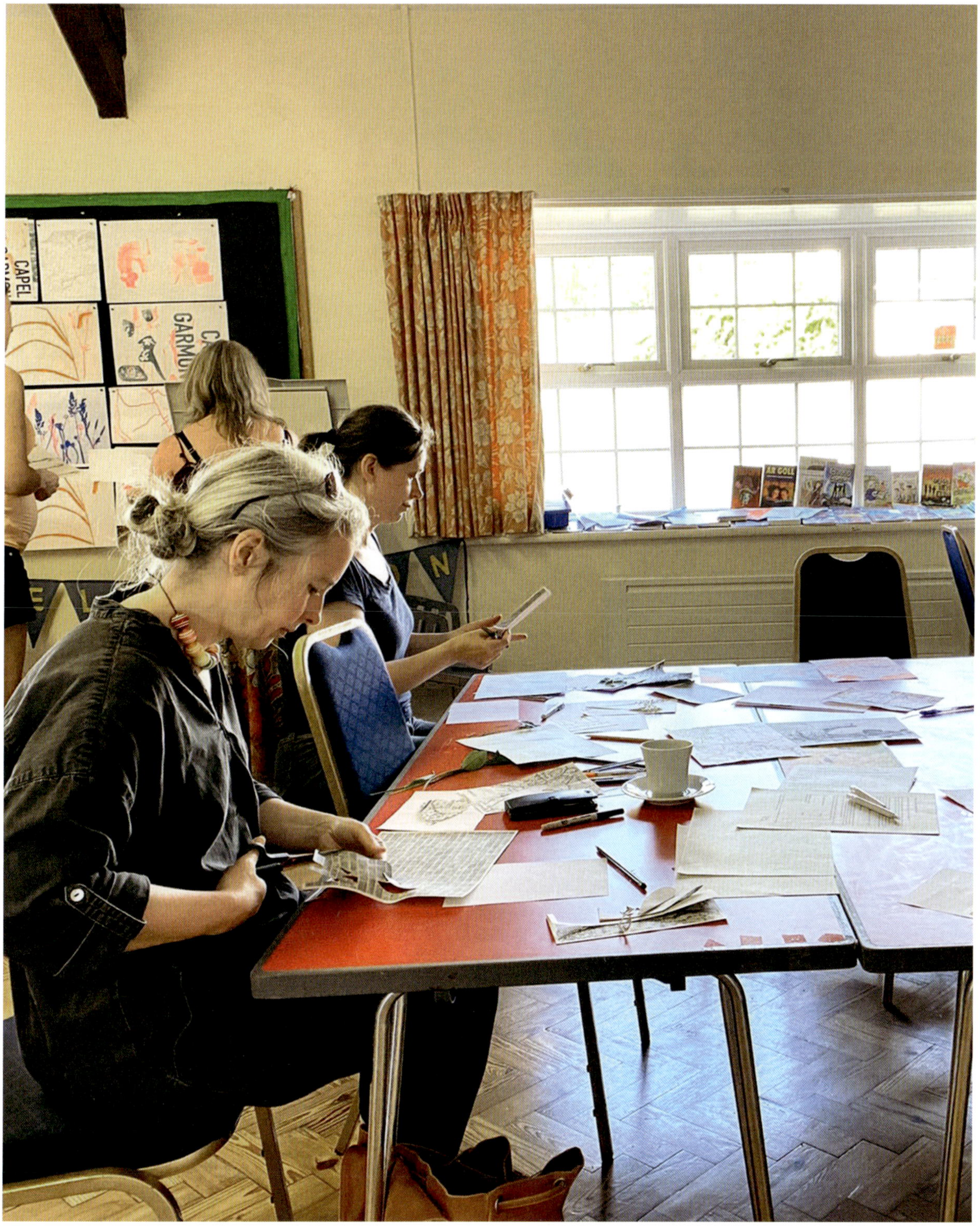

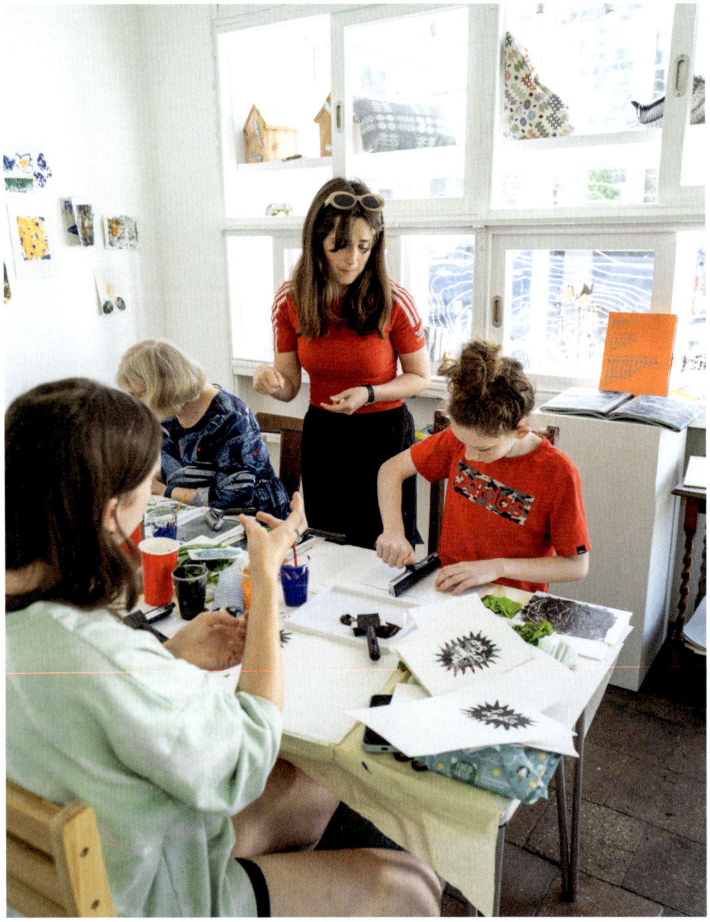

Left: Printmakers in session: a workshop at Oriel Machno. © Mark McNulty

Right: Three-colour flair and local talent: results of a Risograph workshop, Capel Garmon. © Kristin Luke

Other hwbs are in the making: up the road is Pentredwr, where shearers are trying to create markets for low-grade mountain sheep wool, an alternative to more commodity fleece which is only profitable at scale (a scale, presumably, beyond what Welsh sheep and farmland can sustain).

With every day registering concern over long-term climate change, the UK National Trust – which manages 46,000 hectares of Welsh farmland dotted with sheep – is promoting what it calls nature-friendly farming practices. Will Bigwood, who's just taken a National Trust tenancy at Foel Farm at the top of the valley overlooking Penmachno, says that means rethinking – and re-designing – the land he'll graze his livestock on. Bigwood comes from a Welsh farming family and studied as a conservationist. He'll be living out some of those concepts through the winter as some of his landscaping takes hold, changing the way the water flows through the ground on Foel Farm. With care it should encourage better development of peat, which can act as a carbon sink.

This is a wrenching time to be a farmer. Postwar Britain encouraged – and needed – high production farming, which included grazing on low-use peatland. Changing directions, however, could make tenuous Welsh farm economics even more dicey. Doing so is very unpopular in some places. Bigwood is partner to Bethan Jones, an archaeologist for Gwynedd county. Like her, Bigwood has set up special greeting days at the Oriel Machno space. This social connecting is part of his job now. And at the Eagles pub across the street, the barkeeper grins and lets slide that he took part in a big tree-planting that Bigwood organised.

Little works like these – they reverberate. Gahan and Luke collected stories for an interactive map of the valley. Josie King, another Clear Villager, has come up from her studies in London to build out community

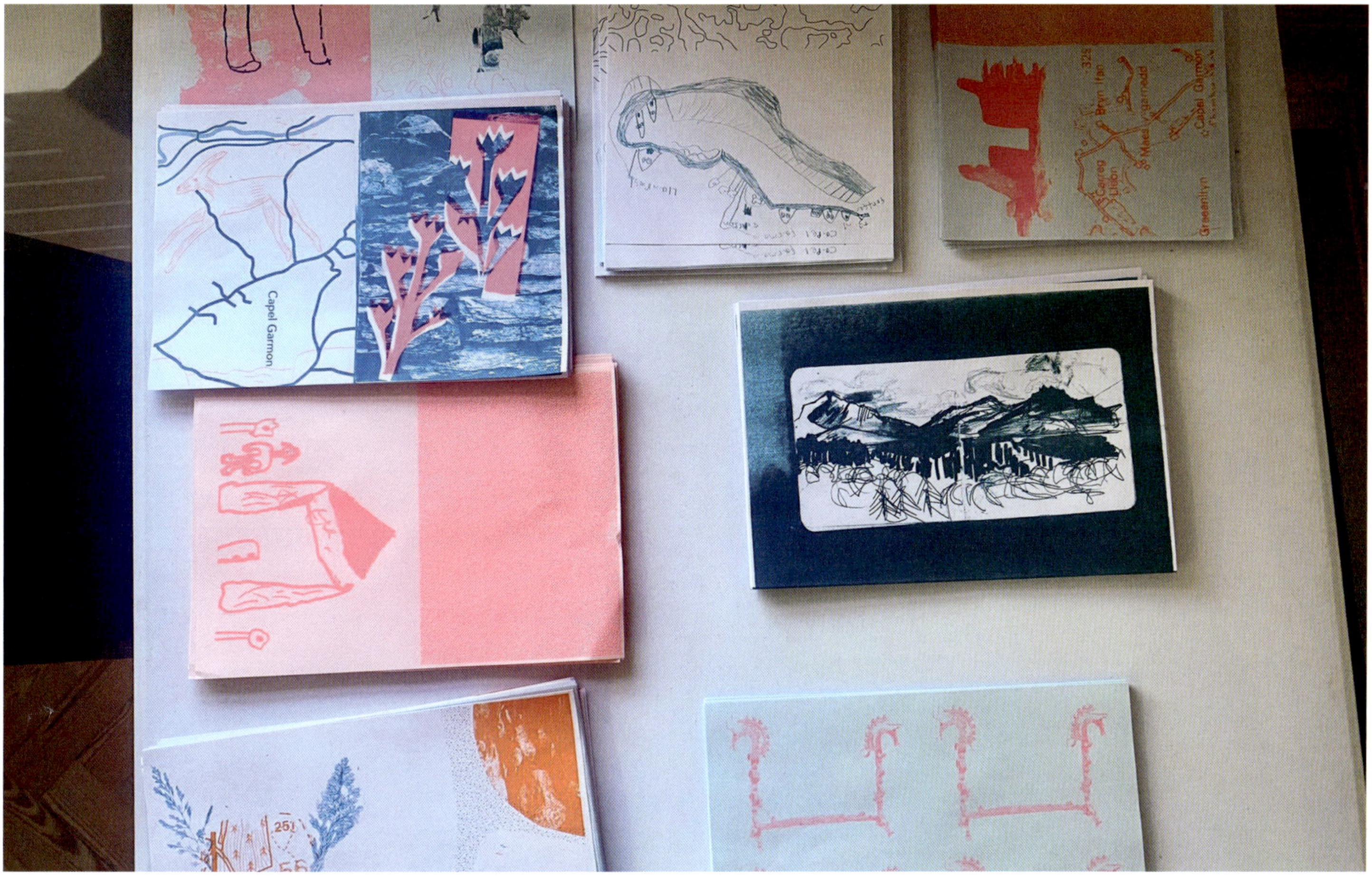

design workshops. These travelling workshops are very local and specific to those involved. On a summer day in 2023, Luke's screenprinting workshop has one taker: and it is a young woman, Awen Dafydd, from a longtime Penmachno family. She is thinking about her schooling. She'd like to work as a graphic designer. Luke has just started her family in Penmachno. She and Clear Village similarly look to broader horizons.

"It feels like that Oriel Machno as a project could be looking outwards and connected to a lot of different other locations, other communities," Luke says. "Not just thinking that it is only about this valley."

“Ürgse loodusega Joaveski on nii kõrvaline, et jäi oma eraldatuse tõttu nii Põhjasõja katkust kui ka COVIDI pandeemiast puutumata.”

“Joaveski, with its primal nature, is so remote that – due to its isolation – it remained untouched by the Great Northern Wars of the early 18th century and the COVID-19 pandemic alike.” René Meimer

Location:
Joaveski, Estonia

In the remote coastal woods lies Joaveski, a remote village at a crossroads with an industrial past. It is a place open for lively experimentation and creative events, with open and surprising spaces; it may one day also be the site for long-term retreats and residences for senior designers and creatives.

SMOTIES Partner: Estonian Association of Designers, Tallinn

The Estonian Association of Designers is a small nonprofit creative organisation that represents Estonia's vibrant design community. Estonia is a small country on the Baltic coast – its population is only just under a million-and-a-half – but the design association makes sure it has a long reach, helping designers to show their work near and far and keeping close links to the country's higher education and trade and cultural institutions.

Joaveski

Key involvement in project

Estonian Association of Designers:
Ilona Gurjanova, communication designer and curator, president, and main organiser of Tallinn Design Night Festival; Kirke Tatar, communication and marketing manager, and Tallinn Design Night Festival.

Kevin Loigu, communications manager and photographer.

Indrek Leht, lighting designer and arts manager;
Enn Eeriksoo, property caretaker and forester;
Andres Õis, property manager, Maru; Sten Berglund, historian;
Karl Joonas Alamaa, case study project manager and designer.

What they set out to do

Seek out ideas and concepts to beautify and add value to an abandoned and historical factory site, and to bring creative activities and events there.

What the project accomplished

Worked with residents and other people with a deep understanding of the local context to set up exhibitions, installations, a history podcast and immersive residences where creative minds can stay and work; developed a long-term concept for a residence for elderly creatives, which could help develop infrastructure and create jobs.

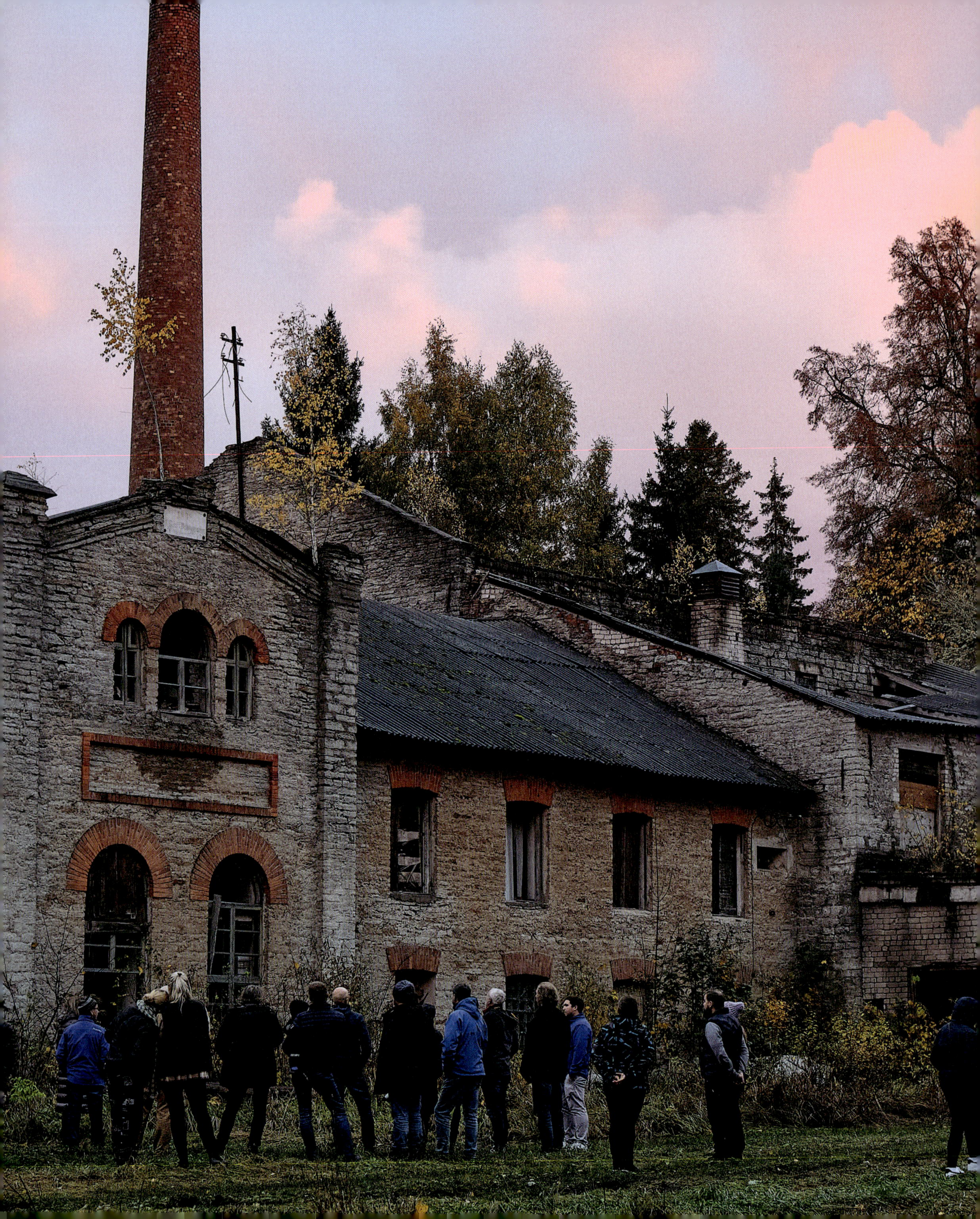

The Café at the End of the World

Joaveski is more cosmopolitan than many villages its size: it boasts an official librarian, forester, and historian. At least, it can do so for the half of the year when everyone is living there at the same time.

Joaveski: population, 23. The forester on this spring afternoon is in the corner of Joaveski's community hall, playing a bass guitar and learning a tune from the American pop singer Miley Cyrus. Enn Eeriksoo, 64 years old, on the shorter side with close-cropped hair, jeans, a coffee, and an energetic terrier at his feet, is carrying on a tradition of music-making in this place. He has been the forester here for 30 years and tends to a generator across the canal in the field outside the hall, which is the only functional remaining piece of the Joaveski Pulp and Paper Factory.

The factory – and the fast water running it, diverted from the nearby Loobu River – was the reason Joaveski developed at all. The water still spins a hydro turbine supplying local power. Eeriksoo is playing the bass on the same site where workers and their families would entertain themselves with a polka or folk-song in previous incarnations of the community hall. A brass band would play for the midsummer night party.

The factory itself is in ruins.

Joaveski still needs a forester, though. The woods once supplied the pulp for the factory. Now the deeper forest, and the sea beyond, is why the people who do come to Joaveski still come.

Striding through the door into the hall, René Meimer has brought a burst of energy with him and he's got a car full of Nordic walking sticks outside. "I have run 50 marathons," he says, right away. Meimer is white-haired, fit. He is here to guide a brisk walk through the surrounding forest to the other side of the river, where some of the factory water channels still stand like alien temple artefacts.

On the tour are the two principals of the Estonian Association of Designers, Ilona Gurjanova and her daughter, Kirke Tatar. The association has placed itself for the Joaveski project as an interlocutor among designers, architects and architecture students, with the mild-mannered researcher who probably knows more about Joaveski's social history than anyone, and with the construction giant that manages most of the land in the region. That includes the factory.

Joaveski is located in the Lahemaa National Park, Estonia's largest and the first like it established in all of the former Soviet Union. Meimer, 74 – a former university fitness lecturer – runs a hiking trail company. He was also Enn Eeriksoo's neighbour for 35 years. Meimer finally moved, thinking he needed to live somewhere a little easier. "I love this place," he says. But the nearest bus stop is eight kilometres away. The nearest shop is in Loksa, 15 kilometres away. And the nearest doctor is 70 kilometres away.

Meimer leads the group into the forest, sun-shaded with patches of melting snow among the spruce and silver birch. It is strange and exciting to suddenly come across moss-covered giant concrete works among the big trees. There is a set of rising berms, arranged in a circular pattern, now obscured in the woods. During Soviet times, a lot of this area was off-limits for military purposes.

The concrete running through the woods used to channel the Loobu water to Joaveski factory for pulp-making and to the hydro-electric turbines for power. The mild-mannered researcher, Sten Berglund, knows a lot about this. He's assembled a remarkable archive and brings an academic perspective to local oral history: *Joaveski küla lugu*.

Berglund, sporting a thin goatee, a baseball cap and a Helly Hansen windcheater to beat the now-and-again bracing Baltic gusts of April, holds up a set of cardboard pieces of varying thicknesses and colours. Factory samples. "When I started collecting material for the book, local people brought me all kinds of different things," Berglund says.

P. 30: Showcase of the updates in Joaveski as part of the "Joaveski REstart" event in October 2022. © Kevin Loigu

Top: Meeting Joaveski's premises in winter 2022. © Kevin Loigu

Bottom: Prototyping studio in Joaveski as part of the "Joaveski REstart" event in October 2022. © Kevin Loigu

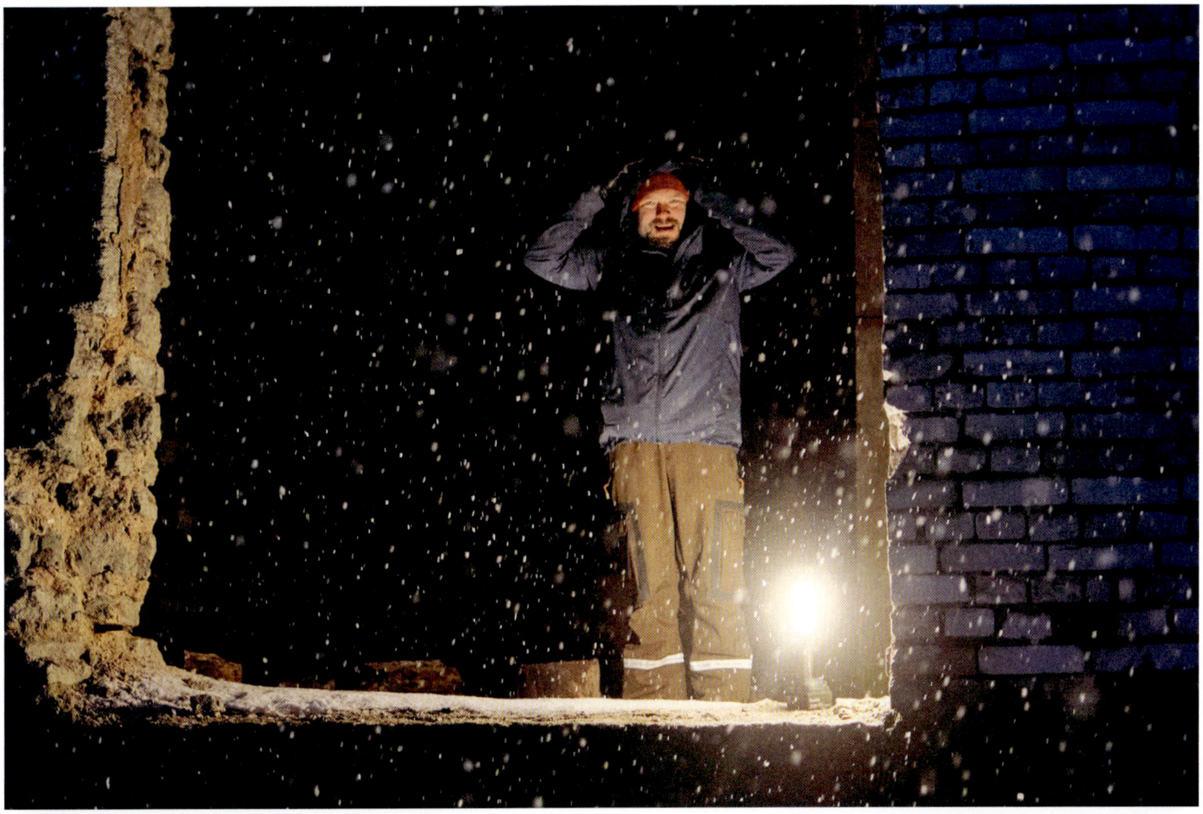

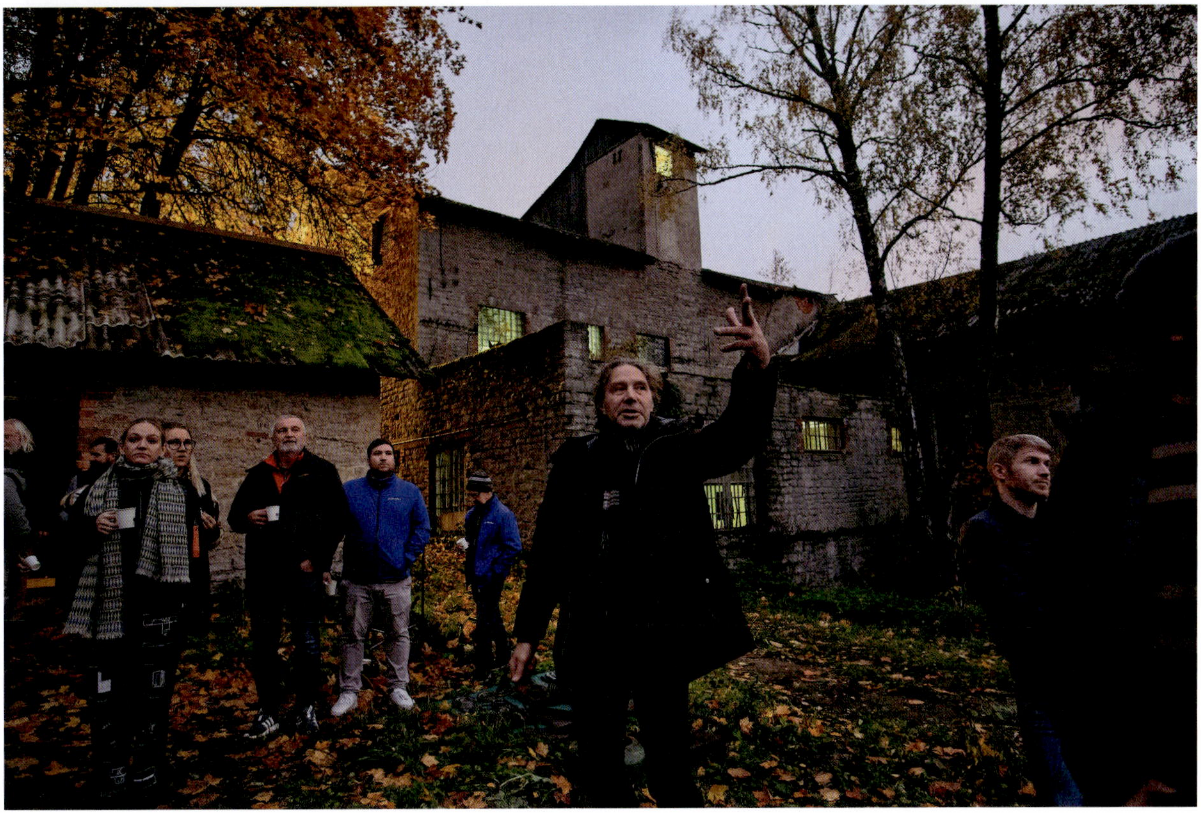

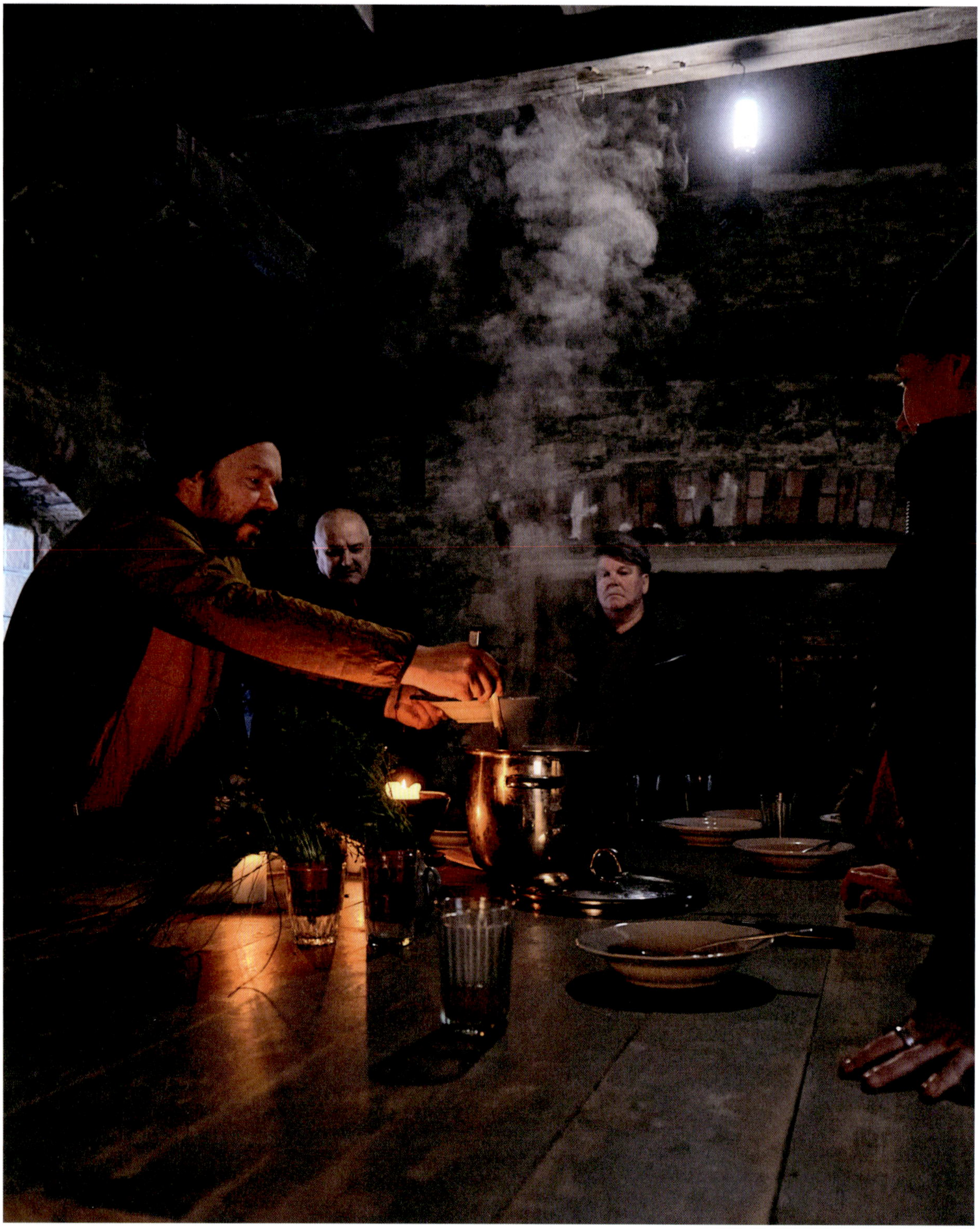

Left: "It's like the cafe at the end of the world." Indrek Leht serves a hearty stew at Joaveski. © Kevin Loigu

Right: Showcase of the updates in Joaveski as part of the "Joaveski REstart" event in October 2022. © Kevin Loigu

Recording oral history in remote places can be instrumental in understanding what people want today. It's one of the practices proving valuable to the SMOTIES teams in considering their creative works. Sten Berglund has a vast archive on hand. He was an important find for the design association. He can point to objects and tell stories; he is a walking map of memories. It is a way to make initial and then lasting connections.

Because that recent history is always disappearing.

"I got these with the drawings for the Nõmmeveski hydroelectric turbine," Berglund says, waving the factory samples. "It was my uncle who rescued all this stuff, because they wanted to heat the boilers and put it all in there. Normal in Soviet times."

The factory produced a cornucopia of cardboard as its fortunes waxed and waned and changed; by the mid-1970s they had binding machines installed and were producing hand-pressed weighted paper albums with cellophane strips. Stamp collectors prized them. It was the only place in the Soviet Union in the stamp-album-binding business. This soon became a lonely place to be. And now snow caves in the eaves of the building, Berglund says, and the forester Enn Eeriksoo's son, a farmer, stores hay bales in the main engine hall under what's left of the roof.

On the other side of the engine hall, the long industrial canal channels the water from the Loobu River into the dormant factory works, and a light is on in a low building as the sun sets.

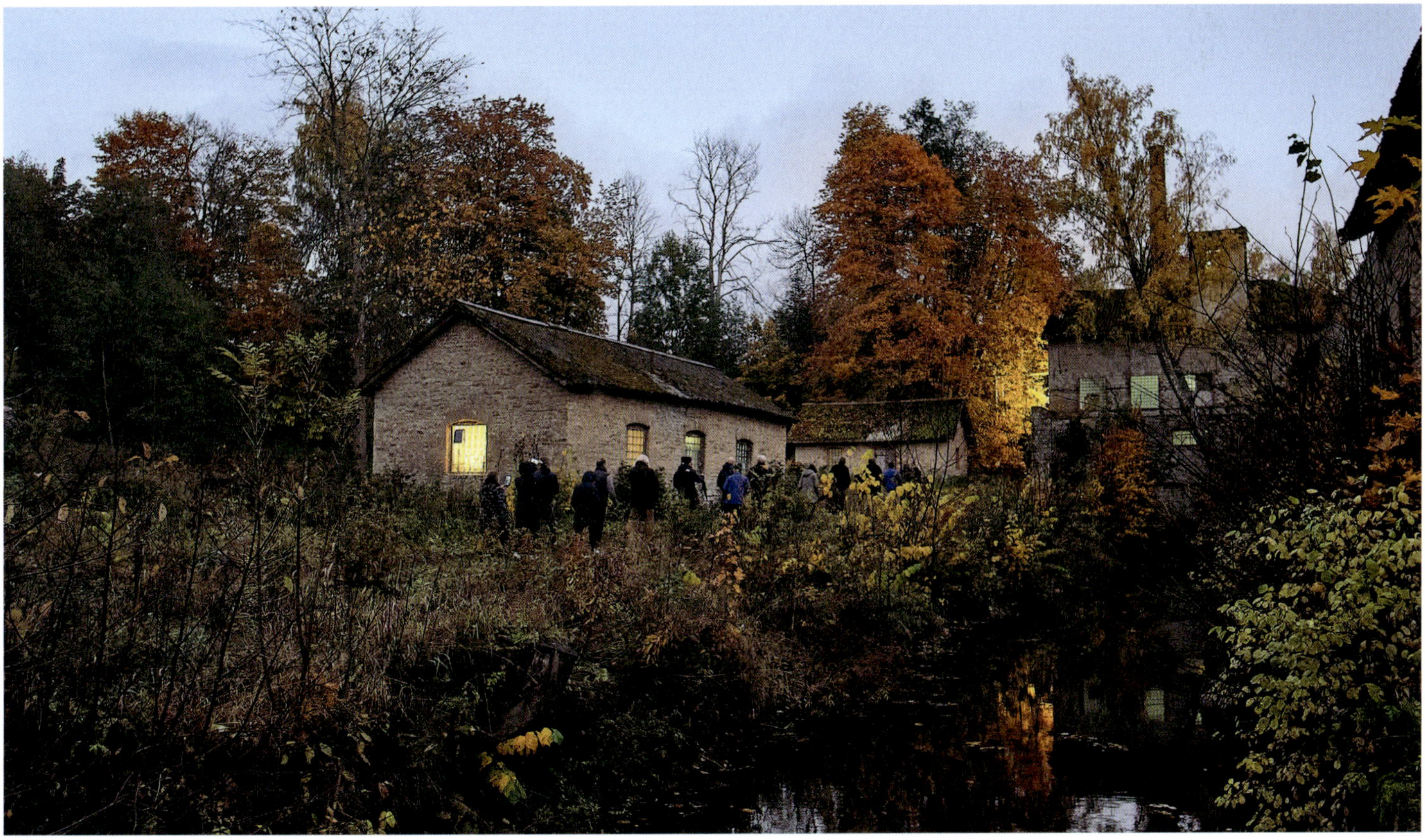

In the building, there are jacket potatoes roasting inside a hot potbelly stove. Ellery Powell, head chef in a restaurant in a restored country villa in the southwest of the country, and Indrek Leht, lighting designer and arts manager – and once a drummer with a Tallinn band that recorded a metal version of a Boney M. disco number – put the finishing touches on thistle-and-berry aperitifs, cricket snacks, and beaver brisket sourced by the forester. The brisket has been marinating for three days.

Leht is a pivotal member in the web of connections that brought Joaveski to the attention of the SMOTIES enterprise. At the table, being served a small dish of cricket snacks, is a white-haired and long-bearded gentleman: Andres Õis. Õis is a property manager for Maru, one of Estonia's largest construction companies and a huge developer. It administers a lot of the land around the Joaveski Pulp and Paper Factory. Maru wants to revitalise some of the fallow areas. Õis and Indrek Leht come from the same village.

In October 2022, the Estonian Association of Designers hosted history and art events at Joaveski alongside Leht, the historian Sten Berglund, and Raoul Kurvitz – a well-known artist in Estonia – soundtracked by musician Lauri Lest.

Vestiges of those events remain. This is one of the reasons Õis is contentedly munching on dried cricket snacks. Leht's lighting installations are set up throughout the Joaveski ruin: one sits on a disused stamp binding machine. He is deeply interested in the filmmaker Andrei Tarkovsky, particularly his masterpiece *Stalker*, which was shot in Estonia. Leht and Kevin Loigu, a Tallinn-based communications manager and photographer working with the design association, are experimenting with short events held in post-industrial locations that possess the feel and visual language of *Stalker*. This is one of those events.

"It's like The Café at the End of the World," Leht says.

Building on their initial programming, the design association worked with Leht to set up themed rooms on the factory site where creative minds can come to write or film or get away from it all in blissful post-industrial seclusion. It also developed an audio play about Joaveski past and present, a podcast called *Sauna MF*. Visitors can listen to it while in a repurposed pop-up sauna by the factory canal. The sauna is a vestige of a nudist festival that used to take place here. Meanwhile, Gurjanova has been talking with Maru about another part of Joaveski: a big, run-down house where the old managerial offices used to be. Their idea is that it could be a kind of retreat for older artists. The house would have to come down, but Maru's management is open to the idea of having creatives who are seniors on site in Joaveski. Estonian architects Peeter Pere and Martin Melioranski are already engaging with students about concepts for it.

René Meimer gets up and heads back outside with his Nordic walking sticks. His current business is hiking, and the moss-covered factory canal appears more and more ancient in the forest as the light fades.

The Loobu River ripples in the dusk.

Top: Pop-up sauna in Joaveski during summer 2022. © Kevin Loigu

Bottom: Indrek Leht, Kaarel Leht, Ilona Gurjanova, and Kirke Tatar check out post-industrial space, Joaveski. © Kevin Loigu

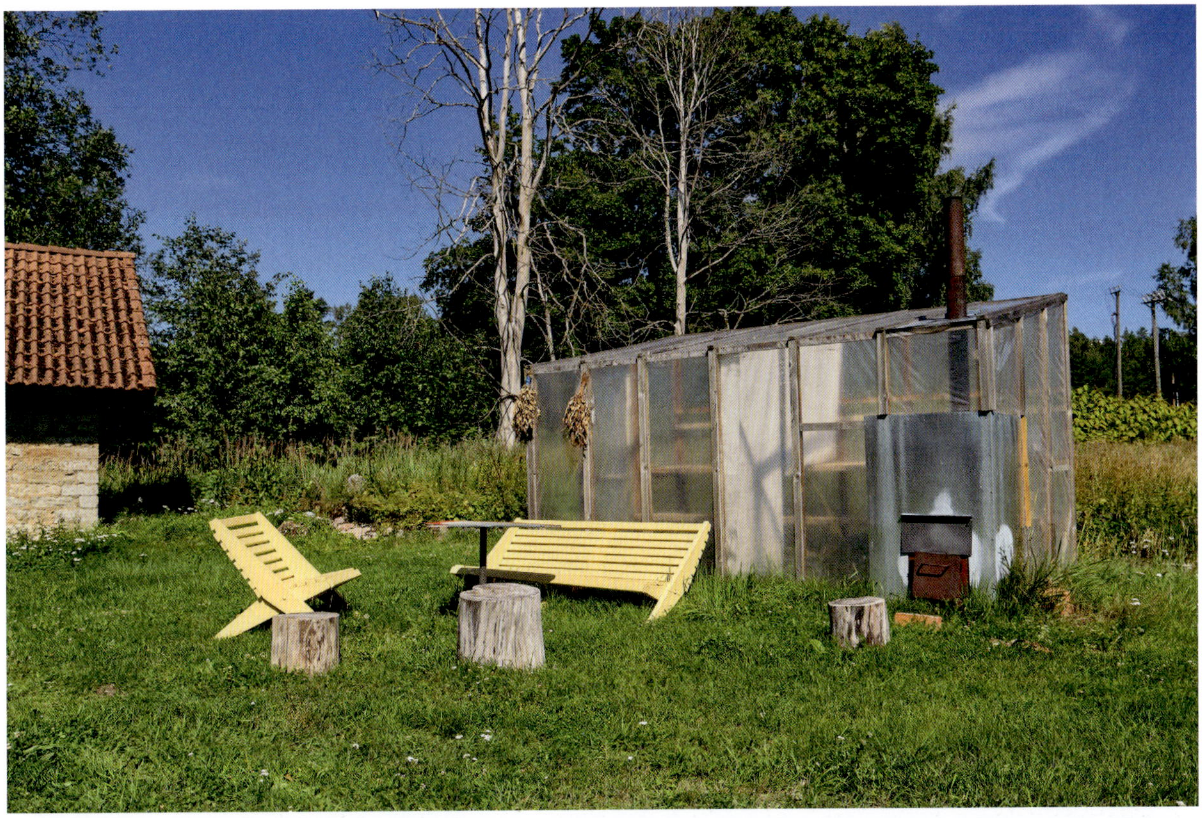

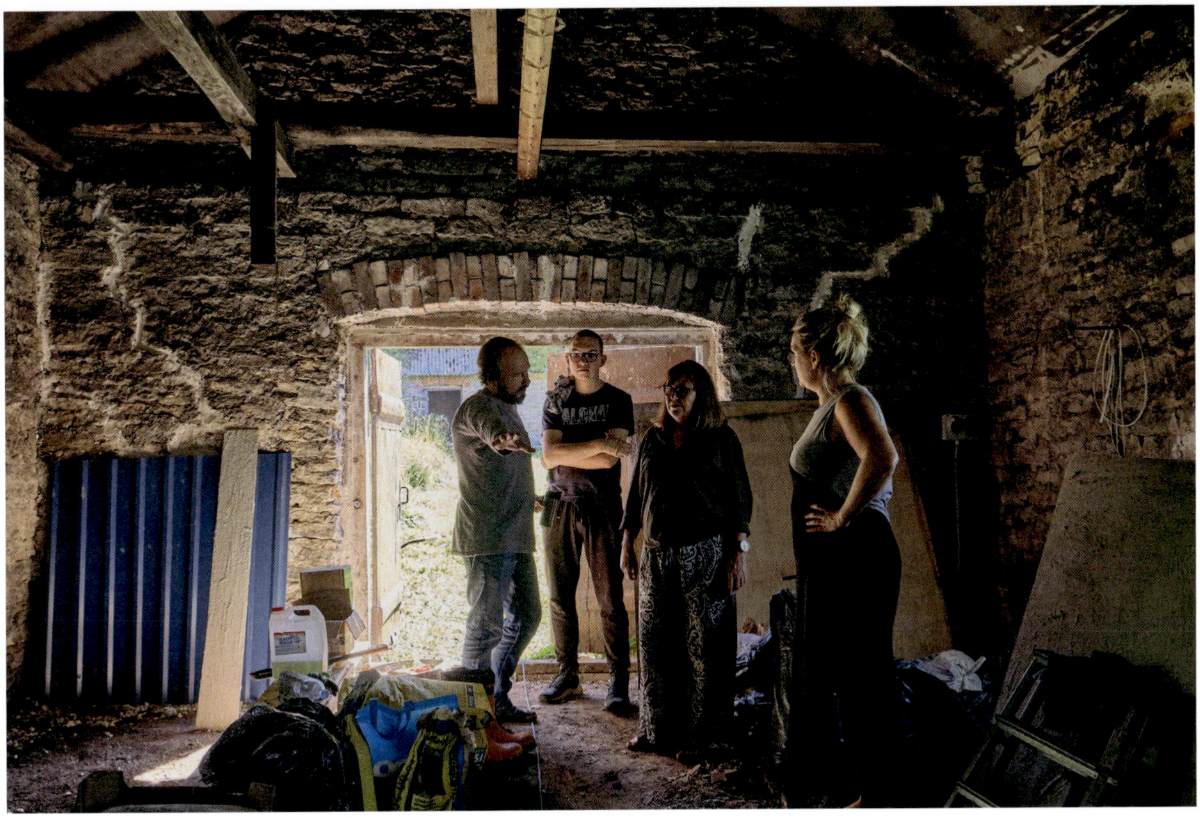

“Sobald klar war, dass der Marktplatz wieder allen und nicht nur dem motorisierten Verkehr gehören soll, haben die Vereine gemeinsam mit den Studierenden von Ausstellungsdesign, eine temporäre Bespielung des Platzes in Angriff genommen. Und es soll weitergehen und vor allem eine permamente Situation geschaffen werden.”

“As soon as it became clear that the market square should once again belong to everyone and not just to motorised traffic, the associations, together with the exhibition design students from Graz, developed a temporary concept for the square. And the plan is to continue and, above all, to create a permanent situation.” Anke Strittmatter

Location:
Oberzeiring, Austria

Remote Oberzeiring has a small market square and once, long ago, was renowned for silver mining. Today, it is a commuter town with 830 residents, a wellness centre and a small but influential theatre. Its public social spaces are not well utilised and its social organisations somewhat detached from public view. One positive step would be to free its central square from its traffic woes.

SMOTIES Partner: FH Joanneum University of Applied Sciences, Graz

FH Joanneum's architecture and engineering school supports faculty in a full range of design disciplines, including media arts, printing and graphic production, laboratory technologies, and digital interfaces. FH Joanneum's Anke Strittmatter led the college's partnership in the Human Cities: Challenging the Human Scale enterprise in Graz from 2014 to 2018.

Oberzeiring

Key involvement in project:

FH Joanneum:
Anke Strittmatter, architect, urbanist and associate professor, urban planning and exhibition design; Bettina Gjecaj, lecturer, strategic communication management; Lucia Jarošová, research assistant, graphic designer, exhibition design and communication; Sigrid Bürstmayr, senior lecturer, exhibition design and communication; Anika Kronberger, researcher and senior lecturer, interaction design; Christoph Neuhold, lecturer, communication, media, sound and interaction design; Professor Erika Thümmel, exhibition design.

Hannes Pfandl, Schaubergwerk Museum, Oberzeiring; Peter Fasshuber, THEO Theatre; Tanja Perchtold, resident; Robert Reif, local parliament.

What they set out to do

We knew that many architecturally beautiful old buildings urgently needed renovating before their doors and windows rotted away. Since many people have been leaving the area, owners are reluctant to renovate because it is unlikely they will get tenants. We did not have a specific goal, but we knew we needed to make contact with active residents. In conversations and workshops with residents, we realised Oberzeiring's Marktplatz, its main square, was a problem area.

What the project accomplished

During a three-day festival in the summer of 2023, we did everything we could to build a prototype of how the square could be used and designed, with the key aim of making it permanently car-free. Since then, the population has been working to meet this goal in the near future.

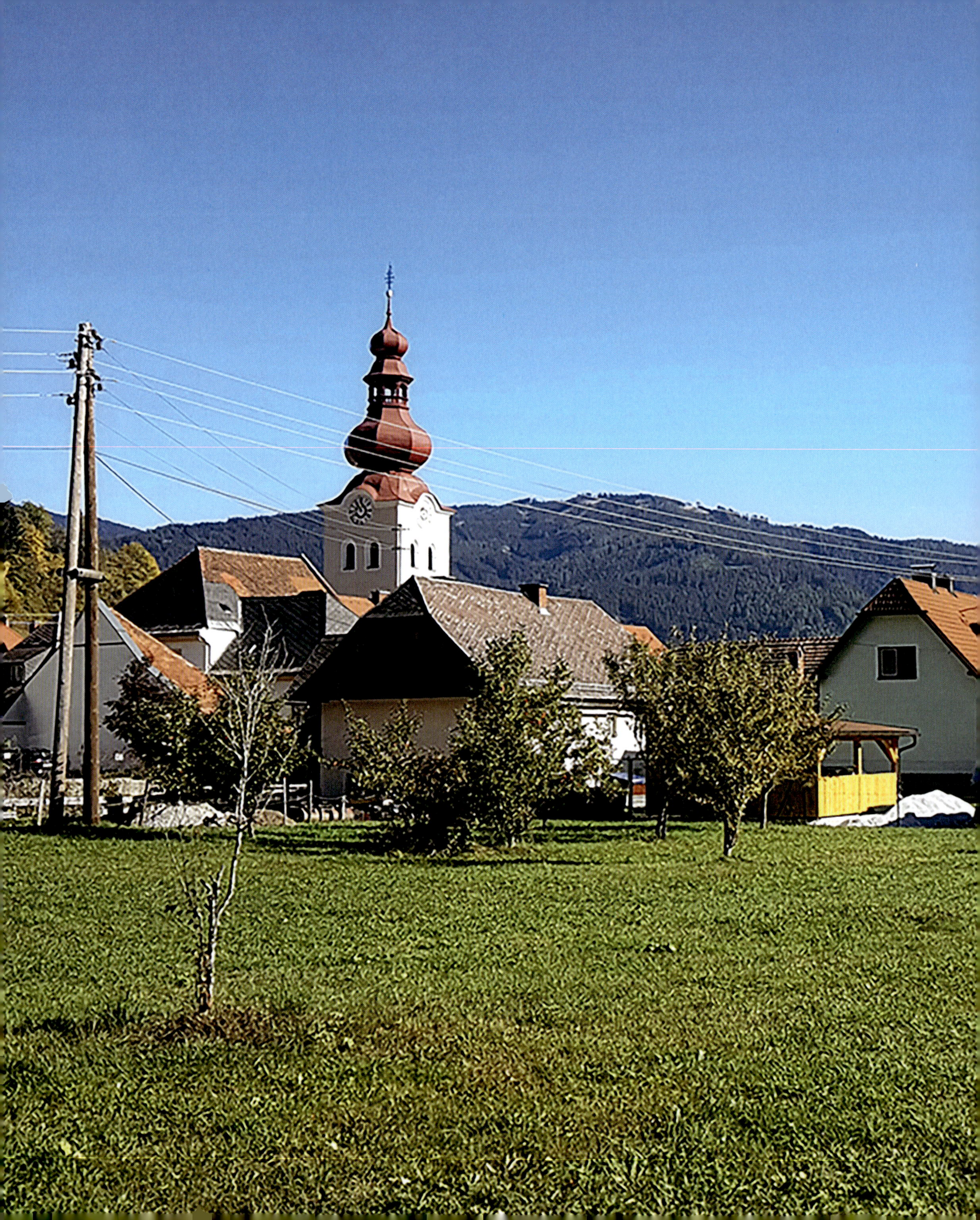

Next Stop, Please

The big green bus rumbles into the square with the haloed statues of Mary, St. Florian, and St. Roch in the centre delivering mercy and fortitude in memory of the plague years, 1714-1715. Barely clearing the building walls as it wheels around, the bus stops; a group of kids spills out ready to play.

The only other feature in this paved square is the outlines of three car parking spaces. It is not very big. But it is the point from which a lot can flow through the commuter town of Oberzeiring, Austria.

This is the Marktplatz, the town's main square. Making changes to it is not a simple thing.

It took six months to convince local officials to shift the bus stop down the road just for a weekend village fete. The former mayor hurled rude names at Hannes Pfandl. But Pfandl is prepared to hear more, and to exchange more ideas with urban design students at FH Joanneum in Graz, 90 minutes away, because he'd like the town to benefit more from the square.

"To make the place more lively, more animated again and better known in the area. Simply to revitalise it," Pfandl says. There's a deeper concern. "We want to keep the generations going in the village, so that it continues here. That the youth have a future, that work lives on and does not die out."

Pfandl is an electrical engineer. He works at a municipal utility in a nearby town. He also heads a little mining museum in the square and for some time now has been keen on building links between the village and the college in Graz. In 2015, a design team from Graz including Joanneum's Erika Thümmel came to give a makeover to the Schaubergwerk Oberzeiring, as the mine museum here is called.

Pfandl got to know about the SMOTIES initiative through Thümmel and he and a few other key Oberzeiringers began thinking about how to improve the square. Because, frankly, it's a conundrum.

Oberzeiring is in Austria's Obersteiermark, or Upper Styria: a few hundred homes sit by a running water source in forested upland. It's steeped in medieval history, and today some villagers farm in the heights of the more industrialised valley of the Mur River, which flows into Graz.

Oberzeiring's once-prized silver mine has been silent for hundreds of years. In 1361, labourers tunnelled into underground water sources, leaving the mine – and 1,300 miners – under water. Still the mining fables and culture echo through the years, and the uppermost levels of the mine galleries, a geological point of interest, have been reimagined.

If you ride along the road running into and out of Oberzeiring's main square, you will find the village's three main institutions: the high school, the 14th-century Catholic church (with its altar tiles alternating between fleur-de-lis and mining symbols) and the Kurhaus.

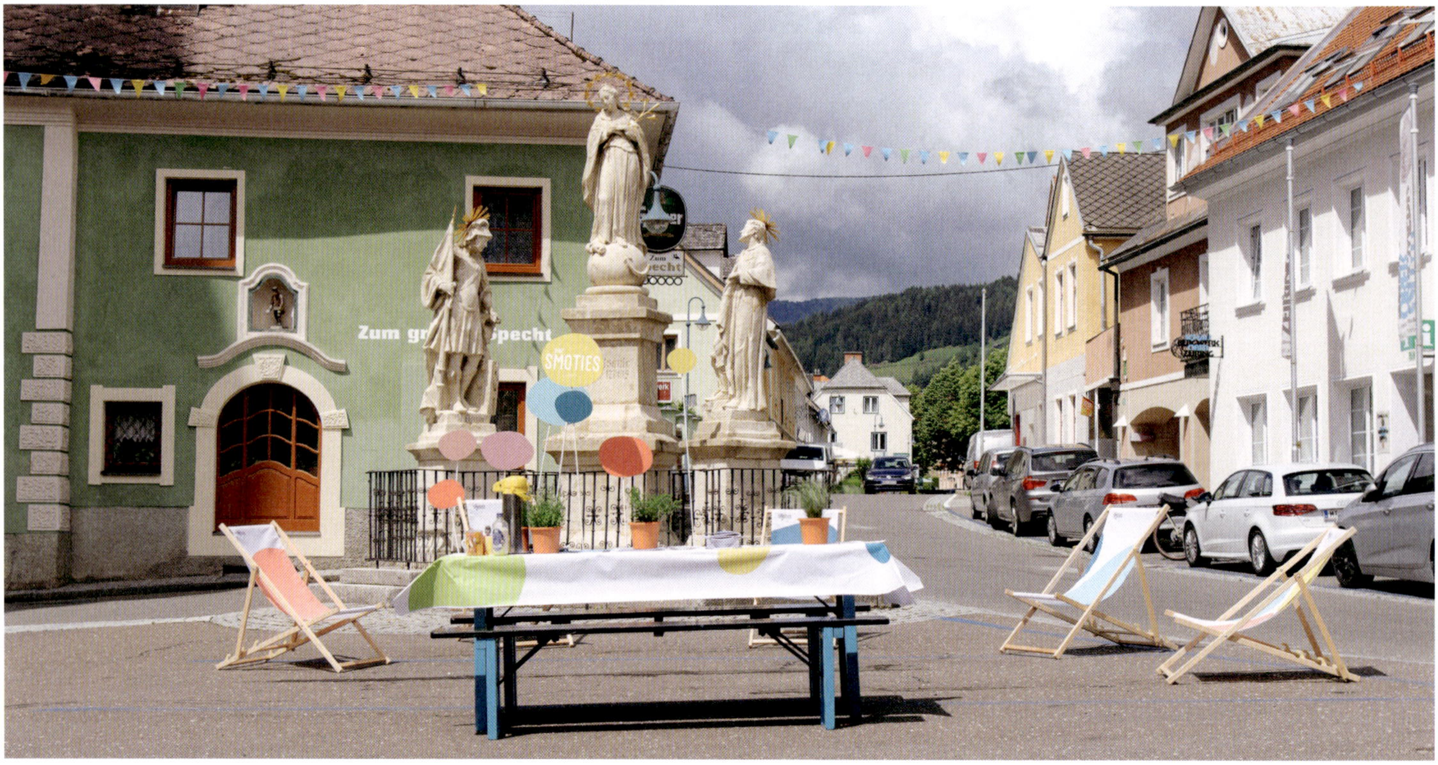

P. 40: Oberzeiring is part of the municipality of Pölstal and is located in Upper Styria, 2021. © thuemmel

Left: Taking over parking spaces and creating alternative concepts for the Marktplatz, 2022. © Katja Krug, FH Joanneum Gesellschaft mbH

Right: The cocreations were accompanied by a SMOTIES exhibition where all partners were also introduced, 2022. © Katja Krug, FH Joanneum Gesellschaft mbH

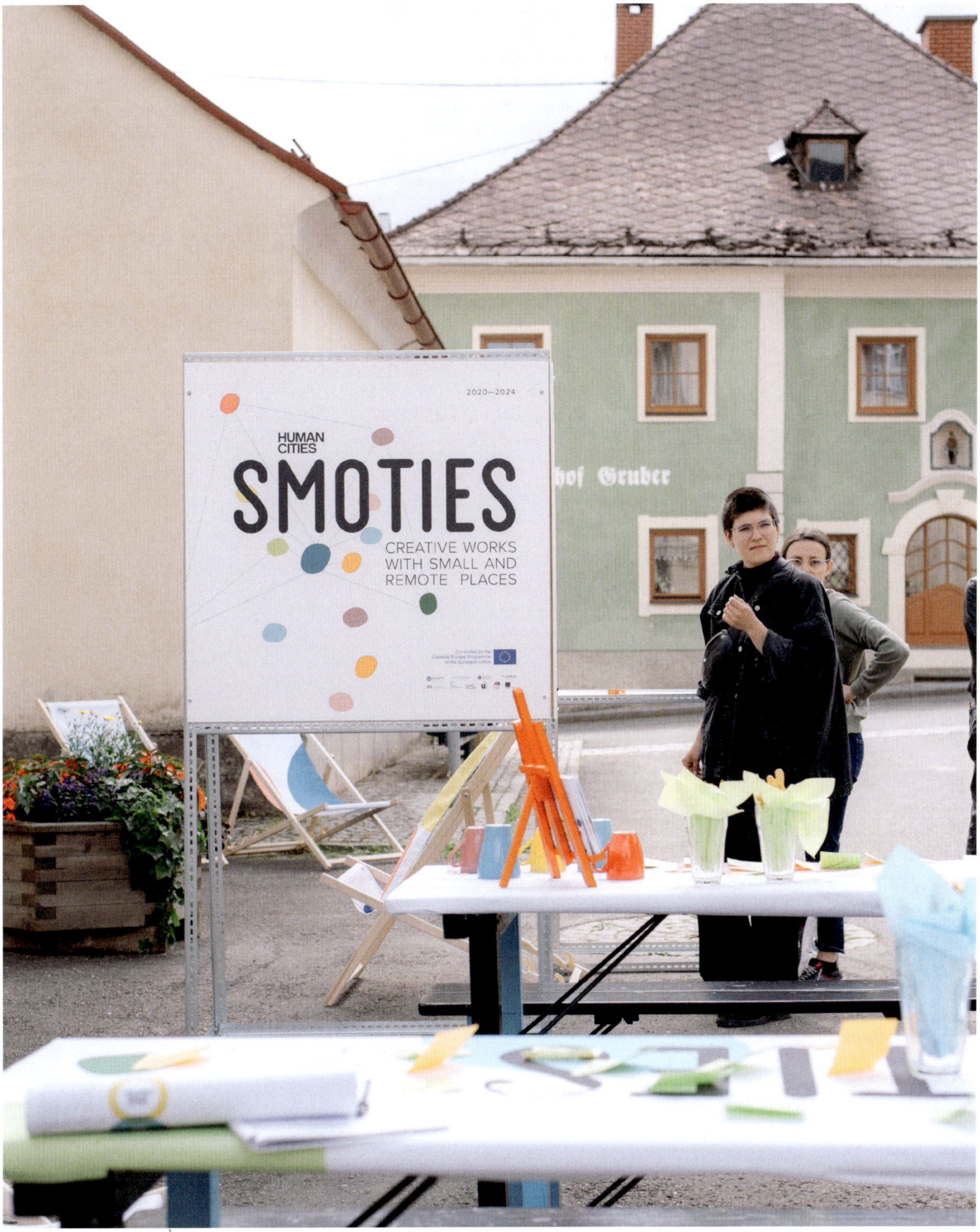

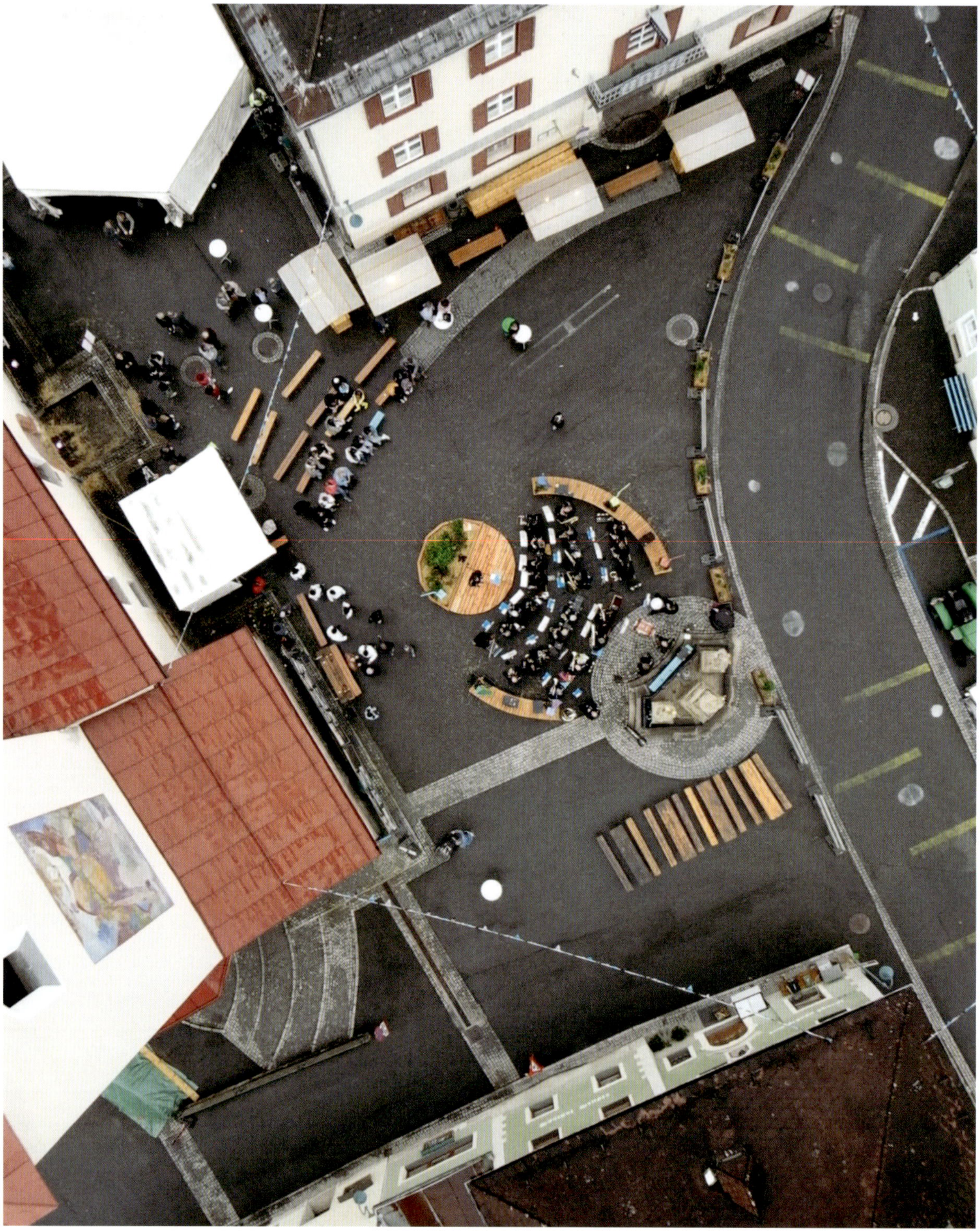

Left: A busy road runs through Oberzeiring, currently with a speed limit of 50 kilometres per hour. By relocating parking places and moving the turnaround point for the buses, quieter and safer areas can be created. © FH Joanneum Gesellschaft mbH

Right: In the future, another option will be created outside the town centre for the bus, which as of 2024 was still using the Marktplatz as a turnaround point. © FH Joanneum Gesellschaft mbH

The Kurhaus offers a wellspring of wellness to the Steiermark region. At the Kurhaus, people enter the old mining chambers to take in the air there, which is reputed to have therapeutic properties against breathing ailments. Whether that is medically true, it is certainly true that people love natural wellness resorts. The Kurhaus is a unique attraction (so much so that thriller writer Eric Ambler featured it in his hit novel *The Care of Time*).

As Oberzeiring's main business, the Kurhaus – located just off the Marktplatz – is linked to other landmark institutions nearby. There is the Schaubergwerk mining museum on one side of the square, its banners fluttering; the Grünen Specht public house (setting for a gruesome folktale about the medieval mine involving ninepin bowling, a beheading and a curse); and a small theatre down the road.

Oberzeiring is served by the number 871 and 846 buses, which pull in to the square every three hours or so, not on Sundays. Being able to offer a bus service, even infrequently, links the village centre to a broader network and increases accessibility. The bus stops close to the Kurhaus. The primary school kids living in Oberzeiring take the bus to neighbouring villages, as the local primary school was closed a few years ago.

The paved Marktplatz makes it easier for the bus to turn around. But it's not ideal for playing or socialising. It is something of a tumbleweed zone; depending on when you go, the whole village can feel empty. The beautiful but fading facades and empty buildings around do not help. And even when boisterous kids spill out of the bus and immediately start boinging around the square, a reasonable person might wonder why they are playing in the road.

The dilemma presents itself in trying to trade a central but less-than-ideal bus stop for one that is possibly inconvenient and further away, and if so, how. And then, what to do with the square.

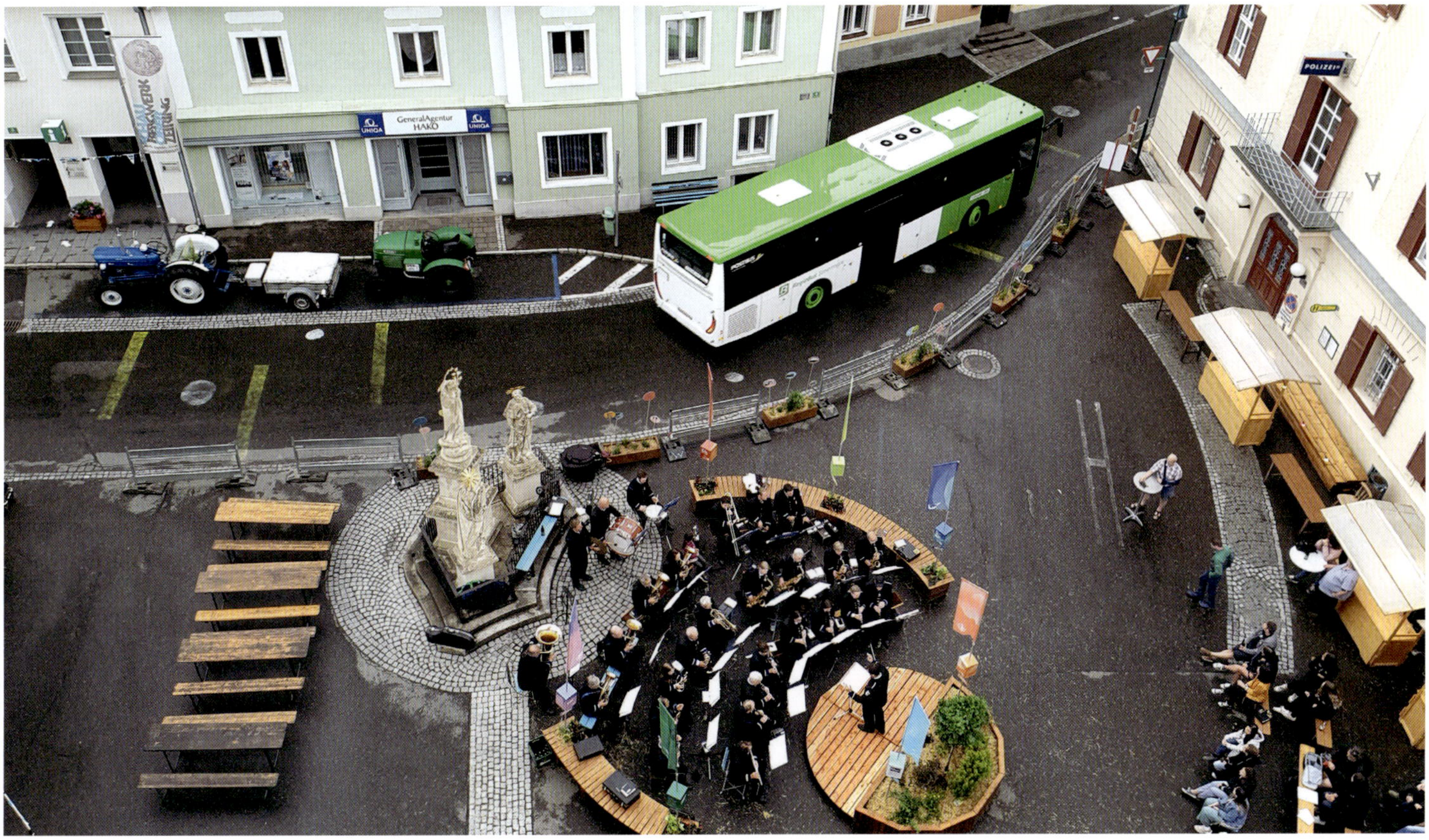

Joanneum students weighed up many options over the months as they were ferried in by SMOTIES partners Anke Strittmatter, Bettina Gjecaj and Lucia Jarošová.

Pfandl met the SMOTIES team on a cold February morning in 2021, as the COVID-19 pandemic was still ferocious. By November, the group was able to screen a film at one of the associations. *Rettet das Dorf!* or *Save the Village!*, played at the village brass band clubhouse. By June 2022, the Joanneum group sat down with the owner of a pastry shop across from the Kurhaus. For four hours a day over three days, they worked with residents and local middle school students. Pfandl became the engine behind the network-building.

He so relishes stories that he wears costumes and grooms his facial hair to suit the occasion. On an April morning in 2023, he had a beard to match his role as a mule-driver in a series of historical films about the Middle Ages in the Mur valley. Altering the way the Marktplatz works, though, may be a little harder than mule-driving: inertia will play a prominent role. Who do you have to speak with to change a bus route? It's not always clear.

Concepts for the market square start with shifting traffic flows. Streets lead off all four corners. That's complicated. The most vocal Oberzeiringers want the square to play a role in promoting the town's clubs: the shooting club, volunteer firefighters, theatre and farmers' association. A bit of colour. A bit of life.

For one weekend in June 2023, the square did change. Joanneum's suggested modifications were used for Frischer Wind, a village summer festival.

The main street curving into the square had yellow stripes to signal a slowdown to through traffic; wooden planters directed traffic flow past the square; concentric curved benches and a central wooden hangout spot took centre place by Mary, St. Florian, and St. Roch. The bus routes were also amended – the buses stopped at a ski lift parking lot a kilometre down the road, just outside the town limits.

But after that weekend, everything was back to normal.

All back to how it was earlier, says Tanja Perchtold, looking at the schedule for March 2024. The 24-year-old Oberzeiringer grew up in the village, studied languages, dresses in grunge rural style, works in an office, is an aspiring writer. Her mother works with Pfandl at the mining museum.

"People want to come and do things here," she says, walking across the square. "It would have been absolutely great when I was still a teenager, doing my things and hanging out with people." Where did she hang out? "I didn't."

But it is also no longer apparent that people socialise as much in a village dynamic marked by the market square, the crossroads. This is a common gap faced when trying to make sense of public spaces in rural places (and not just rural places). If everything is virtual now and contained on screens and phones, if the club is a group chat, will people come out of their living rooms to a public outdoor space?

But then the bus pulls up.

And when the kids spill out of the bus, they play in the square, paved over as it is.

Right: A throwback experiment from Joanneum: just off the square they've designed and placed a rideshare bench (Joanneum's last Human Cities initiative also deployed benches). Flip the card to show where you want to go, and share a ride. Returning, though, might require more resources. © Katja Krug, FH Joanneum Gesellschaft mbH

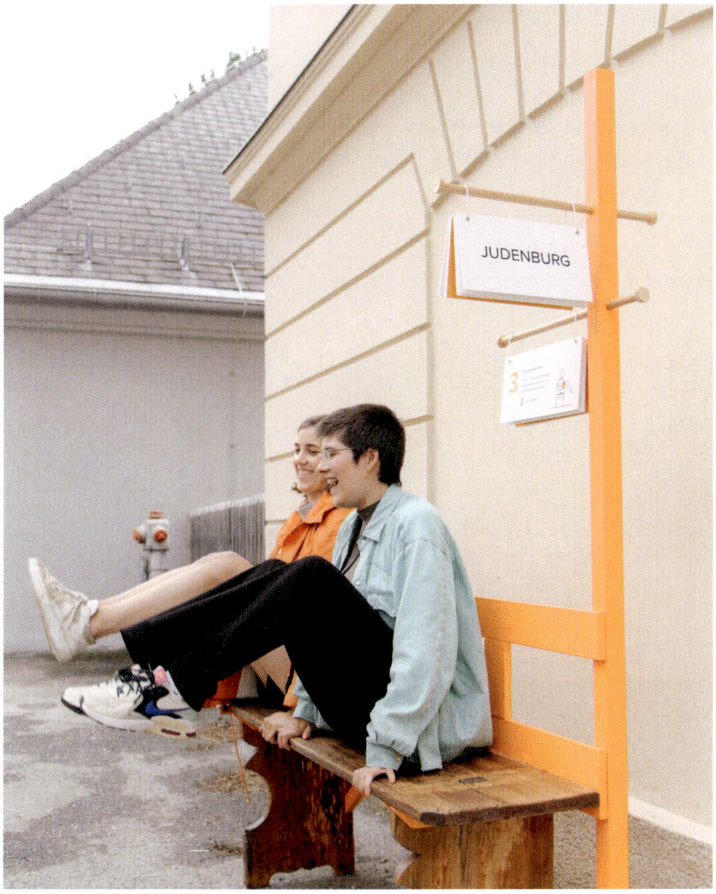
JUDENBURG

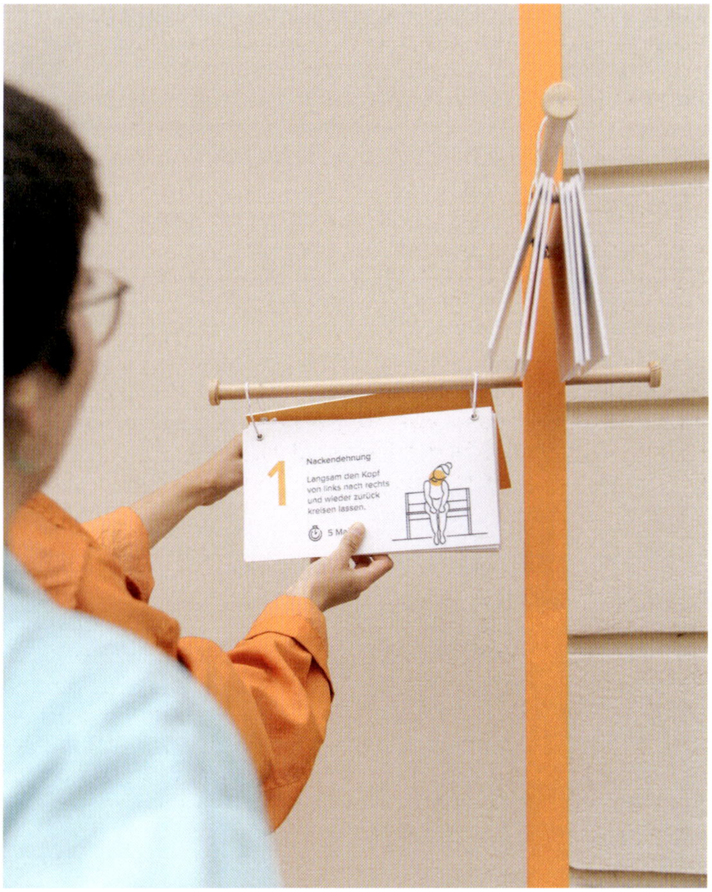
1
Nackendehnung
Langsam den Kopf von links nach rechts und wieder zurück kreisen lassen.

“To, czego to miejsce potrzebuje najbardziej, to aktywna wspólnota.”

“What this place needs most is an active community.”
Anna Sowińska

Location:
Cieszyn, Poland

Cieszyn is a historic market centre and border town to the south of Katowice and Krakow in Silesia, south-central Poland. Years ago, a hilltop village on the outskirts was emptied and relocated to make way for the Bobrek housing estate, composed of Bobrek Zachód (Bobrek West) and Bobrek Wschód (Bobrek East), somewhat removed from the town below. Residents there are managing ongoing change in the neighbourhood and trying to resolve community differences over what to do with the green space on their doorstep.

SMOTIES Partner: Zamek Cieszyn, Cieszyn

Founded in 2005, Zamek Cieszyn is a public cultural institution run jointly by the town of Cieszyn and the Silesian state. The institution is a research and documentation centre for material culture and design that works with companies, NGOs, and public institutions to promote good design and collaborate with putting it to good use.

Bobrek

Key involvement in project

Zamek Cieszyn:
Magdalena Chorąży-Suchy, director; Anna Sowińska, sociologist; Agnieszka Niczyporuk, interior designer, lawyer, painter.

Pronobis Studio:
Grzegorz Pronobis, architect, urban planner, place maker; Sylwia Widzisz-Pronobis, researcher, architect, urban planner, place maker.

What they set out to do

To engage with and help the residents of the Bobrek housing estate improve the green space available to them and make it suit the varying ideas for it; and to help bridge divides within the community and link the different areas of the complex to one another.

What the project accomplished

Prompted discussions among younger and older residents about how best to use common areas; built connections between the estate and local municipality, which could lead to further improvements; installed communal outdoor furniture, including benches, tables, bike racks and litter bins; and developed a plan for future additions, including a picnic zone, sport zone, and multifunction / reading zone with an outdoor library.

The Cieszyn municipality will continue to mull utility and improvement ideas for Bobrek through 2024.

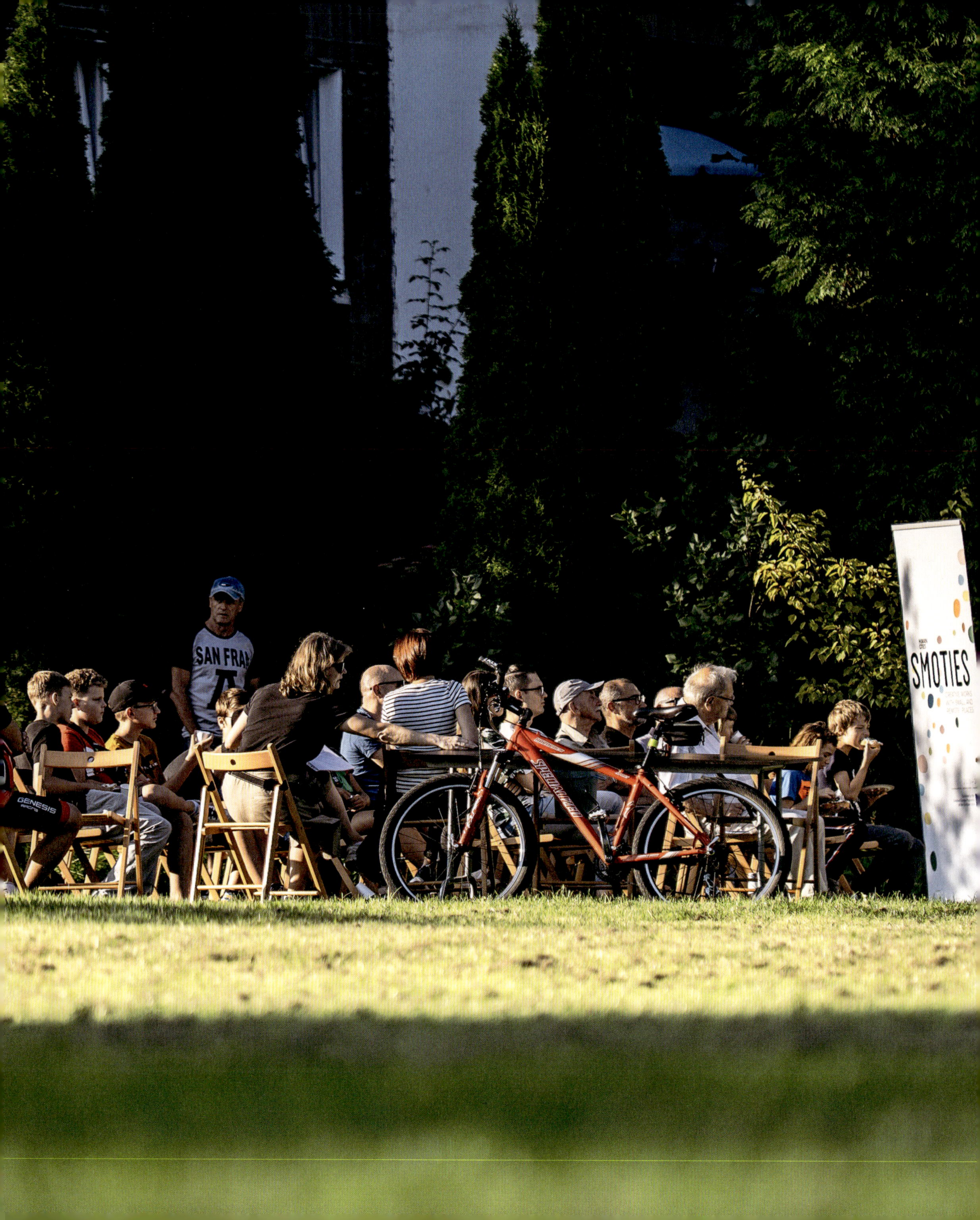
SMOTIES
GENESIS

The Grass is Greener

Twin Peaks was a series from director David Lynch that was, for a brief time in the late 1980s, the strangest thing on prime television at a time when truly mass media was still possible.

But Zdzisław Ciuk was unusually startled when he heard this show through his windows. It was his first night at the Bobrek estate in Cieszyn, Poland, near a breezing stand of pines and a small creek.

Ciuk, now 63, had at that time just graduated from university. By May 1991, he had the new keys to his Bobrek flat following a flurry of applications in the apartment allocation system that still operated during the last days of Eastern Bloc communism. Televised noir surrealist American *Twin Peaks* through the window? Here was yet another sign things were changing, and changing fast.

"This place was supposed to be for coal miners only," Ciuk says. He is relaxed, sitting on his sofa next to an upright piano. "We got this flat based on the fact that we are teachers and were then newly married, and potentially a growing family, and that was it." He and his wife, a music teacher, raised their two children at Bobrek.

Together they've seen generations from their top-floor balcony, looking over a big green field and basketball court and the woods and a stream behind. Bobrek sits at the top of a hill at the end of a road. The first residents have greyed; new generations have been born.

Coal miners actually did wind up living in Bobrek, Ciuk says. They came to his house-warming party. Soon that part of the mining industry went away, and the miners retired or tried to find other lines of work.

On a warm late-September afternoon in 2023, these are some of the 35-odd people who come out to the green field in the corner of the estate to a table laden with Cieszyn's special sandwiches – open-faced *kanapki*, heavy with egg, pickle and mayo – baskets of them, the subject of great interest. The block residents sit on chairs set up near to an array of architectural posters. Kids are in the front row; they'll head later to a table to paint and play.

On the field setting up are the designer, Agnieszka Niczyporuk; the project manager and organisation leader, Magdalena Chorąży-Suchy; architect Grzegorz Pronobis; and a sociologist – and Bobrek resident – Anna Sowińska. The group represents Zamek Cieszyn, which can loosely be called the town design centre (loosely, because they are more than that, having started as a municipally sponsored entrepreneurial accelerator).

The issue at Bobrek is, as Pronobis says, connection: connection of space with function, with how residents want to live.

"One important thing for the people who live here is that they want to connect two parts of Bobrek," Pronobis says, drinking a coffee before the September lawn gathering. "And maybe some place for appointments. Where they can meet. Maybe a little area with green space."

Looking out at the oaks and mown grass behind the estate flats, it's clear the discussion among residents is a bit more nuanced – as, technically, there already is green space. But a metal post sticking three metres out of the lawn from a nearby small rectangular concrete slab, a court, is a clue: there's dandelion and hairy bittercress tufting between the flagstones, and no backboard on the post.

P. 50: Prototyping workshop with residents, Bobrek. © Krzysztof Puda

Bottom: Animated field game for children and youth. In the background old basketball court and footbal pitch. © Rafał Soliński

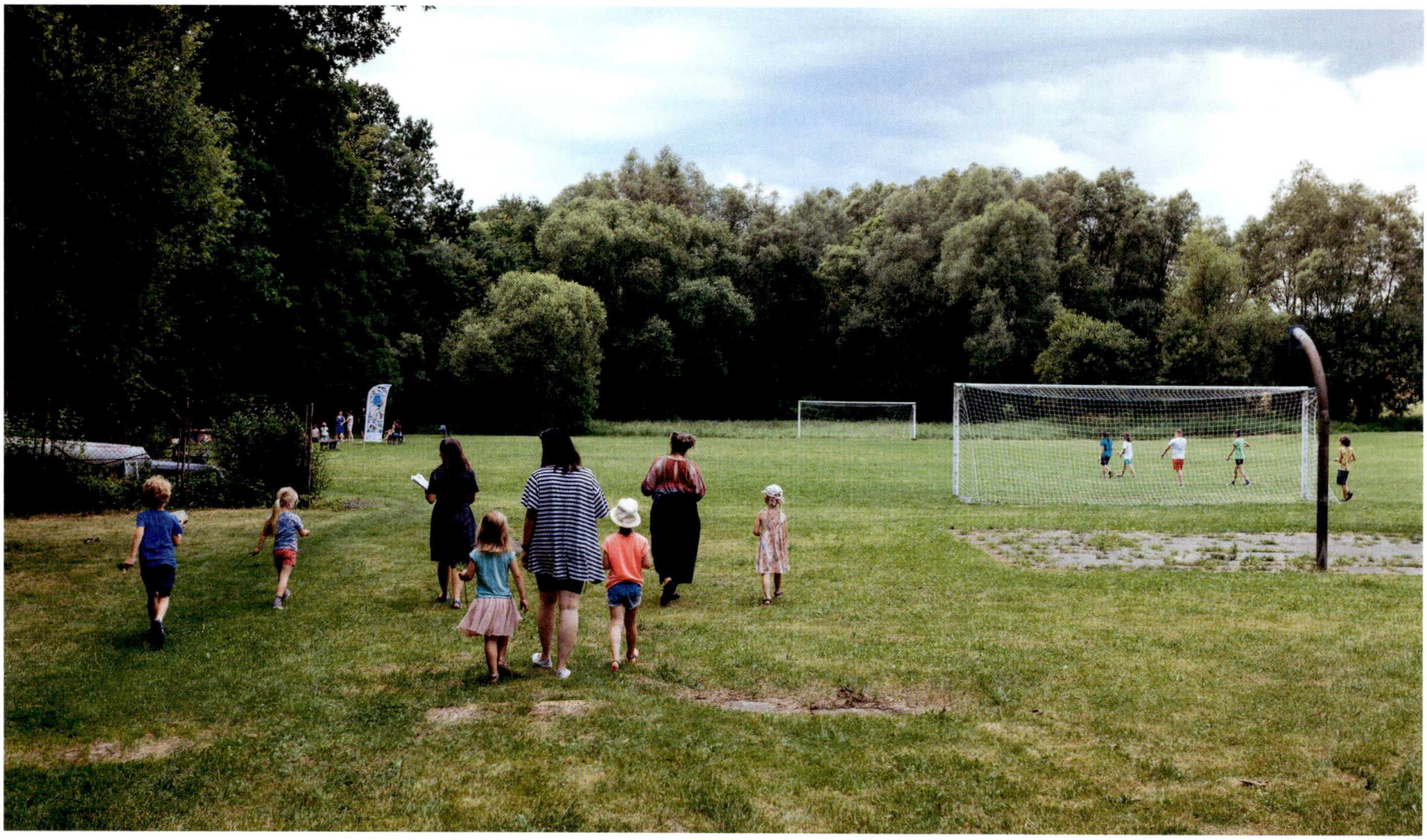

The Bobrek estate is home to some 1,200 people in 24 rectangular blocks across seven streets on the outskirts of Cieszyn.

Cieszyn's origin story is that a thousand years ago, three brothers (Leszko, Bolko, and Cieszko) found a spring, and so founded a town on a bend on the Olza River. Cieszyn now straddles the frontier, partly in Poland, partly in the Czech Republic. At its highest point overlooking the river, the 14th-century ruling Piast dynasty built a castle with 30-metre defensive towers. One remains.

Two kilometres away from that tower is the hill on which Bobrek sits: the hill slopes up from a busy avenue to a clump of trees. A road moves sharply to the estate's brown tiled modular blocks and its tinted globe streetlights. It's peaceful, but without a car, you're cut off from the town unless you walk down the hill. There's a broad, open green pitch behind Building 7. At the first stand of trees, there's a steep bank to a creek. There are two parts to Bobrek, one on either side of the wooded creek gully.

When the Zamek team began contacting residents, many of them recalled playing games in that wood and catching crawfish in the creek. Meadows near the estate for dog-walking are now paved over for parking.

The little brook is called Sarkandrowiec. Ciuk, a skiing enthusiast, calls it Beaver Creek, after the high-end Colorado resort. Bobrek means beaver. He remembers the crawfish in the creek, too. "And our kids spent hours playing football, you know," he says. Now there is more likely to be molehills and breeze in the trees than knots of kids out kicking a ball around in the field. It's unused, not really playable.

Bobrek got its start under communism. When the system collapsed, the estate was never finished, not well connected to surrounding neighbourhoods and services. It has never really attracted civic interest.

Zamek spotted a chance to steer municipal attention to the future of this overlooked part of Cieszyn. It started with walks around the estate, bringing in historians and naturalists to talk about the hill and creek; they got Bobrekers to start telling their stories. Then it got complicated.

At first, some wariness. Then 40 people signed a petition and sent it to the cooperative: no changes to the field, please. In fact – we'd really rather you did nothing. Diverging views had arrived.

Zamek had for some time been running into obstacles. The cooperative said it would put up flyers promoting upcoming events. When that failed to happen with the first batch of flyers, Zamek's Anna Sowińska – who lives

Prototyping meeting on green area development concept. Architect Grzegorz Pronobis is presenting students' proposals. © Krzysztof Puda

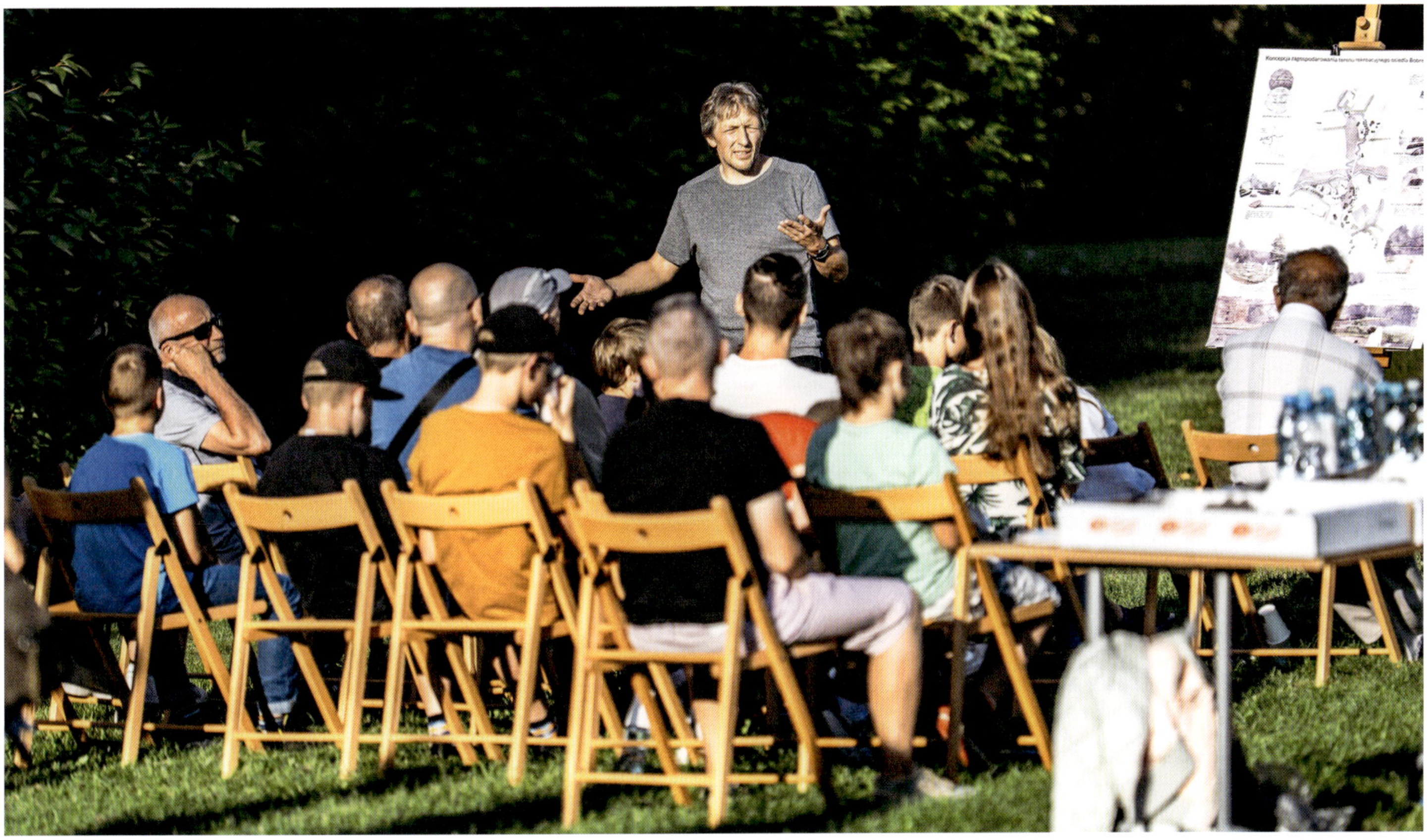

in flat 9 with her husband and two young boys – posted flyers in the stairwell herself.

The lawn gathering with the sandwiches last September had a big turnout: maybe because two weeks prior, Zamek had brought in mediators to make sure different views would be aired in person, in real time. A basic exchange, but increasingly unusual. There are very few digital platforms to get a retired coal miner talking at length to a teenager.

It may seem like low stakes, but there really was generational tension. "You have different groups of people that see the same space different ways," Pronobis says. "They are not bad people. They use the space differently. To get them to see other perspectives takes skill in encouraging conversations." Older people and people working late shifts want quiet. Teens (including at least one who's in a model government club) want a place to do something. There was at least one sharp quarrel. Pronobis conducted one sit-down; the mediation nonprofit Do!Pamina Lab, from suburban Katowice, another.

The back-and-forth is along simple but closely held perspectives: my environment is changing and getting loud. People have loud parties and leave trash or they bounce balls by my window while I'm trying to sleep. Or, improvements mean the rents go up, my parking is gone and I have to leave. Or, okay: there's a play park, but there's nothing for me and my friends to do, and nowhere to go. Why not a place to exercise, even a little climbing wall?

That clash got things moving, got the petition-signers engaged. Perhaps a quiet zone closer to the flats, a more active or sporty area further away?

"It was a good development to have kids in there and to get them all in the same room," Pronobis says. "Maybe just seeing their neighbours reminds them, hey, kids are great. They're loud, but they're great."

Prewar Bobrek was a village, a farming village. It was cleared out to build the housing estate. By the time Ciuk heard *Twin Peaks* wafting through the window from his neighbour's television, the country was heading straight for another system-wide and wrenching economic upheaval. Maybe it's not so surprising that some Bobrek residents are sceptical of plans to improve it. There is more to it than just what to do with a patch of green.

"Sometimes it's difficult. But at the same time, this is the first moment probably, when they are talking, that they have the idea that someone is listening to them," Pronobis says.

Ciuk thinks he may leave Bobrek soon: the stairs are getting harder for him and there is no lift.

Maybe it will be up to the new tenants to see what happens to the fields under the balcony.

Prototyping workshop with residents view from basketball court.
© Krzysztof Puda

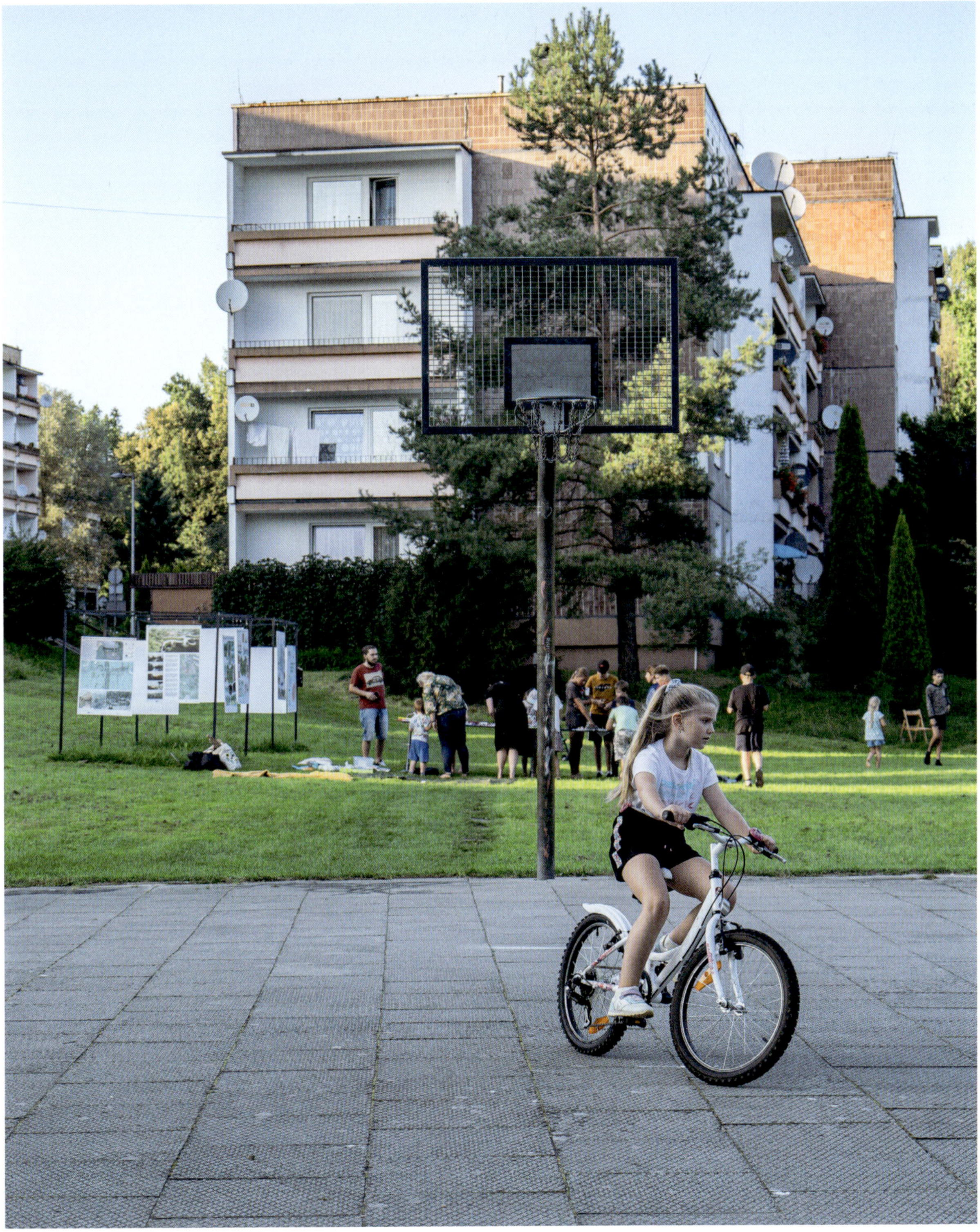

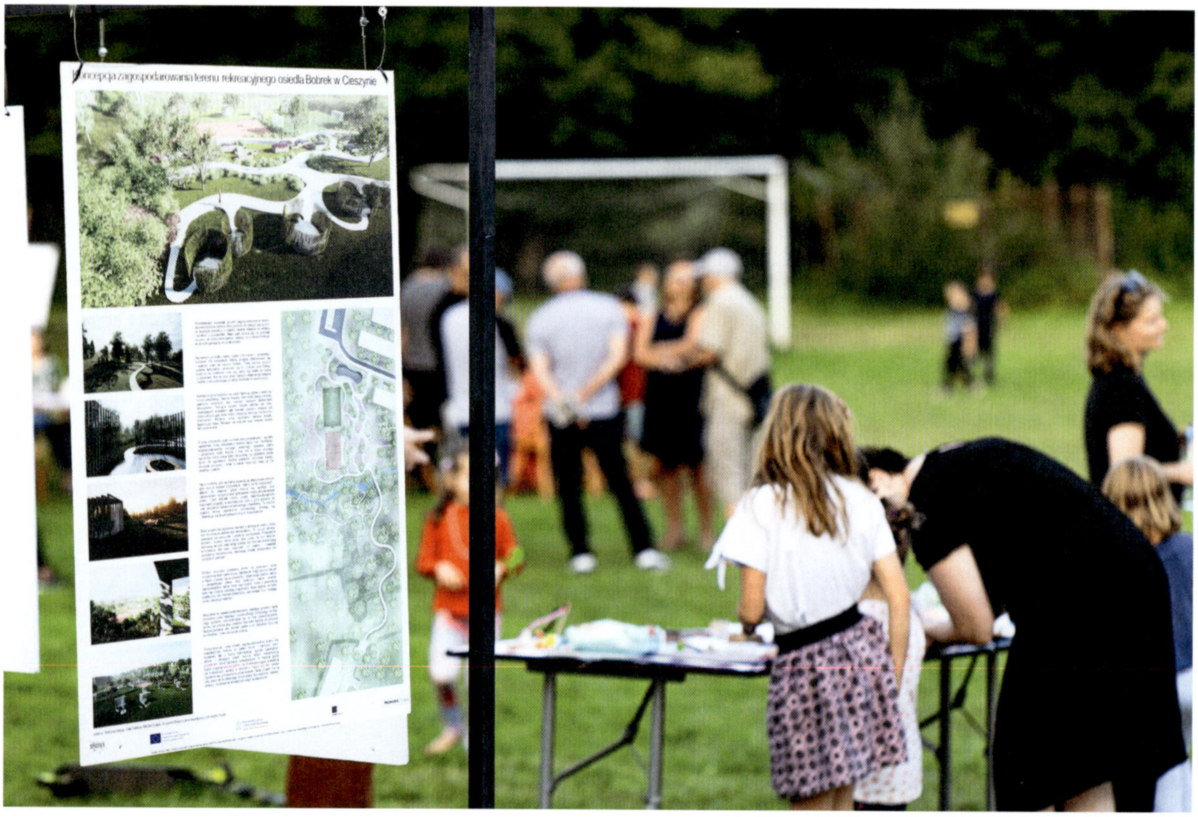

Prototyping meeting with residents – children and adults. © Krzysztof Puda

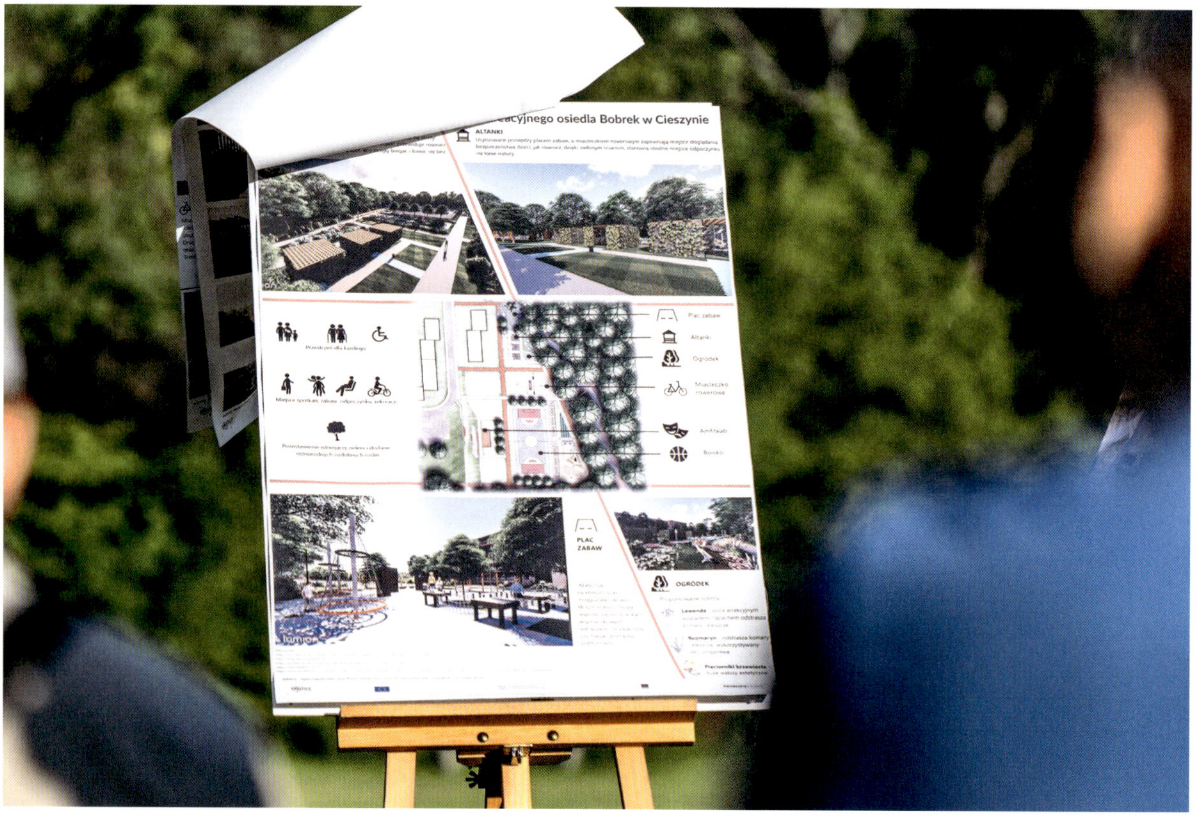

One of the students' projects. © Krzysztof Puda

Children have their own paths and places to play in the woods in between Bobrek housing esates. © Anna Sowińska

Animated workshop for childern with Modulo stamps. © Krzysztof Puda

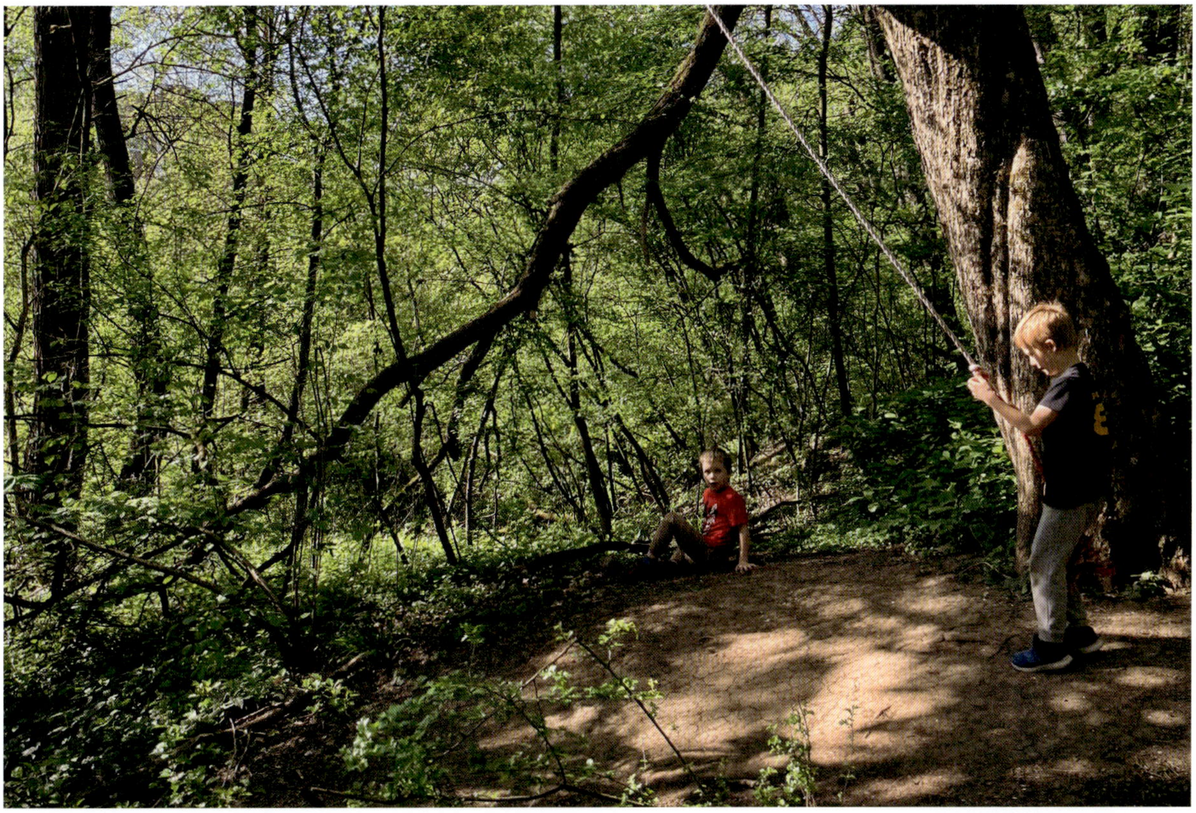

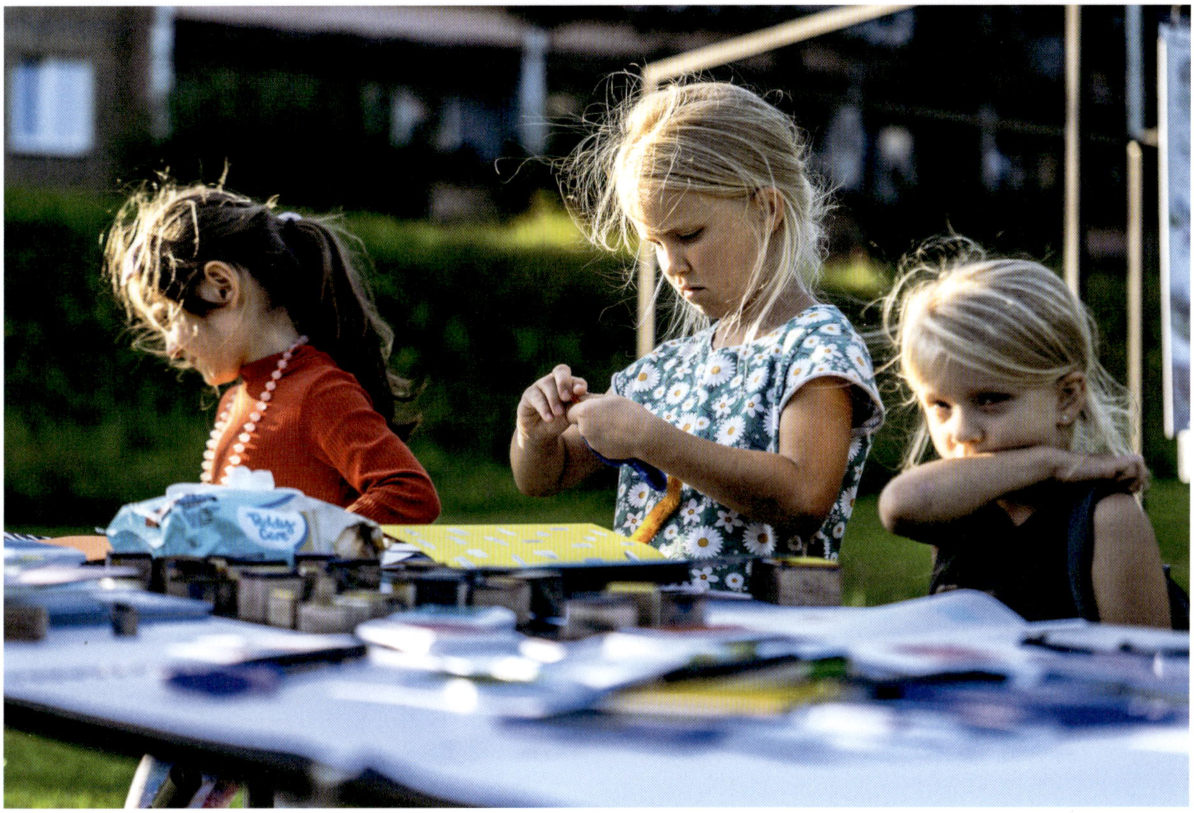

“Révéler le potentiel créatif des petites communes pour un développement durable de nos territoires est au cœur de nos projets.”

“Revealing the creative potential of small communities for the sustainable development of our territories is at the heart of our projects.”
Nathalie Arnould

Location: Pilat Regional Nature Park, France

The region around Saint-Étienne in southeast France is hilly and rural. It is the site of a large nature park of great beauty, though it remains influenced by its experience with textiles, which came and went with the industrial revolution.

SMOTIES Partner: Cité du design – ESADSE, Saint-Étienne

Cité du design is a centre for teaching, research, and the dissemination of design culture. Together with the Saint-Étienne Higher School of Art and Design (ESADSE), they form a public establishment for cultural cooperation. Founded in 2005 after a successful Biennale Internationale Design Saint-Étienne, Cité du design led the most recent Human Cities initiative, Challenging the City Scale, from 2014 to 2018.

Sainte-Croix-en-Jarez and La Vallée du Dorlay

Key involvement in project

Cité du design – ESADSE: Inge Eller, European and international programs manager; Isabelle Vérilhac, head of innovation and international affairs; Anouk Schoellkopf, teacher; Cécile Van Der Haegen, teacher; Nathalie Arnould, design manager, Saint-Étienne metropolitan government; Josyane Franc, former head of international affairs.

Costanza Matteucci, graphic designer; Monica Olszak, designer; Isabelle Daëron, designer, Studio Idaë; Pauline Avrillon, designer, Studio Idaë; Juliana Gotilla, designer.

L'Atelier Mobilité, les Nouveaux Ateliers du Dorlay: Hoël Ascouet; Jean Marie Gaide; Cécile Matricon; Jean-Louis Mauricout.

Luce Chazalon, Maison des Tresses et Lacets; Emmanuelle Gaide, la Turbine Créative, les Nouveaux Ateliers du Dorlay; Didier Lazzareschi, Parc du Pilat; Jean-Philippe Porcherot, Mayor of Doizieux; Christian Ducceschi, Mayor of La Terrasse-sur-Dorlay; Norbert Lacroix, Deputy Mayor of La Terrasse-sur-Dorlay; Myriam Dorel, Deputy Mayor of Saint-Paul-en-Jarez; Jean Michel Chauvet, Association de Sauvegarde et d'Animation de Sainte-Croix-en-Jarez; René Vassoille; Vincent Noclin, videographer and photographer.

What they set out to do

To present soft mobility alternatives to automobile use and link them to the heritage of the Dorlay Valley.
This project focused on three villages: La Terrasse-sur-Dorlay, Doizieux, and Saint-Paul-en-Jarez. For a project focused on Sainte-Croix-en-Jarez, the goal was to gather information about residents' past experiences and create a means of dialogue between generations.

What the project accomplished

Collaborated with residents to establish tools to identify and promote soft mobility, including a map with useful walking and cycling paths in the valley, temporary signage to draw attention to heritage sites, and shoelace designs depicting mobility data. Created a memory card game for the village of Sainte-Croix-en-Jarez.

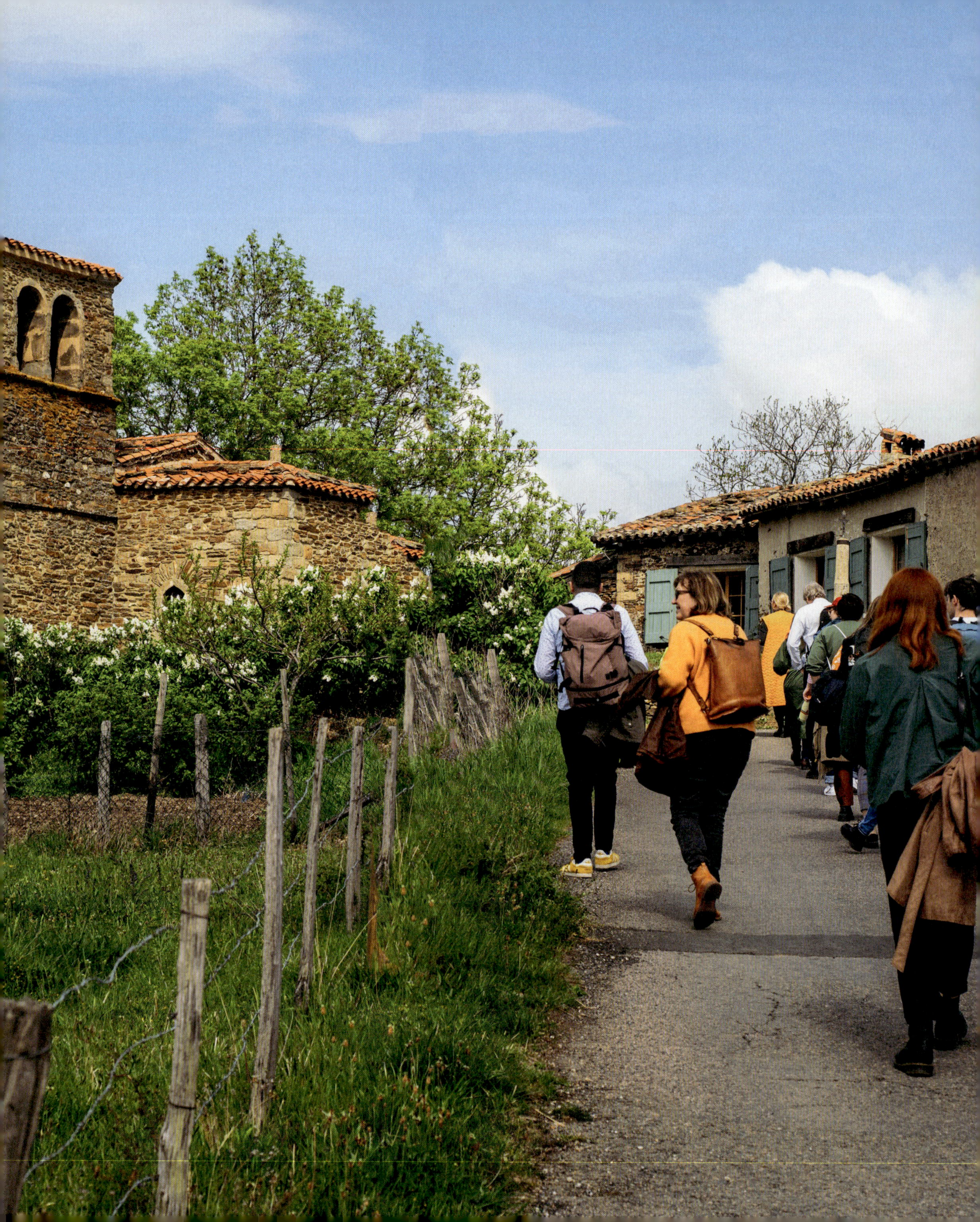

In a French Industrial Valley, Commuting with History

Serious cyclists piston furiously up the hills in the Parc du Pilat. But you don't have to be one. An electric bike will do nicely for an easy glide away from the railway bridge and faded metallurgy plant in town, ascending to the hilly heights of the green and yellow valley of the Dorlay River. While you're at it, you can take in the view of the valley's factoried past while sitting, maybe, in the saddle of its mobile future.

In this commune, 19th-century French industrialists built their looms and perfected the braiding machine: squat metal desks with spinning platters that can make 50 bobbins whirl their thin threads in a fast and endless clattering quadrille. Out came intricate flat ribbons. Corsets. Colourful shoelaces. Textiles dominated the valley for more than a century.

You would not know this on your whirring e-bike along these narrow farmroads unless you were from here (and even then, maybe not). But one late summer afternoon, bright, stylish signposts let you know every so often that you're on what once was the morning commute for generations of textile workers.

In some parts of the valley, the commute wound up the Dorlay River in what was called *la Galoche*, a kind of three-carriage miniature steam train.

Rather than giving a nod to train heritage with some sort of rubber-wheeled trolley passing along the Chemin de la Galoche, we are instead following a pleasant and low-key winding pop-up heritage path.

The signs along the path are only temporary, to see whether people will take to them (and because putting up permanent signage in a public space is difficult). It is, however, an upgrade from a virtual trail on a mobile app that may well go unfound and unused – and the waypoint signs are appealing. They are further represented on a stylised map featuring 30 points of interest, new and old, based on ongoing conversations with villagers, local historians and cultural figures.

Costanza Matteucci, a graphic designer with close-cropped hair, quick smile and prominent spectacles, created the signs with her colleague Monica Olszak. The pair were zip-tying and securing the green signposts in place one morning in mid-September, 2023. Joining them were members of the SMOTIES team that commissioned the work: Inge Eller from Cité du design in nearby Saint-Étienne and Nathalie Arnould, who for more than a decade has been Saint-Étienne's design manager.

"Through the trees here is a viaduct," Eller says brightly. "Yes, this is the old train viaduct over the Dorlay River!" Arnould says, smacking the first of many late-summer mosquitoes coming to greet them.

Under the SMOTIES initiative, they've knit a web among little villages here, aiming to draw on *le patrimoine*, or the culture of history, and spool it into moments of everyday life in these places that have seen so much

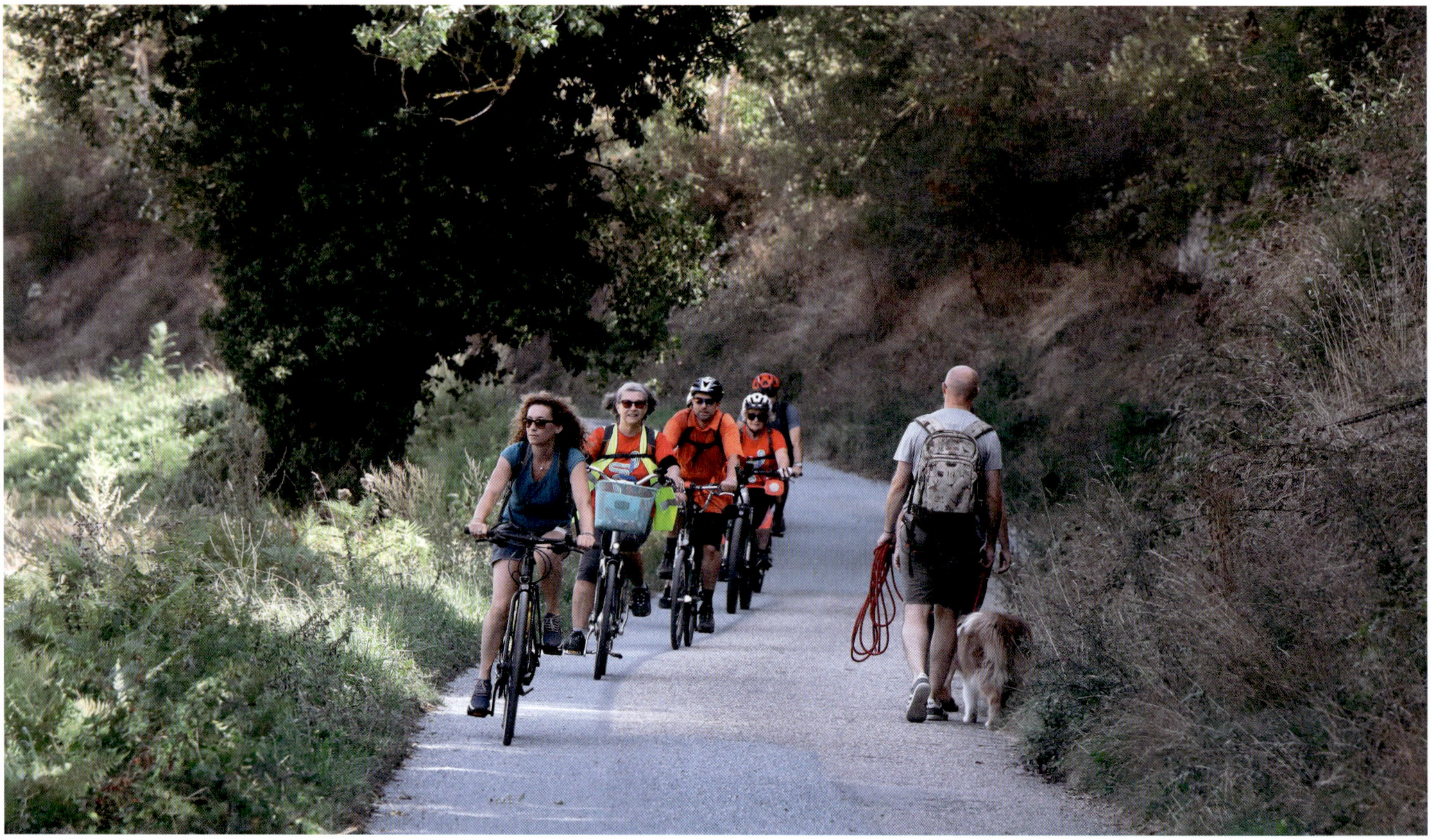

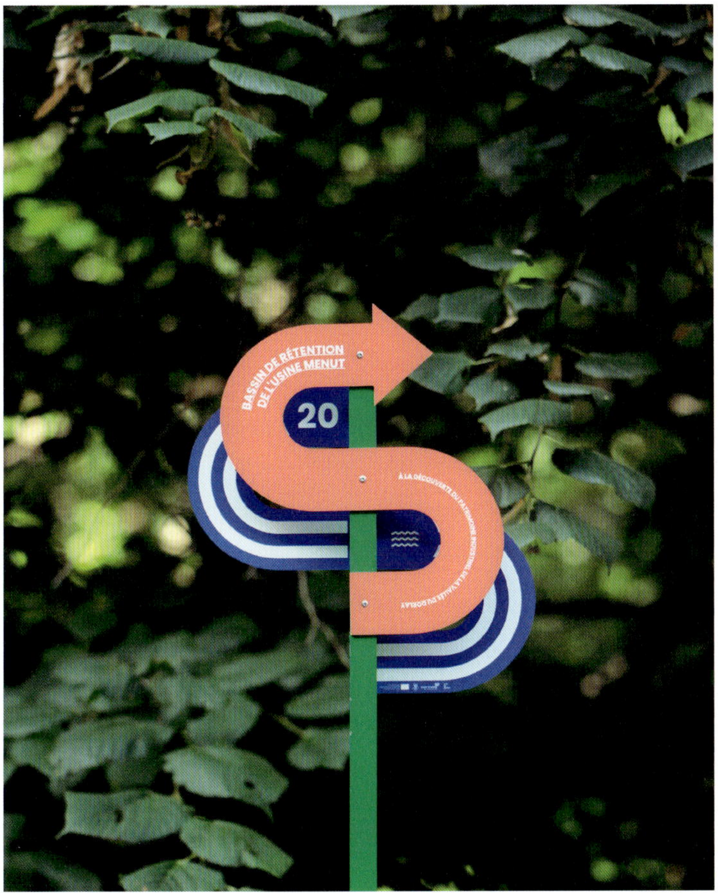

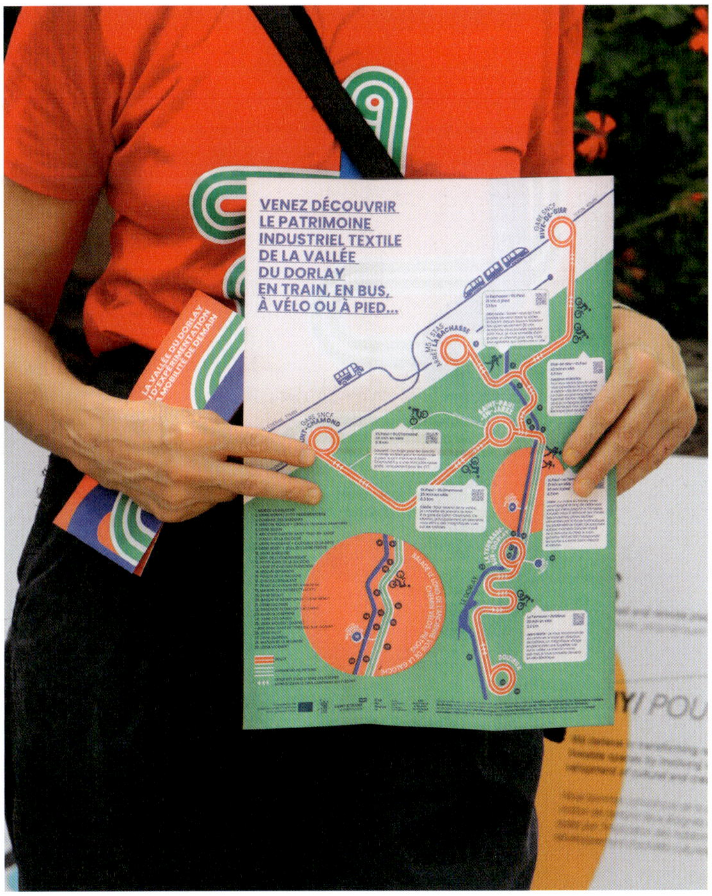

P. 60: Le Chemin des Roches à Cieux trail in Sainte-Croix-en-Jarez. © Vincent Noclin

Bottom left: Participants of the European Heritage Days discovered the industrial heritage of the Dorlay Valley by bike or on foot thanks to the map and the temporary signposting in September 2023. © Fabrice Roure

Top left: Temporary panel on the heritage trail, linking soft mobility routes with the promotion of the Dorlay Valley's industrial heritage. © Fabrice Roure

Top right: Creative wayfinding and a map for mobility in the valley. The aim of this map is to share with the local population and occasional visitors “intelligent routes” taken by bike or on foot, with sensitive descriptions and detail not found on conventional maps. © Monika Olszak

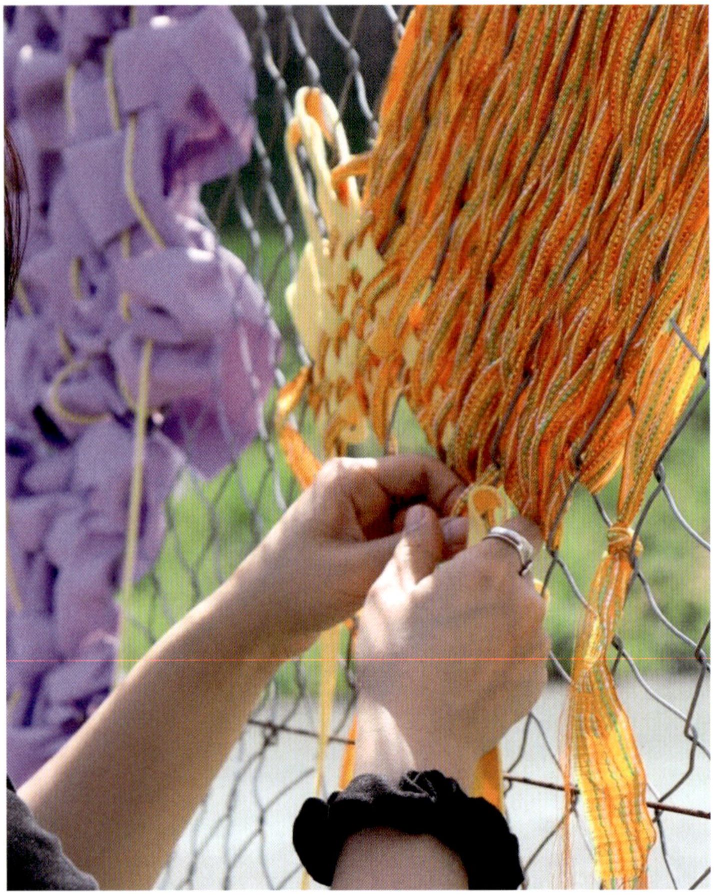

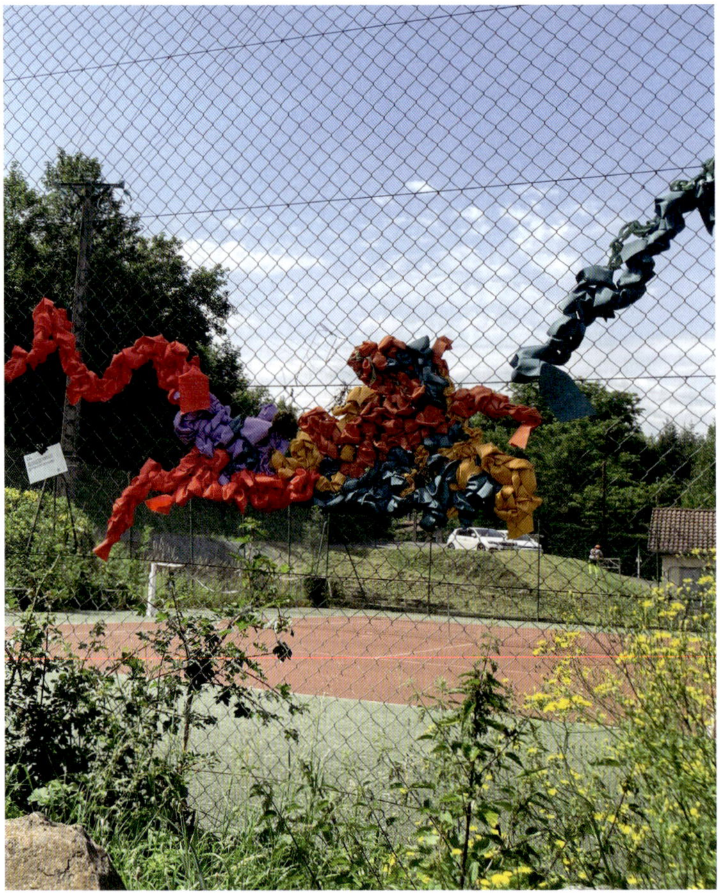

Left: Student textile work brightens the scene at La Terrasse-sur-Dorlay. © Cécile Van Der Haegen

Right: La Terrasse-sur-Dorlay. © Coline Vernay

change. The idea is to tacitly connect it to how we move around today. In the valley, most of the time, that means by car.

The group shoulders its signs and sets off. The path past the former textile rail station, now an ordinary garage hidden by hydrangea bushes, has been designated as the Ancienne Gare de la Galoche. No rails, no auto: just bicycle and foot.

A few days later, a large group of valley residents cycle over the flat footpath, crossing the viaduct and climbing an ever-steeper hill. They've just pedalled past Effet Passementeries, one of the few textile plants still in operation (making artisanal ribbons for Parisian name brands).

Soon they arrive at La Terrasse-sur-Dorlay. It's one of four villages where SMOTIES is at work within the large Pilat Nature Park, through which the Dorlay River winds. The other villages are Doizieux, Saint-Paul-en-Jarez and Sainte-Croix-en-Jarez, which is a village completely contained within the ancient walls of what was once a monastery.

Coming down the path we see patches of yellow and red and lavender cloth woven into fences as art on the way past a restored brick mill. It is a dash of colour in the afternoon.

Those textiles were woven in La Terrasse-sur-Dorlay at a place called La Turbine Créative, a workshop with four training looms; it is located next to a burger grill and across from the town's post office. It is run by the former milliner Emmanuelle Gaide, who kept her hat-making studio for 25 years in Lyon, to the north, before moving to Doizieux, where she took up residence. A book on Pilat first sparked her interest. The park administration supports La Turbine. Saint-Étienne design students moved to La Terrasse-sur-Dorlay to live and work in November 2021 and May 2023; theirs is the lavender and yellow cloth art in the fences on the way into town.

The Turbine did not just spin in the past. Cécile Matricon comes here every month to participate in a 'mobility group' – L'Atelier Mobilité – urging valley residents to think more about how they get around. Suburban America is often cast as the spiritual home of

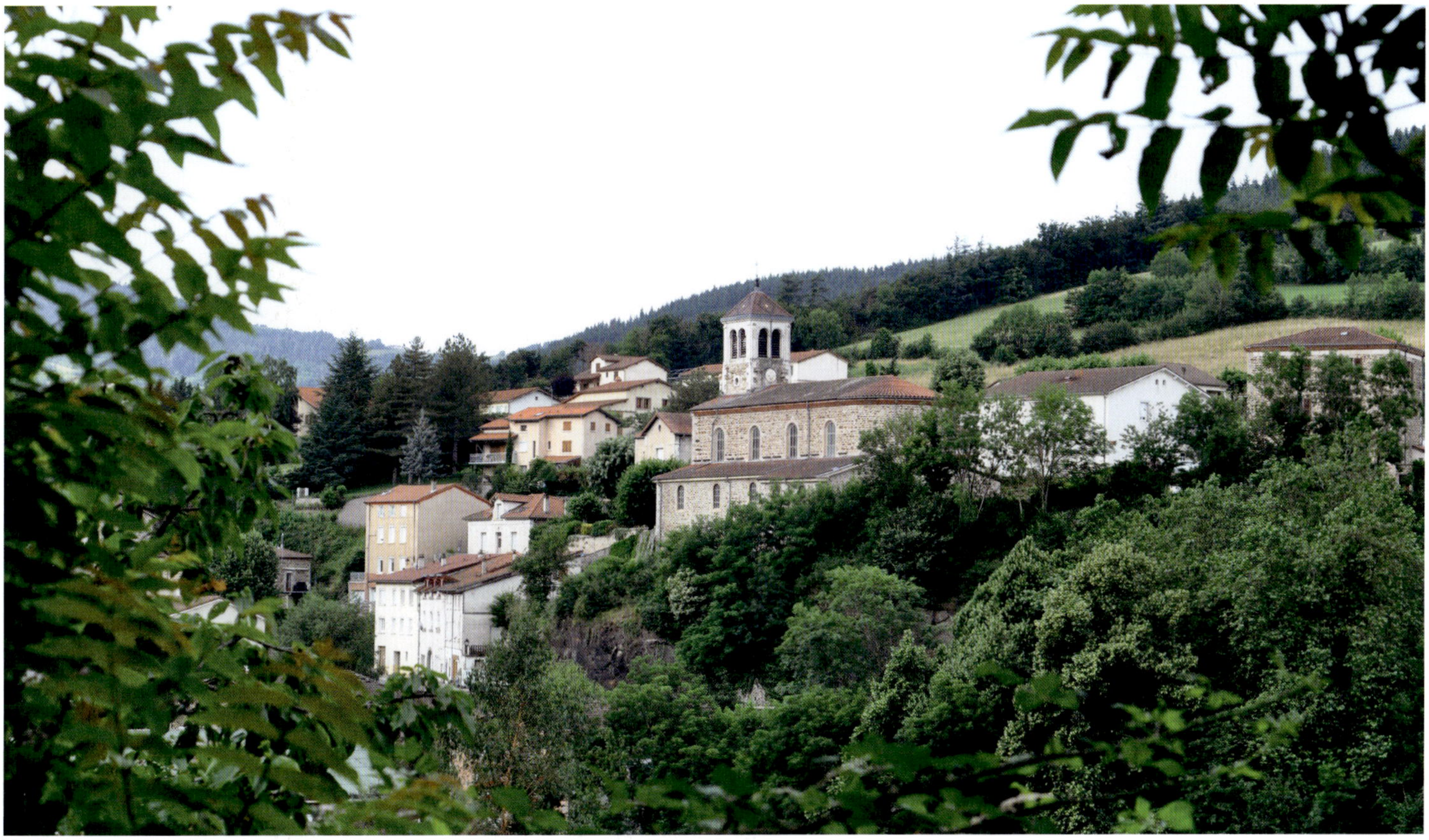

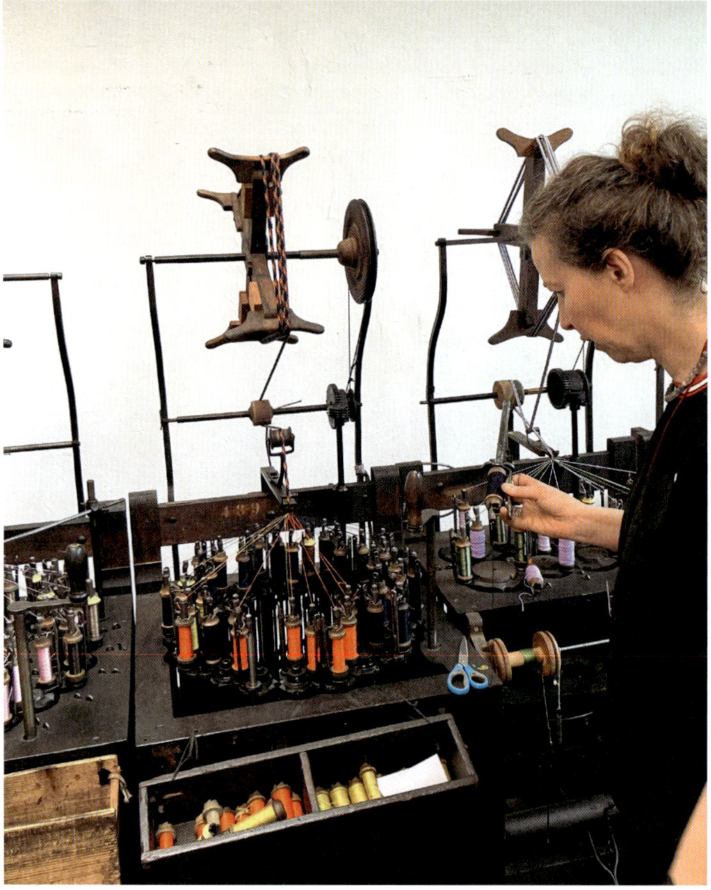

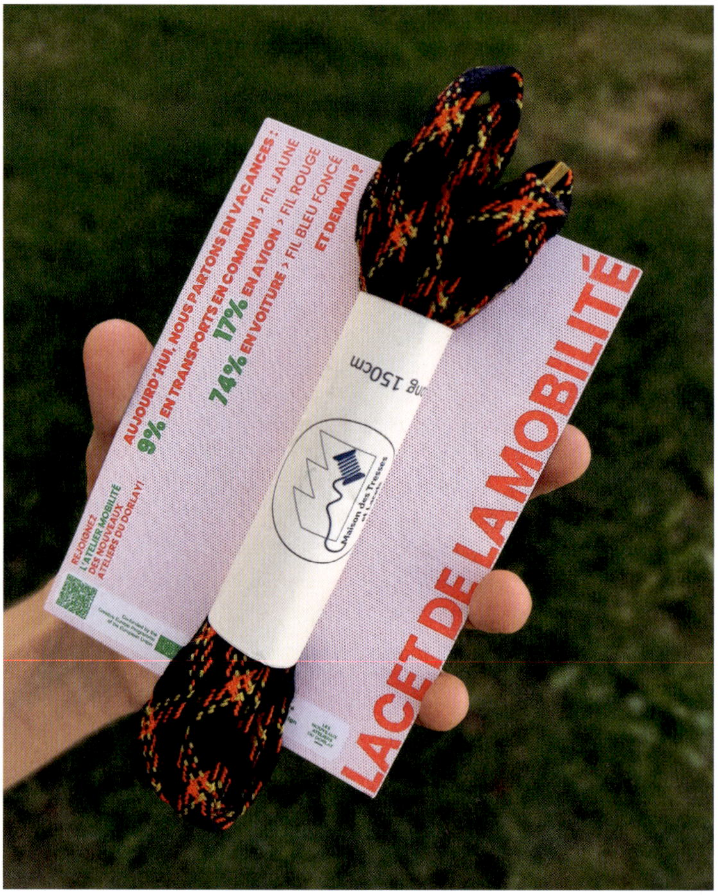

car culture, but the car really rules just about anywhere rural, including Europe. The idea for the map and trail began to take shape as SMOTIES partners worked with residents following a village festival in Doizieux in 2022. Getting by without a car is not practical here. What's the alternative? Even an e-bike is something you'd need to own, and they are expensive – the nearest rentals are in Saint-Étienne, 27 kilometres away.

Matricon holds up a colourful flat shoelace. Eller explains that each band of colour and its thickness represent something meaningful about transport in the valley. SMOTIES will hand out these *Lacets de la mobilité* at an upcoming village festival. They were produced on the still-functioning braiding machines at a local textile museum. Lacing them up in your shoes can remind you that without a car, life here would be very difficult.

In Sainte-Croix-en-Jarez the atmosphere is even more reflective. Carthusian monks first settled here 744 years ago. It's a summery September afternoon, and Isabelle Daëron and Pauline Avrillon, designers from Paris, are laying out tarot-sized cards on a table in a cloister. These cards are *Le Jeu des Cartusiens*, a memory game Daëron devised.

Top left: These braiding machines may be museum pieces, but they still operate. © Monika Olszak

Top right: Holding the *lacets de la mobilité*. © Monika Olszak

Right: Designer Pauline Avrillon lays out the cards in Sainte-Croix-en-Jarez. © Fabrice Roure

Life is pleasant and full of greenery for the residents of Sainte-Croix-en-Jarez, even though the monks have long been gone from this walled village. Deputy mayor Jean Michel Chauvet says if you want to see your neighbours, you work in the yard; if you want to be alone, you work in the garden. You walk there.

Daëron once attended Cité du design and worked on a previous Human Cities project. By the end of 2021, she was finishing a Saint-Étienne-sponsored residency at Sainte-Croix-en-Jarez. Daëron absorbed the local rhythms. She often considers how memory is imbued in objects, creating visible totems and an invisible landscape. A meadow is not just a meadow, but a place where perhaps there was once a barbecue and someone fell in love; a tree there is significant; a road once saw Tour de France participants flashing by. Local history can be plotted on a map. Or in other ways.

She organised a workshop for village residents, who voted for something untethered to the historic monastery walls, more representative of living village memory: the card game. During her time in the village, Daëron says she also became inspired by the monastic habit of *spaciement*: a weekly meditative walk.

This may not be an answer to everyday car travel in the rural valleys. But it is a kind of consolation.

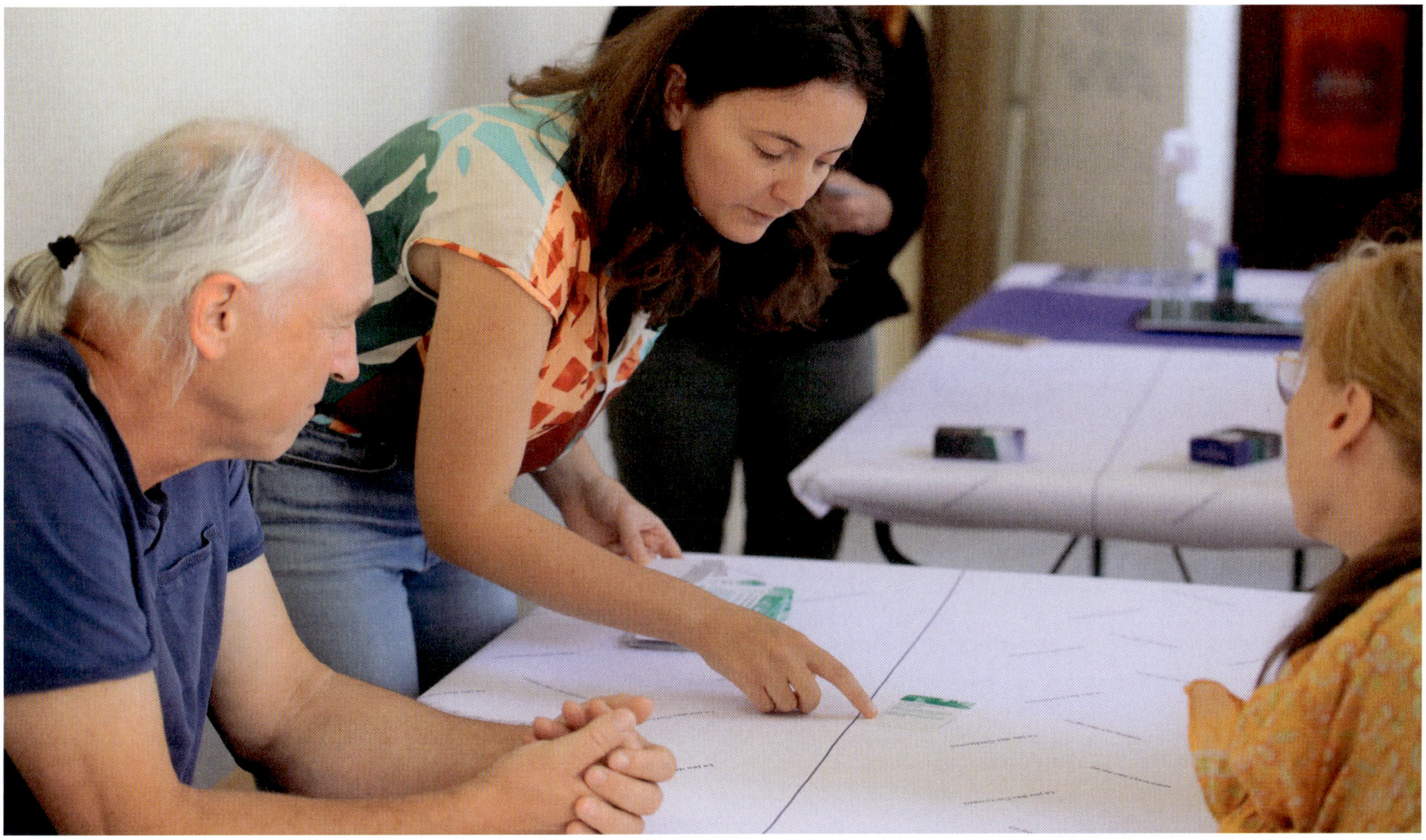

"L'approccio del progetto SMOTIES ha fatto sì che percepissimo Albugnano e noi stessi come parte di una rete sociale interconnessa. Questa nuova prospettiva ci ha spinti ad ampliare le nostre iniziative, come il festival, coinvolgendo anche le comunità circostanti."

"The SMOTIES project's approach has led us to consider Albugnano and ourselves as parts of an interconnected social fabric. This perspective has motivated us to broaden our initiatives, such as the festival, to include neighbouring communities as well."
Marco Gobetti

Albugnano

Location: Albugnano, Italy

The small hilltop villages of Albugnano, Aramengo, Gonengo and Pino d'Asti in the Italian Piedmont lie to the east of Turin, have strong ties to viticulture and tourism, and feature old Romanesque churches. Albugnano hosts an annual culture festival. Its sites command views of the Asti countryside. This is an area that has taken in outsiders – a large group of Peruvians once settled near there to work – but villages struggle with depopulation and buildings falling into ruin.

SMOTIES Partner: Politecnico di Milano, Milan

Founded in 1863, Politecnico di Milano is a leading research and educational institution; its Department of Design was Italy's first institution for research in design. The research team involved in the Human Cities research project is part of the Polimi DESIS Lab within the international DESIS Network. The Polimi DESIS Lab is a group of researchers adopting a strategic and systemic approach to design, with a specific focus on design for spaces, services and design activism.

Key involvement in project

Department of Design, Politecnico di Milano: Davide Fassi, professor in design, coordinator of the Polimi DESIS Lab, coordinator of the SMOTIES project; Annalinda De Rosa, researcher in design, co-coordinator of the SMOTIES project; Paola Russo, research fellow; Valentina Auricchio, associate professor; Vanessa Monna, postdoctoral research fellow; Alexandra Coutsoucos, research fellow; Marco Finardi, service designer collaborating with the Polimi DESIS Lab; Nadia Pirovano, research fellow.

Andrea Pirollo, co-founder of Albugnano 549; Dario Rei, former sociology professor, expert of Basso Monferrato region; Enoteca Regionale dell'Albugnano; Lo Stagno di Goethe ETS and its founder, Marco Gobetti.
The mayors and municipalities of Albugnano and Aramengo towns (Aurora Angilletta, Giuseppe Marchese, Alessandro Nicola), Pro Loco di Aramengo and Pro Loco di Albugnano.

What they set out to do

Use design tools to bring visibility to local cultural heritage and tourist itineraries; to create spaces for residents; find ways for residents to work together towards these goals.

What the project accomplished

Creative ferment: residents felt encouraged to network and create initiatives and associations. There is now a set of landscaped and redesigned small community spaces in formerly under-used corners of the villages. The team co-designed the main square with a tactical urbanism approach and modular "totem" columns and signs and placed them in eight key spaces in Albugnano featuring informative and historical texts, linking them to one another.

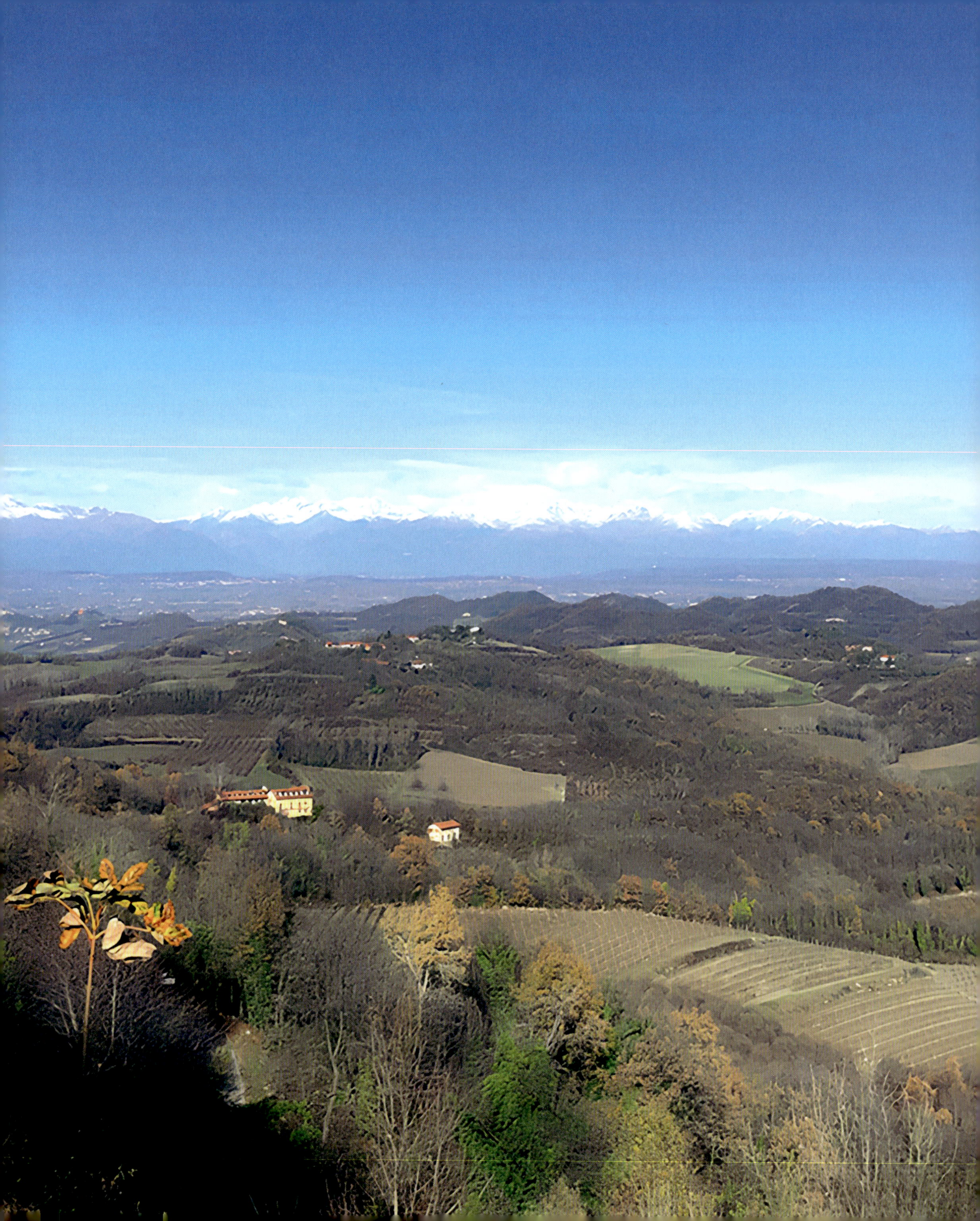

Basso Monferrato: Totems and Stories

"People are needing to reflect after being forced to stay locked in their houses for months, without the possibility to act," Marco Gobetti says, sitting at an early-evening picnic table in a beautiful and crumbling former rectory in the medieval village of Albugnano, on top of a low, steep hill.

We are about to be inundated with a truly biblical swarm of bloodthirsty mosquitoes but don't know it yet. Gobetti, a theatre person and culture festival director, is describing the recent pandemic. Though our memories about it have quickly become indistinct, here in the Basso Monferrato region, on the southern reaches of the Italian Piedmont, we are not so far away from one of its most brutal and tragic European epicentres.

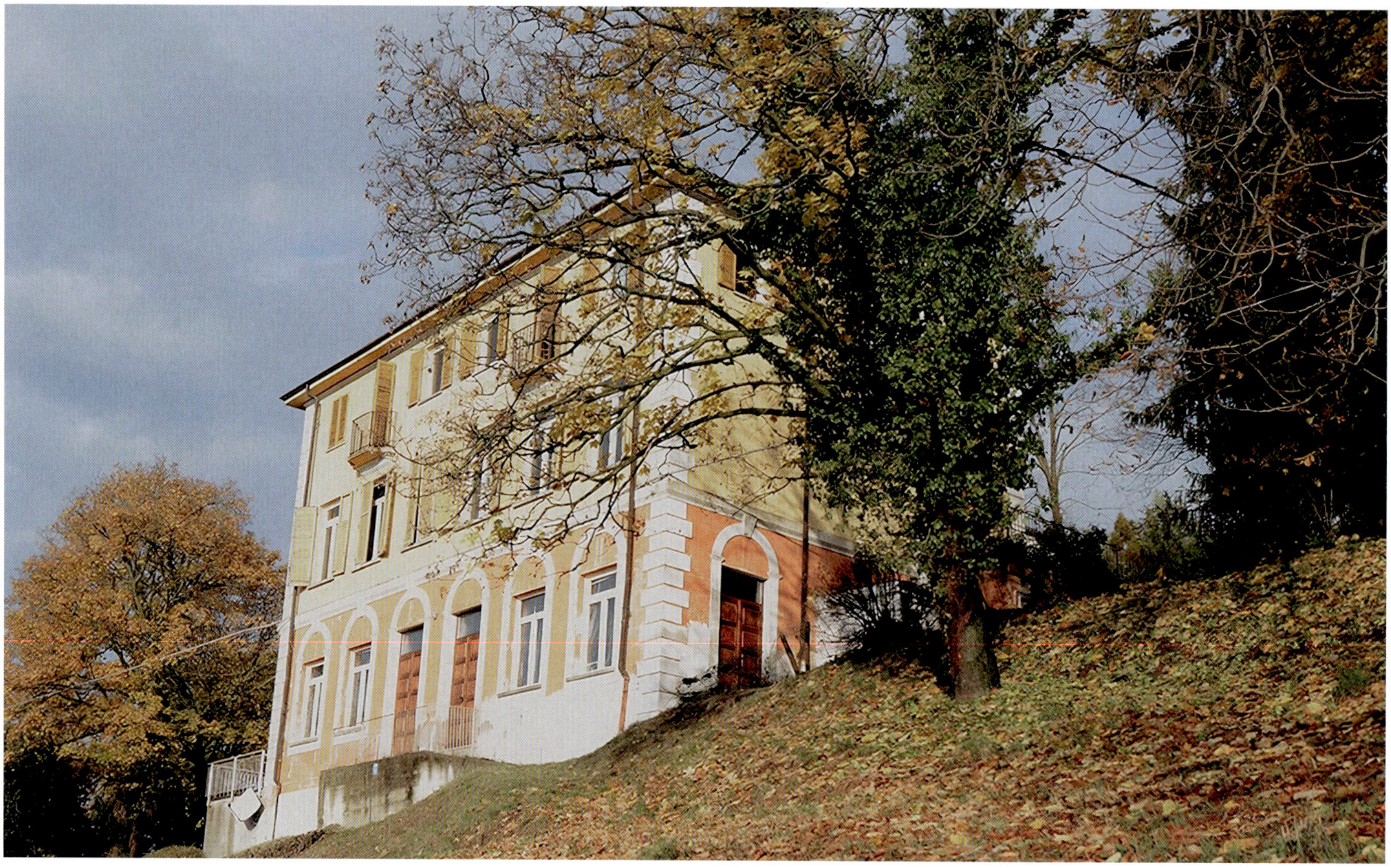

P. 70: The view over Basso Monferrato. © Polimi DESIS Lab

Left: Regional Winery, Albugnano (Enoteca Regionale dell'Albugnano). © Polimi DESIS Lab

Right: Vezzolano Abbey. © Polimi DESIS Lab

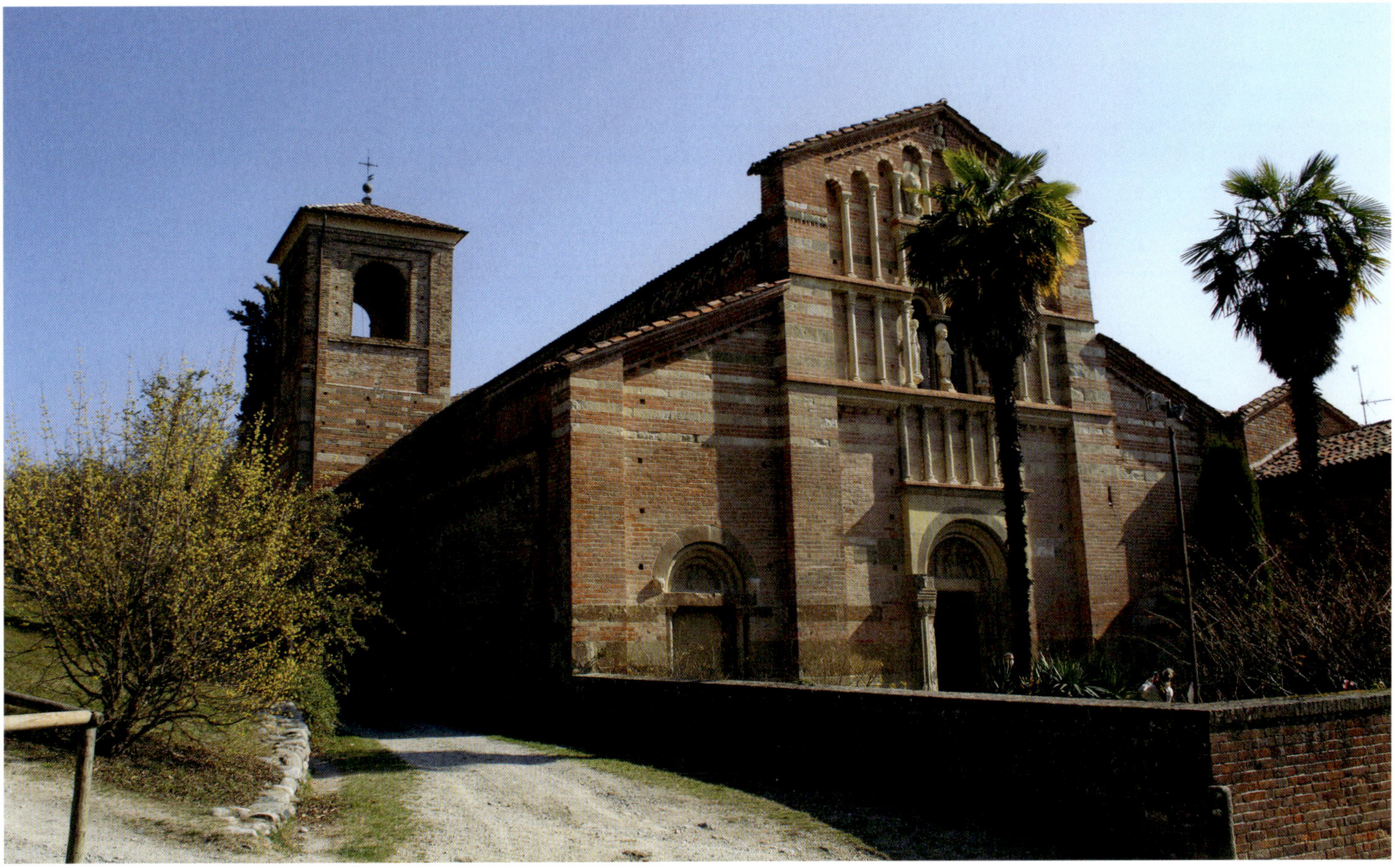

Lockdown meant disconnection, staying still. "Reflection is necessary more than ever now, because it generates actions, movement, cooperation, communication. Getting reacquainted with the taste for thinking is essential," the bearded director says, cup of the local Nebbiolo in hand.

That's the vital role he sees for the theatre: live theatre, itinerant theatre, touring small and out-of-the-way places. He sees the same role for people aiming to bring design into the lives of everyday people – and this is why he was keen to connect with a group of researchers from Politecnico di Milano putting out feelers in Basso Monferrato.

Then the mosquitoes descend and we act: we have to run. We wind up in a building that once was the Camilla Serafino elementary school, but which is now an outlet for regional wine production – the Enoteca Regionale dell'Albugnano, it's called – with a tourist information point and community space at the top where classrooms used to be.

It is packed and sweltering: an actor from Turin is starting a monologue about the misadventures of the man who patented the automatic transmission. It is the second-to-last night of the QUADILA festival, run through Gobetti's troupe, Lo Stagno di Goethe. It runs for three weekends every summer in Albugnano. The Enoteca is also the place where in March 2021 design leaders from Politecnico assembled to launch efforts for SMOTIES.

Albugnano is close to Turin but does not feel that way. It is at least old enough to have been settled when the Saracens sacked nearby Vezzolano Abbey in the tenth century. Vezzolano is an anchor of what's now known as the Romanica di Collina or Transromanica, an informal network of trails and heritage sites tied to the Romanesque period of the Middle Ages. Vezzolano is a still-startling show of its art and architecture and of the Abbey's fixture in daily life.

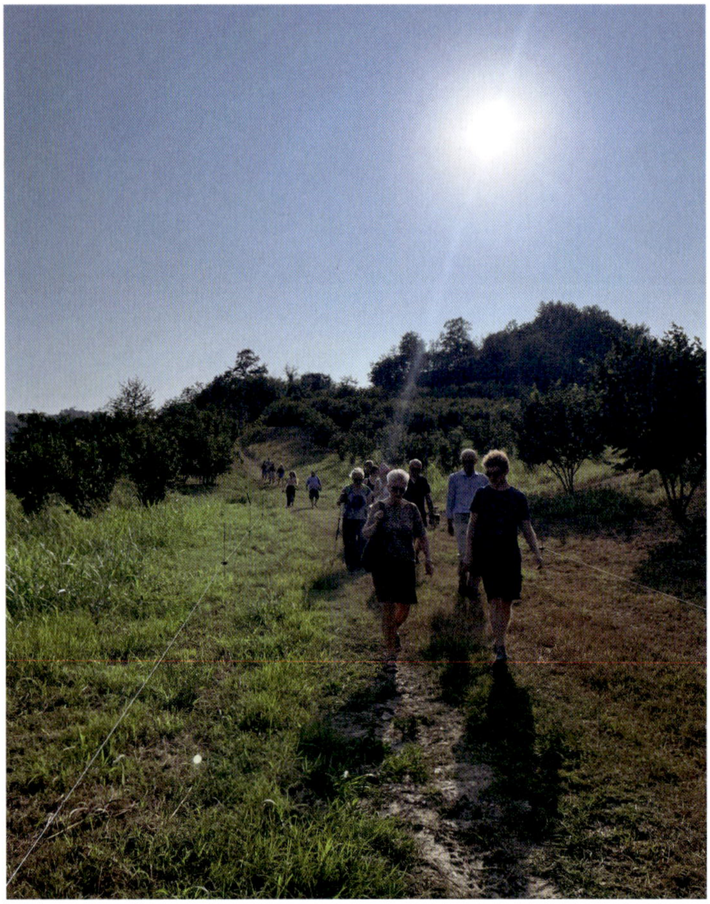

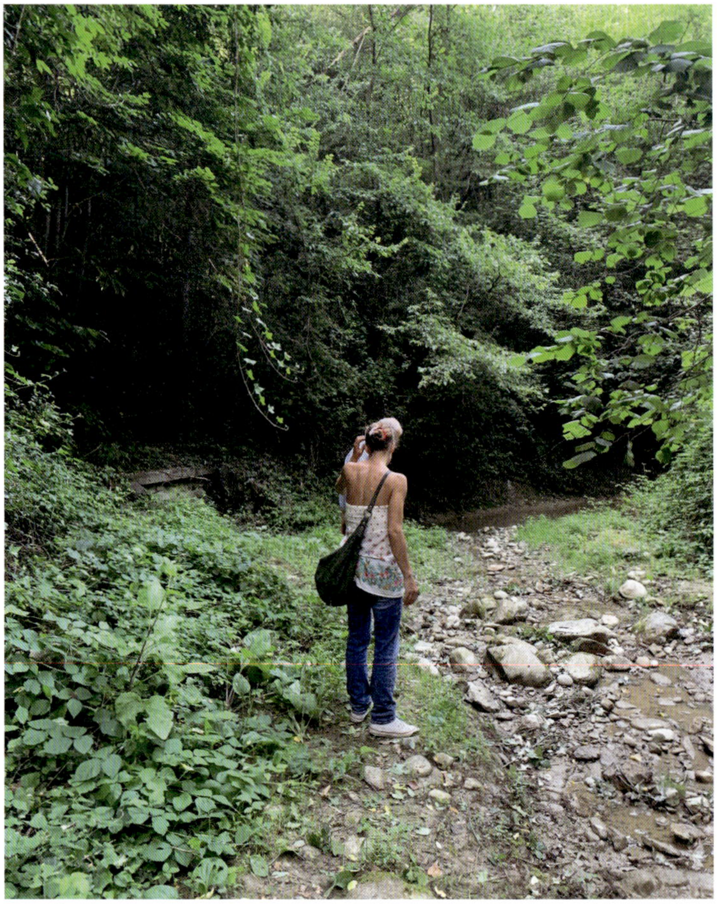

Itinerant storyplaying during the local QUADILA festival 2023, reaching Fonte Solforosa (a sulphur source). © Polimi DESIS Lab

Five hundred people live in Albugnano now; the average age is about 50. Polimi had its eyes first on this village. It then branched out to villages that dot Basso Monferrato.

It was a winding trail. Not only did the team need to negotiate the ebb and flow of the COVID-19 pandemic – at the time still sharply resonant in Italy – but move through a challenging local political environment.

Wine is essential to this lush area of the Piedmont. Polimi had developed a mailing list as it started to visit the Basso Monferrato, launching master classes and huddling with residents to draw up ideas with students and understand the villages. A lot of this happened with the help of the Enoteca and local municipal council. It's a small village, though – when the leadership of the Enoteca and municipal council clashed, it would eventually prompt new elections, and Polimi had to tread carefully.

Every design project runs through political hurdles, especially those involving civic or public space, but it takes a deft touch to do so in village civics, where everyone knows everyone and the procedural is personal. While the electioneering took place, the Polimis busied themselves elsewhere.
"I was asking people, hey, can you introduce me to your nephew because I'm trying to find someone younger than 35," laughs Marco Finardi, who's recently finished his master's work involving public performance, design and narrative community participation. He collected stories from villagers, plotting them onto maps and creating storytelling walks.

"They are places you would not really know without talking with someone from Albugnano," he says. This is a specific way of reading landscape: it reveals what is often hidden in plain sight. "A lot of important places for them were for me really anonymous in the sense they were like a tree or a

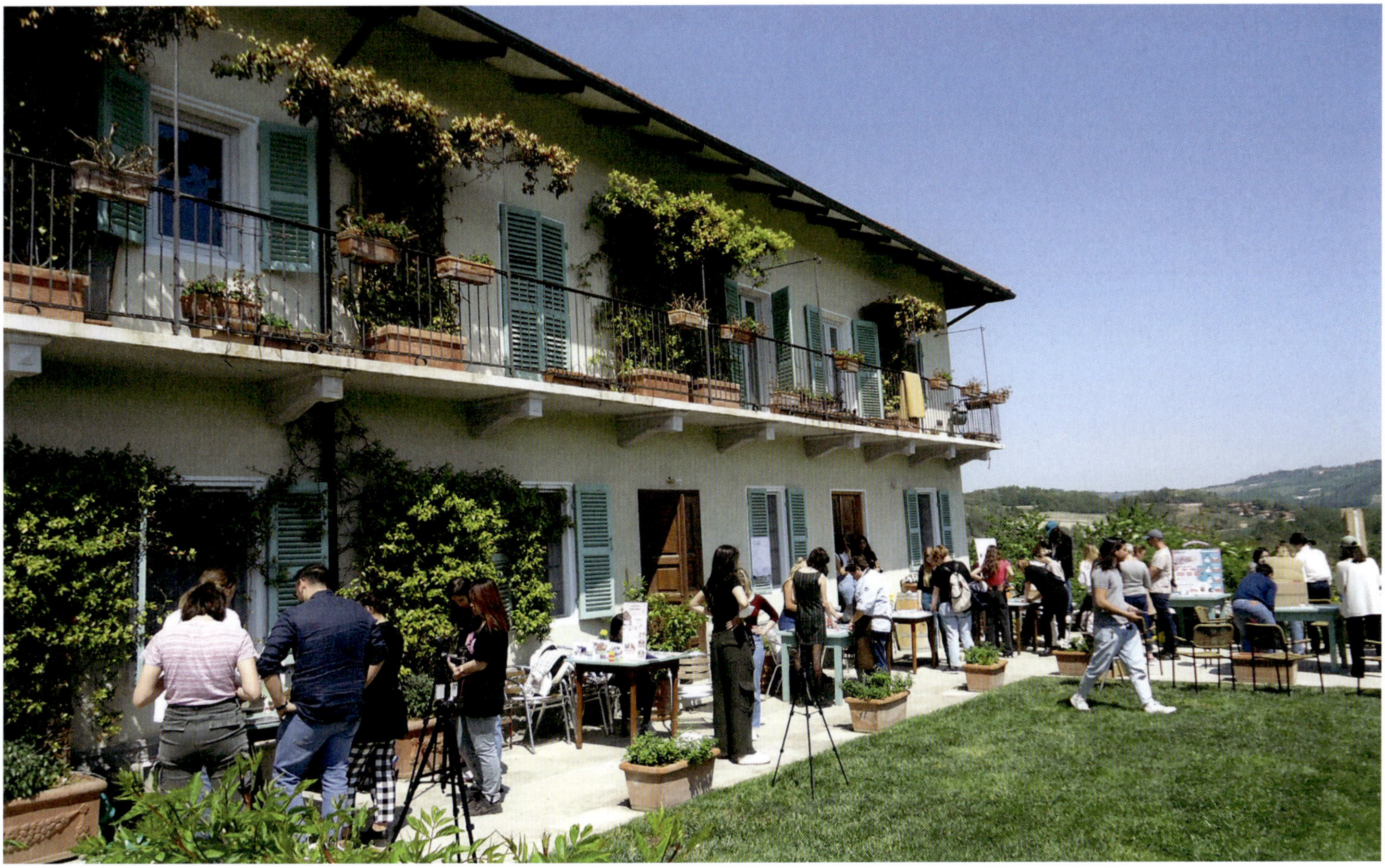

Co-design workshop with design students and citizens at Cà Mariuccia ethical and organic farm in Albugnano, April 2022. © Polimi DESIS Lab

field or a specific spot on a specific side of a hill," he says.

These storytelling walks fit neatly alongside the QUADILA festival. Behind Vezzolano Abbey there is a dirt road rising into the vineyards. Gobetti, the festival director, is escorting a group. After the show, there's a detour, up one path, turn around, down another. There's a wooden cross in the trees. One of the Polimis holds up a speaker; it's Finardi's narrative, and the voice of a neighbour.

L'abbazia e tutta questa zona emanano una serenità davvero palpabile.

"The abbey, this area is truly serene, a peace of soul that I rarely experience. But in those places, I do," she says. Then another voice.

Per noi quella era la crocetta e la crocetta erano proprio i primi baci.

"For us this was the little cross. And this was the place where you had your first real kisses. If a couple was coming together, they had to come all the way down here."

Then we're off again, as the mosquitoes have found us. On the next day of the festival, another story, on the other side of the village. Aramengo mayor Giuseppe Marchese joins on his red Vespa, riding through a hazelnut orchard. In deeper woods finally there is a trickling stream with a faint hint of sulphur and a fountain. The group spreads in a wide circle in the trees. Finardi holds up his speaker. *La giungla.*

"The jungle. The farmers would come down here because the water quenched their thirst, it was rich in salts. But for me it was a place of wandering, through rain and snow. It was Indiana Jones." A place for exploring. A little up the hill on the Via Roma in Albugnano, a wall stretches along the street across from a stand of trees that pulse and buzz with cicadas. It's a crumbly courtyard,

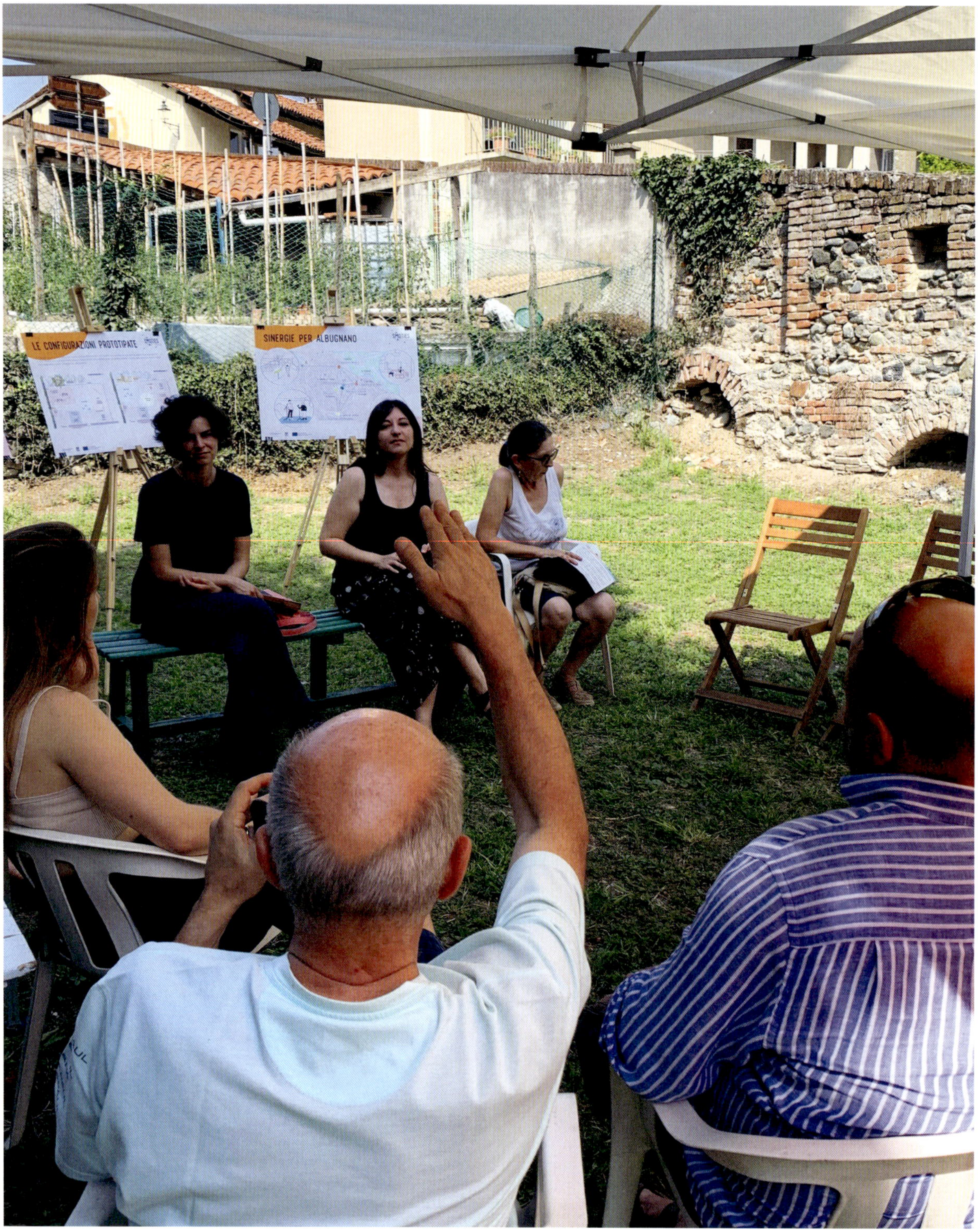

Left: Talk with citizens at the Via Roma Garden during the local QUADILA festival 2023. © Polimi DESIS Lab

Right: The totemic panel and the *book crossing* spot in Piazza Cavalier Serra, Albugnano. © Polimi DESIS Lab

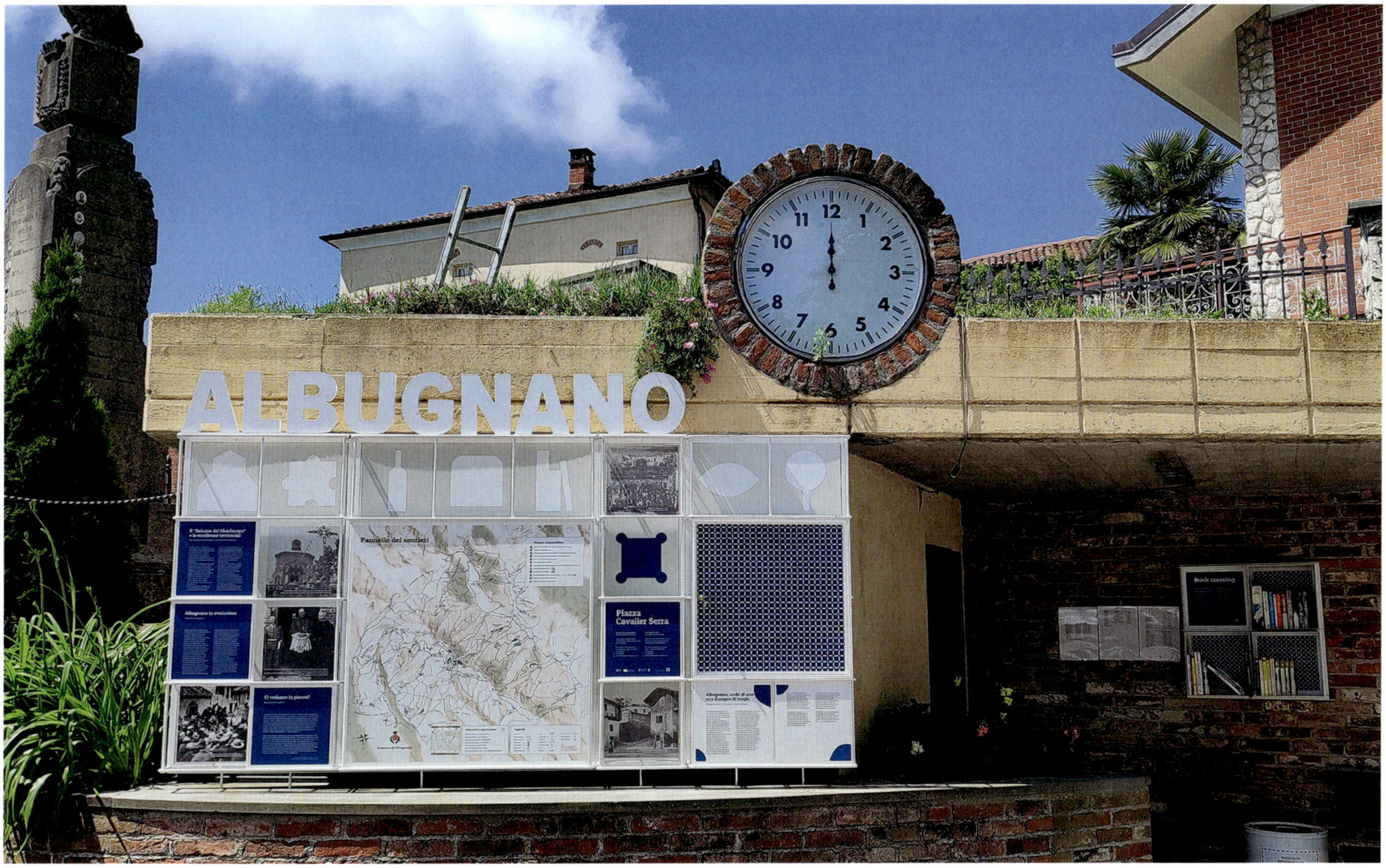

green and uneven; there's a vegetable garden at the top and a leaning tree to one side. It needs work, and available funds can't cover everything. There are more interesting parts of the village that people use. It's hot and out of the way. But it is available. The owner, Mario Conrotto, gave the village a concession to it for the next 30 years. Polimi came back with renderings of the Via Roma Garden, tiered slopes and places to sit and gather. A small amphitheatre. Or, if it were garden enough, it could also be used just for hanging out, talking: for getting outside and taking a break from digital life. There is no real piazza in Albugnano (though a table at the hilltop serves as one). Plans call to mark that area more significantly, linking it to the garden amphitheatre, saying: here are public spaces for gathering and activities.

Here also will be one of eight totemic panels signed with texts and symbols about the place, its uses, its history, its connection to seven other public places in the village, now also marked with totems. They catch the eye. They present an opening to visitor and resident alike to imagine the village by what you can do: here's the veranda, the garden, the study, the living room, the chapel. They also remind residents that the keys are available to the rectory for public events just about any time they like.

Albugnano has a curious geography. It is pretty, and the local wine is fantastic, and QUADILA draws big crowds, but the village also participates, so far unsuccessfully, in the one-euro-housing programme that dots similar villages across Italy: municipalities taking up dilapidated properties and offering them for a symbolic euro. Abandonment and depopulation of the countryside is real. Young people are leaving. Garden plots and views won't keep people around if there's no work. But places that show signs of life also show possibilities; they can be spots for dreaming new dreams and making new memories. The stories they tell here show a hunger for it.

“Απρόσμενες συναντήσεις με τα ζώα και φυτά με τα οποία μοιραζόμαστε το οικοσύστημα, μας καλούν να επαναπροσδιορίσουμε το ρόλο μας ως άνθρωποι.”

“Unexpected encounters with the animals and plants with which we share the ecosystem invite us to redefine our role as humans.”
Helen Charoupia, Kypriani Bartzoka

Location: Apano Meria, Syros, Greece

The remote northern part of Syros, a small Greek Aegean island in the Cyclades, is called Apano Meria. It is protected under the European Union's Natura 2000 programme, but its future is uncertain. In this environment, negotiating civil administration requires patience and creativity to realise design initiatives.

SMOTIES Partner: University of the Aegean, Department of Product and Systems Design Engineering

The department is part of the Polytechnic School of the University of the Aegean and focuses specifically on the integrated design of modern and emerging products, systems, and services. It is a forerunner in Greek higher education, recognised for its high-quality, broad research; it is the only design engineering department in Greece.

Apano Meria

Key involvement in project

University of the Aegean, Department of Product and Systems Design Engineering: Helen Charoupia, researcher, sustainable futures through design; Kypriani Bartzoka, interdisciplinary designer, engineer, and researcher; Paris Xyntarianos Tsiropinas, design researcher, street art.

Spyros Bofylatos, former team member, University of the Aegean; Jenny Darzentas, former administrator; Io Stavridi, Apano Meria SCE.

What they set out to do

Engage communities and draw attention to a place that is remote but still local to the university's design faculty; record local narratives and create memory maps; focus public attention on considering ecology, water shortages, a fragile environment and the challenges of overtourism; highlight cultural heritage and sustainable local economy.

What the project accomplished

Built memory maps and developed a concept for community-maintained shelters and rest stops near the start of many hiking trails using existing underutilised infrastructure.

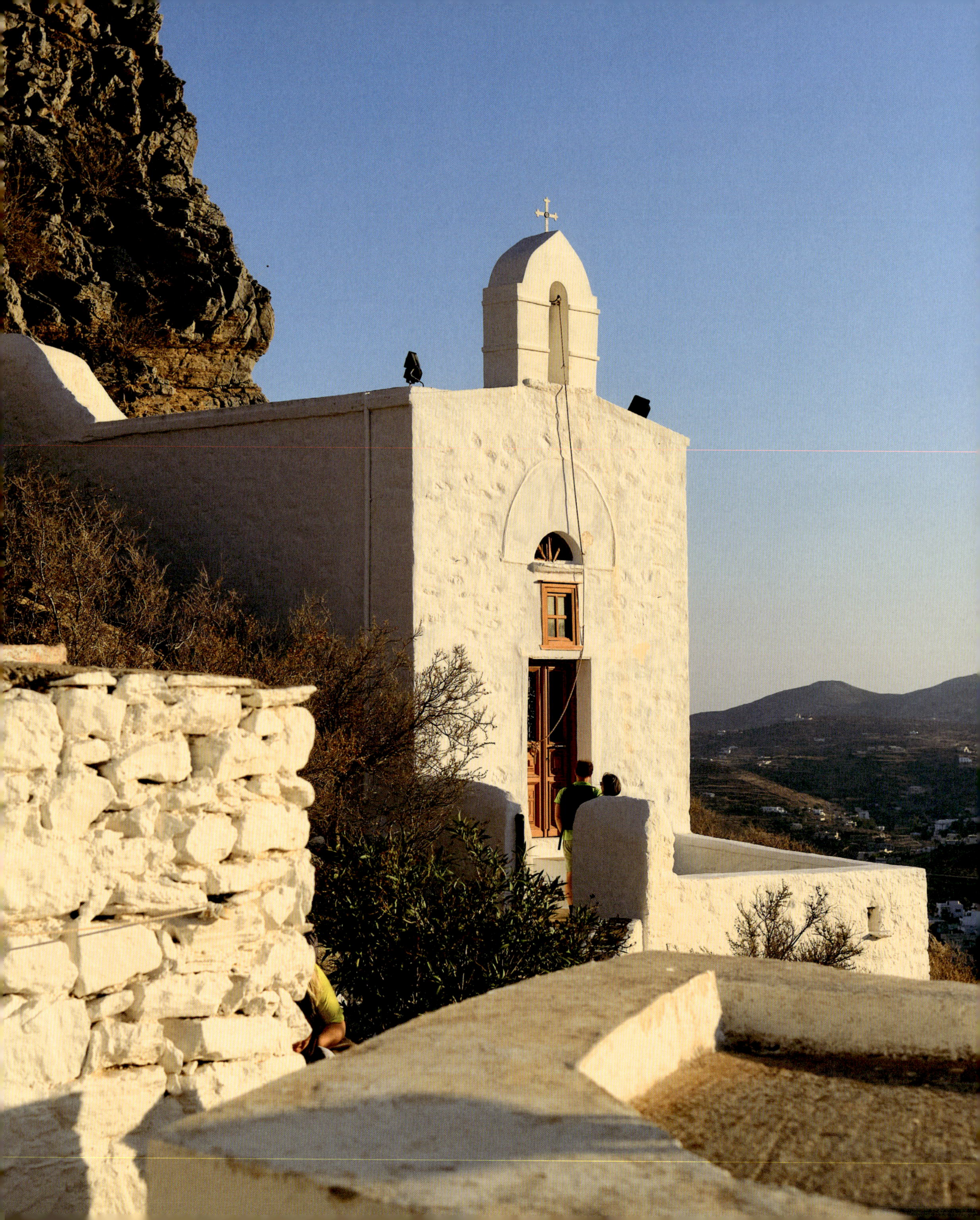

Shelter Island

As the hazy outline of the island of Syros comes into view the murmur on the ferryboat is curious, even startled: look, there, it's so arid. It must never rain. So dry.

Most people on the boat will not disembark here and will carry on to Mykonos. But in their first view of Syros, they at least have a point. Blue is the water along the coast, but it does not rain much there: 40 centimetres a year – as dry as Mali south of Timbuktu (but not as dry as the Sahara).

But onshore there are other things to notice. There are twisted grapevines tucked into and hidden by winding stone walls among the empty hills, vines that predate phylloxera, the bug that destroyed wine production across 19th-century Europe.

And there are no roads that take you to the beaches on this part of the island. You have to either walk or go by boat. When a developer tried to build a road as part of a lease deal on one of these municipal beaches – ostensibly for a food cart – it caused a ruckus.

That sparked the creation of the small nonprofit Apano Meria SCE. Opposition grew strong enough to nix the road.

"We're saying no to this kind of development that opens new roads and installs canteens and recliners and umbrellas," says Io Stavridi, a group organiser. Umbrellas may sound harmless enough but are contentious at a time of kinetic postpandemic tourism. Businesses are mushrooming on public beaches and charging 70 euro for a chair. Only sad gravel patches are left free. "We say no to this. But we also want to know, 'What can we say yes to?'"

Apano Meria SCE is named after the place known as Apano Meria, a nearly deserted triangular-shaped area on Syros. This is the place SMOTIES partners at the University of the Aegean have chosen to focus on. Helen Charoupia, a young design researcher at the university, has been doing communications for Apano Meria SCE for three years now.

Settlements on Syros are 5,000 years old. "Human activity has always been here," Stavridi says. In her view, Apano Meria should not be in a protective bubble where there are no people. But it is a precarious place. A September walk is eye-opening under the baking sun along dry rockwalled terraces and tiny village paths. Holiday homes are already boarded up and quiet. Some houses have sagging roofs and no water connections and are uninhabited and have gone to seed. Others further along the road have smart gates and jewel-blue pools, even though the sea is in sight and water is scarce.

Through these dusty hills it is still possible to hear a tinny radio coming through an open window with the cascading notes of Markos Vamvakaris playing the bouzouki. Markos, as he is known, was a master player from Ano Syros; a statue of him graces the main Syros harbour as a champion of *rembetika* folk style. Pointing it out on this hot September afternoon is Paris Xyntarianos Tsiropinas, a graphic designer and street art scholar.

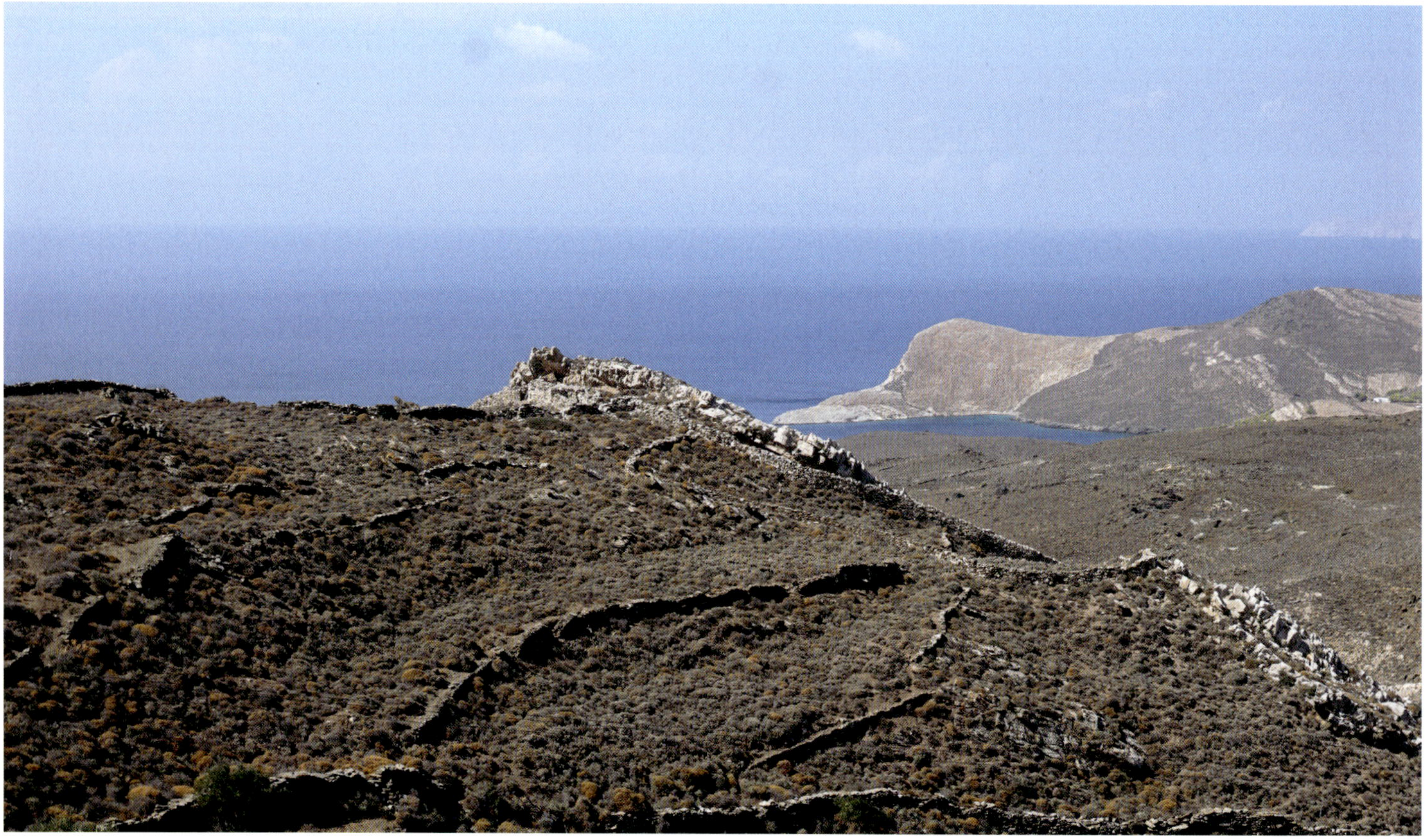

P. 80: © Kevin Loigu

Left: Dry stone walls wind their way to the Aegean in Apano Meria, Syros. © Kevin Loigu

Right: Paris Tsiropinas, centre, leads a group of SMOTIES partners through fields below San Michalis. © Kevin Loigu

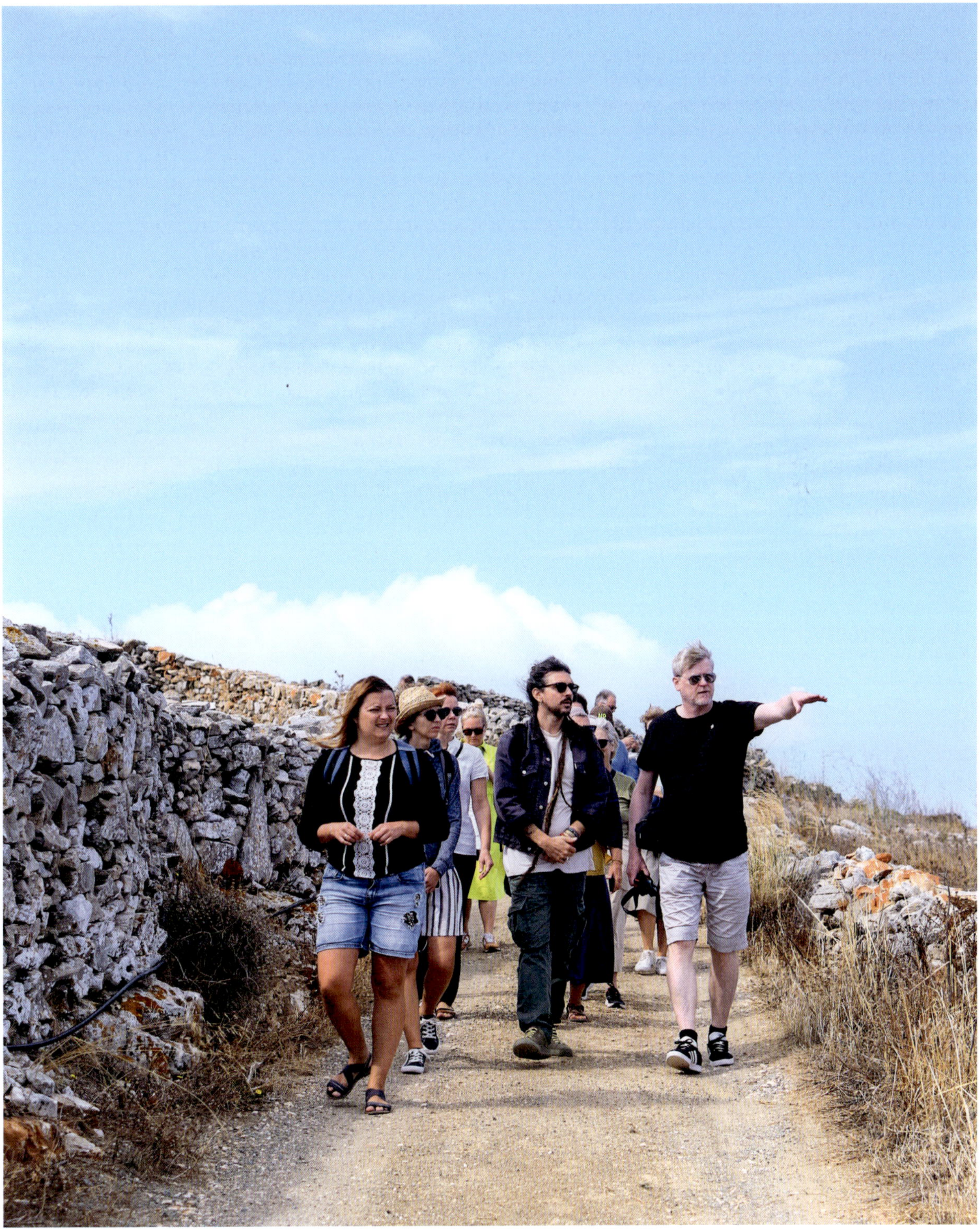

Paris also plays the bouzouki. It was in cafés listening to live music that he got to know Nikos Chatzakis and the wine writer Nikoleta Makrionitou. Nikoleta and Nikos run a small winery at the top of a hill in Apano Meria. Paris painted the logo above the winery's patio trellis; its barrels overlook sinuous terraces made from rocks set without mortar, these dry stone walls winding down to the shoreline. Today the winery is harvesting Serifiotiko grapes for pressing, a variety found only in the Cyclades, the group of islands to which Syros belongs.

"A lot of people here had vineyards and wanted to abandon them," Chatzakis says, bearded, agreeable, a little doleful. He describes himself and Nikoleta as poor people from Piraeus, a rough harbourside in Athens. They rent their place. They started elsewhere on Syros and moved to Apano Meria, in spite of the harsh winter wind, because they love it. Here you can make honey, wine, San Michali cheese.

But the water situation is hard. Syros gets its drinking water from desalination plants. For two months in summer, the winery doesn't see any water at all.

"We have a big tank. We try to fill it up, and then work with it," he says. Cultivation is okay. Bottling, a joy. Daily life? Rugged. "Only because you are a romantic, do you have vines." A little further down the hill, though, it's easy to spot a few well-appointed patios with their bright blue pools. Water doesn't seem to be a problem there.

Chatzakis does not export. "We try to keep the situation calm," he says. "We want to live from what we do, but don't want to be very touristic. We want the tourism but in a good way." Because tourism makes up one fifth of the economy, this is on the mind of many Greeks. Across the street from Nikos is a little white concrete shelter with an open entrance and shaded interior. When Helen, Paris and their colleagues canvassed people in workshops, the idea arose to focus on the shelter.

The shelter occupies a mysterious space at the roadside. It looks like a bus stop. But there are no buses. There very well may never have been buses. One hypothesis is that it was a drop-off point for farmers to distribute local milk and cheese. Or workers going into the fields ducked in to escape the sun or strong winds. There are four of these shelters on the switchback up to Apano Meria from Ermoupoli, Syros's small harbour city. There is one where Chatzakis is set up at San Michalis, a village with somewhere between five and 11 residents.

The Aegean designers are working with a civil engineer to blueprint a landscaped shelter, drawing up little mod spots framed by indigenous climbing plants; a corrugated bin on top could funnel what little rainwater there is into a communal watering can.

Locals expressed initial concerns. "They were most afraid of the touristic stuff," says Kypriani Bartzoka, one of the Aegean designers. "That we might create something that is more for tourists. They didn't want that."

Paris Tsiropinas says their goal is to create an initial project. "Plant the plants. Make people active, get them to water the plants, meet, have an event," he says. If work at the first shelter goes well, move on to the others. "Maybe one like a small garden, another like a small terrarium or a place for animals. Or book exchange."

Drawing up the concept is not the challenge; what they've created is easy to grasp. Keeping up healthy green space in such an arid and depopulated environment would be tricky and require creativity, but it is possible. The real challenge will be – as in so many civic design initiatives – negotiating a labyrinth of administrative offices. It is often unclear who has ultimate authority and responsibility over a small public space. Expending effort for an underpopulated, remote place where there is no real money involved, no clear lines of demarcation and among offices that are already understaffed?

The designers have enquired; they are waiting for responses and given conflicting answers.

If a planter is to go up on this shelter, most of the real labour will be in being meticulous and patient.

Top: Vines, cats, music: the logo at Chatzakis Winery in San Michalis village. © Kevin Loigu

Below: Detailed rendering of a concept for converting Apano Meria bus stops into new spaces. © Paris Xyntarianos Tsiropinas, Helen Charoupia

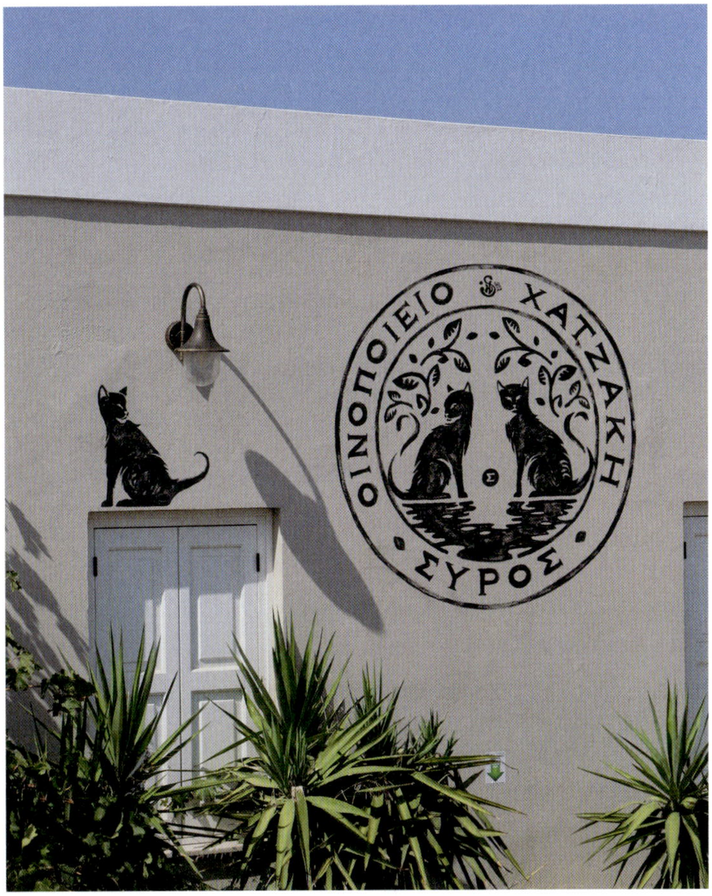

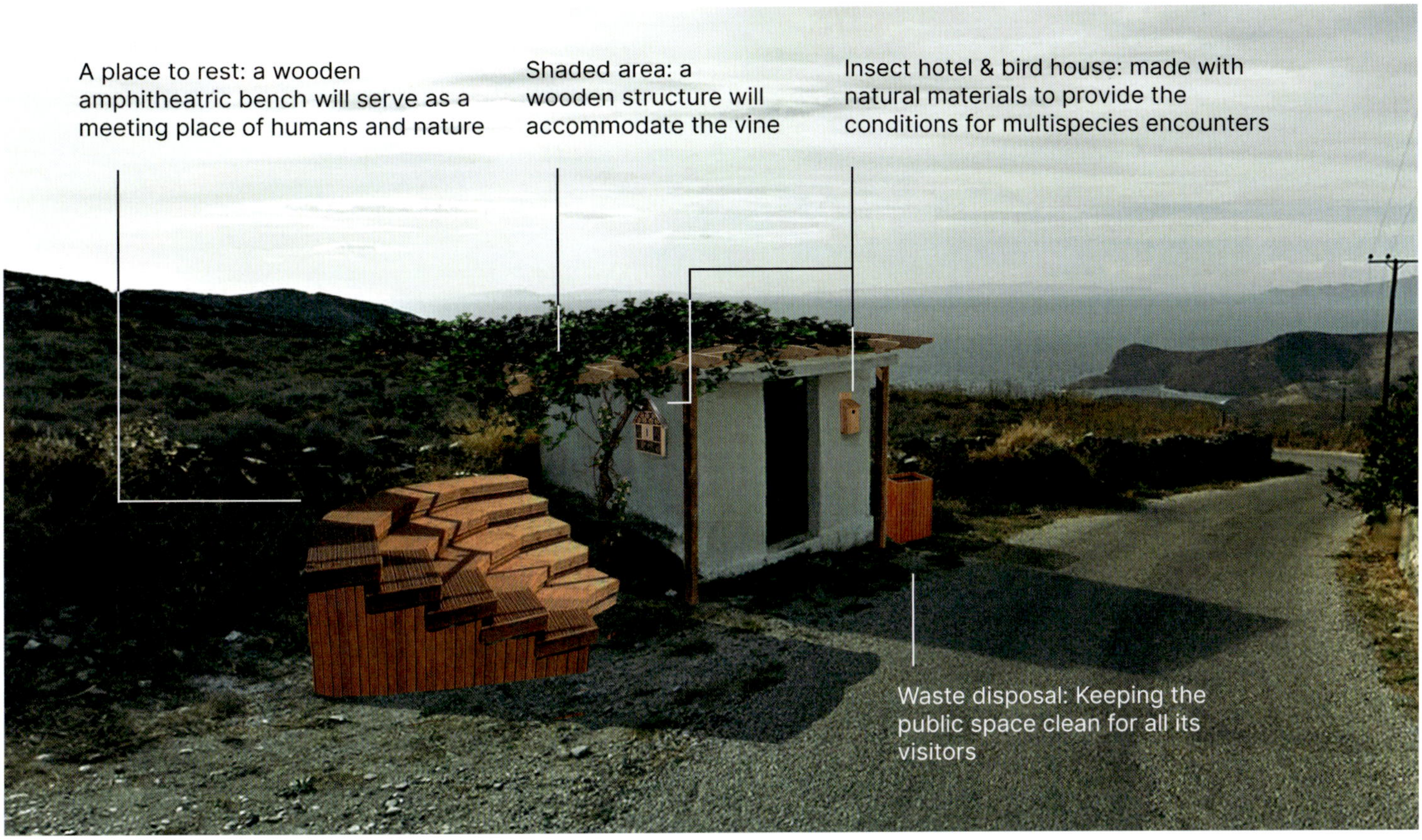

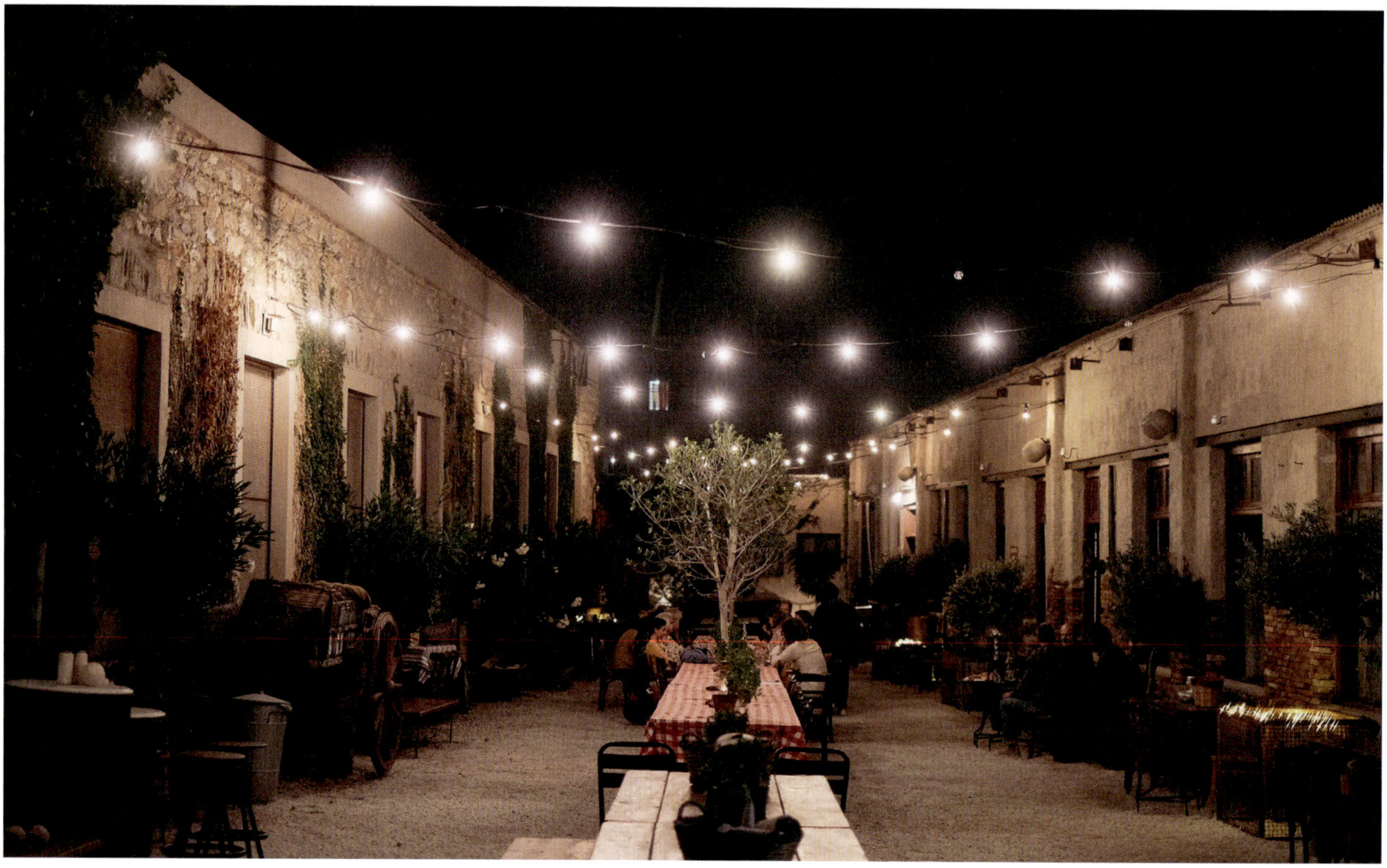

Back in Ermoupoli, Paris tunes up his bouzouki. He is with a group in a long rectangular courtyard, about to play Vamvakaris and rembetika under the stars for a full table of guests.

The north of the island may still be wild, but Syros was also once the only Cycladic island with industrial muscle. Until it went bust overnight in 1986, the venue about to resound with *rembetika* was a textile mill, one of dozens in Ermoupoli. It has been restored as a museum and event space, its mighty jacquard looms and last days frozen in time.

Just a few blocks away is the rented Apano Meria SCE house. It is modest, big, and unfinished downstairs, and it sleeps ten with a patio garden that has not yet been planted.

Apano Meria SCE wants to keep itself solvent and, even so, attract a certain type of visitor: people who swim and have fun, yes, but who get involved in the community. The house is set up to host environmental policy researchers or volunteers who travel out to the *Βιγια* organic farm, picking lemons or harvesting capers. It's a sharp contrast to the superyachts just offshore.

It's not clear which kind of development will have more sway on the island.

The balance, however, will surely influence what Apano Meria looks like a decade from now.

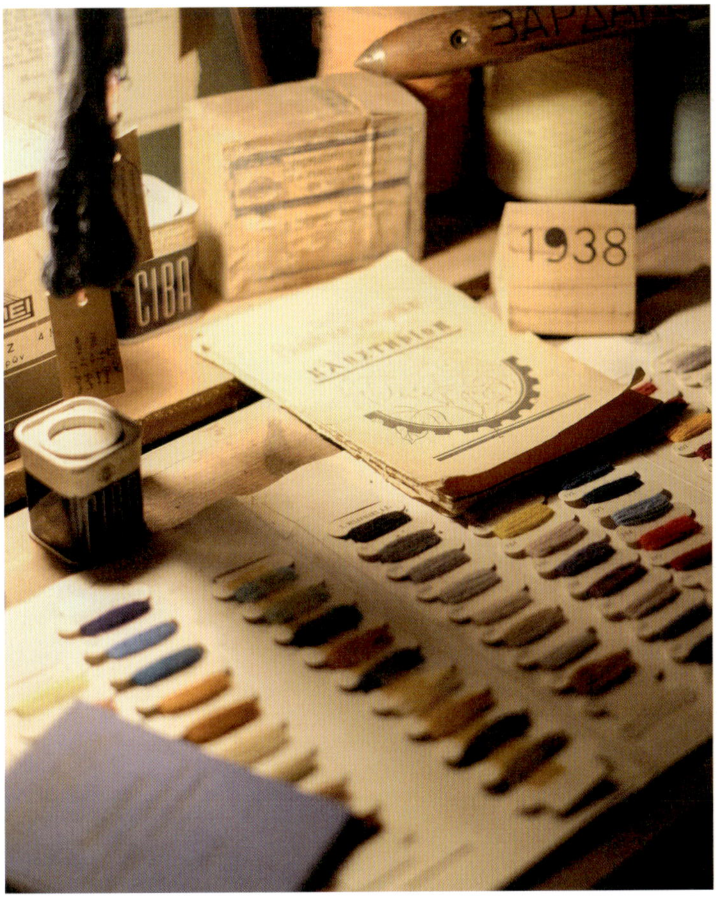

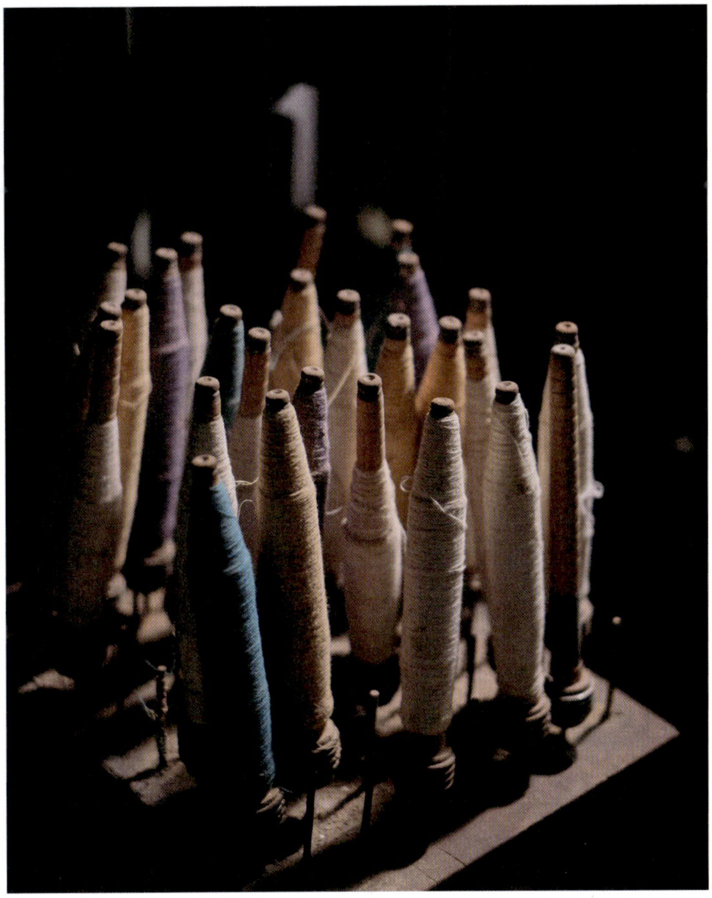

Left: Bouzouki resounds with life in the court of the former Zisimatos textile mill, now an event venue. © Kevin Loigu

Top left: Thread samples lend colour to Syros's industrial past. © Kevin Loigu

Top right: Looms are silent on the island now, bobbins for show. What next for Syros? © Kevin Loigu

“Madeira é uma ilha. É daqueles lugares onde tudo é concentrado. Como um concentrado de sumo de fruta. É um território complexo que precisa de tempo para ser percebido.”

“Madeira is an island. It’s the type of place where everything is concentrated. It’s like a concentrated fruit juice. It’s a complex territory that takes time to understand it.”
Susana Gonzaga

Location: Estreito da Calheta, Madeira, Portugal

Madeira is famed as a garden island and it is just that, 750 kilometres off the coast of Morocco in the Atlantic. But it is also a place of steep ridges and deep valleys that shape the island's agriculture, economy and village life. Estreito da Calheta is a town clinging to a steep and narrow hillside. It gained access to electricity within living memory. Some of its 1,600 residents went as far afield as South Africa to find work and send money home; it is now rapidly changing, and flagging in its cultural production and sense of self.

SMOTIES partner: University of Madeira, Art and Design Department

The University of Madeira is a state university based in Funchal. Professor Susana Gonzaga is the SMOTIES partner coordinator from the Art & Design Department.

Estreito da Calheta

Key involvement in project

Researchers from the Art and Design Department, University of Madeira:
Susana Gonzaga, PhD, assistant professor in Art and Design Department, Faculty of Arts and Humanities, University of Madeira;
Elisa Bertolotti, PhD, assistant professor of Communication Design in Art and Design Department, Faculty of Arts and Humanities, University of Madeira; Pau Galbis, PhD, assistant professor in Art and Design Department, Faculty of Arts and Humanities, University of Madeira; Luisa Santos Freitas, junior researcher; Sara Patrícia Abreu, junior researcher.

Stakeholders:
Priest Rui Sousa, Estreito da Calheta Parish; Abelhinha, Associação de Agricultores; Estreito da Calheta, Parish Council; Calheta Municipality.

What they set out to do

Enhance local culture by promoting engagement and activities between the young and the elderly, revitalising local products and helping the community boost its civic pride and identity.

What the project accomplished

Local museum and community center; producing and screening the 90-minute documentary *Estreito é o Tempo* (Narrow is the Time), an oral narrative history from Estreito da Calheta inhabitants; book *Romagens e Cantigas de Natal da Dona Antúcia*, a written memory about old Christmas songs and traditions; prototyping studio sessions with students and residents; festivals and community Christmas market.

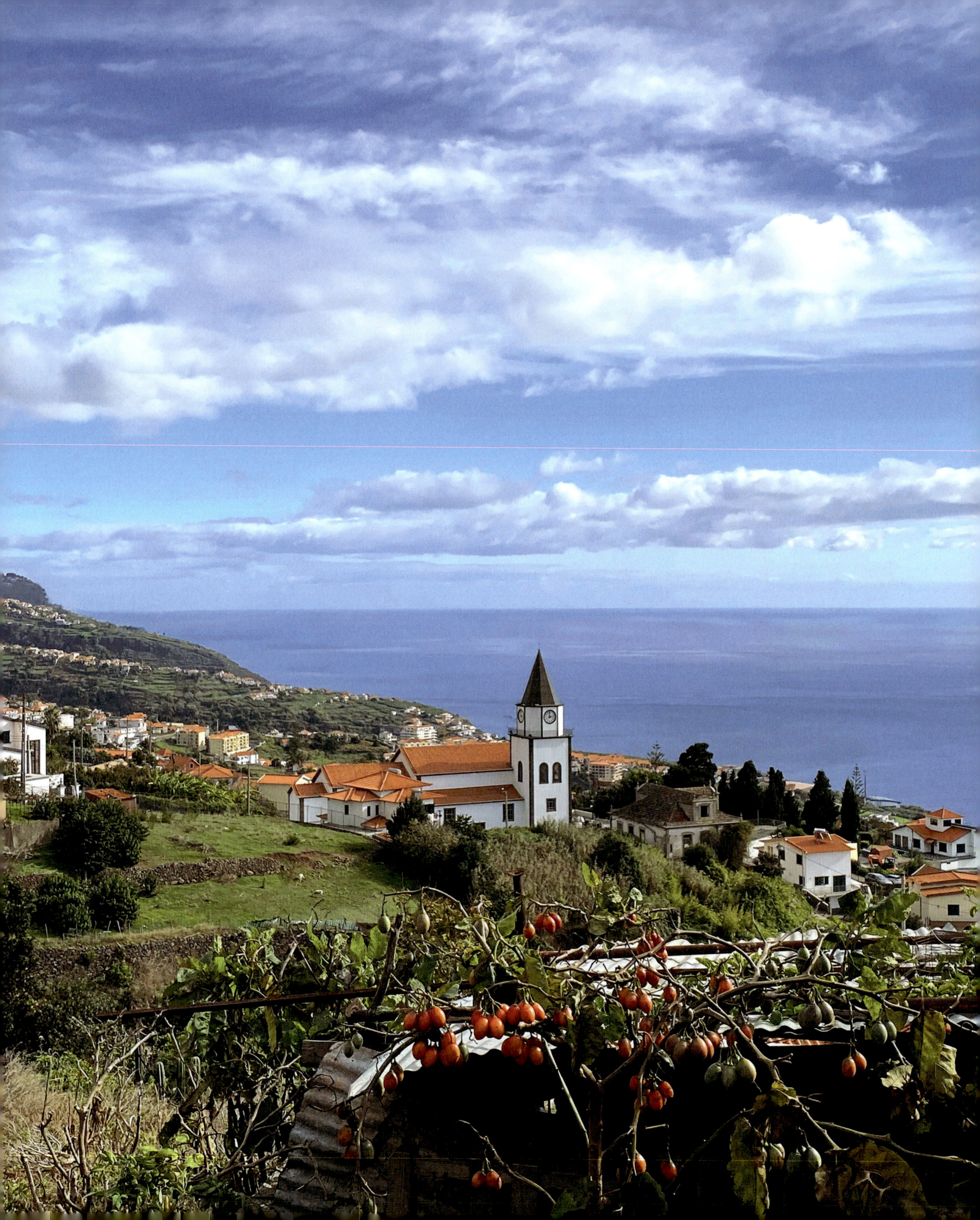

Pixels and Crops

The memory comes easy for Lidia Pereira. “There were no fridges and freezers.”

She leans forward in her wicker chair, raising her hands to her chest, smiling and pursing her lips, looking to the left of the screen. Emilia da Silva joins in from her kitchen, brushy white hair, beige cardigan over her shoulders, mischievous and knowing. “We had whatever God would provide us. Now they have yoghurts,” she says. “My children never ate yoghurt. Cheese? I wouldn’t hear anyone talking about cheese. They’d never eat such things. Neither would I. I didn’t even know what it was.”

She pauses, glowing onscreen. “I discovered it recently.”

They're all laughing and carrying on, enjoying the warm still evening, sitting and clapping on the side of a deep green slope overlooking the Atlantic Ocean on the southern tip of the Portuguese island of Madeira.

A big projector below them is showing Hugo Olim's 90-minute documentary film *Estreito é o Tempo*, or 'Narrow is the Time', and the film's protagonists – the grandmothers, sons, the winemaker, the priest, Lidia Pereira and Emilia da Silva – are also in the audience on this midsummer night in 2023.

And oh, what it is they say. Most of the people onscreen are middle aged or a little older, but only just so. Some are students, teenagers. They describe what can loosely be called a village – Estreito da Calheta, where the film gets its name – but what is really only a steep narrow ridge with small houses, arable land and small crops, of all kinds, scattered on top. Its boundaries are permeable and blurred, almost like a suburb. But it is not a suburb. Its geography and circumstances demanded a rugged life, as in much of the rest of Madeira: until quite recently, this was often very poor. And now it is a place that also features million-euro second homes overlooking the blue sea. Narrow indeed is the time for these stories.

Olim knows the SMOTIES lead partner in Portugal, the nature-focused designer Susana Gonzaga, because the two were colleagues at the University of Madeira in the administrative capital Funchal, where Gonzaga is a faculty member. They've also both worked with the priest who was instrumental in producing *Estreito é o Tempo*, Padre Rui Sousa, whose mission of delivering the gospel brought him out into the fields. These are threads that wind through SMOTIES' work in Estreito.

Rui arrives at a cafe on a slow afternoon: he's in his mid-fifties, energetic and greying, with heavy-lidded eyes and distinctive brows that always look surprised (or worried, or calming). He's brought a big jar of lychee nuts in a cloudy liquid with him; he has made a kind of pickle. It is...unique. He likes to experiment. But more than that, Sousa says he tries to see what is being discarded that could potentially be useful.

All along the ravines on either side of Estreito are precarious terraces of banana plants, the small sweet bendy kind that can be found across this garden island. But there are also pockets of apple orchards. As he took up his parish work, Rui says he would notice endless apples discarded in fields – varieties that were too acidic for table use and would just rot. He thought they could be made into cider.

He began experimenting. Now the Sidraria dos Prazeres produces fresh bottles for local distribution, giving new life to a practice that had gone by the wayside.

The work Rui inspired is established in Prazeres, the next ravine over from Estreito. By comparison, Estreito is a bit more indistinct in its personality and forms. Its winding road from the sea follows the ridge crest up towards the nearby mountain forest. Scattered along the road are a vibrant school (with two school sheep), a little grocery store, a bit of green space, a small but smart municipal centre (the kind where you might find watercolour classes), a playground and a café.

And there is the Igreja do Estreito, Rui's church, as an anchor.

The first foray as Gonzaga and her colleagues started engaging with Estreito was to consider renovating the Venda Grande villa, a once elegant and stately home directly across from the Igreja. It is a ruin. Birds roost in the dormers and rafters. It is overgrown and boarded up. As a community hub? It could be excellent. Resources for such an enormous renovation seem far out of reach, however.

But *Estreito é o Tempo*, the film project, came together in three months in 2023. Olim had left Madeira and gone to Nepal in the Himalayas but returned; he went to stay with Rui. The priest helped to introduce him to people who might be in the film. As they saw Olim with the priest, they got over being camera-shy. Olim often shot indoors with the Estreito residents speaking directly into the camera.

P. 90: Estreito da Calheta © Susana Gonzaga

Top: Screenshot of the documentary © Susana Gonzaga

Bottom: Banana trees in Estreito da Calheta. © Susana Gonzaga

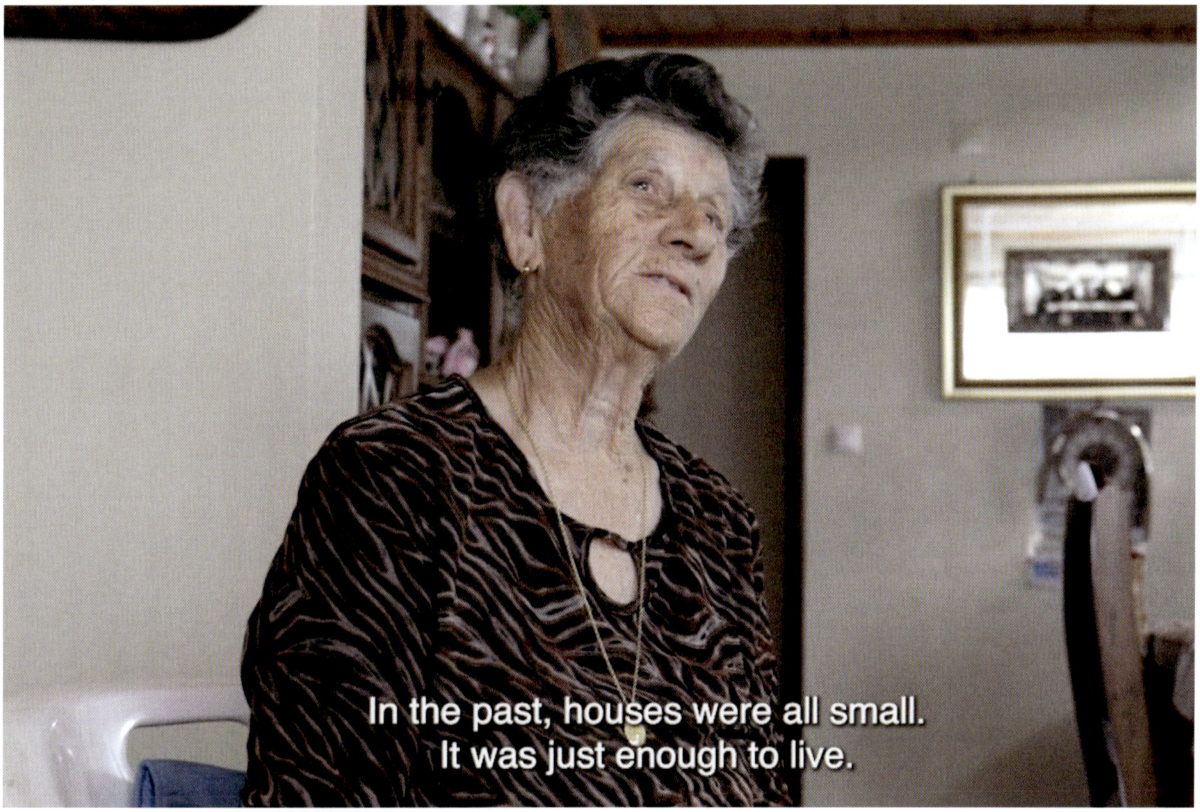

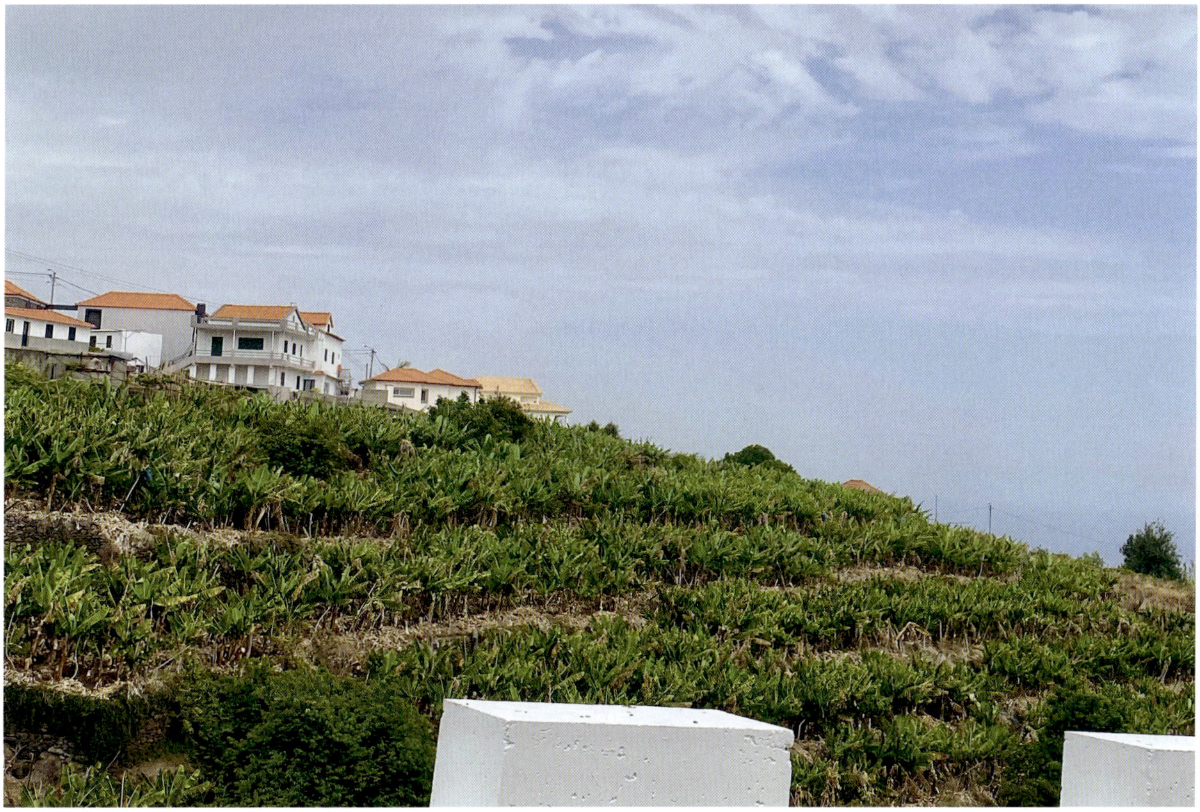

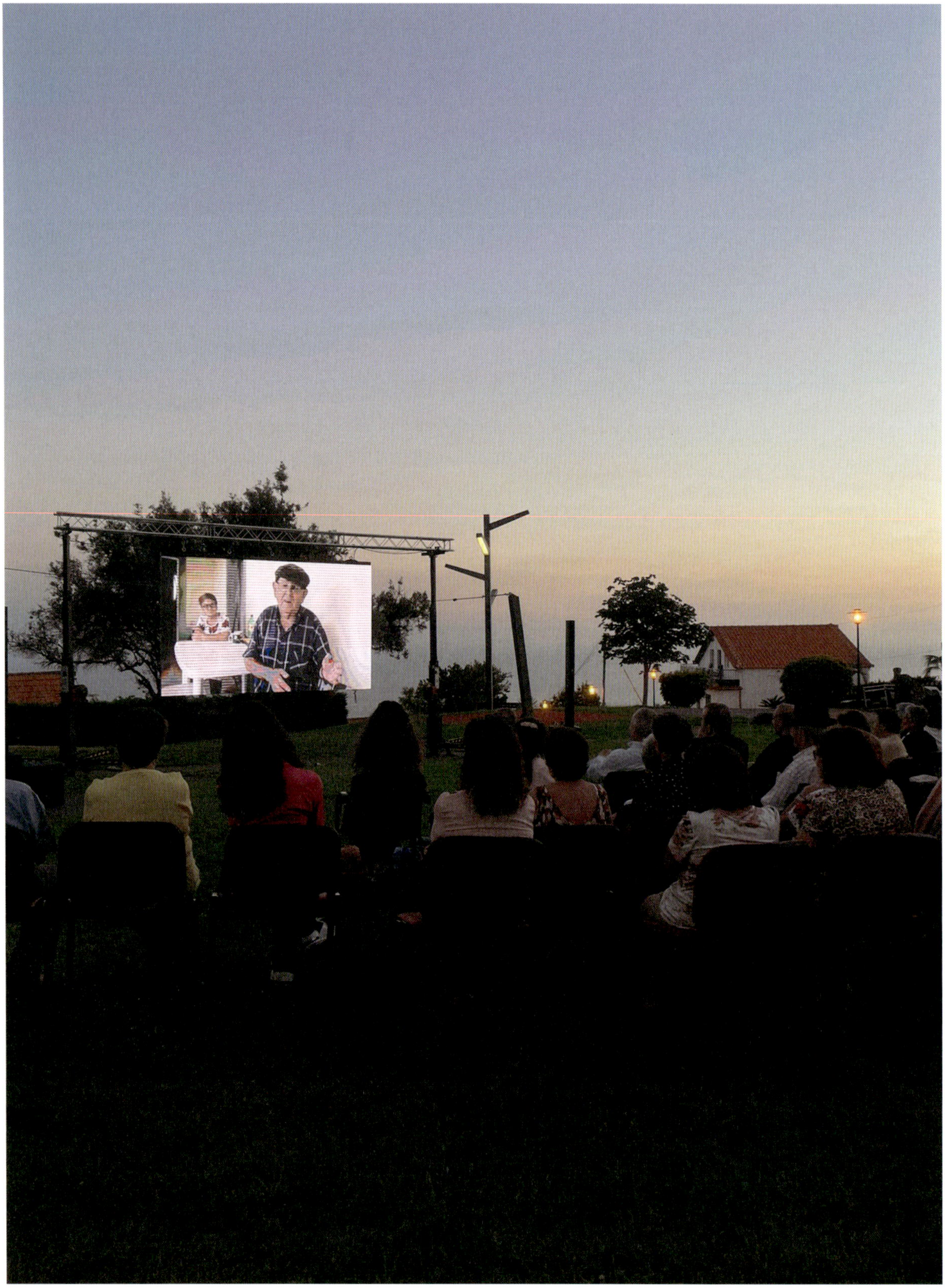

Screening of the documentary in Estreito da Calheta. © Luisa Santos Freitas

In July 2023, 150 people watched *Estreito é o Tempo* on a big screen on the summer lawn next to the municipal centre.

About an hour in, Olim holds a long shot of a lush plant as a woman named Noélia Paiva describes a kind of healing spell that a village elder taught to her grandmother. Together, grandmother and elder would take on the evil eye, sunstroke, the *bicho virado*. There's a quick cut, and Noélia is chanting the incantation.

Heal in the Name of God, the Virgin Mary, the Holy Trinity. You have the evil eye. From the three drops, the second two spread apart. During the Divine Holy Spirit days, we traverse the houses with the girls who sing, and we play and sing the Divine Holy Spirit songs. One, two, three. Allow me to exit through these doors.

Noélia is grinning, and the mood is light-hearted; among the audience, too. But Rui lends a reminder.

"At a time when there were no doctors, and someone would get sick, they'd have to find a way to get well. At hand they'd have herbs," he says.

Medicinal plants and folk remedies are still used by 80 percent of the developing world. And *Estreito é o Tempo* is a window on a fairly recent past in Europe. In one interview, a resident describes it as "the old days, until 1993". Even at that point the school building had no electricity, running water, or a bathroom. "There was a lot of willingness to learn and respect for the teacher."

Other SMOTIES partners in the audience took inspiration from the screening; it would come up unbidden among them even weeks later. "This film will stay. It will stay forever because there is a really fast change going on there. This is going to be the last generation that really knows how they lived before," says Nina Goršič, recalling it while driving back to her office in Ljubljana, Slovenia (see "An Orchard, a Nest, a House on a Hill", next section).

At the end of November, Gonzaga was workshopping ideas with her students for another desire expressed by Estreito residents: a Christmas market, either outside the church or where the film screening took place. The vision isn't there yet. The student designs need more consideration. "If the model does not work, it will not work in real life," she tells her students, for neither the first nor last time.

In Estreito, she takes a drive to one of the last banana terraces at the bottom of the hill. This was once part of an invisible landscape, with paths running between fields, and villagers claiming status depending on whether they lived uphill or downhill. Sleek new jet-set houses now command the lower curves of the road, walled and gated, where nobody is seen going in or out. She's not sure what will develop here.

A few weeks later, the new Christmas market, with its updated designs, is a big hit.

Olim, impressed by his time in Estreito, sees a bright side. "They could use a place to hang out, I heard this from the residents. Sure, it's also difficult. People are in their houses, they don't have the same interactions as they did years ago," he says. "In general though, they are quite happy. Because they come from a situation where they didn't have anything."

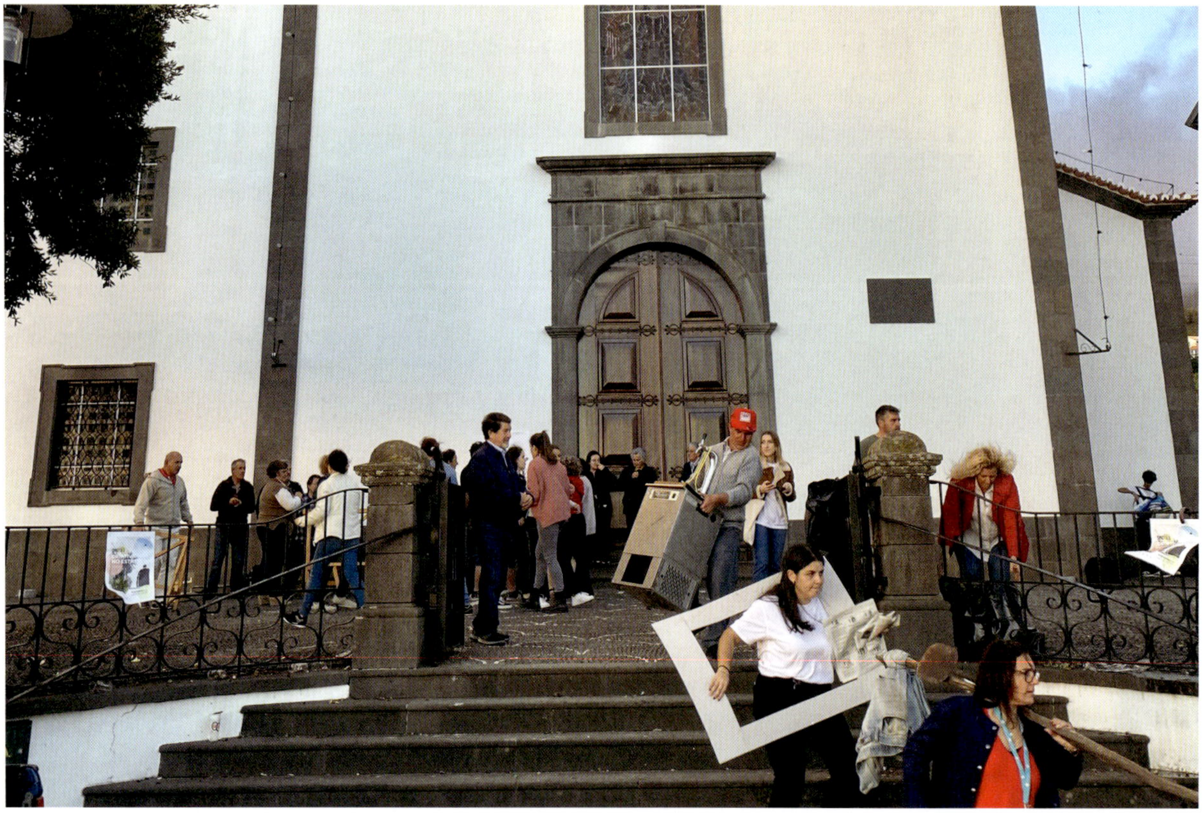

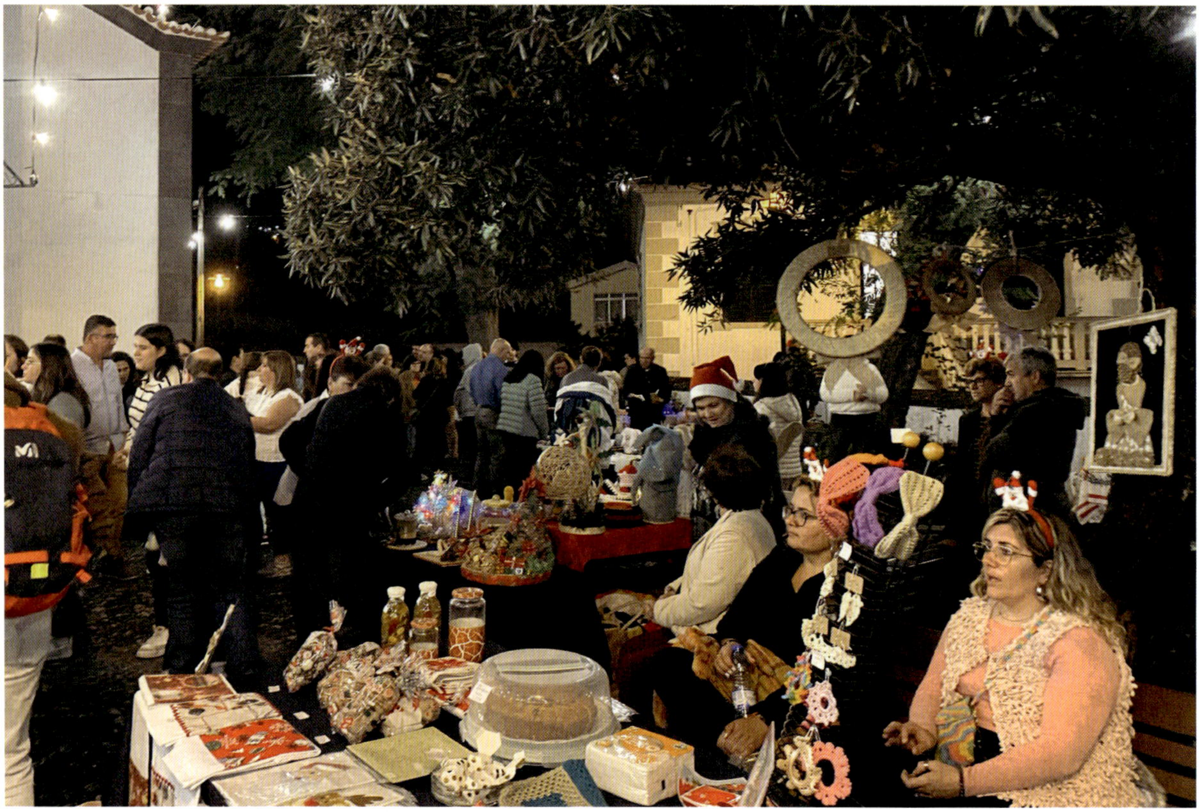

Top left: Estreito da Calheta's Parish © Susana Gonzaga

Bottom left: Christmas market © Susana Gonzaga

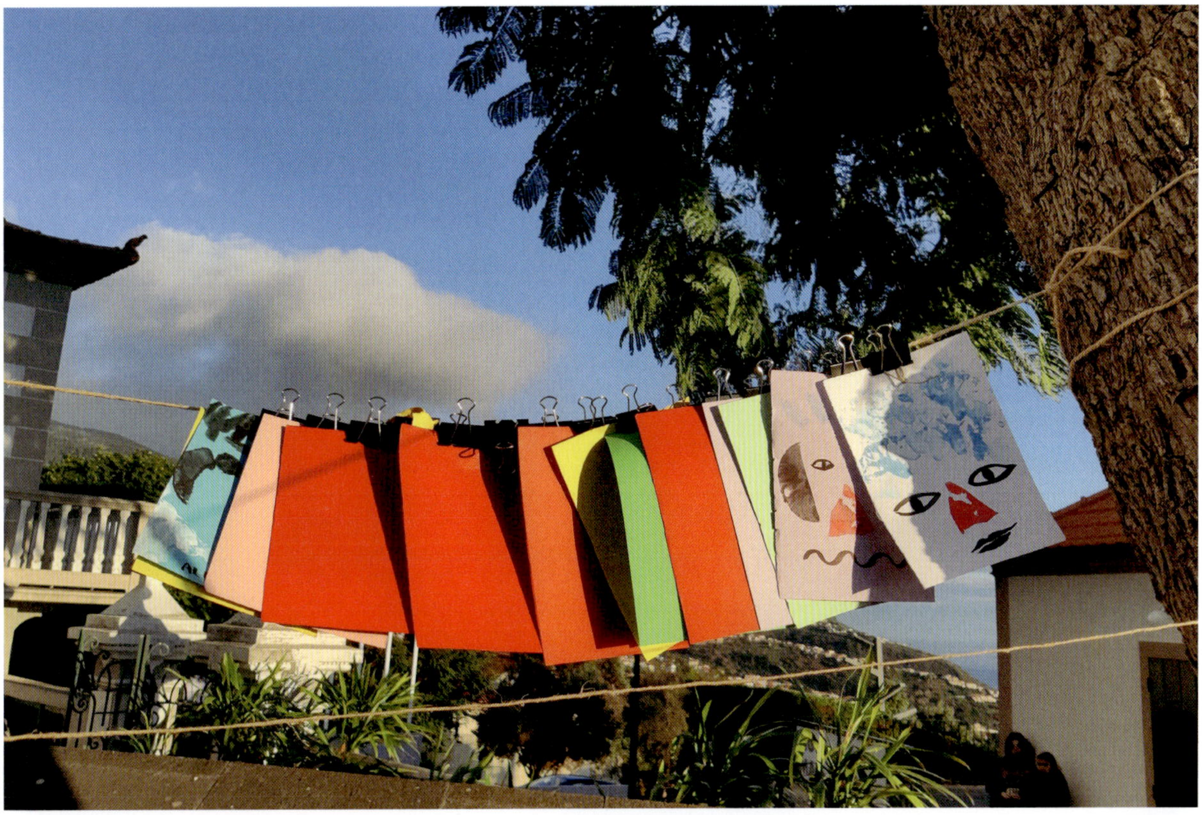

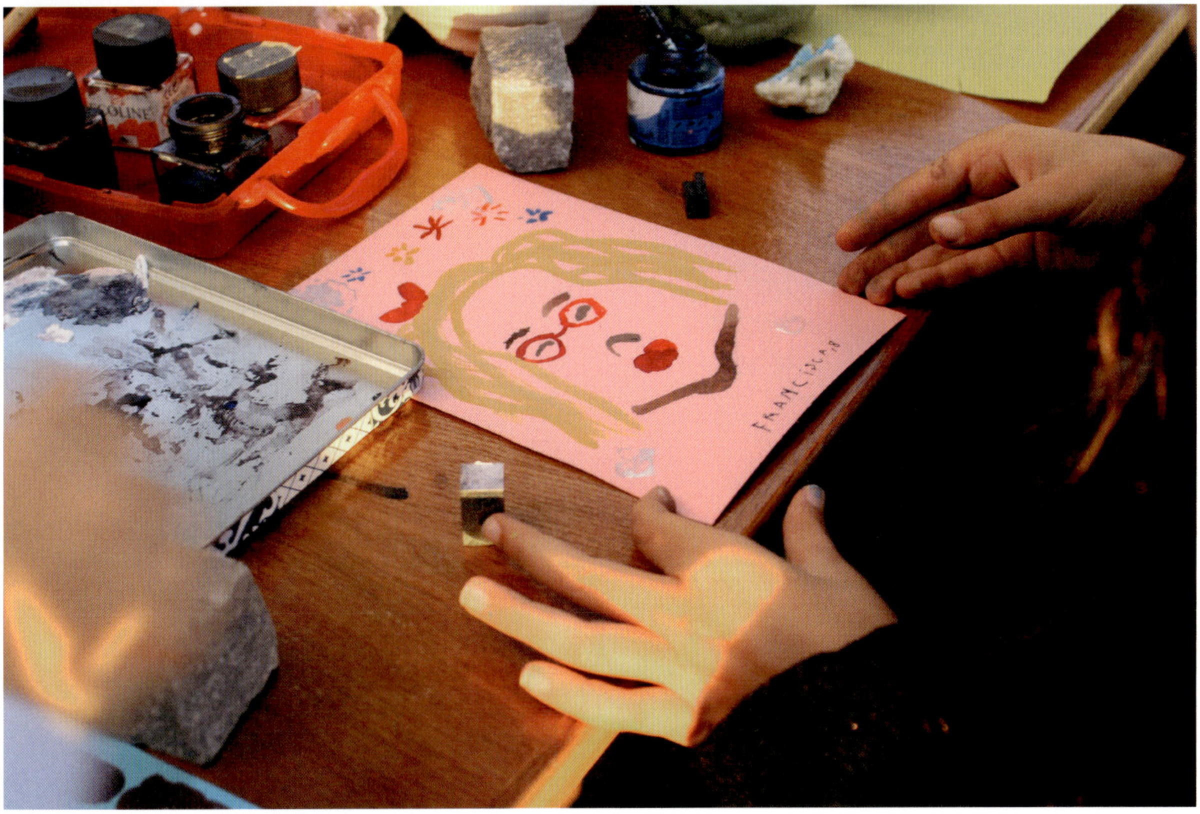

Results from the collaborative drawing workshop with Elisa Bertolotti, a member of the design faculty at the University of Madeira. 2022. © Sónia Freitas

"Prostorsko-socialne inovacije v oddaljenih krajih so ključne za krepitev lokalnih skupnosti in njihovih javnih prostorov – pomembno je povezovanje tradicije, naravnih virov in programov, ki so usmerjeni k skupnosti in človeku. Z inovativno arhitekturo in prostorskim načrtovanjem lahko ustvarimo funkcionalne, trajnostne prostore, ki so povezani s kulturno in družbeno identiteto. Kulturni sektor spodbuja to preobrazbo, javne prostore obogati z ustvarjalnostjo in živahnostjo ter podpira dinamične in vključujoče družbene izkušnje."

"Spatio-social innovations in remote areas are crucial for strengthening local communities and their public spaces – it is important to integrate tradition, natural resources, technologies and programmes focused on the community and human-centred design. With innovative architecture and spatial planning, we can create functional, sustainable spaces that are rooted in cultural and social identity. The cultural sector catalyses this transformation, enriching public spaces with creativity and vibrancy, and fostering dynamic and inclusive social experiences."
Matej Nikšič

Location: Polhograjski dolomiti Landscape Park

Mountain forestry and farming over centuries has marked this landscape and its rich built heritage, which includes well-preserved homesteads and hayracks. The Polhograjski dolomiti Landscape Park was established in 1974, but it is not a nature reserve: there are several villages here among its pristine natural settings. It is facing pressure from the suburbanisation of nearby urban centres and increasing traffic from recreational visitors. Three villages within the park are near one another and have particularly interesting features. They are Žlebe, Belo and Topol pri Medvodah.

SMOTIES Partner: Urban Planning Institute of the Republic of Slovenia (UIRS), Ljubljana

Founded in 1955, the UIRS is Slovenia's main research organisation for spatial planning and related disciplines. It has been working with SMOTIES since March 2021 in the rural region of Medvode, outside the capital Ljubljana.

Belo, Žlebe, Topol pri Medvodah

Key involvement in project

Urban Planning Institute of the Republic of Slovenia: Matej Nikšič, architect and researcher, urban planner, lecturer in urban design; Nina Goršič, architect and researcher, urban renewal, cultural heritage and accessibility.

Mojca Sfiligoj, manager of heritage renovation and cultural programmes at Homestead Pr' Lenart, Belo; Zvonka Simčič, artist and cultural programme manager, Hiša na hribu/House on the Hill, Žlebe; Mojca Senegačnik, artist/painter, organiser, Hiša na hribu; Jakob Šubic, forest garden visionary, Topol pri Medvodah; Žiga Kršinar, farmer and president of Polhograjski dolomiti Tourism Board, Topol pri Medvodah.

What they set out to do

To find active residents and foster development in tangible and intangible ways; and to organise events that draw in residents, encourage creative community engagement with local public spaces, and build connections among the scattered villages of the landscape park.

What the project accomplished

Created cultural programmes that raised the profile and development of two cultural places where residents came together – one a homestead with an orchard, the other a gallery in a former sexton's house at a prominent church; organised several communal walking events and gathered people to create communal tablecloths with painting and decorative art. Village residents at diverse levels continue to independently pursue creative projects in public spaces such as in a community garden: these are spin-off effects.

After several years of Human Cities activities in Slovenia, participatory design is now a nationally recommended practice for the country's 212 municipal spatial plans.

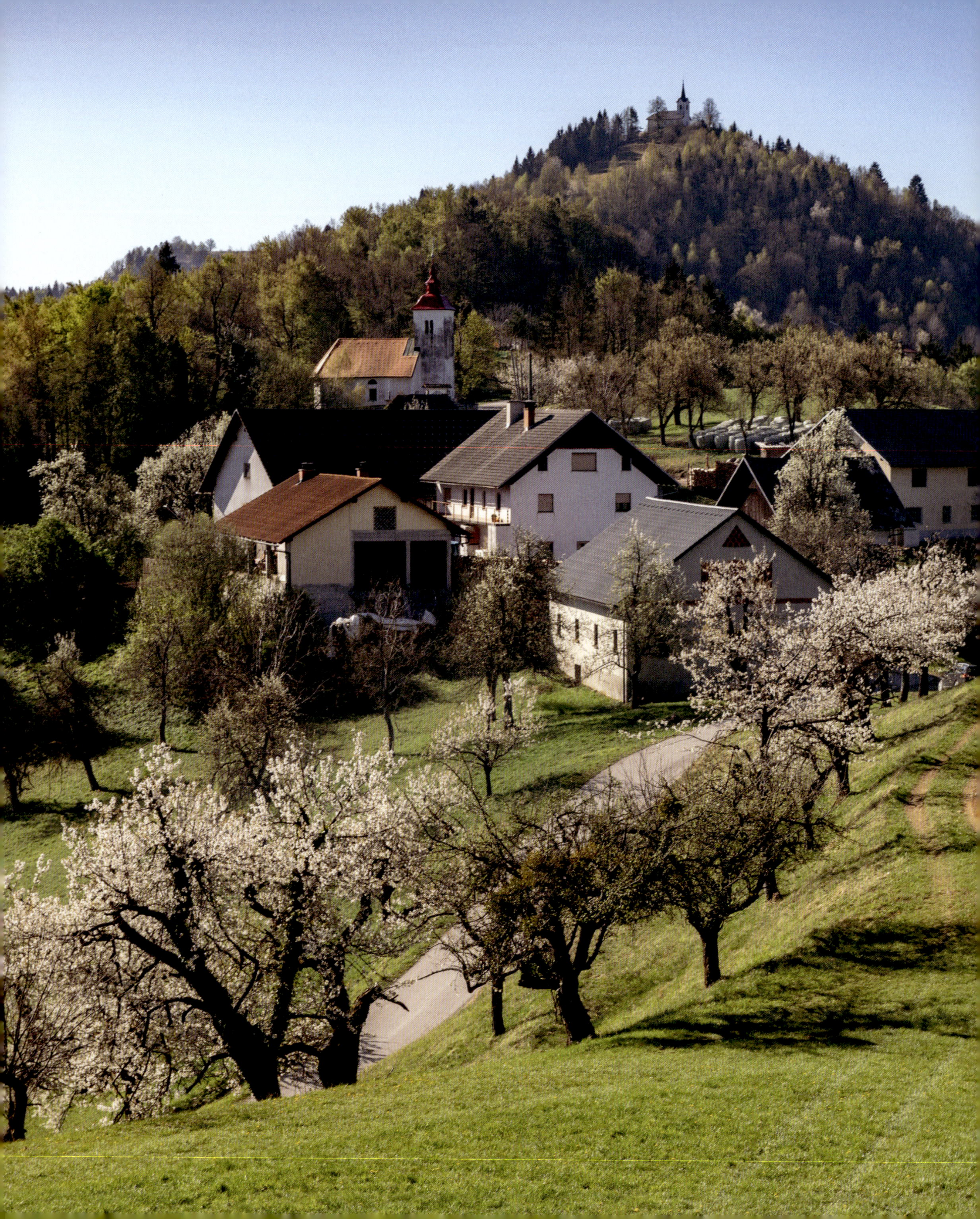

An Orchard, a Nest, a House on a Hill

The bell rings from the tower at St. Marjeta's on the hilltop over the Slovenian village of Žlebe, a big *klanngg* rolling down the steep slope and over ribbons of roads to the faraway woods.

This sound has tolled from here for the better part of five hundred years. The artist Zvonka Simčič, 61, knows it from the time she was a girl, and the memory is out of the ordinary: her father was the St. Marjeta sexton. It was his job to ring the bell. He did not have to go far. Next to the church was their house, where it still stands. She was born in this house. She had to leave it when she was six and when her father died, young, in a rail accident. After that, the house stood empty.

But almost a decade ago Simčič was able to start restoring it with her friends, residents, and fellow artists, including the painter Mojca Senegačnik, with the idea of making a creative, communal place called *Hiša na hribu*, the House on the Hill. It is still a work in progress, but it's an ideal address for the SMOTIES partners to call on. Last summer it became the go-to place for community tablecloth-making.

The villages of Žlebe, Belo, and Topol pri Medvodah are within three kilometres of one another as the crow flies, in the high hills to the west of the capital, Ljubljana; from Belo to Topol is a pleasant walk through the woods. Technically, so is Žlebe, though that's more of a two-hour hike up and down through dense Alpine forest; it is 20 minutes by car around the big hills.

These three villages are part of the 14,000-hectare Polhograjski dolomiti Landscape Park, and it took the better part of a year's research for Nina Goršič and Matej Nikšič of Slovenia's Urban Planning Institute to mark them as potentially fertile places for their socially engaged design practices.

"Some places are not going to want what you are bringing," Goršič says. "Every village has its own history, own locals; its own people who have arrived more recently. You need to be sensitive and think hard about what really you can give."

In 2021, she and Nikšič began looking to build connections with villages in this rural municipality, which is administered from the nearby industrial river valley town of Medvode. It is tricky territory, and even three villages can get complicated. "It's hard to be in contact with a lot of people and at the same time do something," Goršič says. "And you can't promise them we will do something – and then, at the end, have nothing happen."

Years ago, she had worked with a woman named Mojca Sfiligoj in a cultural heritage office. Sfiligoj was managing an old family homestead, using it for small cultural events. It seemed like an opening. It is called Pr' Lenart, the Lenart homestead. It is in Belo.

Pr' Lenart is low, big, and old and commands the top of a forested hill. On the side of the long farmhouse plaster wall is a little memorial plaque with a red star and a name, Lizika Jančar. She was 23 in 1943, when she was shot here as a partisan wireless operator by an anti-communist militia of Italian sympathisers during the Second World War.

The homestead is a quiet place surrounded by whispery trees. But inside it is cosy with heavy furniture, Hiša na hribu flyers in the hallway, installations outside, and posters on display for upcoming cultural events. There's a huge warm stove and broad communal table – it could probably seat 20 around its worn and comfortable edges. At the table are Nikšič and Goršič from the Urban Planning Institute, Mojca Sfiligoj, Simčič and Senegačnik from Hiša na hribu, and a man from Belo named Peter. Two others join: Jakob Šubic, a local activist and promoter of mindful forest walks, and Žiga Kršinar, an influential farmer. They've come from nearby Topol pri Medvodah. They're sitting down with coffee and pastries and apples.

As Matej Nikšič puts it, the table was the idea: to bring people around a common table to talk about their future. They've promoted these evening sit-downs, and over the last two years they've organised community walks between the villages. Distinct parts of the community are sitting down together here.

"You produce goods. Food always has high value," Senegačnik, the painter, says to Kršinar, the farmer. "Producing art is treated like, pffff. Useless in our community." It's certainly hard to make a living with it. But it's hard to make a living being a farmer, too.

And House on the Hill has attracted little communities. It began with printmaking to line the inside of glass jars called *potovke*, referencing a tradition of hand-carrying messages and small produce along the paths in Polhograjski dolomiti. Many times in 2023 area residents gathered to join Simčič and Senegačnik for a day of painting and designing dyed tablecloths. The tablecloths are not for show, though some have been put on display in Ljubljana. Nina and Matej organised these gatherings with Simčič and Senegačnik under the SMOTIES banner to make communal tablecloths on which to put baked bread and local produce, and to bring people together. There's personal meaning for Simčič too, who recalls her father taking care of the altar linens at St. Marjeta.

Behind Pr' Lenart is a bird's nest made to surreal size by a local art collective. It's based on an idea first tried out at Hiša na hribu and then reproduced in Belo. It was a SMOTIES idea to promote orchards as a semi-public space (more open than a private garden, not as open as a pavement). The nest at Pr' Lenart is in a fruit orchard.

Slovenia exports 6 million euro of air-dried fruit a year, mostly to Austria and Germany. A fair amount of that is pears.

It's not much. But it resonates here. In Slovenia, one of the things they do with dried pears is make flour for bread. They use tepka pears. These have tart, coarse brown flesh and are found in just a few parts of the country. Two years ago at the behest of the Austrian Fruit-Growing Association, the Slovenian newspaper Delo declared a "Day of Meadow Orchards." It drew attention to the disappearance of meadow orchards.

P. 100: Polhograjski dolomiti Landscape Park, recognised in 1974 for its unique topography, natural beauty and cultural heritage, includes the eastern hilly part of the Medvode municipality, where SMOTIES focuses on integrating local cultural activities and promoting sustainable living despite the area's remoteness and lack of public facilities.
© Peter Košenina, Javni zavod Sotočje Medvode

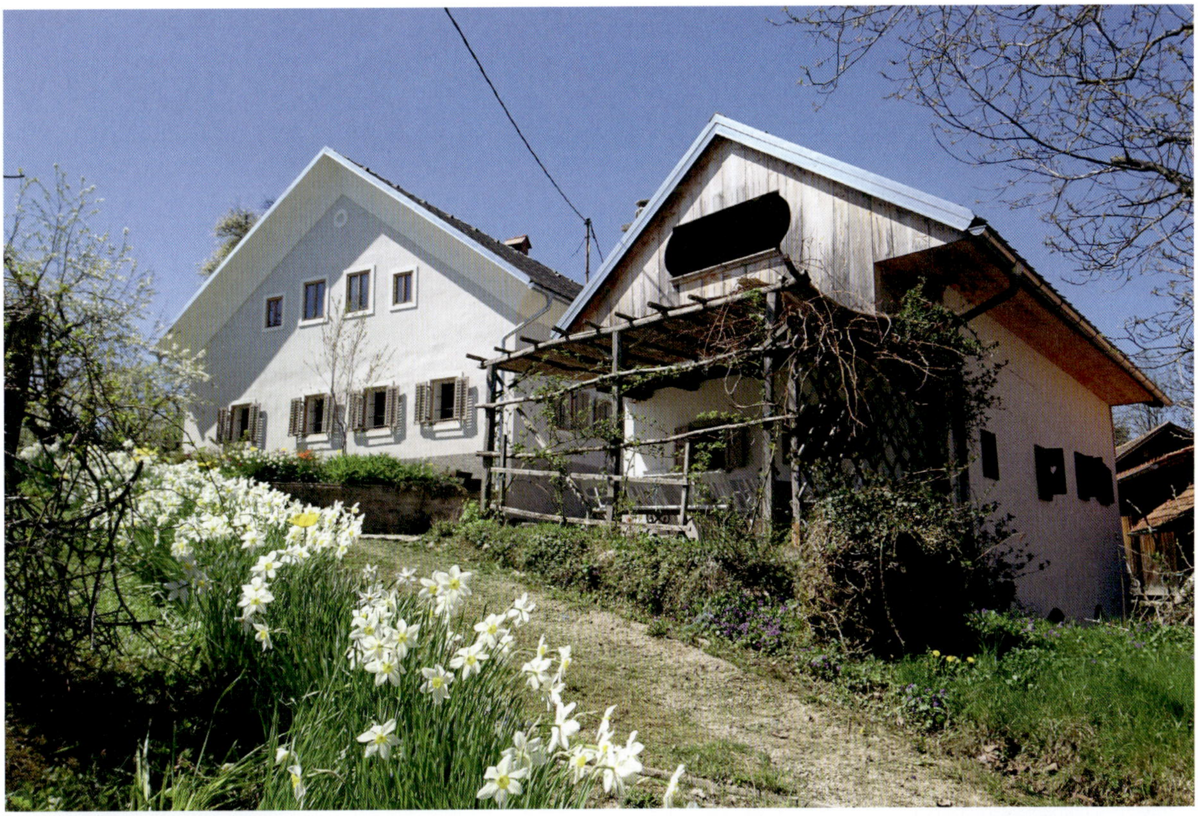

Top: The Homestead Pr' Lenart in Belo, an important site for local heritage, is now repurposed: it hosts exhibitions, workshops, concerts, and summer accommodation alike.
© Mojca Sfiligoj

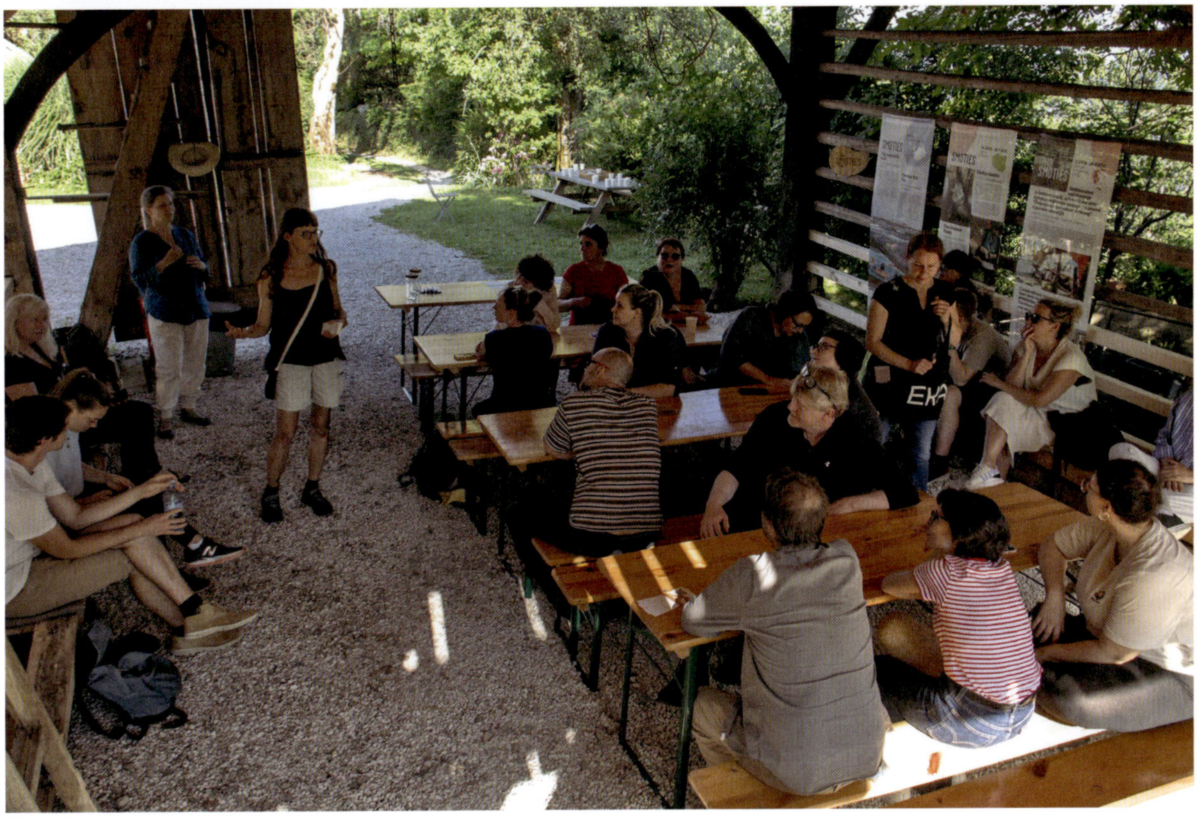

Bottom: The hayrack, traditionally used for drying grass and storing farming equipment, now serves as a remote cultural venue hosting workshops, exhibitions, and other gatherings.
© Simon Koblar/UIRS

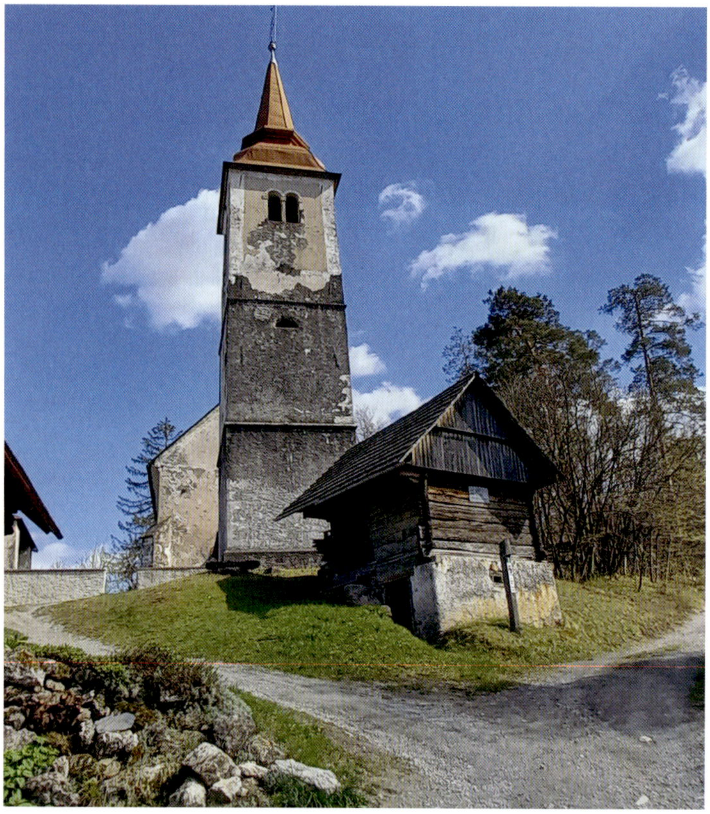

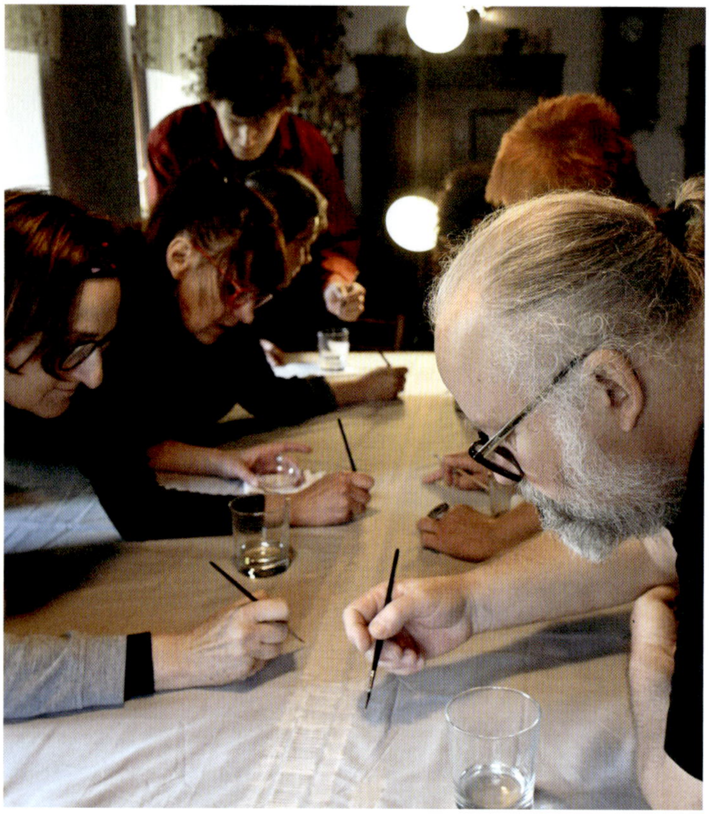

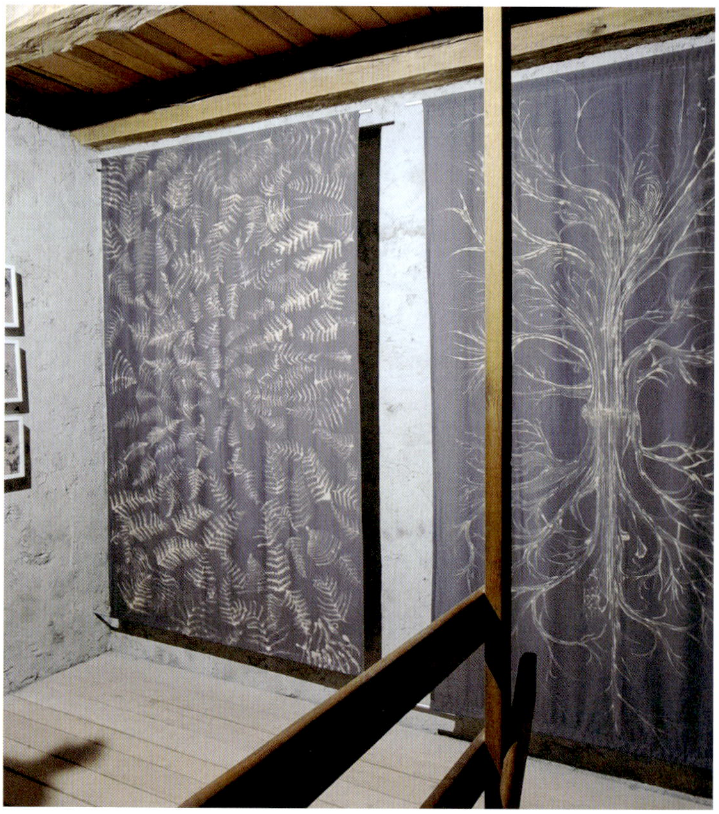

Top: The built cultural heritage of Polhograjski dolomiti, exemplified by the St. Marjeta churchyard and sexton house, holds significant potential for creating public spaces. Through activities organised by SMOTIES, these sites have enhanced their roles as central community spaces.The major cultural event is the yearly Festival Hiša na hribu, produced by Zavod CCC (a community institute for media arts and social research projects). © Nina Goršič/ UIRS

Bottom left: The community interpretation of artistic enhancement of tablecloths in curated workshops by local artists from House on the Hill (Hiša na hribu) brought locals around the same table, thus keeping old traditions alive and promoting joint endeavours of residents. © Matej Nikšič/UIRS

Bottom right: In the belltower at Žlebe the exhibition of codesigned tablecloths promoted the values of this common work. The exhibition brought contemporary community art to rural areas. © Nina Goršič/ UIRS

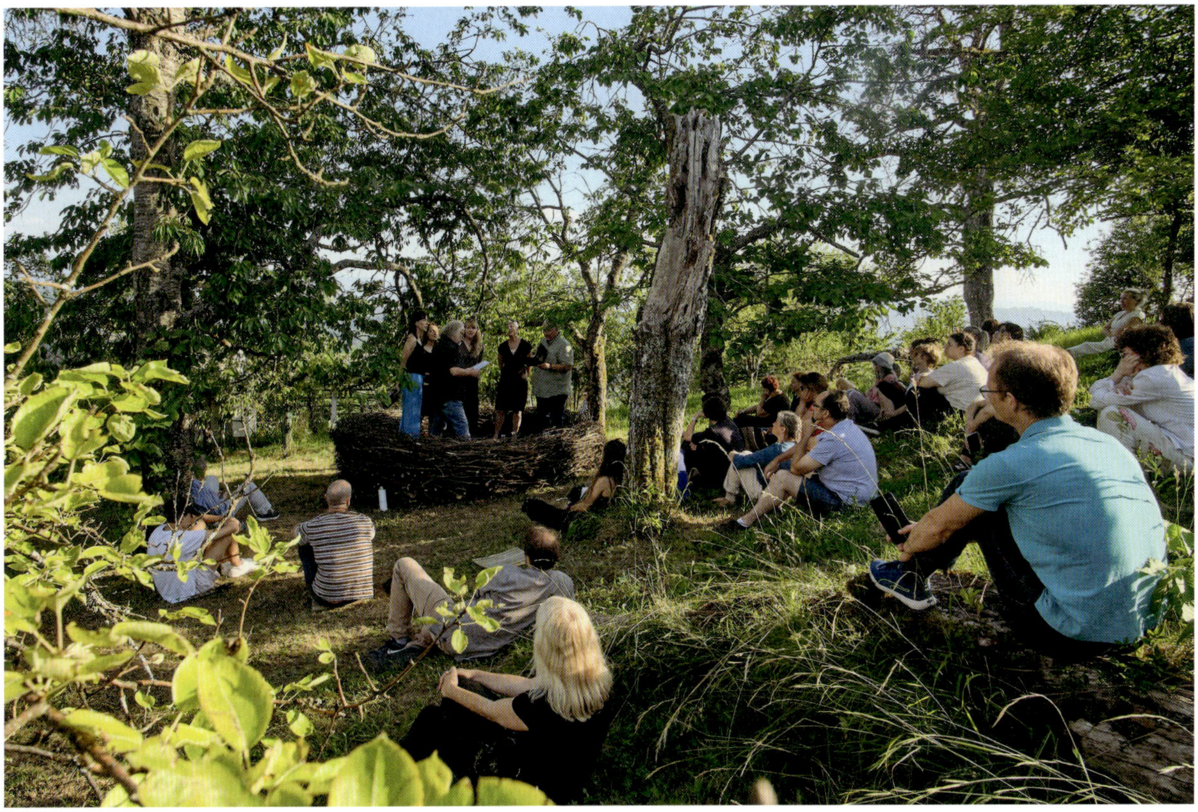

Gathering at the Big Nest, an experimental piece by the artist Mateja Kavčič located at Pr' Lenart in Belo. A place to bring people together for socialising and cultural exchange. © Kevin Loigu

Belo and Pr' Lenart is one stop along the 'Path of Dried Pears' through the forest. It is marked with the sign of a pear. The path runs through the orchard outside and into the deeper birch woods. Follow it up and down the hills and eventually you will come back out through the orchards to the schoolhouse at Topol pri Medvodah, the trailhead marked by the large flat gravel car park. Nikšič and Goršič think something can be done with the car park. But that's a path with a longer horizon.

Just up the road from the car park Žiga Kršinar is in rubber boots on a Thursday, having walked through poplar forests looking for clearings with fruit trees he can pick up and replant. He and Šubic are talking trees. Particularly they are talking about a 10-metre patch of wood-chip garden on the roadside of the hillside. Set back from the road are young herbs, grapevines on a fence, a bench, and a fig tree facing south.

Kršinar and Šubic didn't always agree on the concept. Šubic long had a vision for a forest garden, but didn't have tools and couldn't gain enough support. Kršinar followed a different idea for the slope. He also has an excavator. Nina wonders how the garden will be used, with its entry paths not yet clear.

But the village now has what could grow into a new communal space. Kršinar returns to his tree-planting. He is putting down tepka pears. He and his partner are clearing out and building what Kršinar calls an educational farm, working with all the animals and produce you can imagine, but also creating a place for schools to visit, integrating traditional wood-pin nails into the architecture. It'll also be a place for guests to stay and they could take home honey from the hives and pears from the trees. Would not even need to be greedy – even a small set of filled guestrooms could well earn more than an entire farm.

And so he is planting new orchards.

Left: Walking through the "Pot suhih hrušk/Path of the Dried Pears" initiated the idea of turning local orchards to (semi) public spaces at Belo by refreshing knowledge on tree pruning and planting new fruit trees of old, locally distinctive tree varieties (tepka pears, apples, plums etc.). © Mojca Sfiligoj

Right: The surroundings of Topol pri Medvodah are criss-crossed with forest and other walking paths. Mindful walking offers an alternative way of experiencing rural landscapes. © Kevin Loigu

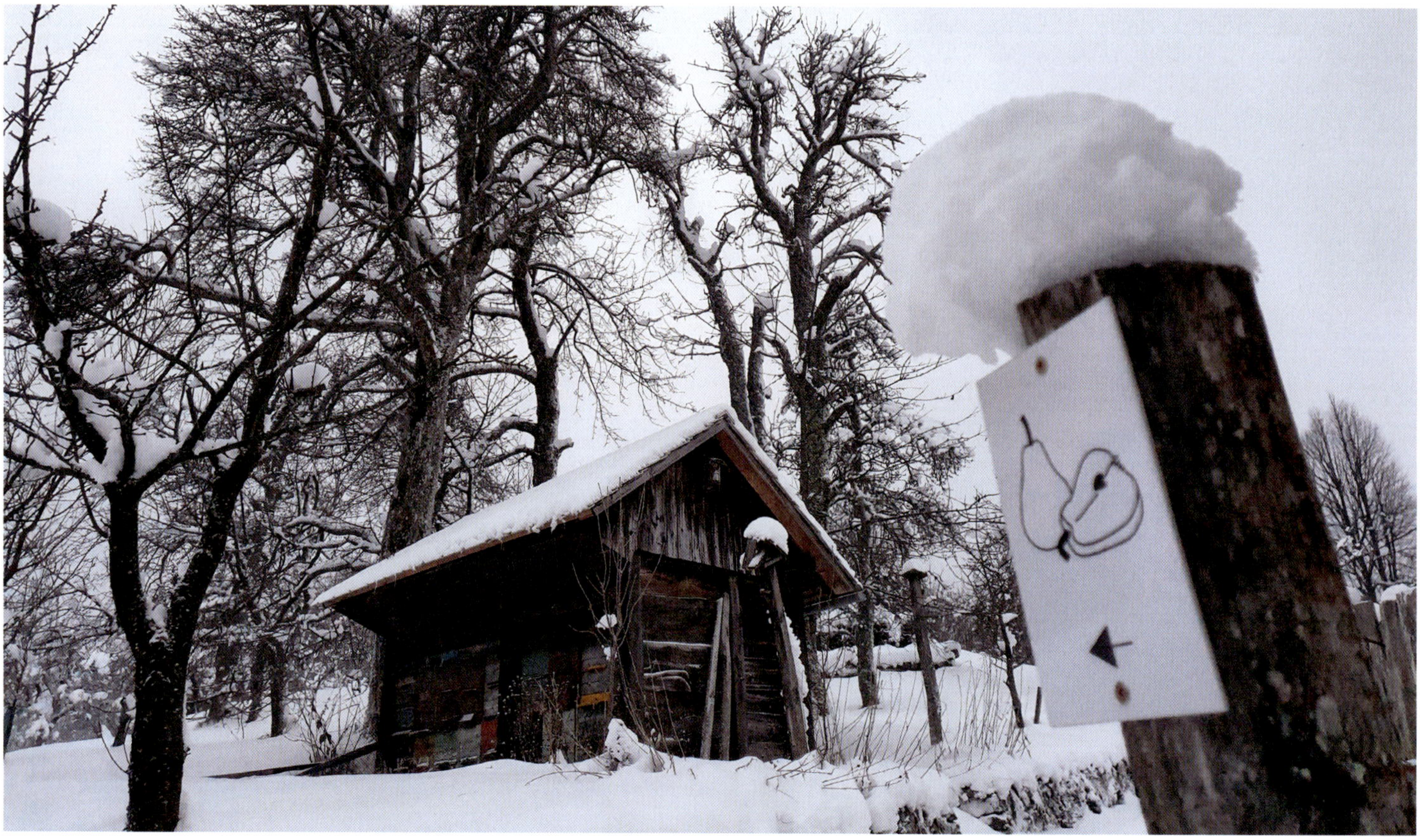

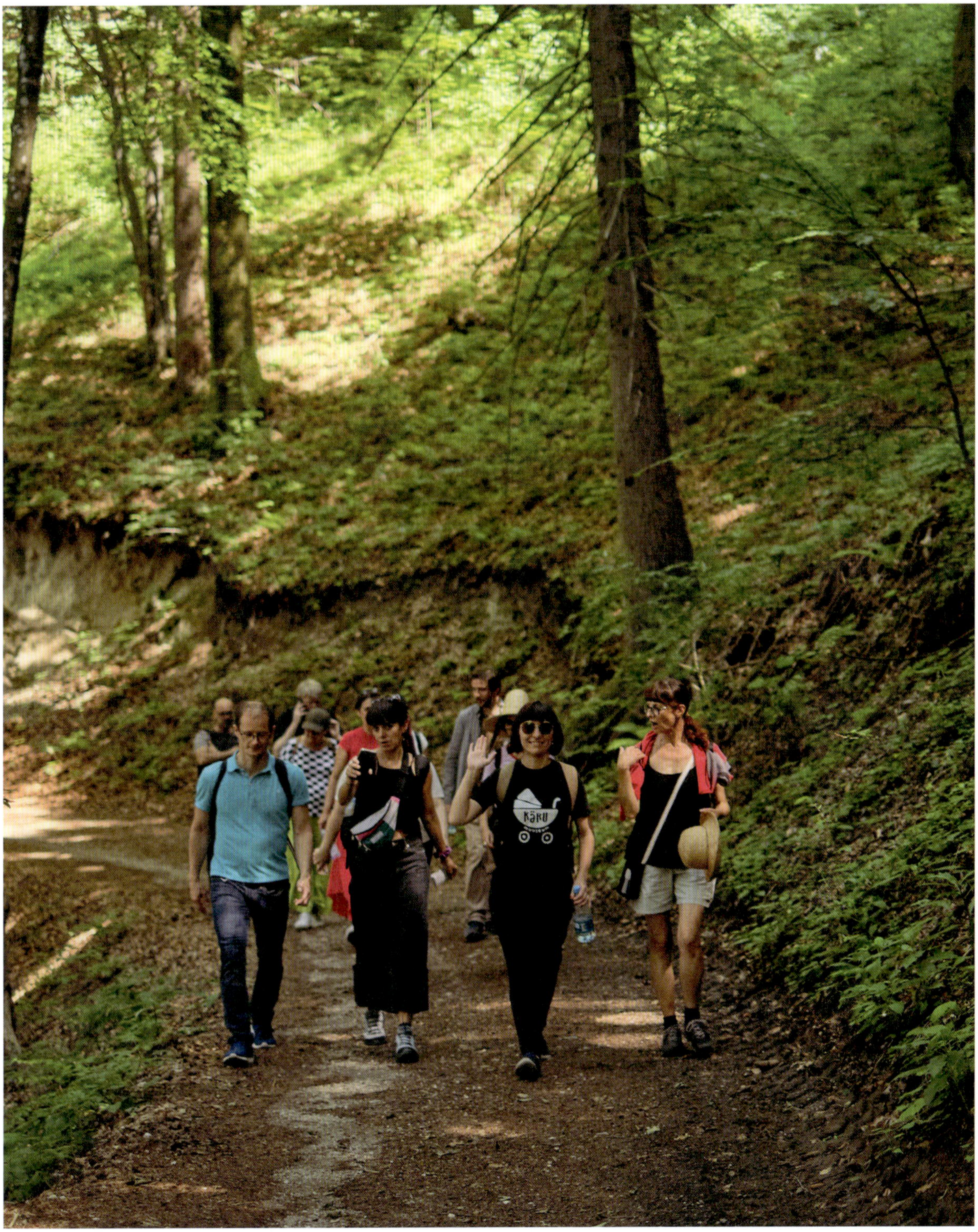

“Hérna er einstakt tækifæri til nýta hönnun til að upphefja byggð út frá sinni mögnuðu sögu og minjum frá víkingaöld og nútíma.
Hér langt út í hafi eru möguleikarnir og tækifæri til að skapa frábært umhverfi, hér þar sem fjársjóðinn er erfitt að sjá því hann er beint fyrir framan nefið á okkur.”

“Here in the far north Atlantic we have the possibility to use design to valorise a town using its incredible history and monuments from the Viking age and late modern times. Here where the treasure is so close that it is difficult to see, we can catch the opportunities and make a great environment.”
Birgir Þröstur Jóhannsson

Location: Borgarnes, Iceland

Stretching to the tip of a small peninsula in western Iceland, Borgarnes is a regional agricultural outpost in transition and a gateway to a remote area of great natural beauty.

SMOTIES Partner: Alternance Architecture and Urban Planning, slf, Reykjavik

Alternance is a small research-based design and planning studio based in Reykjavik, Iceland. From the perspective gained through a methodology it calls MAPS – multidisciplinary assessment of a public space – it aims to assess the quality of public spaces and deliver recommendations to improve them.

Borgarnes

Key involvement in project

Alternance:
Astrid Lelarge, historian in urban planning, project manager, faculty, Agricultural University of Iceland;
Birgir Þröstur Jóhannsson, architect, urban planner; Pall Jakob Líndal, environmental psychologist; Sigriður Kristjánsdóttir, geographer and planner, former dean of faculty of planning and design, Agricultural University of Iceland; Gabriel Cauchemet.

Borgarbyggð municipality, township of Borgarnes;
Sigursteinn Sigurðsson, culture and welfare administrator, West Iceland Regional Office;
Hafþór Ingi Gunnarsson, Hollvinasamtök Borgarness.

What they set out to do

To raise the profile of local cultural heritage and history and identify public spaces with good design potential in Borgarnes for reflecting and reinforcing those aspects; to highlight natural beauty and develop activities; and to focus attention on an area of historical importance left behind by economic and infrastructure changes.

What the project accomplished

Developed a detailed pre-designed architectural plan for the redevelopment of historical public space; mapped an urban design rubric for municipal use; presented animation and augmented reality models for a central axis of Borgarnes' old town from park to waterfront.

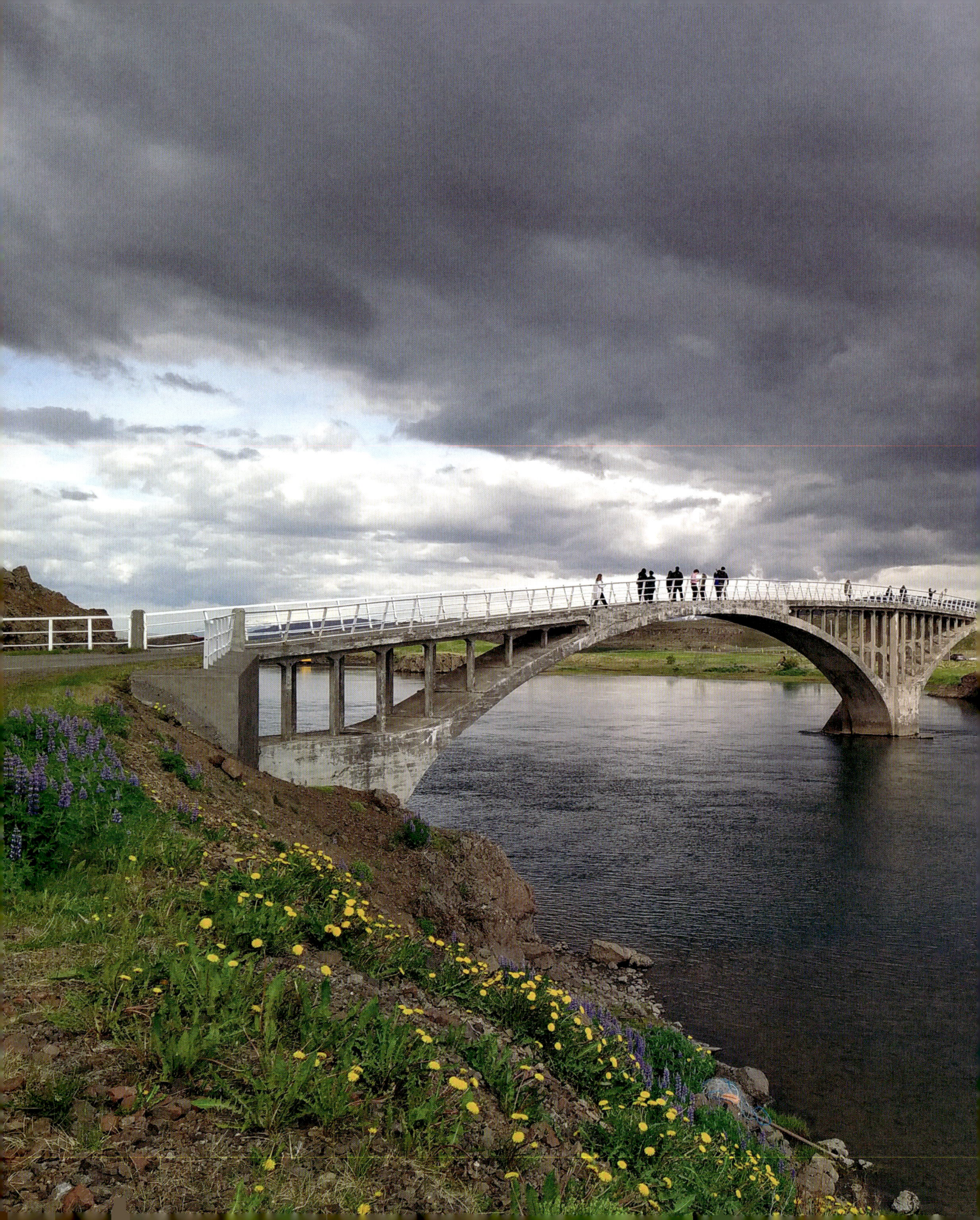

The Road Past Skallagrímsgarður

It was the slaughterhouse at the tip of the peninsula that brought crowds of people into town for two months a year. Sláturfélag Borgfirðinga, it was called. Kaupfélag Borgfirðinga was the co-op that ran it. Sigursteinn Sigurðsson of Borgarnes, an architect by training and cultural advisor to a regional government office in western Iceland, remembers it being so busy when the livestock came to town that his neighbour slept in her bathtub because she'd rented out all of her rooms.

Now the slaughterhouse is gone. And the traffic is gone. But the broad road that runs down the hill to the tip of the peninsula is still there. And Borgarnes is trying to figure out what that means.

"Waking up in the middle of the night, when the post truck was coming? It was just like a freight train going down that street," Sigursteinn says. He is addressed by his given name, as is Icelandic fashion, and is talking about the main avenue that splits the narrow older part of Borgarnes. It is called Borgarbraut.

It is a sharp left turn off the National Route One. Heading downhill, Borgarbraut changes name to Brákarbraut and winds up at the harbour and Brákarsund channel, passing over to a little island. This road was meant to move lots of traffic quickly. It was livestock going down for slaughter, vehicles coming up. No more.

In 2021, Astrid Lelarge and Birgir Þröstur Jóhannsson of the design studio Alternance drove an hour from the capital Reykjavik, through the tunnel under wide Hvalfjörður, skirting a massive basalt ridge shaped like a whaleback–and then, turning left off Route One, down Borgarbraut.

They had a map–a plan, a methodology that drew on planning, environmental psychology, architecture, and applied historical expertise to understand public space. It clarified not only the importance of Borgarbraut and Brákarbraut to Borgarnes but also suggested possible outcomes.

Over three years Alternance refined its understanding of Borgarbraut (and Borgarnes) and applied its concepts to three public spaces along a main axis beginning with a small park at the top of a rocky hill and leading down to the waterfront.

One of many Alternance field surveys observed the area a dozen times.

"Pedestrians are rare; residents and visitors drive past the park, even without noticing, on their way somewhere else." The park suffered from being unable to attract public attention.

Alternance has reimagined the neighbourhood's entire main axis, with ideas touching the park, the traffic flow, and the seashore. A key junction on the road where cars pass would be transformed into a public square; and the route going down to the sea would be recast to the point of envisioning steps down to the chilly waters of Brákarsund, to the rocky beach and a stone pier. Alternance created two-minute 3-D video animations that glide and charm viewers through lively open vistas, showing what would be new public spaces in the old part of town.

It's ambitious. Local government is interested. But it has to find resources: budget, sustained willingness, continuity. This is the same for any ambitious planning scheme in a small town. Long odds.

But the research aims for long-term effects. It has set up signposts.

The project is the kind of survey and analytical close reading of Borgarnes that mayor Stefán Broddi Guðjónsson says is unusual and often well out of the grasp of small cash-strapped towns.

The mayor is excited about it. Because it's probably fair to say the first thing that comes to mind for most Icelanders when they think of Borgarnes is petrol and a handy toilet. This is, in some ways, by design. Iceland's Route One is the loop that connects the country: it is a ring road around the entire island. Route One first came close to Borgarnes in the sixties–close but not that close. Then it came directly to the town's eastern edge via a new bridge in 1974, brushing the fat end of the peninsula before rounding north.

Route One is a magnet that moves things as any rail line would in the American West. Before, Borgarbraut and Brákarbraut funnelled farm traffic through town to the slaughterhouse. Now the town's centre of gravity sits by the petrol stations at the bridge.

"This is a place where you stop for gas and then you keep going," says Hafþór Ingi Gunnarsson over a coffee in a café on the harbour, down the hill. Hafþór grew up in Borgarnes and has been an iron welder, carpenter, and rover; more than anything he is an athlete and basketball player. Hafþór runs the Hollvinasamtök Borgarness, the booster association behind an annual town festival. "In my opinion, there is a lot more to see and do in Borgarnes than taking a toilet break."

P. 110: From Hvítárbrú in Borgarbyggð © Birgir Þröstur Jóhannsson / Alternance

Alternance created a comprehensive design plan for the main axis in the older part of Borgarnes, from Skallagrímsgarður park to the waterfront. The plan would see the following:

Top: to the north (upper right-centre, in this illustration) Skallagrímur's square hosts the medieval burial mound of Skallagrímur, the "commemorative" mound of Kveldúlfur and the music school. To the south (in the corner in the bottom left), Brák's square is created where the town developed in the 19th century. The settlement centre, established in houses dating 1876-1887, is located next to it. A new community building, recalling in its shape the old slaughterhouse, frames the borders of the square. Both are connected by the axis transformed into a shared space. © Alternance

Middle: Skallagrímur's square is formed around two landmarks. The central one is the medieval burial mound of Skallagrímur. The second is the "commemorative" mound named after his father. The square in the centre is intended as a community space for cultural, associative, and festive meetings in the open air, hosting a greenhouse/café, a water space recalling the marsh past of the place, and offers a space that can accommodate a stage in front of the music school. The square starts the shared space. © Alternance

Bottom: Brák's square is located in the south of the peninsula. This space hosts a new public building with a cultural and associative vocation taking the shape of the old slaughterhouse and its conceptual location on the water's edge. The square is a multi-use space centred around a shallow pool of water, which can be heated, frozen, emptied, or temporarily filled, thus accommodating numerous uses and events. The stepped docks, descending towards the fjord, provide historic access to the water. © Alternance

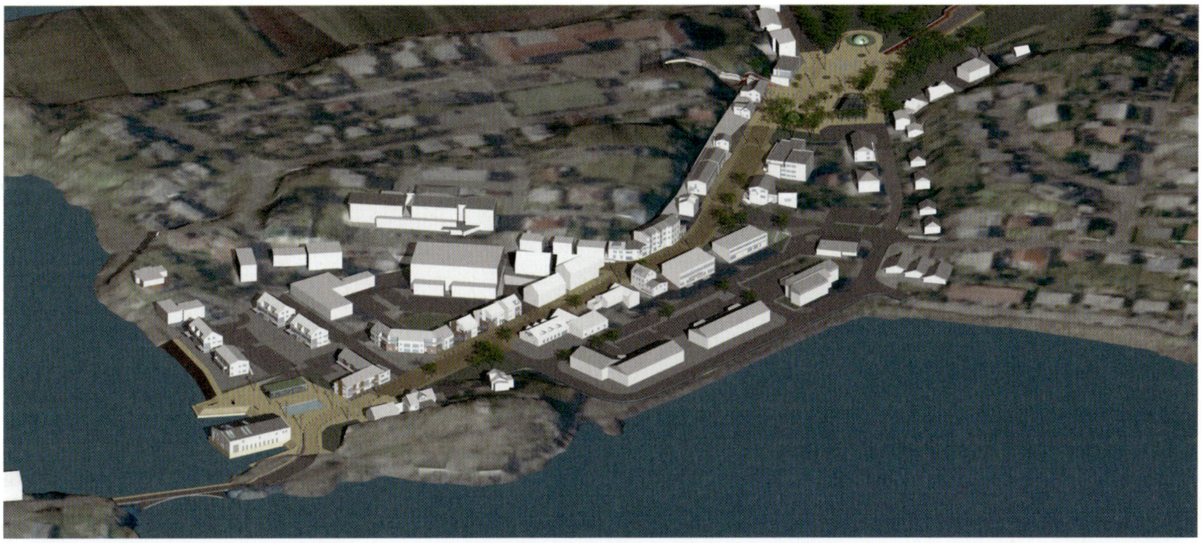

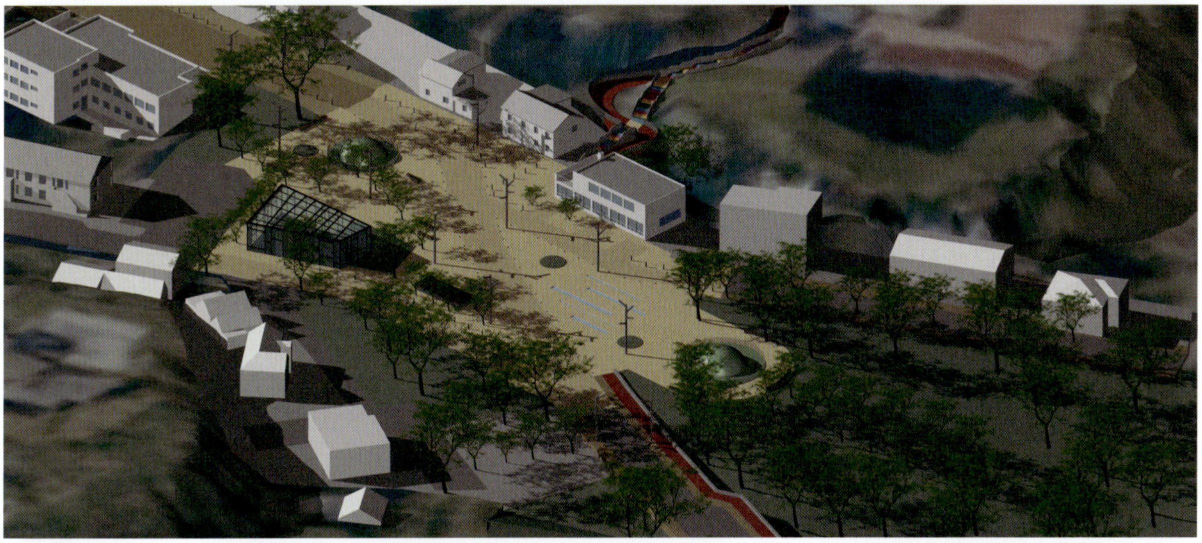

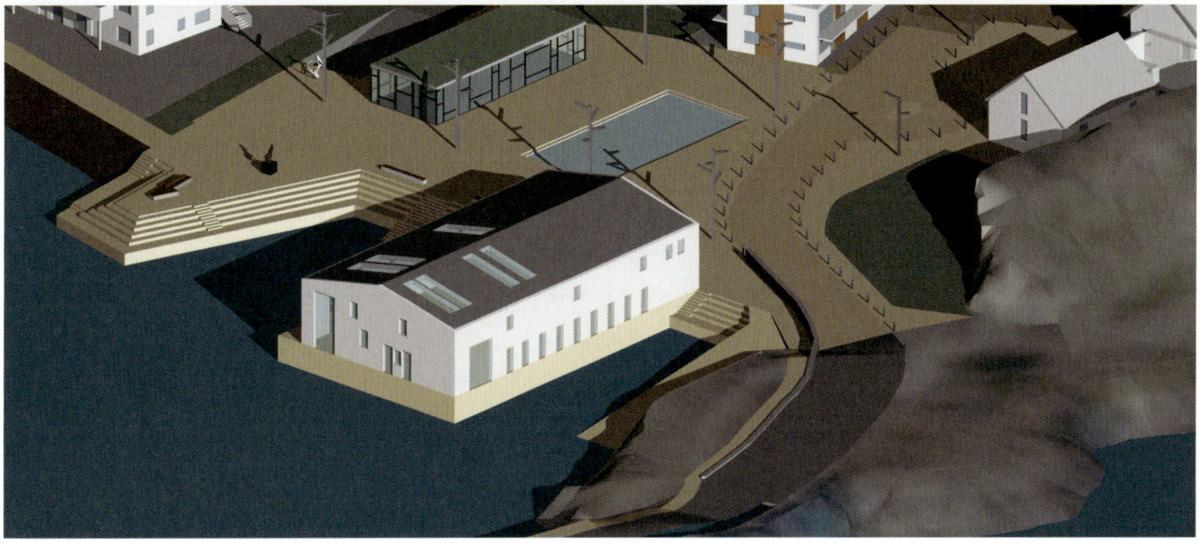

He's been glad to join forces with Alternance to connect with town residents. The architects have set up from time to time at Bara Borgarnes, a nearby tavern that opened in 2021 in what used to be a Filipino restaurant. Sigursteinn sometimes goes there to sing with a little pickup choir. It is a spark of community spirit.

Up the hill from Bara Borgarnes, across Route One from the petrol station, is a care home called Brákarhlið.

Alternance's Birgir Þröstur Jóhannsson, Astrid Lelarge, Pall Jakob Líndal and Gabriel Cauchemet arrive there one afternoon in late October, taking off their shoes in the vestibule and wondering why the sound system isn't set up in the dining hall. Then the residents come in, a dozen at first, dwindling slowly over the course of an hour and a half: there is a vigorous and talkative nonagenarian, and a few that are a little more tired and ill. They all fill out forms after Birgir's pitch to ask them what they'd like to see in Borgarnes. Pall, especially, is interested in quantifying and applying statistical research to design practice.

Afterwards everyone seems a little puzzled. Not all of the seniors come from Borgarnes or know it that well. Pall is reviewing his surveying, muttering about simplifying the questionnaire. Mostly though, the residents are not used to being asked for their opinions in this way – about something outside the home, on equal terms. In a shiny-tech-saturated age in thrall to youth, it is definitely out of the ordinary. And Alternance is making the effort to connect. Even if there's some head-scratching.

Mayor Stefán's office is in the new glass-box bank building on Route One across from the Brákarhlið home; the town administrative centres and bank now overlook the petrol stations. He's recently returned from a trip to New York. Stefán is excited about what he heard there that made him think of home and how Borgarnes can draw people to come off Route One: to turn down Borgarbraut. "There was this new Loki or Thor film coming out, and I looked around at Times Square and there was this huge advertisement and

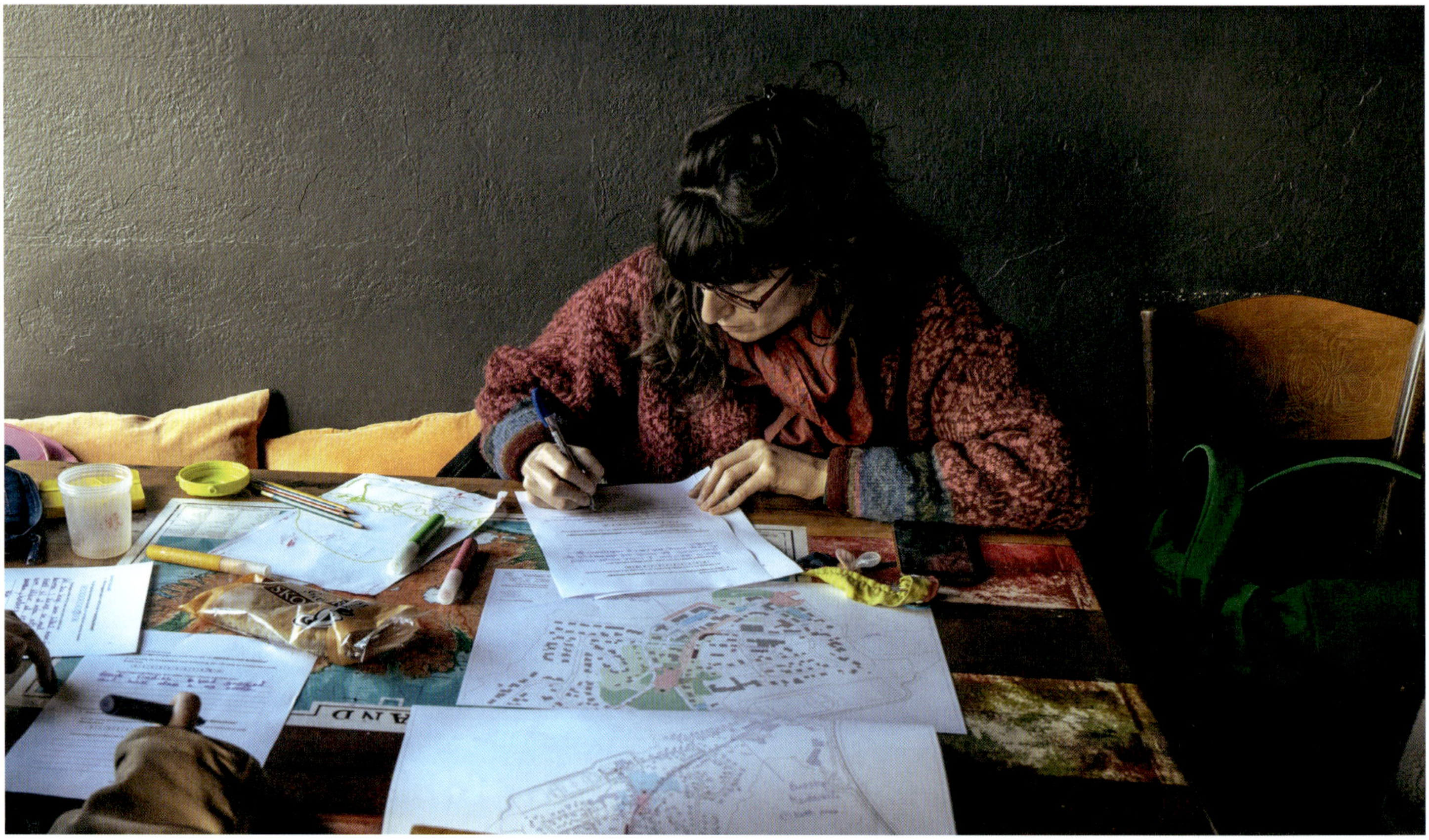

Left: Louise Bassigny, resident in Borgarnes, filling out a questionnaire and a work map on mobility in Borgarnes during a workshop organised at the 'Bara', a pub located in Brákarbraut.
© Alternance/Gabriel Cauchemet

Right: Sögutorgin (Historic place) is a preliminary architectural project designed by architect Birgir Þröstur Jóhannsson in collaboration with the local community in Borgarnes. It aims to regenerate the old town through public spaces development. It includes the preliminary design of two squares (Skallagrímur's square and Brák's square) and the axis between them (Borgarbraut and Brákarbraut).
© Alternance

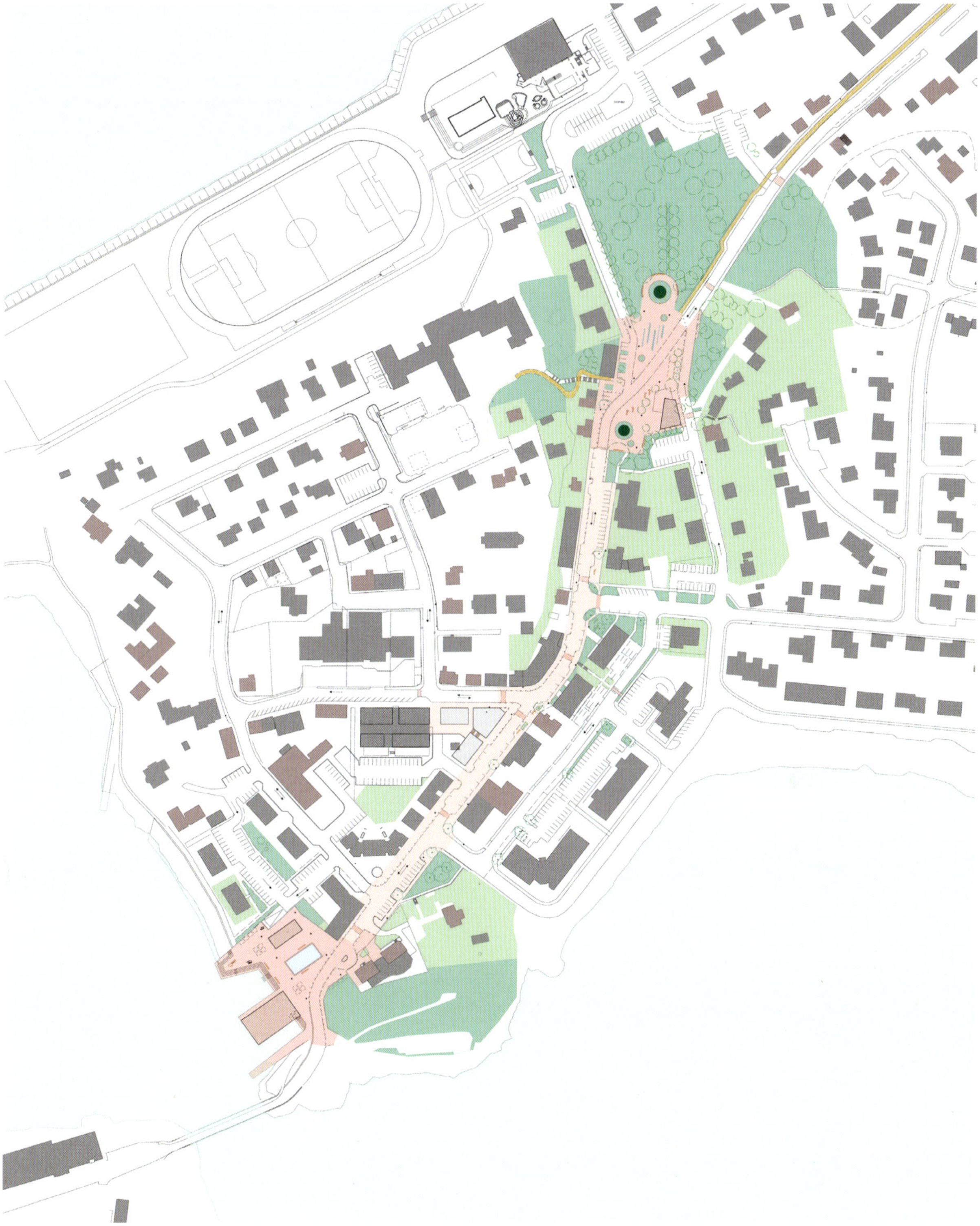

I thought, 'that's us'," he says. "It is built on our heritage."

The mayor means the medieval Icelandic culture set out in the books known as Eddas – the main sources of Norse mythology – and the sagas evoking the Viking age.

The park, central to Alternance's concept for Borgarbraut, preserves the memory of it. That park is called Skallagrímsgarður: the garden of Skalla-Grímr, or Skallagrímur. Skallagrímur is the father of Egill Skallagrímsson, namesake of Egil's Saga. Its mythic story is sometimes dark and it is long and winding. We do not have space for all of its roving turns here. It is – after all – a saga. In it Skallagrímur (boulder-thrower, berserker, Icelandic hero) settles the peninsula that is now Borgarnes.

And a big mound at Skallagrímsgarður garden park carries a sign designating it as the burial site of Skalla-Grímr, or at least the site where he was buried according to folklore.

For Borgarnes it speaks to the importance of folk tradition, of history, and of the old sagas of Icelanders that they have stitched into the landscape here. The Settlement Centre by the harbour where Hafþór sips a coffee is wrapped up in the Skalla-Grímr tale; the town's amateur basketball team is named after him.

A rainy day in a small town with seemingly not much going on suddenly seems much better if it is in a small town infused with a story.

It's a story that might even pull people away from the highway. Even better, it might lead to a fresh lift for the neighbourhood and the people who live there.

Alternance team: Astrid Lelarge, Birgir Þröstur Jóhannsson, Pall Líndal and Gabriel Cauchemet visiting Brák's square after a meeting at Borgarnes seniors' home. The team discusses the project on site and tests a tool currently being developed for 3-D visualisation in augmented reality showing the cultural building imagined in the project. © Michael Dumiak

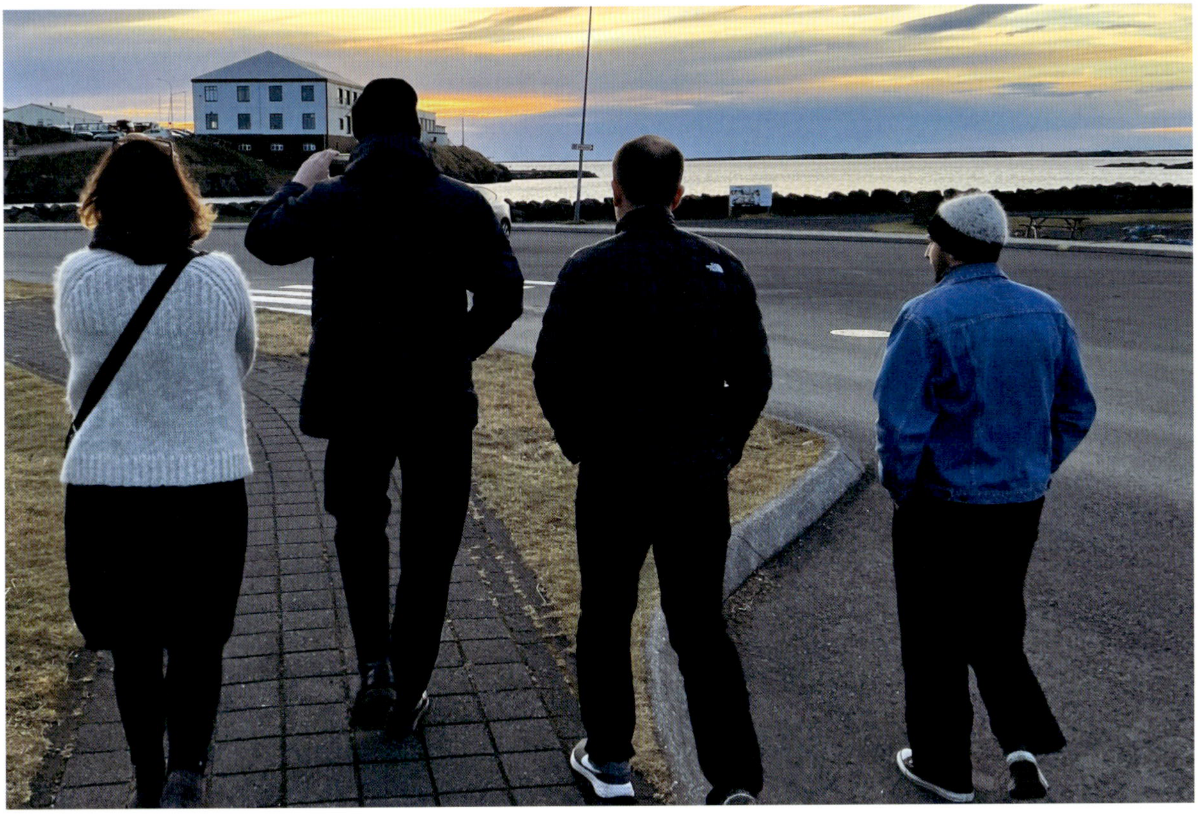

Part 2.

Edited by Inge Eller and Michael Dumiak

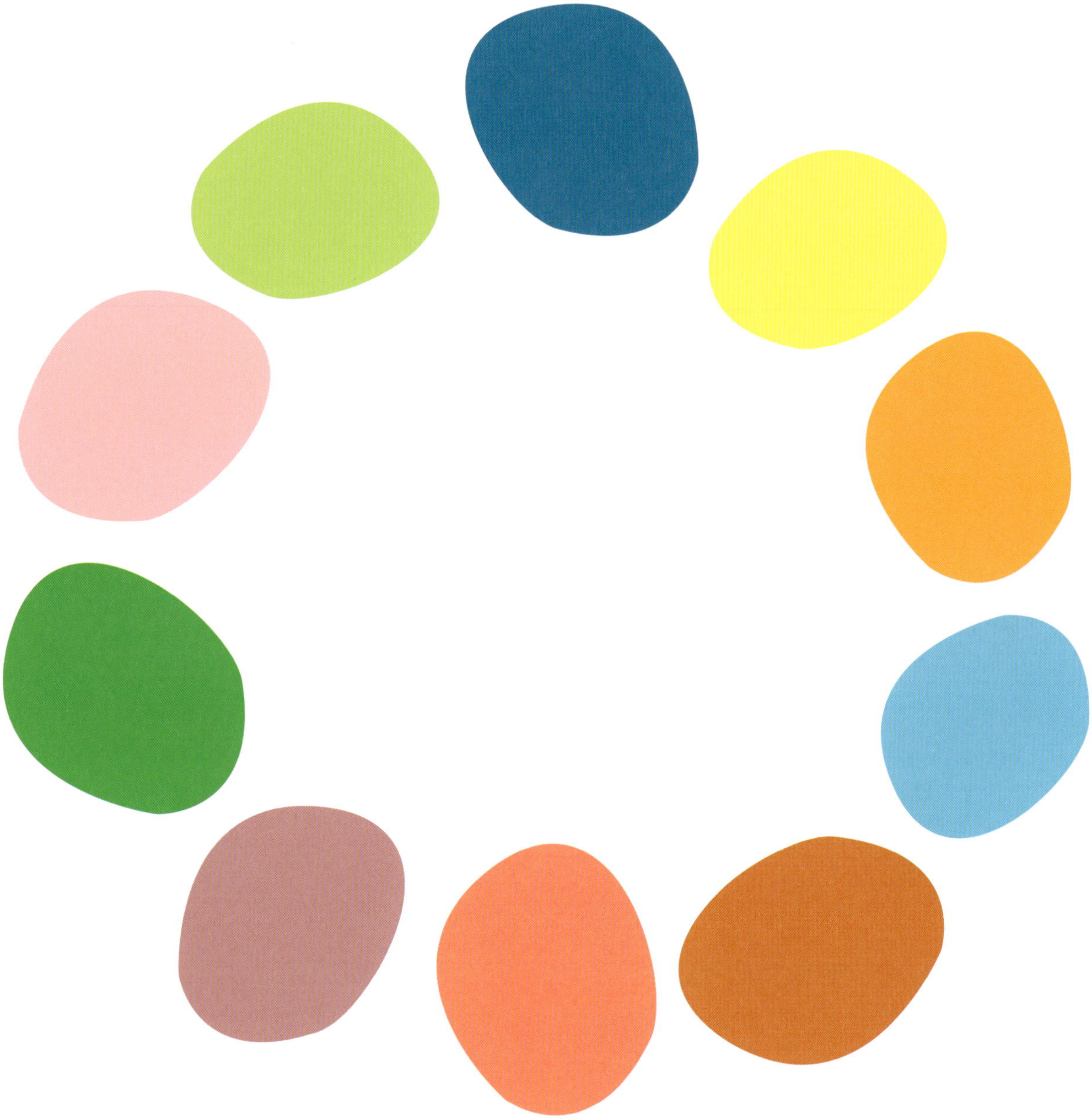

Designers Reflect.

Experience, Understanding, and Notes from the Field

The SMOTIES initiative spanned more than three years and, for many of the designers involved, it meant stepping out of their comfort zone. Left behind was the urban, the abstract, the conceptual and the academic.

The initiative SMOTIES: Creative Works with Small and Remote Places meant engaging with places that are depopulated, culturally varied, often undervalued and overlooked, amid complex and changing community dynamics, and social and economic shifts. And it meant coming into these environments informally, as an outsider.

The SMOTIES partnership includes designers, architects, anthropologists, historians and project managers working in public institutions, design and research centres, national associations, small non-profits, and university design faculties. In each of the ten projects, a surfeit of events, experiences, conversations, engagements, beginnings, accomplishments, setbacks, and surprises took place over years. It is beyond the scope of what we'll be able to capture in these pages. Even so, here we have the SMOTIES partners reflecting on the things they've learned during the initiative and continue to think about.

When you really start engaging with a place or community, some things become apparent right away. Others take a little longer to understand.

[EE] Estonian Association of Designers (EAD)
There are few to no jobs near the remote place of Joaveski. Also, no grocery store within 10 kilometres.

[AT] FH Joanneum
But in the case of Oberzeiring, Austria, traffic is the most important issue. There's a busy road that runs through the middle of the place. The speed limit is 50 kilometres an hour even though it is through tight space. The marketplace – the most important square in the village – is located on that street.

The traffic directly impacts communication in the village. As it is now, the square does not work as a place for either intentional or unintentional meetings among residents. There's no facility for it.

[FR] Cité du design – ESADSE
In the Dorlay Valley, the problem is the isolation of the valley and its villages. This is due to the lack of public transport.

There is a feeling of being between two worlds. You are not far from the towns but still in the countryside. There are contradictory desires: you find pride in the region's textile heritage and a desire to share it, but on the other hand, a concern to be protected from tourist traffic, especially on weekends. You've got a desire to live better but not necessarily to attract people.

[IS] Alternance
The old town of Borgarnes is on a narrow, naturally rocky peninsula. The old town used to be a commercial hub and transit point for the trade of sheep and dairy through the harbour. There are remains from the Viking age, and architectural heritage from the 19th century, when the town was founded.

People rate the current conditions of the squares in the old town as moderate to bad. They want the squares to be renovated to promote public life. They also want to acknowledge its heritage and respect nature and the spectacular views there.

[GR] Department of Product and Systems Design Engineering, University of the Aegean
Meanwhile on the island of Syros, we have water shortages, dropping population numbers, biodiversity loss and community loss. Water scarcity creates environmental and everyday life issues. The community is changing. Our remote place has very few permanent residents, and there are very few spaces where they can meet and interact with each other and share their vision for the community.

Certain assets come into focus at specific points. They help guide actions in what can, hopefully, be long-term collaboration and involvement. But they may change over time.

[PL] Zamek Cieszyn
There is a real lack of infrastructure in the housing estate we are engaged with. There's poor public transport connections and no pedestrian connections linking the two neighbouring estates. This part of town is not well integrated with the rest of Cieszyn.

But the estate has a green space. It's a potential recreational space, or could be a better one. Residents have diverse needs – that's clear. But encouraging communication among them also develops an asset: this feeling of agency.

[IS] Alternance
We pinpointed specific spaces for intervention. They were selected because of their significant history and heritage, and their qualities within the built and natural landscape.

[SI] Urban Planning Institute of the Republic of Slovenia (UIRS)
Our SMOTIES area is part of a landscape park just west of the capital. Mountain farming and forestry are the main economic activities shaping the cultural landscape. We see both tangible and intangible resources there: not only orchards, pristine forests, well-preserved homesteads; but also the local traditions of bread-baking, fruit-tree planting, and tablecloth designing. We experimented with all of these assets to bring people together.

[AT] FH Joanneum
In Oberzeiring, the very local associations and clubs are a valuable resource. They are functioning systems, in a way: it means they can implement projects once something is under way.

But they are not very visible. People visiting the village don't know about them. Young residents who might become members don't have much insight into how they could get involved.

[EE] EAD
It seemed important to try to improve public discussions among local residents about the environment they live in – and to encourage them to dream bigger!

[IT] Politecnico di Milano
A desire for change doesn't wait for a signal from the outside, but that signal can help. Sometimes a project stimulated by an 'outside' presence sparks the flourishing of new initiatives, the proactive presence of citizens. That desire is a resource.

[FR] Cité du design – ESADSE
We also drew on the enthusiasm of a local association to collect and express the history and memory of a very small village located within the walls of what used to be a monastery. In the neighbouring valley, we looked at the industrial heritage and drew on people's strong desire to highlight local history and know-how.

This became an avenue for us to focus our attention. It provided a way in to inspire people to consider soft mobility routes that highlight heritage sites.

[GR] University of the Aegean
The local conditions led to ideas. We were thinking a lot about water shortages and the loss of community. We thought about a small action that would touch on both of these. So, small green spaces that would prompt locals to do something together and water these spaces to keep them green, to nurture them.

Top: Bringing communities together: SMOTIES partners in Poland. © Krzysztof Puda

Bottom: Workshop with residents at La Terrasse-sur-Dorlay. Engaging locals by designing a personalised map with memories. © Cité du design

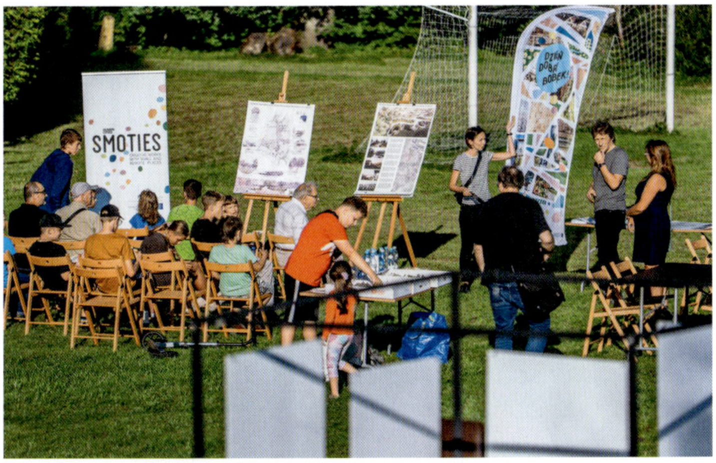

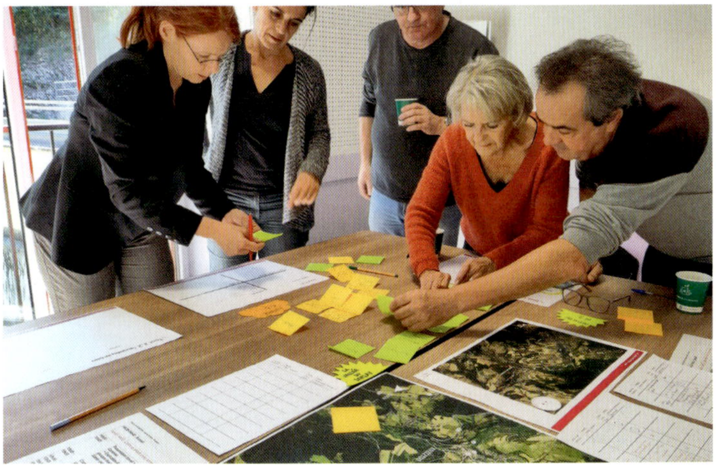

And then it becomes clearer who is really involved, or should be involved, and why. Who either has an impact or could be impacted by your initiative?

[IT] Politecnico di Milano
In Albugnano there is a cultural association and a theatre company. They bring together people that are on different paths, with a variety of cultures and experiences, such as at the annual cultural festival. We also worked with an association promoting the area and its wine culture, and with the local governing institutions: the mayor, deputy mayors and council. We found our local heroes.

[IS] Alternance
The municipality was important. We needed to gain its support. It also actively participated financially. We garnered the support of the residents' association, the residents, and the planning faculty at the nearby university too.

[GR] University of the Aegean
From the outset, we wanted to tap into a diverse group with specific knowledge of these places. And we wanted to collectively cultivate ideas. Our solutions should be useful and sustainable.

People are busy. Persuasion and securing people's involvement takes skill, persistence, convincing, gaining trust, and getting help. Even then, it is hard to widen the circles of those who are really involved.

[PL] Zamek Cieszyn
Memory mapping (interviewing a number of people, and asking about memories tied to a space, and then plotting them on a map) is something that worked well because it brings out people's emotions tied to specific places.

[FR] Cité du design – ESADSE
That way people enjoyed sharing their personal and collective memories linked to the village and its surroundings. The mapping session encouraged them to tell their stories. It created an atmosphere of sharing.

[GR] University of the Aegean
It helped us to bring together people's narratives, and to see the bigger picture of our remote place. It helped us engage locals in a way that was more emotional for them and to bring them into the conversation. But it was challenging to enable everyone to feel equally part of the conversations.

[SI] UIRS
We worked with people to organise public events around themes related to local traditions and contemporary issues in the area, like taking care of fruit trees, rebuilding local drywalls, or seeding honey flowers in grasslands.

[AT] FH Joanneum
In the beginning, we usually had meetings in club rooms. We also actively took 'temporary possession' of public space so we could have more informal contact with people. It happened, for example, when we, teachers and students, worked directly on the market square for a few days at a time.

[EE] EAD
Then we found our 'door opener'. This was a person who knew the locals and was also in contact with our team. It seemed like the best way to attract local people, since it's such a small population.

[SI] UIRS
We also got the students out interviewing while participating in daily activities – like raking and mowing the grass!

Farmers were more likely to talk to them than 'officials' from the capital city. Once the ice was broken, everything went easier.

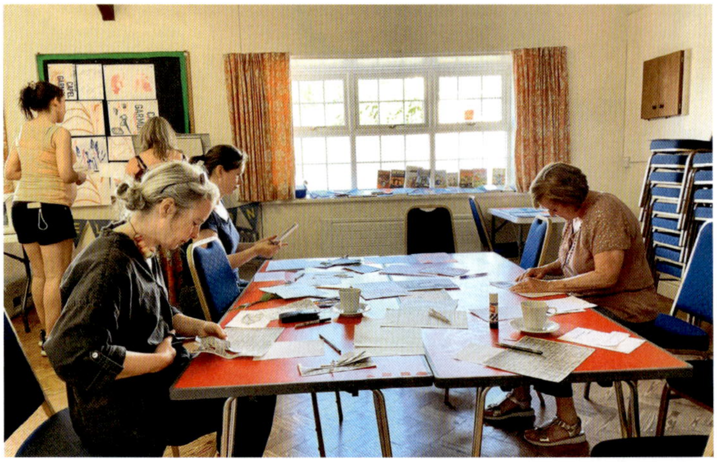

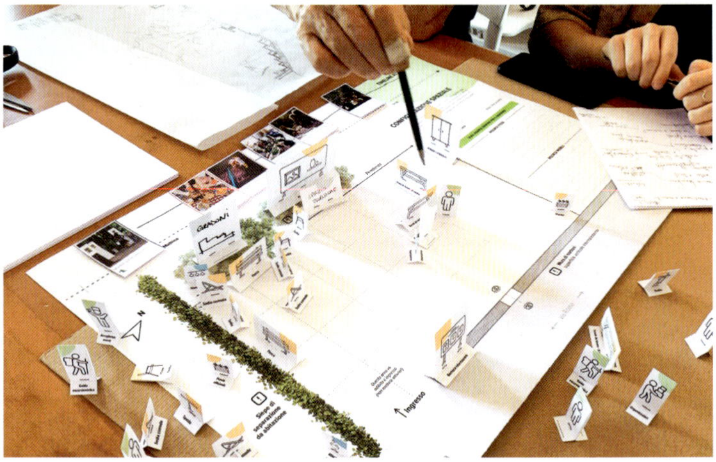

Top: Mapping communities in Capel Garmon, Wales © Kristin Luke

Co-creation workshop for the co-design of the Via Roma Garden in Albugnano, June 2023. © Polimi DESIS Lab

The challenges come regardless. Some are to be expected; others come out of the blue.

[SI] UIRS
It was hard to move past 'business as usual'. People seemed hesitant to start a truly inclusive process. Some residents like the way things are: no changes at all needed.

Nature is unpredictable. Sometimes, it is a shock. In summer 2023, we really thought we had a breakthrough in the central location in front of the local primary school, creating a central public space. Then there was flooding in the area: devastating floods. It changed priorities overnight.

[IS] Alternance
There's a possibility that future outside commercial development will happen in places that would change the public spaces we have been working on. It's uncertain how that might happen, or if it will at all. That makes it difficult to plan. It is also a challenge to get locals to participate actively.

[GR] University of the Aegean
Some of the locals wanted to lead the discussion and made it difficult for others to freely express their opinions. Also, people are very concerned about extreme tourist development happening on Greek islands. So they were sceptical about our interventions: we had to help them understand that this was a collaboration with and for them, and to 'guarantee' that we would not 'hurt' the place.

[UK] Clear Village
We were in an unusual position because a member of our team lives in our remote place. Largely as a result of that, the project has gone very smoothly overall. But it was also striking how careful and diplomatic we had to be. One of our team is American, another is English, the project is European. So we had to be very clear about what we wanted, and that we are not part of the wave that's also bringing in holiday-home owners, that kind of thing.

[IT] Politecnico di Milano
We should mention the pandemic and remember what that was like. Beyond that, often the channels we used to communicate were digital, because of the remote nature of the town. So it was difficult to engage the population that way. Sometimes the language didn't resonate with the population.

And there was a bit of balancing between two types of souls. On the one hand, there were those taking a typical entrepreneurial approach, wanting to bring in new visitors and interest from the outside. On the other hand, some worked by social engagement, involving the local community foremost. We wanted to support both, even if they clashed at times. That could also lead to good results.

[EE] EAD
People got involved only slowly. There was also hesitation from the real-estate owner responsible for future developments.

[FR] Cité du design – ESADSE
We really wanted to solicit and connect with local partners. If it's an association whose members are retired, that is less of a time management issue. But if they are still working and have no time, then the projects sometimes have intense rhythms and tight schedules.

[AT] FH Joanneum
We had to negotiate obstacles with local political actors and in trying to contact the former mayor, who clearly did not want to support the project. A new mayor came into office at the beginning of 2023. Also, the associations we are working with are all small civic organisations: you can't count on being able to communicate with them quickly.

In longer-term initiatives that are by nature socially engaged – that involve actions that can move very slowly and change over time – it can be hard to keep track of the impact. But trying to effectively measure impact and allowing it to shape actions can be an important discipline.

[PL] Zamek Cieszyn
We had to mediate between the differing visions for the same space and the competing interests there. But there were also structural things we had to consider: there are not only budget limitations in real cost terms, but limitations presented by the type of things we can consider due to the rules attached to potential expenditures. We had to manage expectations.

[UK] Clear Village
It struck me that impact measurement sometimes seemed alien. Perhaps it's to do with the culture: it can be that creative professionals are less likely to think about 'measurement' than natural or social scientists. Sometimes it would seem qualitative aspects of a project couldn't be quantified, when it might be reasonably straightforward. I do think impact measurement is quite novel and challenging for design professionals, and it doesn't come naturally to them.

[IT] Politecnico di Milano
We're using a creative tool (that will be made available for open-source use), and it maps a network of public spaces and services. It means we could better visualise the potential impact of the project's improvement on the territory.

[IS] Alternance
Internally within SMOTIES, having an impact assessment strategy and metrics to visualise it was important in creating overall coherence to the initiative. We also have an environmental psychologist on our team. He's encouraged using quantifiable surveying throughout the project and keeping track of a range of data.

[FR] Cité du design – ESADSE
We used questionnaires on site. Our tools were more analogue. We also drew up an oversized questionnaire based on a graphic design mapping out the routes participants had just taken – and whether they were changing their mobility habits. It was a more creative way of soliciting feedback, and it worked.

[EE] EAD
Our site has a pop-up sauna, and we are experimenting with it to see if we can do recordings. In addition to being a place of health and hygiene, the sauna is known to be the place for communication in Nordic countries. The recordings can include interviews between people taking the sauna, but also archival material.

The latest Human Cities initiative, SMOTIES: Creative Works with Small and Remote Places lasted more than three years within a diverse set of environments, regions, and peoples.

Because designers could observe, react to, recalibrate, and engage with very specific places in a variety of conditions, they were able to learn lessons and draw conclusions: to see the aspects and actions which led to successes, large and small.

This work will, in many cases, continue in the future, having built new networks, strengthened contacts, and brought in new colleagues and reference points. The designers have built expertise.

They've used tools and methodologies in a variety of contexts. They've learned.

Inevitably, it also drew out the unexpected.

[PL] Zamek Cieszyn
It was the active participation of children and youth that was a real surprise. We made some efforts to encourage this, but there was no expectation that they would. They are the least favoured group in terms of estate infrastructure – but they are actively striving for change.

[SI] UIRS
The aversion to change, in some ways, was surprising.

[IS] Alternance
We felt this also, not so much aversion as just a lack of participation. You have to be ready for a bit of inertia.

[SI] UIRS
On the other hand, after three years of SMOTIES activities, it was clear that the ideas raised were finding fertile soil. New ideas and projects were coming up spontaneously from residents. There seemed to be spin-off effects on diverse levels. That was nice to see!

[GR] University of the Aegean
One thing we learned – and we learned more than we thought we would – was how to manage change. During the course of the initiative our team changed, and we had to work hard to shift roles and reassign tasks in order to keep continuity.

[EE] EAD
There was not a lot of enthusiasm for the place before we got there. But when we did some interventions, some exhibitions and lighting design works, it revealed some new perspectives: people were able to see it in a new way, and suddenly there was enthusiasm for it.

[PL] Zamek Cieszyn
We collaborated with the Silesian University of Technology and brought in their students to draw up concepts and become engaged with our location. They visited the location and were informed about the needs – but were deliberately not given any additional frameworks. Their projects came in at a super-high and polished level, with a lot of wow! factor.

What that did was trigger enthusiasm and investment in people already interested in the project, and it raised the discussion level – but other residents got worried, became negative about making any changes. That exaggeration is normal in architectural concepts, but it means you also really have to be careful and conscientious about how you talk about it and how people perceive it.

Our conflicts required mediator support. But the mediation was a success.

Also, if you want to get people involved in these contexts, make the events attractive: picnics, a field game for children, plant exchanges, or photo exhibitions of locals by locals.

And bring tasty food!

One of the greatest successes was to help people get together and give them the chance to speak out and engage the youth. To show that their voice matters.

[AT] FH Joanneum
We saw clearly that traffic directly affects social functioning in the village. Our biggest success was creating temporary interventions in the market square. That meant everyone involved sees what a new situation could be like. Not only that, the bus company has shown great interest in the buses in the village being able to turn around at another location in future.

[FR] Cité du design – ESADSE
The game we worked with in one very small village, a historical card game, really got people involved and helped collect memories and pass on village history to people of different ages. It could be a model for other villages.

And participating in a European project puts a small village on the map. It's positive for local authorities. It motivates these institutions. The national park is now inspired by our signage concepts to create sustainable heritage trails.

[IS] Alternance
Bringing in comprehensive research and analysis is a luxury for smaller communities, or it can be if they feel involved, engaged, and listened to. And this methodology helps to give depth and make concepts and projects more convincing.

[IT] Politecnico di Milano
We definitely noticed that working in a remote context meant missing out on having a continuous presence where we could have occasional or more informal encounters. Pandemic restrictions made this even more challenging. It meant difficulties in keeping more isolated groups active.

And we were able to engage beyond planned activities and take part in social life.

One thing we also noticed was that events stimulated by an outside influence – us – prompted the flourishing of new initiatives not necessarily related to our project, rather independent of it.

[PL] Zamek Cieszyn
Your impact should be measurable, and it was good that SMOTIES tried to do this, even if raw statistics are not sufficient to understand influence – that happens on diverse levels of social consciousness.

It affects the way you think about structuring activities, and when combined in the right way, a statistical and humanistic approach together can be suitable for social projects.

[GR] University of the Aegean
Our greatest success was that we gained the trust of local people and felt part of the community, so it created the space for us to have honest discussions and find more local collaborators at a slow and suitable pace.

[EE] EAD
The trust grew every time they saw the progress that we were making in their remote place. The environment woke up. People started thinking about what could be.

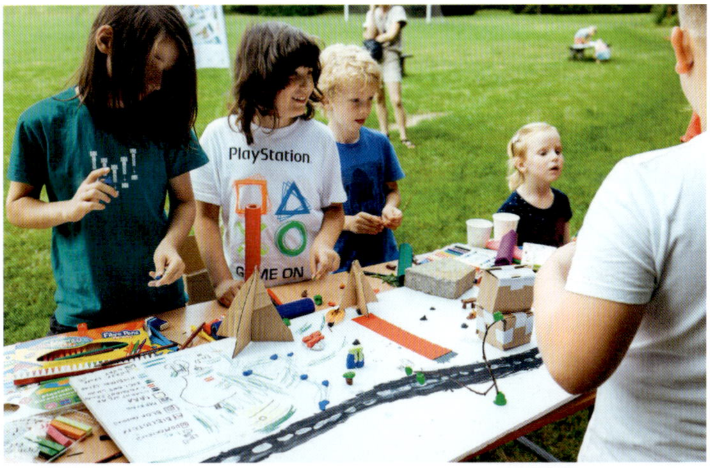

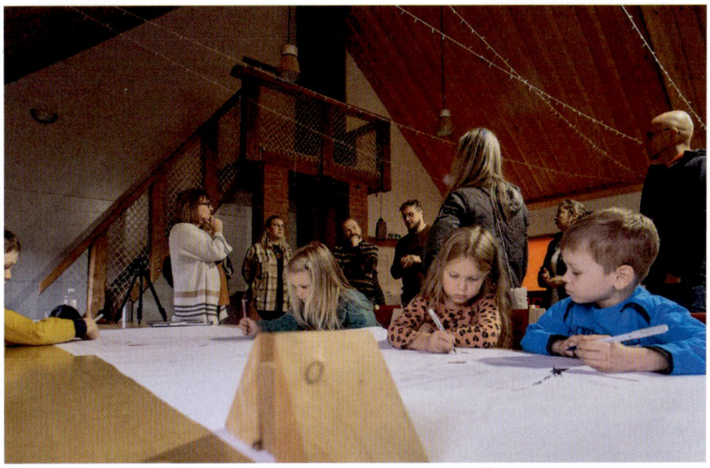

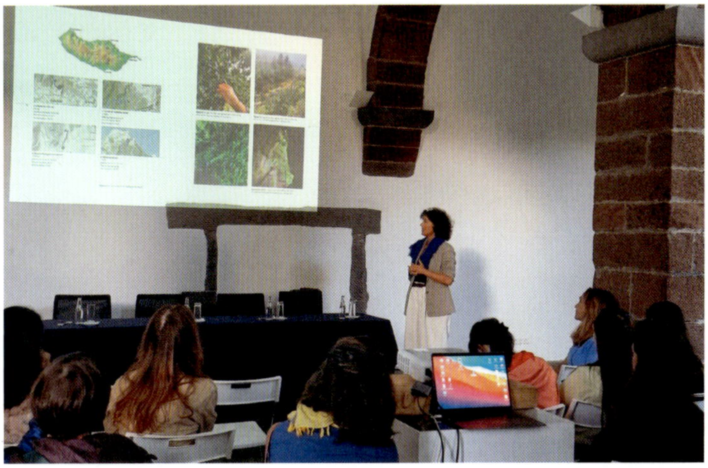

Top: Youth brigade: keeping kids engaged in Poland. © Rafał Soliński

Middle: Children's masterclass in Joaveski as part of the "Joaveski REstart" event in October 2022. © Kevin Loigu

Bottom: Presentation of the publication 'Routes and Roots on the Island of Madeira: Design Practices for Learning Through Nature' edited by Elisa Bertolotti, Valentina Vezzani and Susana Gonzaga, Funchal, 2022. © Luisa Santos Freitas

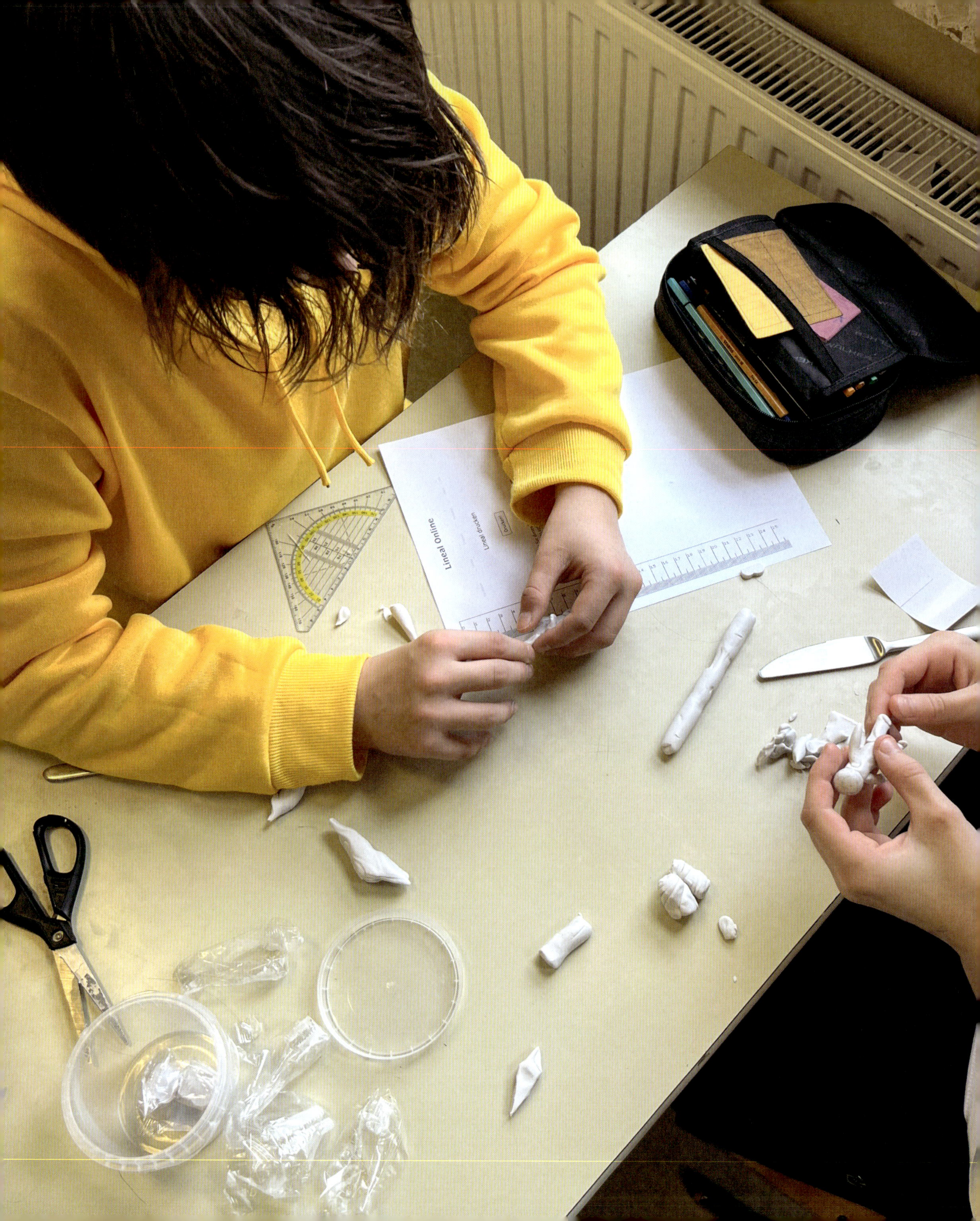
Lineal Online
Lineal drucken

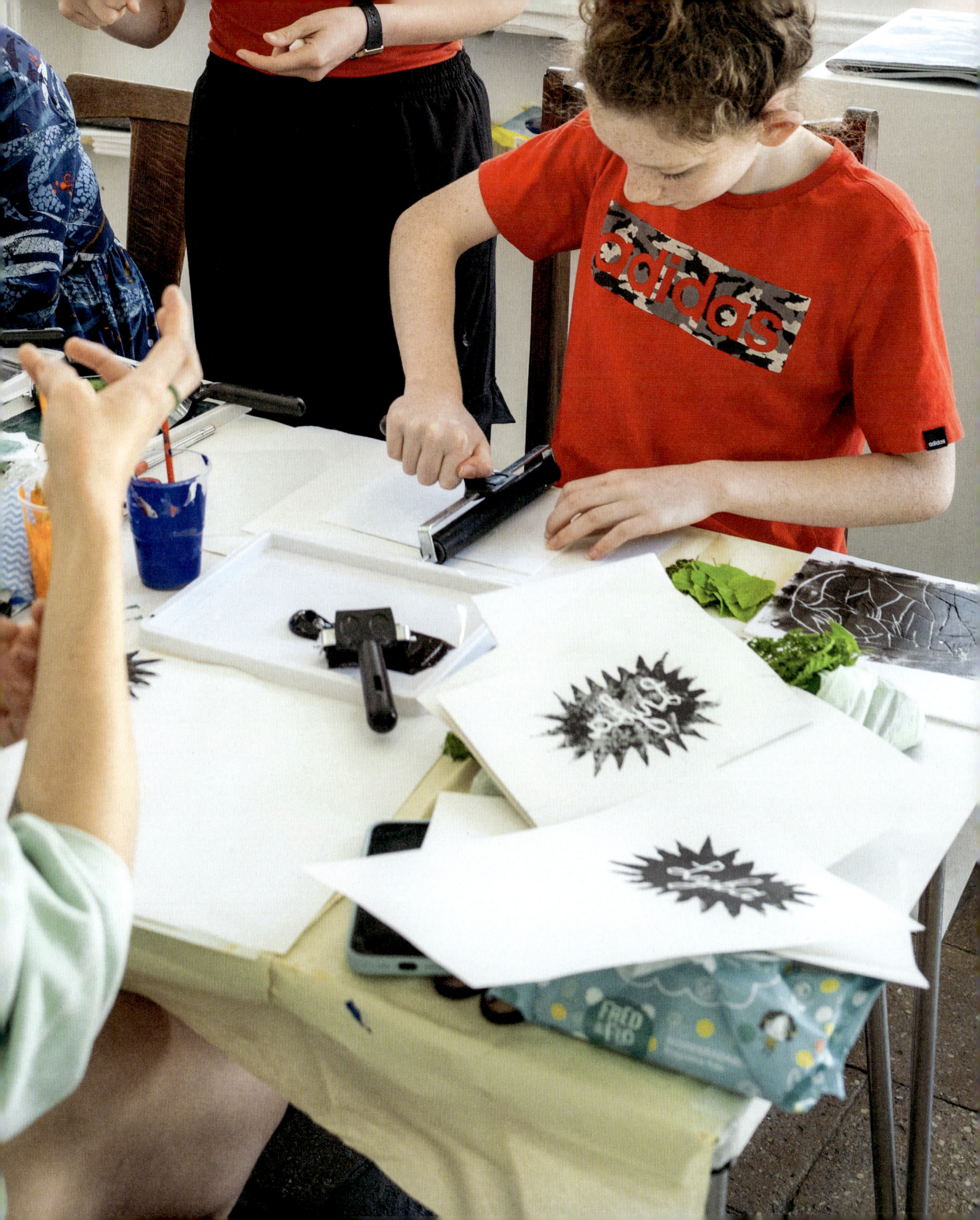
adidas

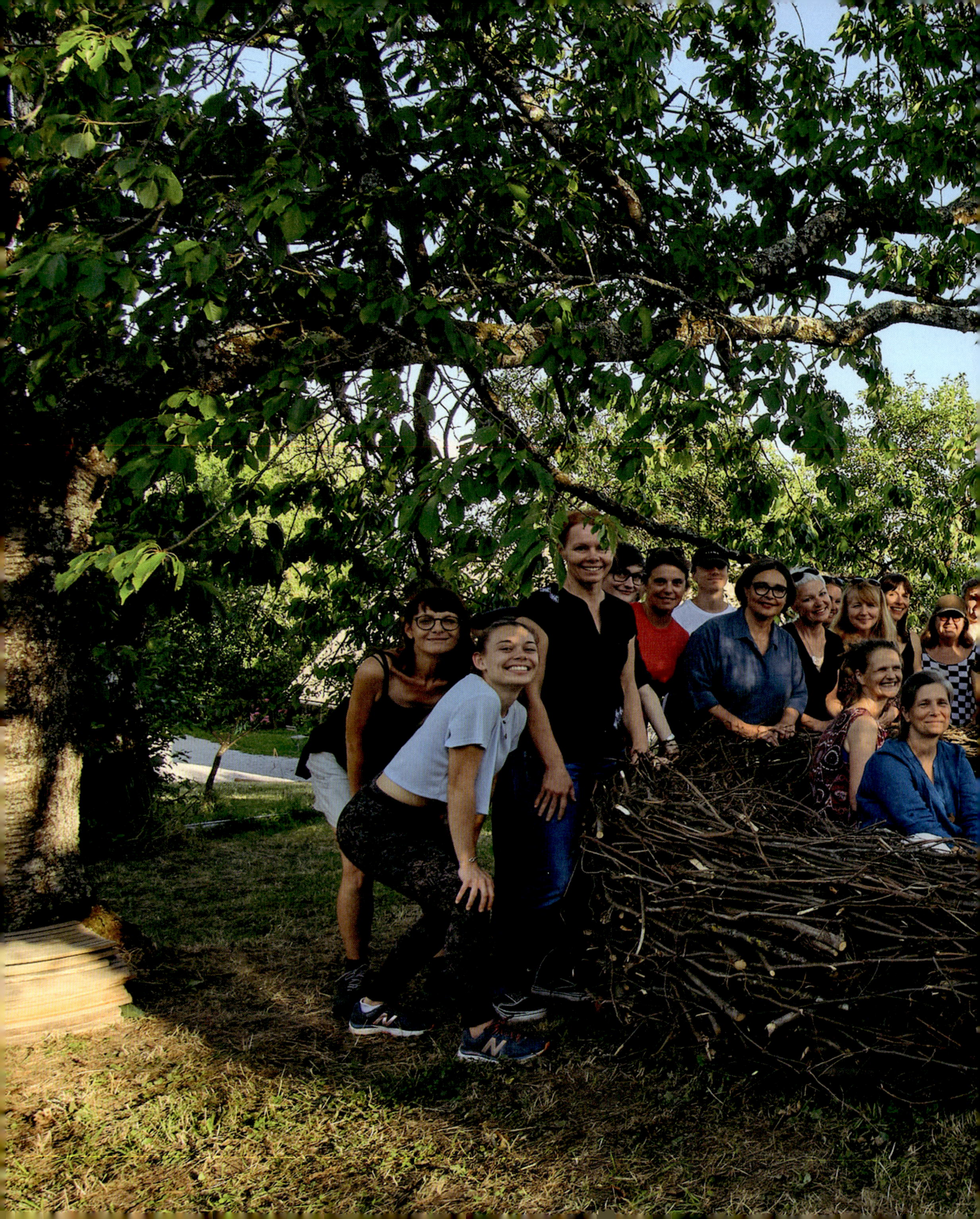

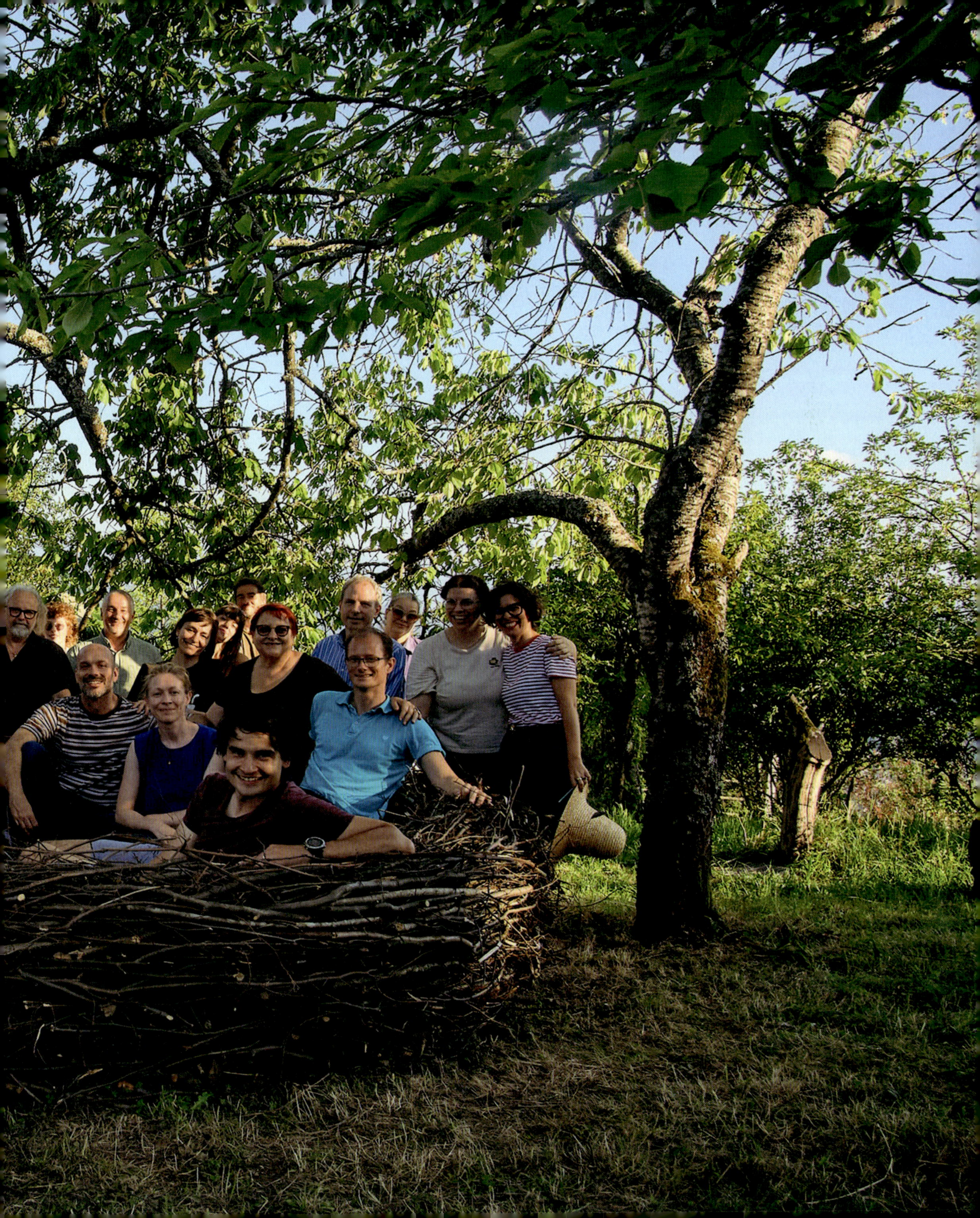

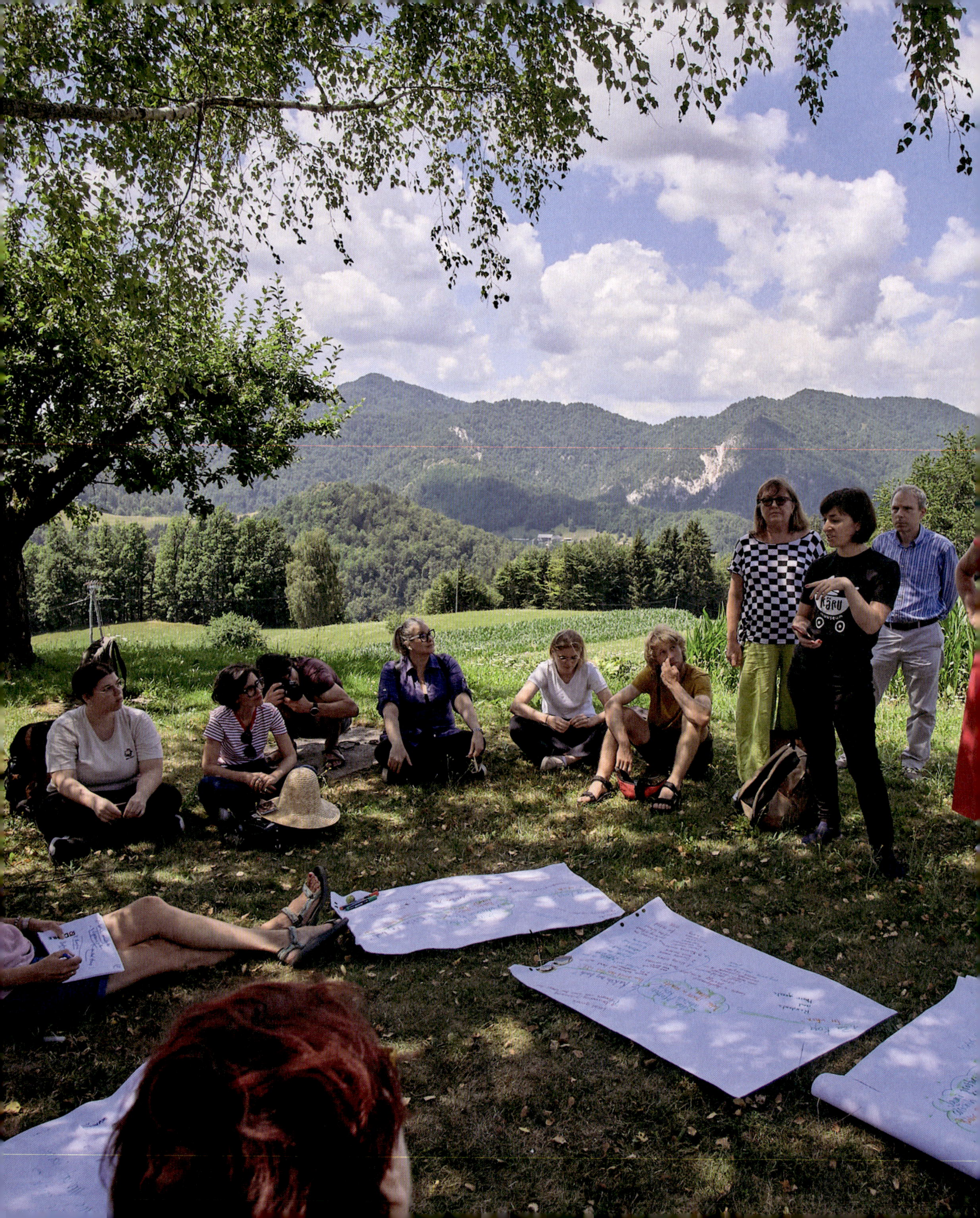

P. 126: Pupils from the New Middle School in Oberzeiring discuss their understanding of the Marktplatz and new ideas for revitalising it. © FH Joanneum Gesellschaft mbH

P. 127: Monoprinting workshop on themes of ecology and non-human perspectives, as part of Oriel Machno's pilot artist residency with Gweni Llwyd. A collaboration between Clear Village and Wales-based arts organisation Artes Mundi. © Mark McNulty

P. 128-129: An orchard at Homestead Pr' Lenart in Belo as an experimental bed for sustainable "street" furniture prototyping – the Big Nest by artist Mateja Kavčič gathering people for socialising and cultural exchanges. SMOTIES Transnational meeting in Ljubljana; June 29-July 1, 2022. © Kevin Loigu

P. 130: Developing future visions for Polhograjski dolomiti with international experts, Topol pri Medvodah, summer 2022. © Kevin Loigu

"Working in a small or remote place is also about this: we can go there from time to time, and you are always an outsider. That is, in any case, correct.

There is a process of understanding each other, of getting to know the kind of activities that we can do together, what is the best approach, in which way we can be useful: being able to go beyond the expectation that funding only serves to build something.

By going there and doing interviews, through observation and co-design sessions, it takes a while to find your place. We are trying in these three months (since coming out of the pandemic) to start reconnecting with them. Every time we are, I think, and I hope, getting to know each other more and more."

Annalinda De Rosa, Politecnico di Milano

“The landscape park is very large. At first we took only one municipality, with ten villages, into consideration. But then we found out even this is a lot for a meaningful participatory process!”

Nina Goršič, Urban Planning Institute of the Republic of Slovenia

“This project is really addressing the question of the public spaces. So, what kind of public spaces do we already have in remote areas? How can we co-create new ones and how can we create them together not only with local people, but also people who work in the cultural sector? And how to include people who visit remote areas only occasionally?”

Matej Nikšič, Urban Planning Institute of the Republic of Slovenia

"So we were saying, for example, that the local orchards, *sadovnjaki* in Slovenian, they have the potential to become open places in remote areas where people could meet, exchange, socialise.

Then we were considering built heritage, like old storage houses, hay racks, these kinds of structures. They were very much functional in the past, but nowadays they're just reminders of the past activities of people here."

Matej Nikšič, Urban Planning Institute of the Republic of Slovenia

"We identified together with citizens three thematic areas of use and need.

And these were: spontaneity and leisure, performance and culture, nature and sports."

Alexandra Coutsoucos, Politecnico di Milano

"You have some people who are really interested. And they attend every meeting. And there are people who don't know about the project. And they don't hear about the project. And there are people who don't want any project."

Anna Sowińska, Zamek Cieszyn

"Sometimes for us it is very difficult because we don't know which boundaries we can cross. I mean, we talk about trees, we talk about our ideas and our vision, but maybe the locals don't really want...

I don't know. We actually don't know what is right to do, up to which point we can do the intervention. So we also try to go step by step and try to listen to their voice and their opinion about it."

Kypriani Bartzoka, Department of Product and Systems Design Engineering, University of the Aegean

P. 135: On the green block. Neighbourhood picnic, Bobrek, June 2022. © Krzysztof Puda

P. 136 European project partners meet in Ermoupolis, Greece, September 2023. © Kevin Loigu

P. 137: Workshop with SMOTIES partners in Slovenia, June 29-July 1 2022. © Simon Koblar/UIRS

P. 138: Joaveski prototyping, March 2023. © Kevin Loigu

P. 139: The most important destinations were identified together with inhabitants of Oberzeiring, 2022. © Katja Krug, FH Joanneum Gesellschaft mbH

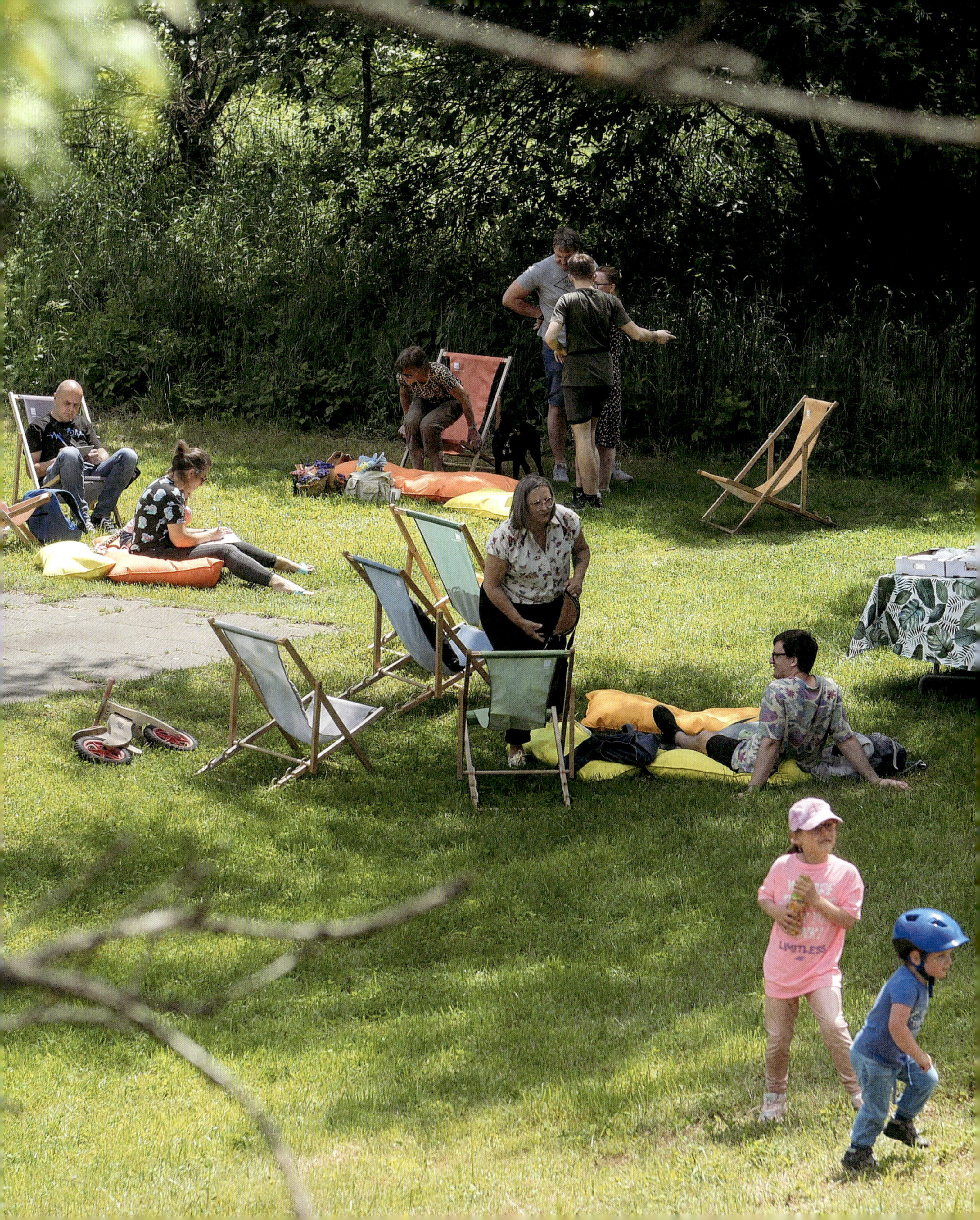

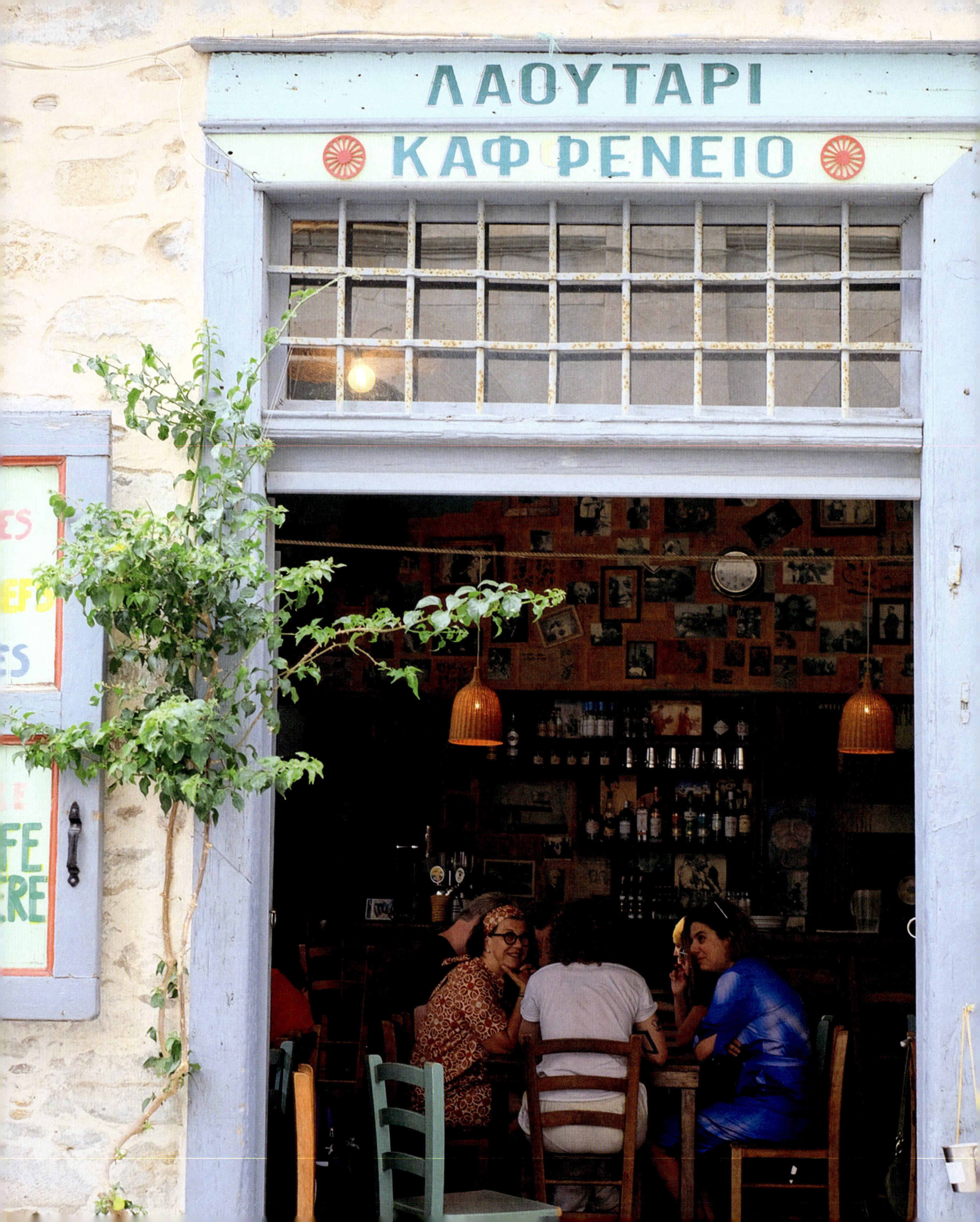
ΛΑΟΥΤΑΡΙ
ΚΑΦ ΦΕΝΕΙΟ

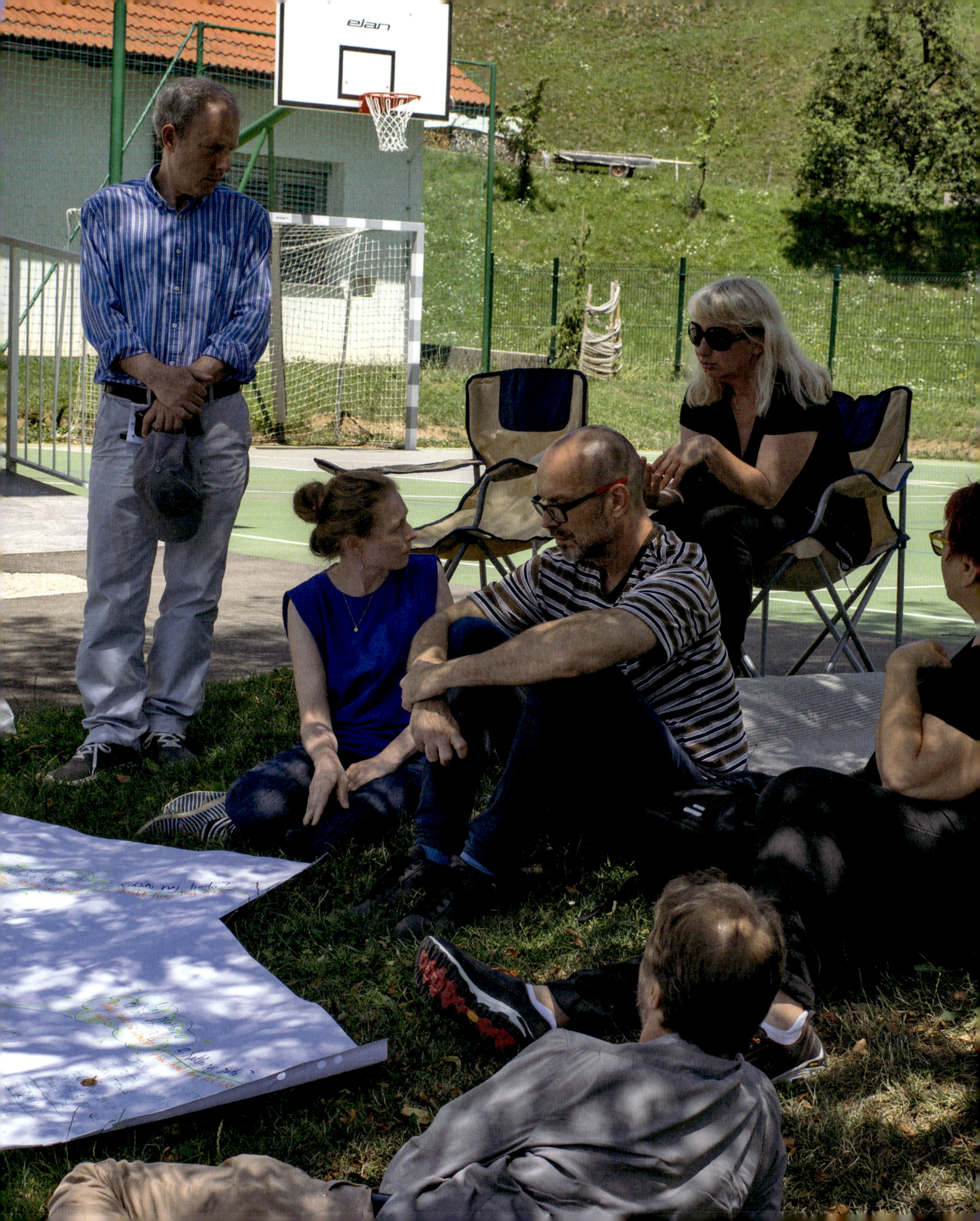
elan

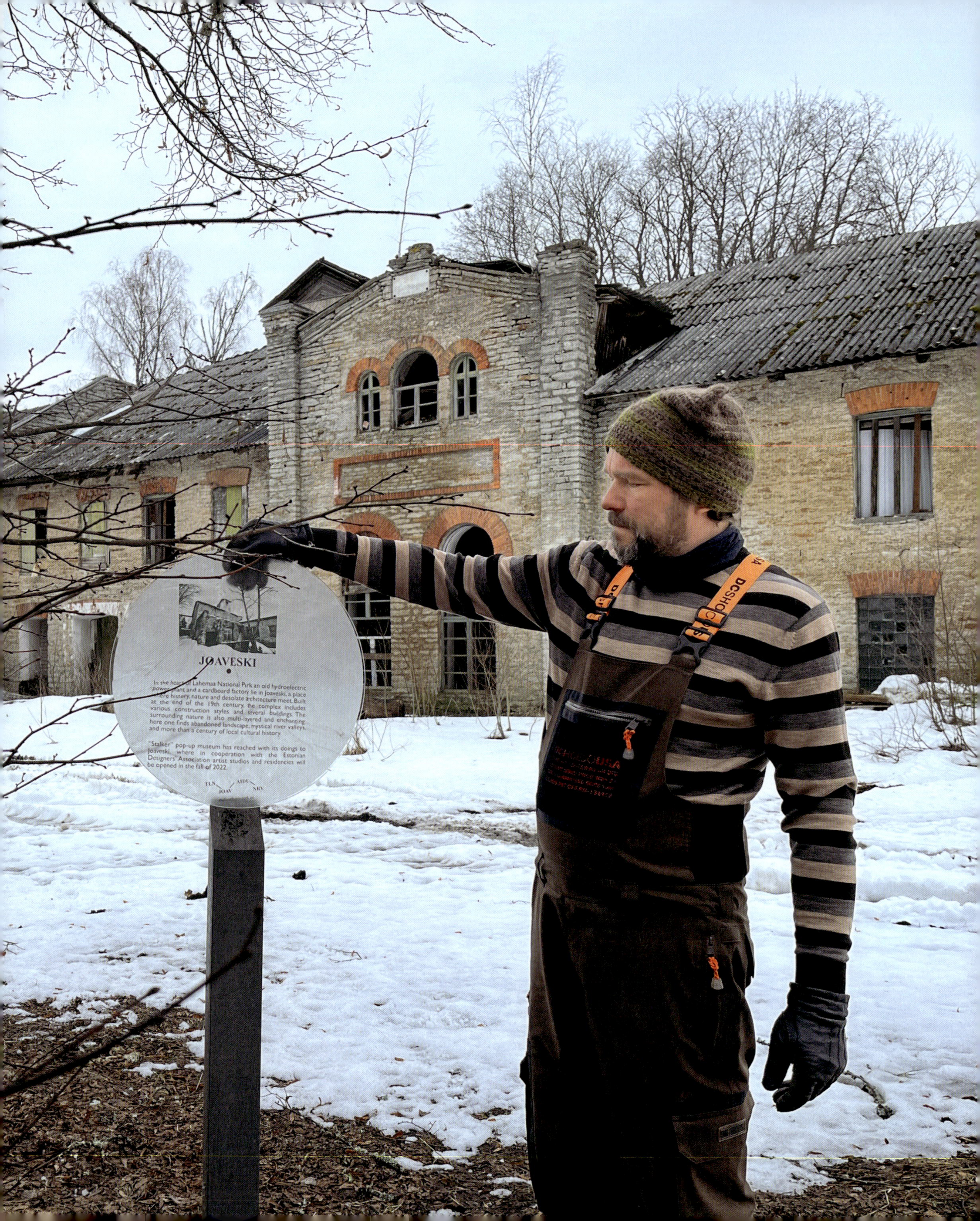
JOAVESKI
In the heart of Lahemaa National Park an old hydroelectric power plant and a cardboard factory lie in Joaveski, a place where history, nature and desolate architecture meet. Built at the end of the 19th century, the complex includes various construction styles and several buildings. The surrounding nature is also multi-layered and enchanting: here one finds abandoned landscape, mystical river valleys, and more than a century of local cultural history.
"Stalker" pop-up museum has reached with its doings to Joaveski, where in cooperation with the Estonian Designers' Association artist studios and residencies will be opened in the fall of 2022.
TLN
JOAV
AIDU
NRV

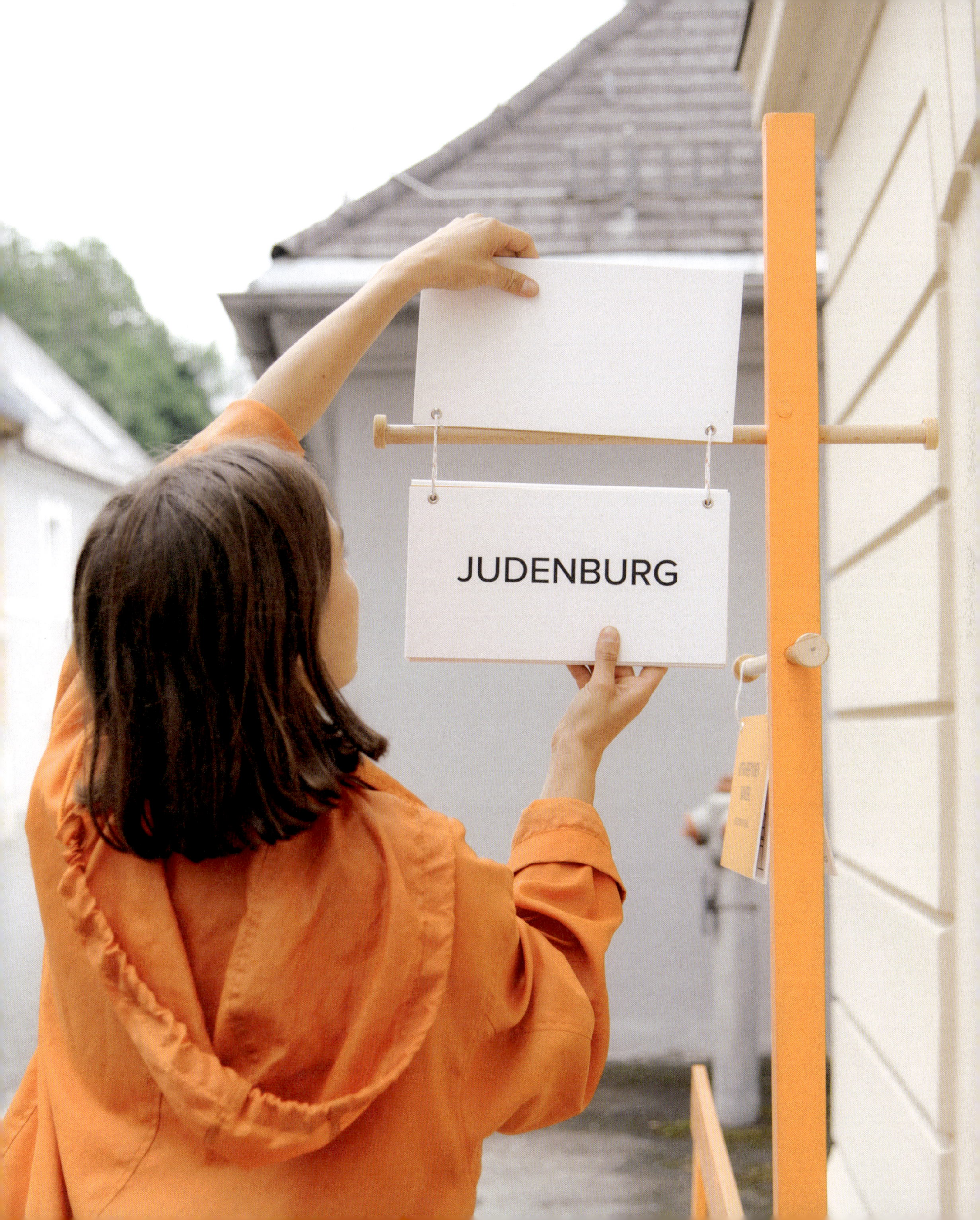
JUDENBURG

Part 3.

Edited by Davide Fassi and Annalinda De Rosa

Transcending Urban Confines, Looking Ahead.

Research Perspectives Gained from the SMOTIES Project and Beyond

1.

Social Innovation and its Dynamics in Small and Remote Places: A Design Research Perspective

Davide Fassi
Full professor, Department of Design, Politecnico di Milano [IT]

In this chapter, we will delve into the expansive realm of design for social innovation (DSI), extending its reach beyond the typical urban settings. Our research underscores the transformative potential of this strategy, emphasising its ability to significantly influence small rural regions, inner areas, and marginalised territories, transcending urban confines. Central to this impact are the designers and creative minds driving change.

This chapter aims to highlight the aspects and effects of DSI, drawing on the knowledge gained from the author's leadership in the Creative Europe project Human Cities/SMOTIES: Creative Works with Small and Remote Places. The project, conducted in collaboration with 10 European creative partners from 2020 to 2024, focused on exploring the potential of design in addressing social challenges. Essentially, this inquiry questions the prevailing belief that social innovation is solely a result of urban dynamics. On the contrary, it asserts that this dynamic and ground-breaking process may reach its maximum capabilities in often-overlooked locations where the environment, challenges, and opportunities undergo significant transformations. This assertion is supported by SMOTIES, which offers a different viewpoint on applying the DSI approach in smaller, rural, and neglected regions. To establish a solid foundation for this inquiry, the chapter starts by delving into the concept of social innovation. This inquiry is not only a theoretical exercise; it serves as a vital basis for comprehending the process by which social innovation emerges when it meets with design and the role of designers. The aim is to analyse the intricacies of this concept to establish a comprehensive framework for comprehending its many manifestations across different settings, with a particular focus on the role of designers in fostering these innovative processes. An essential aspect of this inquiry is examining the interplay between cities, often seen as the focal points of social innovation, and tiny and rural locations, which are commonly disregarded. Exploring the intricate dynamics of designers' engagement with these specific geographic contexts underscores the fundamental considerations of adapting methodologies, strategies, and innovative mindsets to address distinct challenges and possibilities. I will present insights into how design may propel social innovation in unconventional circumstances by navigating the intricacies of small and remote areas. This chapter acts as an entry point to gain a more thorough understanding of the extensive range of DSI, contributing to a more comprehensive and inclusive conversation about the impact of design in fostering positive social change.

Design for social innovation

Social innovation is a dynamic process that emerges from the creative combination of pre-existing resources within a community or society. It aims to tackle and accomplish socially acknowledged objectives by employing participatory strategies and processes. Social innovation is complex and twofold: it transforms societal norms and behaviours and generates specific outcomes, in the form of new design solutions, that contribute to the overall improvement of society.

Social innovation may be defined as a cooperative and forward-looking resource, which restructures ideas and promotes a creative synergy that surpasses traditional problem-solving approaches. It utilises various accessible resources, recognising the significance of social, cultural, and technical factors in promoting beneficial transformation. Consequently, social innovation serves as a comprehensive and powerful influence that not only imagines new approaches to tackling societal problems but also transforms these ideas into tangible solutions, thereby building a future that is both environmentally sustainable and socially inclusive (Manzini & Rizzo, 2011; Manzini, 2014; Manzini, 2015).

Urban areas and small and remote places

The author and his research team have acquired first-hand knowledge in the Milanese urban setting, where many social innovation activities have emerged in recent years. This highlights the role of cities as conducive locations for fostering social engagement and activity aimed at promoting collective welfare. This is shown via a wide range of individuals and backgrounds that promote a variety of perspectives, which ultimately come together in the form of initiatives and activities. The term "project communities" refers to situations when stakeholders come together to transform the requirements for their everyday well-being into tangible solutions (Fassi & Manzini, 2021). The interaction between these "project communities" and public administration is developing into a training hub to uncover cutting-edge tools and techniques for converting individual efforts into systemic endeavours. Therefore, the concept of "project communities" has emerged as a vital topic in urban development, emphasising the need to be actively present in a location to cultivate knowledge, reclaim public spaces, envision new potential uses, and establish new connections.

Local institutions need help adapting to a significant change marked by a growing number of genuine grassroots initiatives. Nevertheless, there are instances where these interactions result in favourable consequences, such as cooperation agreements, public fundraising initiatives, and community development strategies. These initiatives demonstrate that the Milan municipality is addressing new demands using operational methods.

The discourse around social innovation has undoubtedly altered the relationship between society and institutions (Ostanel, 2017), mirroring the continuous changes in the language employed in urban regeneration, which is driven by the declining influence of the State. These efforts now prioritise the distinct attributes of certain areas instead of being dictated by a higher authority. The latter has led to clear indications of gentrification, emerging urban and social conflicts, and instances of marginalisation.

When attention transitions from metropolitan areas to remote locations, certain fundamental factors inherently impacting the connection between local communities and innovation come into play. Various factors, including depopulation, an ageing population, restricted government focused on routine administration, a scarcity of associations, and the distance and connection to innovation centres, all contribute to the situation. We discovered many promising factors in the Albugnano municipality, where our research team conducted its SMOTIES project. We encountered challenges such as a restricted pool of individuals, with an average age of 55 years; sporadic contributions of innovative ideas from external stakeholders about funding; and a lack of enthusiasm towards village administration, particularly during the project's initiation phase when there was a chance of no candidates participating in the elections at the mayor level. Although this framework restricts opportunities for social innovation, there were latent possibilities associated with tangible and intangible culture, exceptional food and wine, cultural heritage sites such as a network of Romanic churches, and the production of wine and hazelnuts. The research team has investigated potential innovation domains over the last four years, capitalising on a revived fascination with these locations.

An emerging focus on small and remote places

The 2020 pandemic redirected focus towards remote regions in several countries. The widespread experience of "suspended time", when individuals cannot engage with others physically and lack a compelling reason (or authorisation) to go to their workplaces, has sparked a new interest in residing and working in locations far from metropolitan hubs. The phrase "doughnut effect" is commonly used to describe this phenomenon, which was first presented during the analysis of dynamics in US cities by Ramani and Bloom (2021). It entails the migration of individuals and the transfer of activity from urban centres to the periphery of the city, suburban regions, or the movement of people from cities to smaller regional towns or rural communities.

Several European examples further highlight this pattern. An increase in population has been reported in small towns in Spain with less than 2,000 residents (Gurrutxaga, 2021). In recent years, telecommuters have been migrating to Italy's southern and inland regions to work for companies in big cities in the north of the country or even overseas (Di Matteo et al., 2022; Mirabile & Militello, 2022). Scotland has observed an increase in population in several intermediate and rural areas following the outbreak of the pandemic (Downey et al., 2022; Brouwer & Mariotti, 2023).

Within this framework, there has been an increased recognition of the possibilities offered by rural areas, a renewed appreciation for local customs, tangible and intangible cultural heritage, and a new way of experiencing life that redefines the concepts of time and space (both in public and private spheres). This has led to a stronger connection between creativity and such places. Over the past few years, many case studies have emerged in urban, suburban, and rural locations. Several of these experiences are triggered in "crisis" situations: environments that necessitate fresh life cycles, theories for development, and transformation processes. These environments have seen the positive impact of the "doughnut effect", since relocating to a small isolated location has redirected people's focus and initiative to enhancing the quality of the areas they live in and utilise.

The SMOTIES project was conceptualised before the pandemic but was implemented and refined during and immediately after the pandemic. This contributed value to the project by capturing people's growing interest in remote locations that offer more comfortable living and working conditions than urban areas. Examining the evolving role of designers and finding the shared characteristics of their engagement with communities have been beneficial in this context.

The role of designers

Designers assume the role of a project activist in numerous projects that entail substantial citizen involvement. They possess interdisciplinary expertise and remain actively engaged in all phases of the process, including conceptualisation and interventions (Meroni et al., 2018). Designers assume the role of facilitators who may foster convergence by discerning and interpreting people's desires. Throughout the on-site activities, we aimed to actively include the local community, generate ideas, work together to develop solutions, create prototypes, share the outcomes, and exchange information. The design researchers studied various attributes developed via the in-field activities conducted over the entire process.

Empathy is the ability to understand and share the feelings of others. This technique enhances the designer's reputation and fosters a trusting relationship with their intended audience. The design and organisation of public spaces in metropolitan settings are seen as a realm of possibility where outcomes are uncertain, varied, and not easily predicted. The effective design of public places goes beyond predetermined programmes, creating possibilities beyond original assumptions. The liveliness of public life frequently depends on impromptu ingenuity and fortuitous interactions (Stevens et al., 2024).

When encountering tiny isolated areas, each interaction with residents is significant, as they embody a community often comprising a small number of individuals rather than collectives. Encouraging empathy with communities entails maintaining an open mindset that allows for inspiration based on people's feedback about what they want, and nurturing connections throughout the entire project. This may be accomplished by leveraging the participation of influential individuals, sometimes called "local heroes", who are acknowledged by local communities for their vital contributions to the village. Alternatively, it can be achieved through chance interactions with individuals during on-site activities in the public areas associated with the initiatives.

The importance of being patient. When investigating an unfamiliar geographical area, the design researcher must prioritise establishing meaningful connections with individuals. This entails tactfully entering pre-existing situations while carefully considering the appropriate timing for active listening, observing, establishing relationships, generating ideas, and executing solutions. Time is essential to steadily develop objectives and organise interactions that address several aspects of the community. The design researcher combines their expertise into tools and methodologies to engage with local people in full respect of ethical and moral principles. This approach guarantees the acknowledgement of local customs and the persons involved, as well as the comprehension and appreciation of the values and resources of the region. Patience is cultivated through a repetitive process in which the design researcher engages in numerous interactions with local individuals and dedicates significant time to actively listening to their narratives. This method tests the researcher's ability to effectively transform complaints and recommendations into viable solutions.

As previously said, very few people accentuate the conflict between the "indifferent citizen" and the "far-sighted citizen". The "indifferent citizen" is depicted as self-centred, primarily focused on consuming services and products to satisfy their immediate needs. In contrast, the "far-sighted citizen" demonstrates a curiosity about their personal history, the history of their community, and those with whom they spend time. Their ability to see, observe, and act is far-reaching, organically overlapping and engaging with other people's horizons. As a result, people readily acknowledge that their satisfaction is closely connected to the well-being of their community. The designer's task is to reconcile opposing forces to provide novel solutions for the social domain. Communities serve as a meeting point for many perspectives, resulting in a diverse and inclusive environment where conflicting ideas and debates occur. Participatory design facilitates the exploration and exchange of diverse perspectives, enabling the identification of shared matters of interest (Puig de la Bellacasa, 2017; Tassinari & Vergani, 2023). Placemaking strategies promote public involvement, can improve decision-making, and aid in resolving problems while instilling trust in democratic procedures and institutions.

Visions, scenarios, and solutions. The designer uses a wide range of expertise to address the problem strategically rather than proposing a specific solution. This methodology adopts a "bottom-up" approach that synergises with the "top-down" approach, resulting in favourable outcomes. In urban settings, this phenomenon is primarily attributed to many social innovation projects that gradually alter how individuals interact with and shape cities. These initiatives, which encompass tactical urban design, slow mobility, guerrilla gardening, and social streets, primarily operate at the neighbourhood level. Conversely, governments implement various mechanisms such as participatory budgeting, collaborative agreements, and civic crowdfunding to support these energies.

Engaging residents in participatory methods fosters their awareness of the project's advantages and actively involves them. Implementing participatory approaches and involving citizens in space regeneration facilitates the development of a new perspective of revitalised public areas. If this assertion holds and is supported by evidence within the urban setting, characterised by many diverse stakeholders and actors, one may wonder about the implications for small and distant locations. In such settings, the population size is often smaller, the number of stakeholders is restricted, and the available spaces are limited. Cultivating a feeling of affiliation – to a specific place, its community, or an endeavour being carried out there – fosters a heightened inclination to engage more responsibly with such a place, thus enhancing the efficacy and durability of the regeneration process.

Through the SMOTIES research, we noted that in small communities, there is a strong correlation between individuals and their surroundings, with a prevalence of local activities at a micro-level. Nevertheless, such activities may only sometimes be related. The project aims to create a system whereby people, at the individual level, can improve innovative projects to limit disruptions in public spaces. This was possible owing to the design researcher's ability to work with locals to create visions, situations, and solutions. Participatory techniques enable small and rural areas to surpass superficial or generic goals of liveability and competitiveness, and cultivate futures with a more profound understanding of local resources (Galluzzo et al., 2023).

Conclusions

This chapter examined how design may bring about transformative change for social innovation in areas outside major cities. It shed light on the substantial impact of design and creativity on small and isolated communities, inner cities, and underprivileged regions when guidance is provided by designers.

Participatory methodologies, which proved advantageous in metropolitan environments, were just as beneficial in small towns, fostering community and engagement. The SMOTIES project focused on creating a framework that connected different initiatives intending to encourage radical innovation in the use of public spaces. Design researchers' ability to work with locals to create visions and solutions was crucial in actualising the potential of these areas beyond generic objectives and fostering a more profound comprehension of local resources.

Ultimately, the chapter illustrated that DSI is not restricted to urban areas but can instead serve as a driving force for positive transformation in overlooked and remote rural regions. The shared experiences of the SMOTIES project exemplify the transformative influence of creativity and design in fostering a sustainable and inclusive future for marginalised communities.

References

Brouwer, A. E., & Mariotti, I. (2023). Remote working and new working spaces during the COVID-19 pandemic–insights from EU and abroad. In M. Akhavan, M. Hölzel, & D. Leducq (Eds), *European Narratives on Remote Working and Coworking During the COVID-19 Pandemic: A Multidisciplinary Perspective* (pp. 9–15). Springer Nature Switzerland. https://doi.org/10.1007/978-3-031-26018-6_2

Di Matteo, D., La Regina, R., Mariotti, I., & Militello, E. (2022). Quali determinanti per il South Working? Una nuova proposta di sviluppo per il Sud, le aree interne e il Paese. *Riv Econ Mezzogiorno* Anno XXXV, 677–702. ISSN: 1120-9534.

Downey, L., Fonzone, A., Fountas, G. (2022). The impact of COVID-19 on travel behaviour, transport, lifestyles and residential location choices in Scotland. Scottish Funding Council.

Fassi, D., & Manzini, E. (2021). Project-based communities: Lessons learned from collaborative city-making experiences. *CoDesign, 18*(1), 1–12. https://doi.org/10.1080/15710882.2021.2001535

Fior, M., Galuzzi, P., Pasqui, G., & Vitillo, P. (2022). *(Re)Discovering Proximity: Generating New Urbanity–An Action Research for Milan*. Springer Nature.

Galluzzo, L., Borin, A., & Giunta, E. E. (2023). *Designing transformative processes in mountain realms*. Service Design and Innovation Conference 44–63. https://doi.org/10.3384/ecp203002

Gurrutxaga, M. (2021). Visualizing the rural population growth in Spain during 2020 triggered by the COVID-19 pandemic. *Regional Studies, Regional Science, 8*(1), 305–307. https://doi.org/10.1080/21681376.2021.1958050

Manzini, E., & Rizzo, F. (2011). Small projects/large changes: Participatory design as an open participated process. *CoDesign, 7*(3–4), 199–215. https://doi.org/10.1080/15710882.2011.630472

Manzini, E. (2014). Making things happen: Social innovation and design. *Design Issues, 30*(1), 57–66. https://doi.org/10.1162/DESI_a_00248

Manzini, E. (2015). *Design, When Everybody Designs. An Introduction to Design for Social Innovation*. Cambridge, MA: The MIT Press. https://doi.org/10.7551/mitpress/9873.001.0001

Meroni, A., Selloni, D., & Rossi, M. (2018). *Massive Codesign. A Proposal for a Collaborative Design Framework*. FrancoAngeli Design International.

Mirabile, M., Militello, E. (Eds) (2022). *South working. Per un futuro sostenibile del lavoro agil in Italia*. Donzelli Editore, Rome.

Ostanel, E. (2017). *Spazi fuori dal Comune. Rigenerare, Includere, Innovare*. FrancoAngeli Design International.

Ostanel, E. (2014). Traces of cultural regeneration in hyperdiverse neighbourhood: Place and planning in mechanisms of social innovation, in Planum. *The Journal of Urbanism*, no. 29 vol II/2014, in *Pratiche di Riappropriazione*, C.Cellamare & F.Cognetti (Eds).

Puig de la Bellacasa, M. P. (2017). *Matters of Care: Speculative Ethics in More Than Human Worlds*. University of Minnesota Press.

Ramani, A., Bloom, N. (2021). The donut effect of COVID-19 on cities. NBER Working paper series, 28876. http://www.nber.org/papers/w28876

Stevens, Q., Daly, J., & Dovey, K. (2024). Designing for possibility in public space: Affordance, assemblage, and ANT. URBAN DESIGN International. https://doi.org/10.1057/s41289-023-00235-y

Tassinari, V., & Vergani, F. (2023). Designing situated vocabularies to counter social polarizations: A case study of Nolo neighbourhood, Milan. *Urban Planning, 8*(2). https://doi.org/10.17645/up.v8i2.6420

Vitillo, P. (2021) Città contemporanea e prossimità. *Urbanistica Informazioni*, no. 295, 124

2. Power Relations in Participatory Design Practices in Small and Remote Places

Vanessa Monna
Post-doc fellow researcher,
Department of Design,
Politecnico di Milano [IT]

Helen Charoupia
Researcher, University
of the Aegean, Department
of Product and Systems
Design Engineering within
Complex Systems and
Service Design Lab [GR]

Small and remote communities, often nestled amid breathtaking natural landscapes, have long been on the periphery of conventional development paradigms. The cultural identities and distinct challenges of remote areas are increasingly acknowledged as essential to the broader socioeconomic environment (Membretti et al., 2022). Sustaining these rural areas is not only necessary but also optimal in the pursuit of equitable and sustainable development.

The necessity for regeneration in these regions has resulted in an increasing recognition that successful rural policies and practices must move beyond conventional top-down and *creative city* approaches (Landry, 2000; Florida, 2002). Smaller communities have more opportunities to overcome their challenges if they give up on formulaic creative city initiatives, which may have been successful in urban areas, and switch to a holistic approach to local development that emphasises embracing creativity across ecosystems (OECD, 2018). Due to its intricate nature, the OECD highlights the significance of involving a wide array of stakeholders in transformation processes, including implementing multi-level governance structures in formulating rural policies and practices (OECD, 2020). This necessitates a fundamental change in perspective, whereby the involvement of local stakeholders is prioritised in the development and execution of practices and policies specifically crafted to align with the distinct goals and ambitions of small and remote communities.

When different but sometimes overlapping 'communities of practice' are involved in the transformation processes and policy development of remote areas, we must consider the various manifestations of power dynamics (Wenger, 1999). To better understand small and remote places' unique power dynamics, we deem it necessary to first unpack the concept of power, presuming neither to be exhaustive nor to be experts in the field.

Unpacking the concept of power: agency, ownership and representation

Most individuals have an intuitive understanding of what the concept of power entails. In the literature about power studies – ranging from political theory to environmental studies, from political geography to social theory – there are two fundamentally opposing perspectives, one perceiving power as dominance, also referred to as '*power over*', and one recognising power as empowerment, commonly conceptualised as '*power to*' (Pansardi & Bindi, 2021; Haugaard, 2012).

Follett (1940) describes the concept of *power over* as a coercive form of power, which later studies (Townsend et al., 1999; Allen, 1998; Rowlands, 1997) identify as an actor's capability to constrain the choices accessible to another actor or group of actors on a considerable scale.

By contrast, '*power to*' can be construed as empowerment. Follett (1940) and Arendt (1957; 1970) understand power to (as well as *power with*, which consists of the collective exercise of *power to*) as a coactive form of power. The power to act in concert has the emancipating potential to liberate and empower people to do something, despite their social status, to achieve a more equitable distribution of power. Hence, empowerment is a process actors take to increase their capacity and contextual power to meet their goals, leading to transformative action (Coy et al., 2021). In their perceived power and capacity to act intentionally, individuals can choose and feel empowered to do so within their environments.

Scholars either align themselves with one of the two sides or attempt to reconcile the two perspectives, conceiving power as a nuanced cloud of concepts (Haugaard, 2012; Allen, 1999). The common threads across these views are that power arises from the presence of or potential for connection among agents (Dahl, 1957; Haugaard, 2012) and that power emerges as an ability to do something in these relationships (Pitkin, 1972; Haugaard, 2012). In other words, power can be said to exist when there is a relationship between agents who are able to do something in such a relationship.

Leveraging these conceptualisations, we have tentatively disentangled and focused on three facets influencing power that we deem relevant in the context of small and remote places: agency, ownership, and representation. The following is a brief overview of these three dimensions, acknowledging that these definitions could be deepened.

Agency is "the power to originate action" (Bandura, 2001, p. 3). It can be defined as the capacity of individuals to act independently and to make their own decisions (Coy et al., 2021). Pitkin (1972) suggests that the concept of agency refers to the concept of '*power to*', or the "capacity to shape action, which partly depends on access to resources, partly on power/knowledge" (Bratteteig & Wagner, 2016, p. 143). It embodies purposeful engagement and acknowledges individuals not as passive entities but as dynamic forces capable of influencing the social, political, natural, and technological landscapes they inhabit. It implies a departure from deterministic narratives to recognise the autonomy and efficacy of actors in navigating their circumstances (Pisor et al., 2022).

Ownership is construed as the acquisition of meaningful stakes in the processes and feelings of responsibility and pride regarding the outcomes of a multi-partner project (Light et al., 2013; Van Rijn & Stappers, 2008). Expanding this definition beyond the conventional notion of holding physical or tangible assets, we interpret ownership as the willingness and responsibility of community members to proactively shape the future trajectories of their small and remote places. In other words, the will to take ownership of the processes and impacts shaping their future. This involves influencing decision-making processes and, ultimately, fostering a collective investment in the results of development initiatives (Light et al., 2013).

Representation concerns the equitable and accurate portrayal of people's identities, perspectives, and needs within social structures. Pitkin (1967) offers possibly the most essential definition: to represent means to "make present again." According to this definition, community representation is the act of making people's voices, ideas, and perspectives "present" in social processes. The concept moves beyond plain visibility: community representation entails the authentic reflection of multiple voices, experiences, and cultures in decision-making processes, institutions, and media that might be fostered through the active participation of diverse, marginalised, and underrepresented communities in these social structures.

The intricate interplay of agency, ownership, and representation takes place at the blurred and ambiguous boundary and intersection between power over and power to, shaping the manifestations and dynamics of power within a context-specific social milieu.

Power dynamics in small and remote places

Power dynamics are primarily evident when different communities of practice interact. Within the scope of our interest, to understand the power dynamics in small and remote places, we will first distinguish between two communities of practice: the 'community' and the 'public administration'.

Communities are the "socio-cultural grouping and milieu to which people would expect, advocate, or wish to belong, (...) the arena in which one learns and largely continues to practise being social" (Rapport & Overing, 2000, p. 63). Communities may be determined based on administrative, geographical, or conceptual boundaries (Alexiou et al., 2013), making them multifaceted, as they encompass individuals from diverse backgrounds that do not "represent a consistent body of individuals sharing the same ideas, perceptions and interests" (Titz et al., 2018, p. 2, as cited in Meriläinen et al., 2021). The community "serves as a symbolic resource, repository, and referent for a variety of identities, and its [success] is to continue to encompass these by a common symbolic boundary" (Rapport & Overing, 2000, p. 63). Hence, communities are neither homogeneous nor singular units (Titz et al., 2018; Walmsley, 2006, as cited in Meriläinen et al., 2021), therefore incorporating inherent conflicts that require recognition and acknowledgement for their challenges and creative potential (Alexiou et al., 2013). This group of actors can often bring empirical knowledge, experience and situated values, legitimisation and support, creating an authorising environment (Moore, 1995).

Public administrations (PAs) refer to diverse groups of people constituting policymakers, administrators, municipal representatives, elected officials who own transitioning political roles, and bureaucracy functionaries with more stable roles. Each of these groups defines, pursues, and enacts their agendas. PAs define, pursue, implement, and coordinate public policies, agendas, institutional tools, services, institutional memory, resource access, and operational capabilities (Moore, 1995). It includes government institutions' systems, performance, and activities at different levels.

When these two communities of practice come together, the actors involved will inevitably have varying degrees of power. These manifest in the amount of tangible or intangible resources they have access to, their positionality, and their connections. For example, a recurring power imbalance occurs when external interventions are implemented without local input. This perpetuates a cycle where affected community members become passive recipients, lacking agency, ownership, and representation in the development of their place. At the same time, public administration may fall short in taking initiative, making decisions, and effectively addressing the needs and priorities of the community it serves (Evers, 2010). The asymmetrical expression of this relationship results in a power imbalance, namely an unequal distribution of power, be it *power over* or *power to*. It is crucial to tackle this power imbalance because reframing it provides PAs with opportunities for a more sustainable, valuable, and democratic change. Power is not fixed; it is dynamic and can evolve over time based on changing circumstances, roles, and capacities. Recognising the need for a more inclusive, community-driven approach, using participatory design methods emerges as an appropriate way to address the imbalances within existing rural policies and practices. We will explore the background of participatory practices and highlight the design's ability to balance the power dynamics embedded in the communities of practice of small and remote places.

Evolution and impact of participatory design

Participatory Design (PD) emerged during the 1970s in Scandinavia as a response to the growing need for inclusivity in decision-making processes related to new technologies and work organisation (Ehn, 1988; Sanders & Stappers, 2008; Björgvinsson et al., 2010). This participatory ethos laid the foundation for co-design, a closely aligned approach that shares its roots with PD. The scope of PD research and practice has broadened beyond the workplace and is now actively engaged in several facets of life. Contemporary PD reflects a paradigm shift from traditional top-down design models to more collaborative and democratised approaches, emphasising the active involvement of end-users throughout the design process. As PD and co-design advance, there is a commitment to moving beyond mere consultation of participants towards higher levels of engagement, striving for genuine partnership and citizen control (Bødker & Pekkola, 2010; Simonsen & Robertson, 2013; Hansen et al., 2019; Teli et al., 2020). Following the evolving discourse on participatory practices, we recognise the imperative of empowering communities to be active decision-makers for their future. Paying attention to power relations and empowering weak and marginalised groups with resources has been the priority of PD research (Björgvinsson et al., 2010). PD advocates a change in democratic design, calling for a shift towards carefully designed processes founded on the distribution of agency and co-created visions for a better future (Rosa et al., 2021).

As design practices move to the public domain, many discourses of participation in design fail to understand the complexity of working in a democratic approach, ignoring that involving users in a project leads to addressing issues of politics and power. Whereas design encourages people to interact in new ways, design often produces (and reproduces) social relationships and systemic power dynamics. These relationships are not only built after using a design product, service, or system, but they are also reproduced in the PD process, where actors with different access to power exchange with one another (Tomasini Giannini & Mulder, 2022, p. 111).

In the realm of design, PD, which puts emphasis on empathy, user-centred methodologies, and community engagement, has become a transformative force, influencing power dynamics in small and remote places. These principles empower local citizens to partake in decision-making processes actively, extending their influence to the planning and development of public spaces, local infrastructure, and social services. Such active involvement not only fosters a sense of empowerment but also contributes to the cultivation of increased horizontal manifestations of democracy. Democracy requires that participatory processes redefine power relationships, which would bring to the surface essential matters pertaining to ownership and sovereignty, and the governance structure (Herlo & Joost, 2019). This shift transforms governance into a collective endeavour that empowers local authorities, public administration, and the communities they represent. Incorporating participatory elements into the design and planning process ensures that development projects align with the distinct requirements and aspirations of these smaller and remote regions.

Participatory design: shifting power relations

Before outlining the differences in power allocation among the different communities of practice in small and remote places and their subsequent shift thanks to PD practices, we need to consider a third community of practice: designers. Designers often introduce resources and methodologies that, through PD, can shift power dynamics within a community (Meriläinen et al., 2021) while assuming the role of facilitator, guide, and interface between the community and the public administration. At the same time, we must consider the managerial aspects potentially introducing imbalances in project ownership, mostly stemming from designers' professional knowledge and over-guidance. These complexities create a challenging arena for project realisation in any context, especially in distant and sparsely populated areas.

Given the nature of small and remote places, notably their number of inhabitants, these communities of practice tend to overlap. For instance, a member of the SMOTIES partnership – Clear Village Trustee Limited, working in the small and remote village of Penmachno (Wales, UK) – is both a designer and an inhabitant of the village. Thus, the roles are blurred, and the power dynamics manifest uniquely. Taking this into account, we

Figure 1: The dimensions of power: from domination to empowerment. © Vanessa Monna and Helen Charoupia

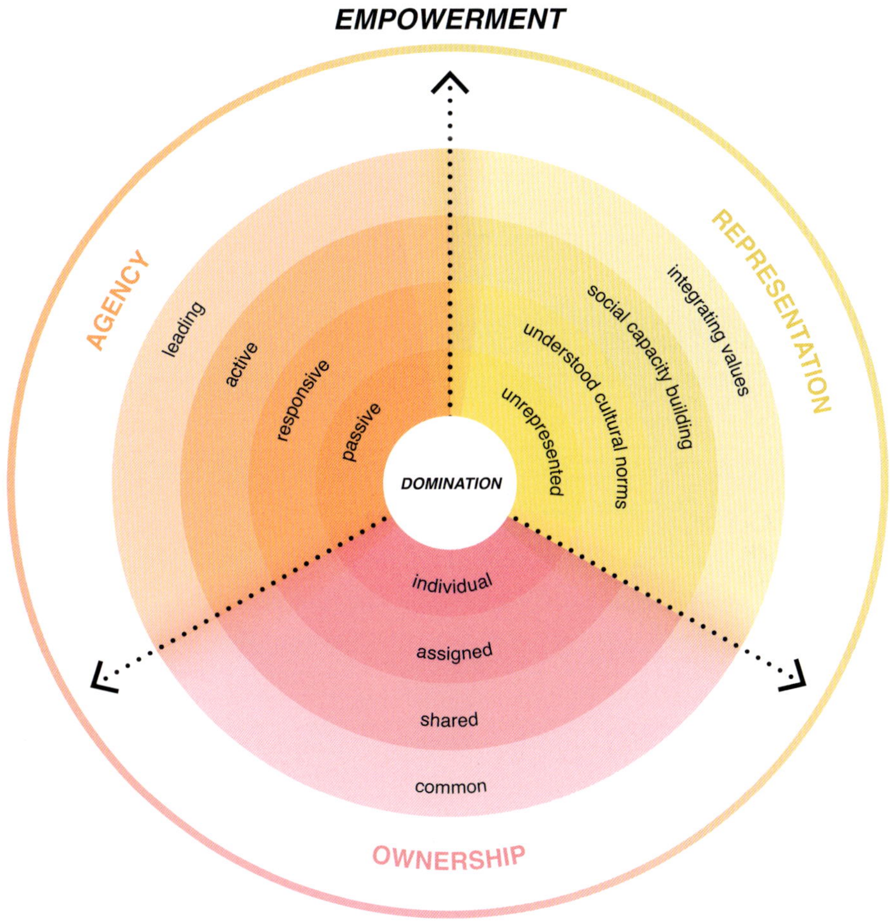

will outline how PD practices can, with the mediation of designers and the active involvement of the respective actors, shift their positionalities concerning the three aforementioned dimensions of power – agency, ownership, and representation – in small and remote places (Figure 1).

In the context of small and remote places, the dynamics of agency distribution between the community and public administration are intricate and multifaceted. The agency of a community varies much, based on, for example, efficient local administration, community activation, education, and economic prospects, which enhance the community's capacity to assume a more proactive or authoritative position in its progress. The SMOTIES project has shown that community agency frequently ranges between little participation and significant engagement. Community members have limited involvement in decision-making processes and initiatives in the former. In the latter, communities actively participate in and initiate communal activities. Certain actors may find themselves on the periphery of decision-making processes, either in design or policy, hindering their ability to advocate their needs. Community members distribute themselves along this spectrum, with some exhibiting a lack of interest for the common good, while some rely heavily on the intervention of public administration to address their needs, from responding to external events to adapting to emerging challenges through small efforts because of their

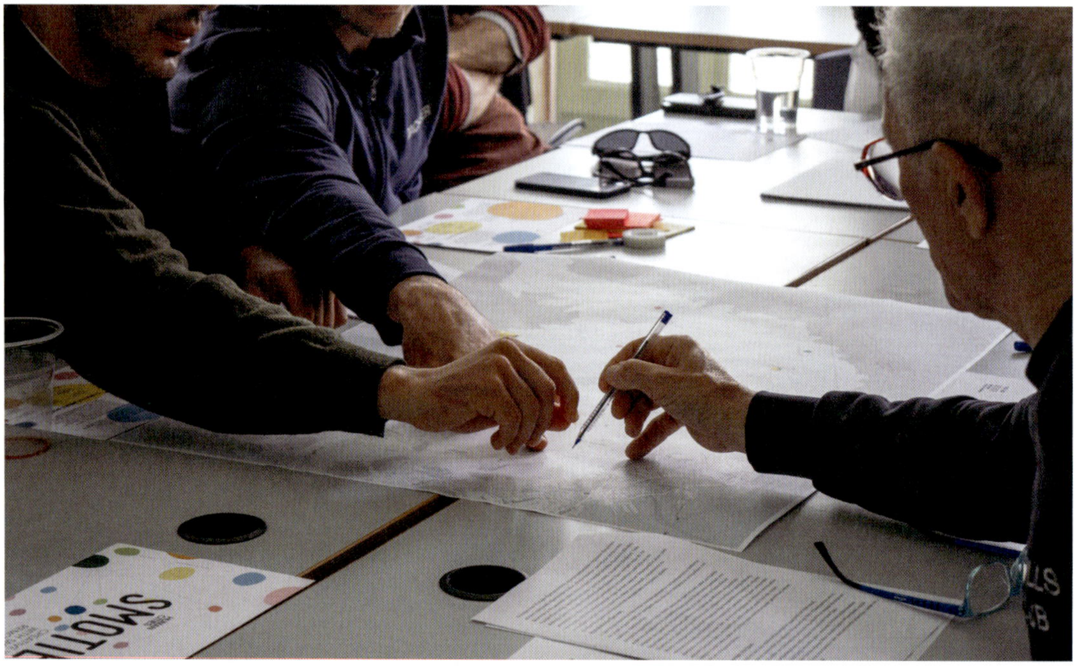

Figure 2: Memory mapping in the initial stages of engaging the local community. © Christina Galani for the University of the Aegean

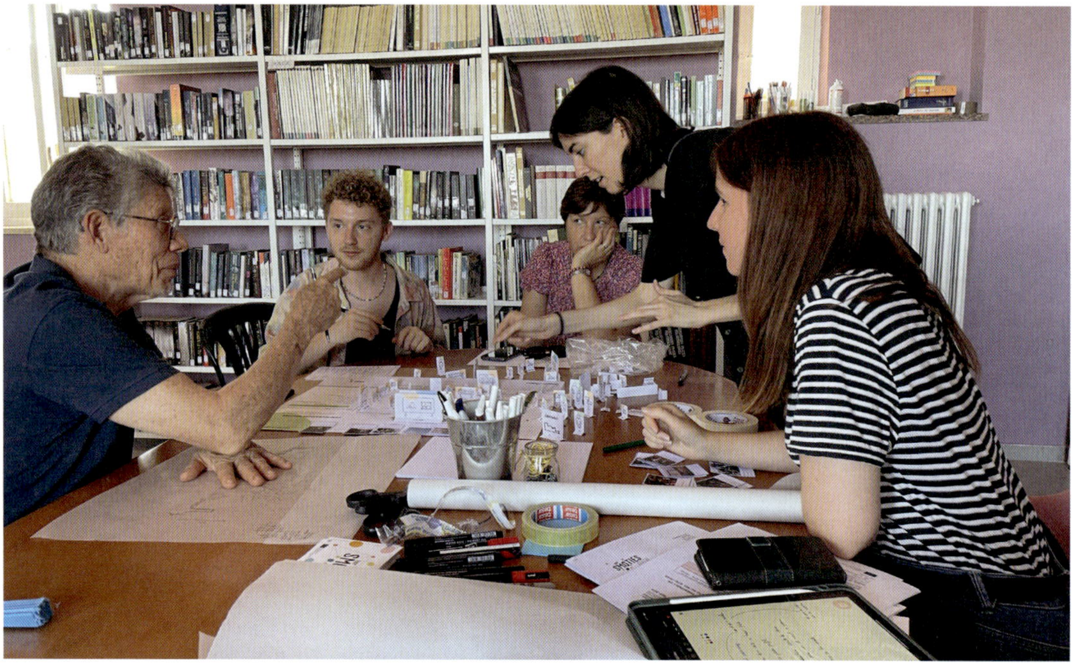

Figure 3: Co-design workshop with the locals to explore the possible and desirable functions of the public space of intervention. © Polimi DESIS Lab

limited autonomy. This may also lead to many of their valuable insights and traditional (even ecological) knowledge being overlooked, leading to suboptimal use of resources and inappropriate decisions. An instance of this challenge, arising from the co-creative processes conducted by the SMOTIES partners at the University of the Aegean (Figure 2), highlighted that, owing to time constraints, numerous well-informed members of the local community were only able to contribute to the discussions minimally and only during specific phases of the project. This circumstance significantly impacted the pool of ideas and the decision-making processes of the broader team of participants.

Some community members, defined as their village's "local heroes" in the SMOTIES project, may develop an interest in governing the municipality. Therefore, most of the highly engaged residents in small remote places assume the responsibility of public administrators, thereby blurring the lines between their being part of the community or the public administration. As in any other context, the public administration agency is defined by institutional power, authority in decision-making, and access to resources. Several aspects, including local governing systems, the efficacy of leadership, financial resources, community participation, and the overall capability of the administration, determine a public administration's level of agency. Assuming a more active or leadership role typically entails having more local autonomy, engaging with the community more significantly, and having the authority to develop and execute policies and programmes customised to address the unique community requirements they serve. Public administrators substantially impact the direction of community development by introducing agendas, institutional tools, and operational capacities. This suggests that the degree of agency within a small and remote community is more significant than we imagine. However, it also hints that the actions of individuals assuming such hybrid roles and qualities could hinder the ability to generate a constructive conversation due to underlying dynamics potentially mixing legitimisation and support with individual interests and community dynamics. For example, SMOTIES partner Department of Design of Politecnico di Milano started working in the village of Albugnano (Italy), because of its connection with local heroes who, at the time, were part of the local PA (Figure 3). Upon beginning the research phase of the project, the differing visions of the PA members became more evident, polarising the members' interests and resulting in a shift in strategy by the SMOTIES team. The SMOTIES team had to reassess its stakeholders and the public spaces it planned to work on, ultimately resulting in an extension of the project. The team therefore highlighted the fact that participatory processes take time to carefully articulate the dialogue and interactions between designers, PAs, and citizens within iterative times for action and reaction.

While the increased authority of a public administration is crucial for efficient governance, it also requires careful balance to prevent potential disparities in power dynamics. PD effectively addresses this dynamic by actively involving community members in projects, aiming to engage them in decision-making processes, thereby empowering communities by granting them more agency. PD challenges PAs to move beyond tokenistic approaches, which not only fail to distribute agency to the community but also result in a loss of trust by the people, who believe that their contributions are not given due consideration. Some PAs may exhibit reluctance towards engaging in participatory activities due to concerns about possible barriers, conflicts, the belief that decision-making should stick to conventional bureaucratic procedures, and, while a shift is conducive to a sense of shared responsibility and inclusivity, the fear of losing authority over a territory. The SMOTIES project has proved that while, in theory, PAs are more than open to engaging with PD when put into practice, they find it challenging to understand the language, methods, and lengthy procedures of PD practices. PAs are built around order and control, and PD questions this, encouraging PAs to genuinely engage in collaborative efforts with the community and providing it with the tools, resources, procedures, and knowledge to act. In the best-case scenario, PD can bring more agency to the community, allowing them to lead and co-manage processes and projects. To achieve this objective, the Art & Design Department of the Universidade da Madeira, a SMOTIES partner, created a feature film in which local actors, including a few local heroes, were interviewed. The video was presented and screened at an outdoor public event, which brought the entire community together. The community welcomed the video, instilling a strong sense of agency and belonging, which encouraged further engagement in participatory practices.

Representation has been commonly associated with the expression of perspectives through voting mechanisms. However, our perspective contends that the intricate processes of representation extend far beyond the confines of voting rituals, permeating our daily lives. This is particularly evident in small and remote places, where the degrees of community representation exhibit considerable variability. Active community members tend to have more visibility and representation than those who do not actively participate in communal activities. Conversely, the voices of individuals less engaged in community affairs may be overlooked and inadequately assessed. This diversity in representation is accentuated in the context of foreign communities, where recognition and consideration of their diversity in government and public service provision often lag. Foreigners grappling with challenges such as linguistic barriers, lack of voting rights, cultural differences, limited access to information, and unfamiliarity with local customs may find themselves excluded from various initiatives. In certain instances, these communities may opt for a more independent existence, leading to what could be perceived as a "parallel" life detached from the mainstream activities of their village. However, there have been instances where embracing diversity has become a cornerstone of small and remote places, fuelling innovative initiatives and inspiring novel business models. For all these reasons, the representation of small and remote communities tends to be less varied, primarily amplifying the voices of the most active participants. This limitation is compounded by the struggle of these communities to cultivate and leverage a social capital representative of their entirety. The exclusivity often associated with the "veteran" community and the low population density of small and remote places contribute to the challenges faced in building a comprehensive and inclusive social capital reflective of the diverse voices within the community. If we take into consideration the fact that often, some of the 'veteran' members of the community are also those who take part in local government, then the representation gap increases even further. While PAs play an essential role in representing the community's voice, the success of their representation depends on, among others, transparency, inclusion, and responsiveness to the varied perspectives within the community. It is crucial to strike a balance between the structured representation of PAs and genuine community involvement to guarantee that the community's collective voice is acknowledged and actively influences decisions that affect its well-being. By incorporating the perspectives of different actors, including those on the periphery of traditional decision-making, PD not only empowers individuals to advocate their needs and provide empirical knowledge, but also incorporates the values of the whole community in decisions and projects.

The low habitation density significantly impacts ownership dynamics in small and remote places. Ownership varies and is present at the individual level and the community public administration level, where ownership is increasing for communities and decreasing for public administrations. Ownership may stay at a personal level, with people having individual ownership of their homes and land, sharing only public spaces. Ownership often aligns with longstanding cultural and communal practices in some traditional contexts. The community may collectively own or manage land and resources, with land tenure systems influenced by cultural traditions. Ownership in this context is deeply rooted in historical practices and reflects the communal ties developed over generations. Finally, the distinctive attributes of small and remote regions have been increasingly seen as an opportunity for developing and prototyping new ownership models. The very constraints that infrastructure scarcity imposes may motivate the investigation of alternative ownership models. In such contexts, where traditional systems may be lacking or inadequately developed, communities are compelled to employ innovative approaches to possess and administer resources jointly. If a community has been formed around or has integrated communal infrastructure, ownership is common to all the community's members, as they deliberately choose to share and collectively own essential infrastructure, particularly in terms of energy systems, water resources, and other utilities. The ownership of these shared resources is often guided by collaborative decision-making processes that prioritise sustainability and self-sufficiency. Residents may actively participate in managing and maintaining shared infrastructure, contributing to a sense of collective ownership over essential services.

Designers play a crucial role in balancing the dynamics within these complex communities of small and remote places. However, more often than not, designers enter a design project as external observers, not fully immersed in the ongoing dialogues, debates, and narratives within these places. Recognising this, it becomes imperative for designers to acknowledge, empathise with, and actively listen to the actors involved in the processes, with a particular focus on amplifying the voices that are often left unheard. In the realm of PD, the success of any practice hinges on the ability of collaborators, including designers, to understand the nuances of the community. Designers, acting as facilitators, guides, and interfaces between non-homogeneous communities, play a key role in translating the actors' needs.

Conclusions

Moving towards just and sustainable small and remote communities necessitates re-evaluating traditional developmental approaches. Prioritising diverse stakeholder involvement and balancing power dynamics in relation to the dimensions of agency, ownership, and representation are essential for a meaningful shift towards equitable rural development. Within an array of options, the discipline of design offers the PD approach, which serves as a democratisation tool. PD integrates fundamental methodologies for equitable power distribution among participants, cultivating a shared trust among community members, officials, and designers.

The implementation of PD practices in public administration encounters challenges for several reasons: i) bureaucratic processes may fear loss of control; ii) PD practices travel on a slower wavelength, which doesn't align with the commonly faster-paced nature of PAs, thus the difficulty to comprehend the "meaningful inefficiency" (Gordon & Mugar, 2020) of the participatory process; iii) the impacts of PD practices may be more valuable from a qualitative perspective, while PAs are more quantitative, which makes it more difficult to appreciate, communicate and take accountability for the results of the work from their point of view; and, finally, iv) all the previous points make PD an expensive process to undertake.

However, if we reflect on the core mission of PAs – to initiate action, make decisions, and effectively meet the needs of the community they serve – we advocate a more forward-thinking approach. We encourage PAs to be visionary, demonstrating the courage to actively engage in and support participatory processes. This involves participating in design processes, embracing uncertainties, making space and time for such processes, and overcoming inherent challenges. It entails entrusting small and remote communities and assuming a safeguarding role in overseeing these participatory endeavours. This approach seeks to mitigate injustices, promote an equitable allocation of power, and foster the development of new narratives concerning those who have influenced our society so far and should be part of its future (Costanza-Chock, 2020). This shift aligns with a governance model prioritising its community's empowerment.

SMOTIES has been an excellent opportunity to put the participatory design approach into practice in complex real-life contexts. It highlighted some very positive experiences and, at the same time, pointed out some challenging aspects. We could have told you a different story, but participatory practices leverage the democratic expression of needs, desires, and ideas, and these might differ within the same community of place, especially if the roles of its inhabitants are blurred owing to the different emerging dimensions of the community.

As SMOTIES has shown, while there may be hurdles along the way, participatory practices acknowledge and act upon balancing power relations, which is a crucial step for constructing a future that is inclusive, democratic, and equitable for everyone.

References

Alexiou, K., Zamenopoulos, T., & Giota Alevizou. (2013). *Valuing Community-Led Design.*

Allen, A. (1998). Rethinking power. *Hypatia, 13*(1), 21–40.

Allen, A. (1999). *The Power of Feminist Theory: Domination, Resistance, Solidarity.* Westview Press.

Arendt, H. (1957). *The Human Condition*. Chicago University Press.

Arendt, H. (1970). *On Violence.* Harmondsworth: Penguin.

Bandura, A. (2001). Social cognitive theory: An agentic perspective. *Annual review of psychology, 52*(1), 1–26.

Björgvinsson, E., Ehn, P., & Hillgren, P. A. (2010). Participatory design and "democratizing innovation". *In Proceedings of the 11th Biennial participatory design conference* (pp. 41–50).

Bødker, S., & Pekkola, S. (2010). Introduction to the debate section: A short review to the past and present of participatory design. *Scandinavian Journal of Information Systems, 22*(1), 4.

Bratteteig, T., & Wagner, I. (2016). What is a participatory design result? *Proceedings of the 14th Participatory Design Conference: Full papers – Volume 1* (pp. 141–150).

Costanza-Chock, S. (2020). *Design Justice: Community-Led Practices to Build the Worlds We Need.* MA: The MIT Press.

Coy, D., Malekpour, S., Saeri, A. K., & Dargaville, R. (2021). Rethinking community empowerment in the energy transformation: A critical review of the definitions, drivers and outcomes. *Energy Research & Social Science, 72*, 101871. https://doi.org/10.1016/j.erss.2020.101871

Dahl, R. A., 1957. The concept of power. *Behavioral Science, 2*(3), 201–215.

Ehn, P. (1988). *Work-Oriented Design of Computer Artifacts.* Arbetslivscentrum.

Evers, A. (2010). Civicness, civility and their meanings for social services. In Brandsen, T., Dekker, P., & Evers, A. (Eds), *Civicness in the Governance and Delivery of Social Services* (pp. 41–65). Nomos.

Florida, R. (2002). The economic geography of talent. *Annals of the Association of American Geographers, 92*(4), 743–755.

Gordon, E., & Mugar, G. (2020). *Meaningful Inefficiencies: Civic Design in an Age of Digital Expediency.* Oxford University Press.

Hansen, N. B., Dindler, C., Halskov, K., Iversen, O. S., Bossen, C., Basballe, D. A., & Schouten, B. (2019). How participatory design works. *Proceedings of the 31st Australian Conference on Human-Computer-Interaction*. https://doi.org/10.1145/3369457.3369460

Haugaard, M. (2012). Rethinking the four dimensions of power: domination and empowerment. *Journal of Political Power*, 5(1), 33–54.

Herlo, B., & Joost, G. (2019). Design for civil society. The model project "Citizens connect neighborhoods – community development harnesses digital transformation." *International Association of Societies of Design Research Conference 2019*. https://iasdr2019.org/uploads/files/Proceedings/pe-f-1027-Her-B.pdf

Landry, C. (2000). *The Creative City: A Toolkit for Urban Innovators*. Earthscan.

Light, A., Hill, K. J., Hansen, N. B., Hackney, F., Halskov, K., & Dalsgaard, P. (2013). Exploring the dynamics of ownership in community-oriented design projects. In *Proceedings of the 6th International Conference on Communities and Technologies* (pp. 90-99).

Membretti, A., Dax, T., & Machold, I. (2022). Thesis 1: Reframing remote places and remoteness as a collective resource and value for Europe. In *The Renaissance of Remote Places* (pp. 17–26). Routledge.

Meriläinen, E., Kelman, I., Peters, L. E. R., & Shannon, G. (2021). Puppeteering as a metaphor for unpacking power in participatory action research on climate change and health. *Climate and Development, 14*(5), 1–12. https://doi.org/10.1080/17565529.2021.1930509

Metcalf, H., Urwick, L. (2003). *Dynamic Administration. The Collected Papers of Mary Parker Follett*. Harper & Brothers.

Moore, M. H. (1995). *Creating Public Value: Strategic Management in Government*. Harvard University Press.

OECD. (2018). Summer academy on cultural and creative industries and local development. The value of culture and the creative industries in local development.

OECD. (2020). Rural Well-Being: geography of opportunities, OECD Rural Studies.

Pansardi, P., & Bindi, M. (2021). The new concepts of power? Power-over, power-to and power-with. *Journal of Political Power, 14*(1), 51–71.

Pisor, A. C., Basurto, X., Douglass, K. G., Mach, K. J., Ready, E., Tylianakis, J. M., Hazel, A., Kline, M. A., Kramer, K. L., Lansing, J. S., Moritz, M., Smaldino, P. E., Thornton, T. F., & Jones, J. H. (2022). Effective climate change adaptation means supporting community autonomy. *Nature Climate Change, 12*(3), 213–215. https://doi.org/10.1038/s41558-022-01303-x

Pitkin, H. F. (1967). *The Concept of Representation*. University of California.

Pitkin, H. F. (1972). *Wittgenstein and Justice: On the Significance of Ludwig Wittgenstein for Social and Political Thought*. University of California Press.

Rapport, N., & Overing, J. (2000). *Social and Cultural Anthropology. The Key Concepts*. Routledge.

Rosa, J. de la, Ruecker, S., & Nohora, C. G. (2021). Systemic mapping and design research: towards participatory democratic engagement. *She Ji: The Journal of Design, Economics, and Innovation, 7*(2), 282–298. https://doi.org/10.1016/j.sheji.2021.04.001

Rowlands, J. (1997). *Questioning Empowerment: Working with Women in Honduras*. Oxfam.

Sanders, E. B.-N., & Stappers, P. J. (2008). Co-creation and the new landscapes of design. *CoDesign, 4*(1), 5–18. https://doi.org/10.1080/15710880701875068

Simonsen, J., & Robertson, T. (2013). *Routledge International Handbook of Participatory Design*. Routledge.

Teli, M., Foth, M., Sciannamblo, M., Anastasiu, I., & Lyle, P. (2020). Tales of institutioning and commoning. *Proceedings of the 16th Participatory Design Conference 2020 – Participation(S) Otherwise – Volume 1.* https://doi.org/10.1145/3385010.3385020

Tomasini Giannini, F., & Mulder, I. (2022). Towards a power-balanced participatory design process. *Data Archiving and Networked Services (DANS), 2.* https://doi.org/10.1145/3537797.3537819

Townsend, J.G., Zapata, E., Rowlands, J., Alberti, P., and Mercado, M. (1999). *Women and Power: Fighting Patriarchies and Poverty*. Zed Books.

Van Rijn, H., & Stappers, P. J. (2008). Expressions of ownership: Motivating users in a co-design process. *PDC, 8*, 178–181.

Wenger, E. (1999). *Communities of Practice*. Cambridge University Press.

3. Exploring Global Perspectives of Co-design of Remote Public Spaces

Matej Nikšič
Urban Planning Institute
of the Republic of Slovenia
and Faculty of Architecture
of the University of Ljubljana
[SI]

Nina Goršič
Urban Planning Institute
of the Republic of Slovenia
[SI]

Anwar Samara
Faculty of Architecture
of the University of Ljubljana
[SI]

This paper delves into the significance of participatory co-design in remote public spaces globally, transcending spatial planning boundaries. It explores diverse case studies worldwide, emphasising the transformative power of community engagement, sustainability, and cultural preservation. Theoretical frameworks, such as place-based approaches and resilience theory, provide a conceptual foundation. The chosen case studies showcase the interplay between global goals and local needs. Insights from participatory design, smart cities, new ruralism and human-centred design offer valuable lessons for spatial planners and designers working in remote areas globally.

Significance of examining participatory co-design in remote places globally

In the broad array of design tasks of places, the participatory co-design of public spaces stands out as a critical thread that connects the communities and shapes the fabric of their existence. The collaborative creation of public spaces in remote settings transcends the boundaries of spatial planning methodologies. Co-creating public spaces in remote areas involves community empowerment, resilience, and cultural preservation, as highlighted by the Human Cities network's latest review (Nikšič, Goršič et al., 2022) of European best practices in that regard. By shedding light on participatory processes in diverse global contexts, this paper seeks out insights into the universal importance of co-designed public spaces worldwide. Extending the lens to remote areas across the globe becomes an academic endeavour and an exploration with far-reaching implications.

Remote areas, often characterised by geographical isolation, possess unique challenges that demand innovative solutions. The concept of remoteness extends beyond mere physical distance; it encompasses socio-economic, cultural, and infrastructural factors that shape the lived experiences of communities. The position of remote areas outside major (urban) areas that dominate the socio-economic discourse may lead to limited access to resources, services, and opportunities (Cumming et al., 2015); however, remoteness also offers distinct advantages, including the preservation of traditional knowledge, cultural heritage, and ecological diversity (Gorenflo et al., 2012). As remote places lack access to the same resources and experiences as more centrally located places, residents in remote places may also feel that the canon is irrelevant to their lives and experiences (Unanue, 2016).

The participatory co-design of public spaces emerges as a catalyst for addressing these challenges, harnessing local communities' collective wisdom and creativity. In examining global cases, the paper explores not only the physical manifestation of these spaces but also the intricate social and cultural dynamics they foster. Understanding the unique context of remoteness is essential for designing interventions sensitive to local needs and aspirations (Lozano et al., 2013). Participatory approaches allow for co-creating contextually relevant and sustainable solutions, empowering communities to shape their future (Reed, 2008, Barraket et al., 2022). As spatial planners, we recognise the importance of this exploration and its potential to inspire a paradigm shift in community planning. By comprehending how public spaces are co-designed in remote places, we aim to unravel the complex interplay between community engagement, cultural identity, and sustainable development in a global context. The participatory approach becomes a catalyst for fostering a sense of belonging, encouraging adaptability, and strengthening the social fabric while addressing some of the most pressing issues of current societies.

As we delve into the participatory co-design of public spaces in remote areas, we recognise its transformative power as a universal language transcending geographical barriers. This exploration aims not only to showcase the richness of individual projects but also to advocate a broader recognition of the global importance of participatory co-design of public spaces in remote areas. It is a call to action for spatial planners, designers, and the broader professional community worldwide to embrace collaborative methodologies, learn from diverse experiences, and collectively contribute to a more inclusive and resilient future of remote communities and places globally.

Methodological framework for reviewing how public spaces in remote areas are co-designed

Public space co-design in remote areas is a subject that has garnered more scholarly attention, especially in the last decade, with various theoretical approaches explored to address its complexity. This short review aims to identify some theoretical frameworks within the community planning domain that are particularly relevant to participatory public open space design in remote locations. Drawing from scholarly works and globally relevant strategic documents, the goal is to lay the conceptual groundwork to review selected cases in the next chapter.

As emphasised by Micek and Staszewska (2019), to understand the dynamics of rural public spaces, one should focus on functions, development issues, and qualitative assessment that are aligned with the needs and values of rural communities. New ruralism developments (Moughtin & Cuesta, 2003) and the exploration of disparities between rural and urban public spaces by Veitch et al. (2013) resonate with place-based approaches. Jaszczak et al. (2017) propose aligning public space planning with village development and resident needs, adding depth to the relevance of place-based considerations. Injecting the dynamics of co-creation into the discourse, as suggested by Sanders and Stappers (2008), resonates with resilience theory and broader cultural sustainability goals. The comprehensive understanding of public space provided by Carr et al. (1992), and later echoed by Gehl (2010) under the theme of human-centric urban design, was well aligned with the Sustainable Development Goals (SDGs), which encompass the globally recognised principles of suitable public spaces (Anderson, 2021). Within the discourse on the SDGs, the exploration of intercultural encounters must also be highlighted (Radford, 2017), which further sheds light on the importance of human-centred design in adjusting to local culture. The impact of a sense of belonging and identity aligns with the emphasis on place-user experience. It underscores the even greater importance of contextual public space design in remote places.

These scholarly works highlight vital factors, including participatory design, place-based approaches, resilience, innovation, cultural sustainability, new ruralism, human-centred design, and strategies in line with the SDGs. Together, they provide the foundation for examining how public open spaces are created in some rural areas around the world. Paying attention to these aspects, we have identified specific global case studies that captured our interest.

Learning from case studies

Based on the above conceptual framework, we identified specific case studies that not only exemplify the previously mentioned concepts but also provide tangible evidence of their feasibility and effectiveness in different parts of the world. This approach aligns with the research methodologies advocated by Yin (2018) and Stake (1995) in case study research, ensuring a robust exploration of real-life situations.

The selected case studies across diverse global regions (Fig. 1) serve as examples of successful co-creation of public spaces in remote areas. They lay the foundation for an illustrative exploration of conceptual approaches, emphasising the global applicability of the unique challenges of co-designing public open spaces.

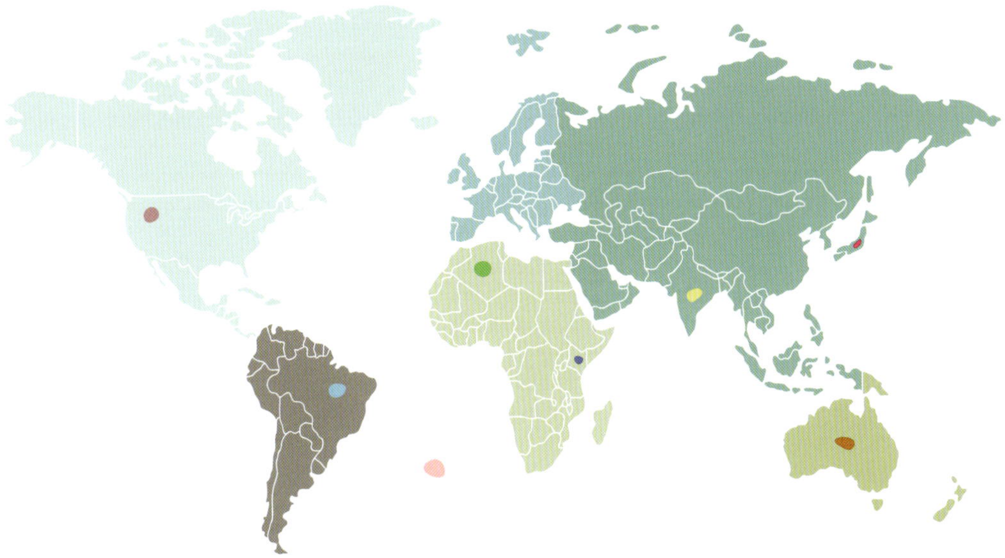

Figure 1: A map of selected case studies from several continents and their varying approaches to co-creation in public spaces. © Matej Nikšič, Nina Goršič and Anwar Samara

Case Study 1 : Tristan da Cunha, British Overseas Territory
Sustainable Community Design for Tristan da Cunha
Place-Based Approaches

Case Study 2 : Tilonia, India
The "Barefoot College Solar Electrification" project
Sustainable Development Goals (SDGs)

Case Study 3 : Rio de Janeiro, Brazil
"Favela-Bairro Project"
Participatory Design

Case Study 4 : New Orleans, USA
Post-Hurricane Katrina redevelopment
Resilience Theory

Case Study 5 : Nairobi, Kenya
The "Digital Matatus" project
Smart Cities and Digital Innovation

Case Study 6 : Mâzab Valley, Algeria
The Ghardaia Oasis Revitalisation Project Cultural Sustainability

Case Study 7 : Byron Bay, Australia
The Byron Bay Farmers Market and Sustainable Community Hub
New Ruralism

Case Study 8 : Kumano Shingu, Japan
Oishii Park by td-Atelier
Human-Centred Design

The choice of case studies relied on the diversity of regions. We began assessing each case study by doing an intensive literature and online sources review to identify its main characteristics: initiator(s), tools to involve the community and ensure public engagement, nature of involvement, mechanisms supporting participatory methods, as well as the types of public spaces that were improved. This was useful for understanding and addressing the complexity of public open space co-design in remote areas and how it contributes to the development of contextualised and sustainable solutions. This approach facilitated the exploration of case studies that not only reflect the conceptual underpinnings of the chosen framework but also demonstrate their practical applications and real-world successes, thus contributing to the advancement of community development knowledge.

Variety of approaches and issues around the globe

This chapter highlights the significance of caring for public spaces in remote areas around the world through eight selected case studies. These places often face challenges such as climate change, limited mobility, and social connectivity. To address these issues, cooperation is required at multiple levels. While the broader international community and politics must develop strategies and tools to solve global problems, the responsiveness of the local community is even more critical in addressing the challenges they face in their home environment. Due to direct involvement, the local community can be more responsive and encourage other communities to come together to solve problems quickly, even in crises. Community action in public spaces encourages individuals to be active, contributes to their education, and empowers them at various levels of life. Ultimately, the care for public spaces in remote areas is not just about the spaces themselves, but also about the people who inhabit and interact with them, fostering a sense of belonging, identity, and well-being within their communities. By nurturing and maintaining these public spaces, not only is the physical environment enhanced, but social cohesion, resilience, and sustainable development for generations to come are also cultivated.

The chosen case studies show global initiatives in remote places spanning diverse locations, thus offering insights into an array of challenges and innovative. In the Southern Hemisphere, Tristan da Cunha, a remote island in the vast South Atlantic Ocean, is a British Overseas Territory. Moving to South Asia, a case study was chosen in Tilonia (India), that reflects the implementation of strategies outlined in the UN SDGs. The third case study is in the South American city of Rio de Janeiro (Brazil). The North American example of resilience theory can be seen in the US in the aftermath of Hurricane Katrina. In East Africa, Nairobi (Kenya), is pioneering digital innovations to improve connectivity. In North Africa, Ghardaia (Algeria), focuses on cultural sustainability to preserve its UNESCO-protected oasis city. Byron Bay in Australia embodies the principles of new ruralism with its sustainable community centre. Finally, in Japan, Kumano Shingu focuses on people-centred design and emphasises public spaces and community engagement.

Place-based approach on the Tristan da Cunha islands

The first case study by Brock Carmichael represents a sustainable community design for Tristan da Cunha, which uses the place-based approach. The project was created in 2015-2016 as a competition commissioned by the municipality and organised by the Royal Institute of British Architects (RIBA) in Tristan da Cunha, one of the most isolated inhabited island chains. With a population of only 268 people living thousands of kilometres away from any other settlement, a life centred on planning for future needs is essential. Architects Brock Carmichael won the RIBA competition, and the Tristan da Cunha Island Council awarded them for their design, which fits perfectly into a sustainable future for the community (Tristan da Cunha, 2016). Thus, the architecture focuses comprehensively on sustainability and resilience, specific to the challenges and opportunities in Tristan da Cunha. It emphasises green building, incorporating renewable energy and neighbourhood-oriented spaces to improve residents' quality of life. This partnership emphasised that the design aligns with the community's values, needs, and heritage.

Furthermore, the island government has also invited architects to present ideas for redesigning Tristan da Cunha government buildings innovatively and cost-effectively (ArchDaily, 2016). Community engagement was an integral part of the design process with workshops during the visit, meetings and open forums in which residents provided their insights, needs, and desires during the architects' visit to the island as a means to respond to the needs outlined in the competition's call for participation. The proposed design enables many well thought-out public spaces that stimulate community cohesion and adaptability, with communal areas, green spaces, and facilities for cultural and recreational activities. This whole-of-project approach emphasises building sustainability, community well-being, and cultural preservation in Tristan da Cunha (Place North West, 2016).

Making concrete steps towards achieving the SDGs in Tilonia

The "Barefoot College Solar Electrification" project in Tilonia was undertaken within the framework of the SDGs. This initiative was started in the 1970s by Barefoot College, a nonprofit organisation from India, and has grown worldwide. It aligns with the SDGs to provide clean energy and alleviate poverty. It adopts a transformative approach by equipping women from rural communities worldwide to become solar engineers, training them to install electricity in remote villages. The project achieved job creation and women's empowerment, specifically targeting illiterate middle-aged women from rural areas (Barefoot College, 2019). This bottom-up strategy facilitates providing practical training to rural women in workshops. The women actively contribute to decision-making in the project and can thus drive electrification in their villages. This initiative focuses on the electrification of public spaces in rural communities, such as community centres, schools, and roads. Thus, the contribution of this project to clean energy not only alleviates poverty and supports sustainable development goals but also promotes the active participation of women in leadership roles (Ministry of New and Renewable Energy, 2019).

Participatory design in Favela Bairro

Participatory design was central to the "Favela Bairro Project" project in Rio de Janeiro, Brazil. This initiative was launched in the late 1990s (Massachusetts Institute of Technology, 2001) and has spanned several years. The Municipality of Rio de Janeiro created it with the support of international organisations to address challenges in informal settlements. It has multiple goals: to integrate today's favelas into the settlement structure through improved infrastructure and better services; to avoid future land grabbing; and to provide affordable housing. Residents actively participate in design charrettes, community meetings, and workshops where priority areas are identified, and decisions are made. These changes can be financed through low-interest loans provided by the government and the city municipality, and residents can become actual owners of the homes. This approach encourages camaraderie and enables participants to develop a trade, improve their skills, and find suitable employment opportunities to reduce unemployment. The state and municipal savings from hiring contractors for this project are instead spent on water and electricity infrastructure. Public spaces in the favelas, such as squares, parks, and community centres, are also impacted by this project. The participatory method of the Favela Bairro project has improved physical infrastructure, empowered residents, and contributed to sustainable development, which is part of a bigger national plan to solve the issue of slums and informal settlements in the country (BBC Bitesize, 2008).

Resilient communities in New Orleans

The case study from the USA delves into the application of resilience theory in the reconstruction efforts following Hurricane Katrina in New Orleans. The recovery process began in 2015 and was facilitated by various stakeholders, including government bodies at various levels, nonprofit organisations, and community groups. This initiative incorporates resilience principles focusing on adaptive capacity, integrating green infrastructure and a comprehensive approach to addressing social and environmental risks (Kates et al., 2006). Residents and actors are engaged in the decision-making process, integrating green infrastructure to help mitigate social and environmental vulnerabilities. Students contributed significantly to this citizen-engagement process at Ohio State University's Knowlton School of Architecture (Johannessen & Goldweit, 2020). They facilitated community-wide planning on the Mississippi Gulf, developing community plans for six communities over two years of studio courses with a team of 12 students. Stakeholder engagement was made possible through town hall meetings, public hearings, and participatory planning sessions emphasising stakeholders' collaborative decision-making. The project's scope extends further, encompassing rehabilitation efforts in parks, waterfronts, and community centres.

Digital innovation in Nairobi

The "Digital Matatus" project in Nairobi operates within the smart cities and digital innovation framework. Initiated in 2012 and still evolving, this project involves local technology companies, universities, and government agencies. The initiative aims to use data from mobile devices to map informal public transport routes. This innovative strategy aims to enhance internet access, improve transport efficiency, and showcase how digital creativity can effectively address community challenges, particularly in remote areas. The project organised a group of students from the University of Nairobi who identified stops based on the preferences of regular users, especially those working within the ICT sector. The data collectors included residents and matatu drivers who participated in mapping workshops. Communities' active participation in the decision-making process was facilitated using mobile technology for data collection. While the primary focus of this initiative is on transport efficiency, it indirectly impacts public spaces by improving accessibility to various locations. The Digital Matatus project exemplifies how digital innovation can support spatial infrastructure and connectivity in far-reaching areas (Digital Matatus, 2015).

Revitalisation through heritage protection in Ghardaia Oasis

The revitalisation project in Ghardaia Oasis in Algeria aligns with the cultural sustainability framework. Initiated in the early 2000s and still in progress, the project involves different stakeholders, including government agencies that have a significant role in UNESCO, given the region's listing for its remarkable mud brick buildings (Zanati, 2018). The initiative protects not only architectural heritage but also culture, skills, and tourism, which are integral to the community and the site's intangible heritage. Therefore, the planning process necessitated community involvement, facilitated through workshops and meetings with local experts and artisans, to ensure the practice and preservation of traditional building crafts (Directorate of Tourism and Traditional Industries of Ghardaia State, 1996). The revitalisation efforts also encompass the redesign of historic public squares, marketplaces, and community spaces, aiming to enhance the quality of life in this remote area (Aqakaba, 2010).

New ruralism approach in New South Wales

Byron Bay Farmers Market and Sustainable Community Hub in New South Wales (Australia) is a community initiative which originated in the late 1990s. It was set in motion when Helena Norberg-Hodge organised a workshop as part of the Byron Bay initiative. It gained momentum through local public forums and was taken up by several farmers looking for a way to directly sell their produce and promote local sustainability (John, 2003). Launched in 2000, the project brought together local farmers, community organisers, and the Byron Shire Council. The principles of new ruralism are embodied in this initiative – the farmers' market and sustainable community centre integrate sustainable agriculture, community participation, and intentional design of public spaces. The development of these facilities was characterised by active community participation achieved through public meetings, workshops, and design events (Banyan Tree, 2022). Residents played a pivotal role in designing the marketplace and community spaces, as well as in developing sustainability initiatives. The project's ongoing activities encompass regular community events, sustainable living workshops, and gardening, all of which ensure continuous community engagement. The marketplace functions as a centralised community space with well-designed areas for vendors, communal seating, and interactive spaces for events and workshops (Adams, 2002). The market's layout encourages community interaction, supports local businesses, and promotes innovative, more sustainable practices in the rural community.

Human-centred design in Oishii Park

The last case study is centred on the Japanese Oishii Park project, which originated with the establishment of the Engawa Youth Library in 2013. This library, created by renovating an old privately owned house, was designed as a "live-in library," providing both travel accommodation and a public space for residents. It catalyses a subsequent project to create a private, public space encompassing a park and a library. During the COVID-19 pandemic in 2020, the Engawa Youth Library sought new ways to utilise the outdoor public space, leading to the conception of Oishii Park (mooool, 2022). This park opened a community space linked to the library, creating a conducive environment for reading books. The project involved extensive studies in creating a multifunctional meadow where people can gather, linger, and read. Factors such as sunlight, shade, and the site's aesthetics were thoroughly analysed under the human-centred design approach. This led to the design of a long, three-dimensional bench that meanders along the site's western end, inspired by the natural features of Kumano. The design was created to be easy to construct without advanced skills, offering a learning process for carpentry techniques (ArchDaily, 2016 and n.d.). Collaboration with students in Kumano over seven years laid the foundation for the project. However, with the challenges brought on by the pandemic, parts were manufactured at the university and assembled on-site to minimise contact with older residents. The planning and design factored in goods transportation, assembly procedures, and

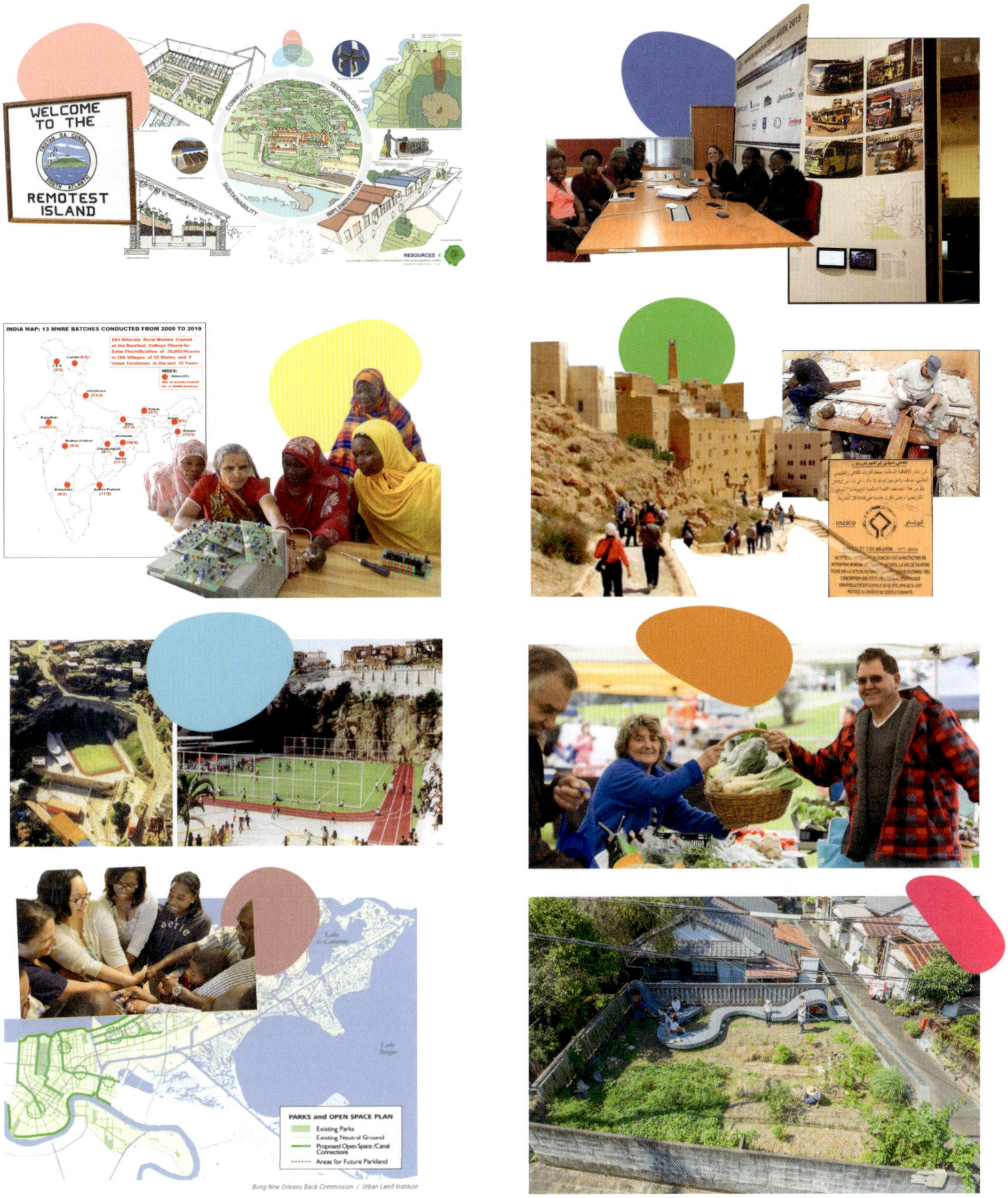

Figure 2: Photographs illustrating selected case studies of good practices in co-creating remote public spaces.

From top left by columns:
© Brock Carmichael studio UK
© Barefoot College / Bindi International India
© Urban upgrading Australia
© Urban Land Institute
© Catholic Charities Archdiocese of New Orleans
© Digital Matatus Kenya
© Ministry of Tourism and Handicrafts – Algeria
© Our community AU
© Photographer Matsumura Kohei

a reduction of the local labour force. Oishii Park aims not only to harvest delicious food but also to foster enriching experiences, encounters, and community-building in the wider region.

The insights from global case studies

Exploring diverse global case studies in participatory co-design of public spaces in remote areas provides insights into universal implications and challenges. Across various continents, from Tristan da Cunha to Tilonia and from Rio de Janeiro to Ghardaia, the common thread lies in the recognition that community engagement is integral to the success of such projects. The participatory design process in the Favela Bairro Project in Rio de Janeiro and the Ghardaia Oasis revitalisation initiative in Algeria highlights the transformative power of involving local communities in decision-making. Beyond physical improvements, these projects empower residents, fostering a sense of ownership and community pride. Such empowerment echoes in the participatory planning sessions post-Katrina in New Orleans, reinforcing the notion that community-driven decision-making is crucial for resilient spatial development.

In the realm of digital innovation, the Digital Matatus project in Nairobi and the Oishii Park project in Kumano underscore the potential of technology in redefining public spaces of remote places. While the former focuses on enhancing transport efficiency and accessibility through mobile data, the latter, amid the challenges of the COVID-19 pandemic, creatively utilises outdoor public space, demonstrating adaptability and innovation in the face of unforeseen challenges.

The Byron Bay Farmers Market in New South Wales, Australia, and Tristan da Cunha's sustainable community design are set apart by their new ruralism principles. The focus on sustainable agriculture, community participation, and purposeful design in Byron Bay corresponds with the careful planning observed in Tristan da Cunha, which highlights a harmonious integration of environmental and cultural considerations.

Human-centred design takes centre stage in the Oishii Park project in Kumano, where a meticulous analysis of environmental factors contributes to creating a multifunctional public space. This focus on the human experience, combined with a community-centred approach, results in a space that not only serves practical needs but also enriches the lives of residents. This initiative also showcases the need for quick adaptability in providing public open spaces in remote areas, too – it was a direct echo of how people's needs changed during the COVID-19 pandemic.

The convergence of the SDGs in projects such as Tilonia's Barefoot College Solar Electrification initiative and the New Orleans post-Hurricane Katrina recovery efforts is noteworthy. Both cases demonstrate that aligning projects with global sustainability objectives not only addresses specific local needs, such as mitigating energy poverty and ensuring infrastructure resilience, but also contributes to broader societal goals. At the same time, it points out the relevance of global strategic directions for developing local resources in remote areas.

The selected case studies are an illustration and offer a comparative lens through which we can discern patterns and best practices. They emphasise the interplay between global goals and local needs, the transformative potential of community engagement, and the role of technology and innovation in shaping the future of public spaces in remote areas. This nuanced understanding is vital for spatial planners and designers seeking to navigate the complexities of co-designing functional public spaces and is deeply embedded in the fabric of the global diversity of places and communities.

Conclusions

The global case studies in participatory co-design of public spaces underscore a universal observation – community engagement is pivotal. From transformative initiatives to resilient responses and innovative adaptability, empowered communities shape vibrant spaces in remote areas. The cases also illuminate the constant interchange between global goals and trends on one hand and local realities on the other, emphasising the pivotal role of community engagement, innovation, and cultural preservation in shaping the future of public spaces in remote areas. In simple terms, these lessons are a guide for spatial planners and designers working in remote areas globally; they offer guidance on navigating the intricate process of crafting spaces that authentically mirror and enhance the diverse fabric of local communities across the globe.

Table 1: The global perspectives of co-designing remote public open spaces.

Themes	Actors	Engagement of Community	Public Space Typologies/ Improvements
Participatory design	Local communities, architects, designers, residents	Actively involves residents in design charrettes, community meetings, workshops	Improved infrastructure, squares, parks, community centres
Sustainable development goals	NGOs, nonprofit organisations, local governments, communities	Aligning projects with SDGs, driving transformative change (e.g. in addressing energy poverty)	Electrification of public spaces, community centres, schools
Smart cities and digital	Innovation Technology companies, universities, government agencies, residents	Utilises mobile devices and data from residents to map daily life patterns, needs	Improved transport efficiency, increased accessibility
New ruralism	Community organisers, local farmers	Public meetings, workshops, design events	Farmers' markets, sustainable community centres
Place-based approaches	Planners, architects, local communities	Focuses on functions, development issues and qualitative assessment aligned with community needs	Contextualised public spaces, well thought-out community areas
Resilience theory	Government bodies, nonprofit organisations, community groups and university students	Engages stakeholders and community groups in decision-making for more robust places and communities	Rehabilitation efforts in parks, waterfronts, community centres
Cultural sustainability	International organisations (e.g. UNESCO), government agencies, local experts, craftsmen	Involves the community through workshops and meetings to preserve traditional building crafts	Redesigned historic public squares, marketplaces
Human-centred design	Designers, residents, students/university	Considers human scale and needs and collaborates with residents in design process	Multifunctional public spaces

Acknowledgments

In addition to SMOTIES' support, this contribution was also made possible by the Slovenian Research Agency (Research Core Funding No. P50100) and COST Action 18204 Dynamics of Placemaking and Digitization in Europe's Cities.

References

Adams, J. (2002). The real food revolution: A snapshot of the Australian farmers' market movement, Australian Farmers Market Association (AFMA), inaugural conference proceedings, 21–23 November, Bathurst.

Andersson, C. (2021). Public space and the new urban agenda. In *Public Space Reader* (pp. 420–425). Routledge.

Aqakaba, A. (2010). Reconstruction in Wadi Mazab: Between the imperative of expansion and the prioritization of the preservation of urban heritage. Conference proceedings: Technology and sustainability in urbanization, College of Architecture and Planning, King Saud University.

ArchDaily (2016). Brock Carmichael Architects wins competition to transform the world's most remote inhabited island, accessible at https://www.archdaily.com/796277/brock-carmichael-architects-wins-competition-to-transform-the-worlds-most-remote-inhabited-island

ArchDaily (n.d). Oishii Park / td-Atelier., accessible at https://www.archdaily.com/993776/oishii-park-td-atelier

Banyan Tree (2022). Episode 4 – Helena Norberg-Hodge. On 25 Jan 2024, accessible at https://www.banyantree.com/article/episode-4-helena-norberg-hodge.

Barefoot College (2019). Solar solutions, Barefoot College International.

Barraket, J., McKinnon, K., & Brennan-Horley, C. (2022). 09. Regional and geographical aspects of social innovation. Enabling the change! Social innovation and enterprises for a better future, 231.

BBC Bitesize (2008). Improving the favelas – Management of recent urban change in a developing world city.

Carr, S., Francis, M., Rivlin, L. G., & Stone, A. M. (1992). *Public Space*. Cambridge University Press.

Civic Data Design Lab (MIT) and the School of Computing and Informatics (University of Nairobi), Digital Matatus. (2015).

Cumming, G. S., Allen, C. R., Ban, N. C., Biggs, D., Biggs, H. C., Cumming, D. H. M., de Vos, A., Epstein, G., Etienne, M., Maciejewski, K., Mathevet, R., Moore, C., Nenadovic, M., & Schoon, M. (2015). Understanding protected area resilience: a multi-scale, social-ecological approach. *Ecological Applications, 25*(2), 299–319.

Directorate of Tourism and Traditional Industries of Ghardaia State (1996). Tourist monographs and handicrafts of Ghardaia state. On 25 Jan 2024, accessible at https://ghardaia.mta.gov.dz/en/craftsmans-guide/

Gehl, J. (2010). *Cities for People*. Island Press.

Gorenflo, L. J., Romaine, S., Mittermeier, R. A., & Walker-Painemilla, K. (2012). Co-occurrence of linguistic and biological diversity in biodiversity hotspots and high biodiversity wilderness areas. *Proceedings of the National Academy of Sciences, 109(*21), 8032–8037.

Jaszczak, A., Žukovskis, J., & Antolak, M. (2017). The role of rural renewal program in planning of the village public spaces: systematic approach. *Management Theory & Studies for Rural Business & Infrastructure Development, 39*(4).

Johannessen, M., Goldweit-Denton, D. (2020). The green dot effect: neighborhood recovery after Hurricane Katrina. Conflict Urbanism seminar. On 25 Jan 2024 accessible at centerforspatialresearch.github.io.

John, V. (2003). *Byron Farmers Market: A Case Study of Local Food Advocacy.*

Kates, R. W., Colten, C. E., Laska, S., & Leatherman, S. P. (2006). Reconstruction of New Orleans after Hurricane Katrina: A research perspective. *Proceedings of the National Academy of Sciences, 103*(40), 14653–14660.

Lozano, R., Lukman, R., Lozano, F. J., Huisingh, D., & Lambrechts, W. (2013). Declarations for sustainability in higher education: becoming better leaders, through addressing the university system. *Journal of Cleaner Production, 48*, 101–9.

Massachusetts Institute of Technology (2001). Favela-Bairro Project, Brazil. On 24 Jan 2024 accessible at mit.edu.

Micek, M., & Staszewska, S. (2019). Urban and rural public spaces: Development issues and qualitative assessment. *Bulletin of Geography. Socio-economic Series*, (45), 759–3.

Ministry of New and Renewable Energy (2019). Barefoot College, Tilonia. Barefoot College International.

Mooool (2022). Oishii Park by td-Atelier.

Moughtin, C., & Cuesta, A. G. (2003). *Urban Design: Street and Square.* Architectural Press.

Nikšič, M., Goršič, N. (Eds). *SMOTIES: Creative Works in Small and Remote Places: European Best Practices Exploration* (2022). Ljubljana: Urban Planning Institute of the Republic of Slovenia (UIRS). Available at: http://www.uirs.si/pub/smoties_creative_works_in_small_and_remote_places.pdf

Place North West (2016). Brock Carmichael to redevelop loneliest island on planet.

Radford, D. (2017). Space, place and identity: Intercultural encounters, affect and belonging in rural Australian spaces. *Journal of Intercultural Studies, 38*(5), 495–513.

Reed, M. S. (2008). Stakeholder participation for environmental management: A literature review. *Biological conservation, 141*(10), 2417–2431.

Sanders, E. B.-N., & Stappers, P. J. (2008). Co-creation and the new landscapes of design. *CoDesign, 4*(1), 51–8.

Stake, R. E. (1995). *The Art of Case Study Research*. Sage.

Unanue, M. G. (2016). Ensinando fora do centro: As referências no ensino de introdução à concepção em arquitetura e suas possibilidades para uma pedagogia do projeto no contexto pericêntrico. Universidade Federal do Rio de Janeiro, RJ, Brazil.

Tristan da Cunha (2016). Development and Public Works: RIBA Tristan da Cunha Design Competition 2015–2016. On 24 Jan 2024 accessible at tristandc.com.

Veitch, J., Salmon, J., Ball, K., Crawford, D., & Timperio, A. (2013). Do features of public open spaces vary between urban and rural areas?. *Preventive Medicine, 56*(2), 107–111.

Yin, R. K. (2018). *Case Study Research and Applications* (Vol. 6). Thousand Oaks, CA: Sage.

Zanati, D. (2018). Urban development in the heritage cities, Wadi Mazab. *KnE Engineering, 3*(4), 405–424.

4. Challenges in Working in Remote Places: Measuring Social Impact

Annalinda De Rosa
Researcher, Department of Design, Politecnico di Milano [IT]

Valentina Auricchio
Associate professor, Department of Design, Politecnico di Milano [IT]

Frank van Hasselt Chief Executive of Clear Village Trustee Limited, London [UK]

Beatriz Bonilla Berrocal
PhD candidate, Department of Design, Politecnico di Milano [IT]

The SMOTIES project is part of a broader debate that seeks to challenge current trends through academic research and practice to understand how design can improve social innovation. Design for social innovation is a field of investigation that is constantly evolving, creating knowledge that emerges in the dialogue between reflective practitioners and researchers who aim to define the processes, methods, and tools needed for social change, and measure the social change achieved. In this chapter, the design concept for social innovation will be linked to impact and the measurement of social change. The introduction explores a broader understanding of the topic, underlining the gaps in defining specific impact assessment methodologies in the design field. These gaps have been addressed in the SMOTIES project through co-design sessions with partners and residents involved in developing creative works in small and remote places in Europe. This chapter will examine the work done throughout the project, while presenting new possibilities for further reflection.

Measuring social impact in public space projects: a design perspective in European contexts

Innovations have long been seen as essential drivers for advancement and development, and primarily accepted as a positive good in the framework of human technoscientific progress, as opposed to stagnation and resistance to change (Suchman & Bishop, 2000). Although the focus has predominantly been on economic and technological innovations, a shift in perspective has emerged over the years, leading to a more comprehensive view of innovation, its sustainability – environmental, social, and economic – and, specifically, social innovation and its impact. Social innovation has become a key focus and one of the integral components of the innovation ecosystem at various levels (Murray et al., 2010; Terstriep et al., 2021; Manzini, 2015), including local, regional, national, and supranational levels (Kleverbeck et al., 2019). Accordingly, its developmental process entails change within complex systems, often multidimensional and uncertain, and involves aspects not easily captured or mapped through conventional approaches. This change requires long-term, responsible investment to enhance how social relations transform and grow, are interwoven into the socio-environmental fabric, and are embedded in processes of situated relationality (Mouffe, 2000; Rooke, 2013; Tsing, 2015; Di Salvo, 2015; Akama et al., 2019; Huybrechts et al., 2021).

Social innovation must be evaluated to understand the effectiveness and quantify the estimated value of related initiatives in addressing societal challenges and improving the well-being of communities (Krlev, Bund & Mildenberger, 2014) However, despite its relevance, insufficient data and measurement approaches to social innovation are among the primary obstacles practitioners face when supporting and evaluating projects (Krlev et al., 2014). While there are existing frameworks and methods for measuring impact in various sectors, such as economic or environmental, measuring social impact poses unique challenges. Unlike other forms of impact, social impact encompasses a wide range of subjective and intangible factors that are difficult to quantify and standardise. Measuring social impact, which originated in a positivist approach, narrowly defines social innovation as a product or service instead of a process (Antadze & Westley, 2012). The evaluation questions, range of impacts and values considered, and assessment methods used within this established paradigm are limited compared with what is necessary to fully capture all impacts when considering social innovation as a process involving change within complex systems. However, this broader understanding of social innovation has the potential to bring significant social change by contributing to extensive and enduring change in social relations, communities, and behaviours. Measuring and assessing the impact of social innovation initiatives is often conducted informally and qualitatively, if at all. Given the complexity of the evaluation process, it is essential to recognise that there are various evaluation criteria applicable to social innovation. Stakeholders have different concerns, interests, and evaluation requirements, which evolve throughout the stages of social innovation and within various contexts (Antadze & Westley, 2012). The aspects evaluated regarding impacts and targets vary across evaluative criteria, as would the extent to which impacts are potentially felt. Evaluation purposes and criteria call for diverse types of evaluation, evaluation approaches, methods, and tools. The criteria would also change depending on the social innovation, stage of the social innovation process, and implementation environment. Different evaluation approaches would also be necessary in the case of different interpretations and views on social innovation, particularly regarding whether it is primarily characterised by tangible outcomes, such as products, services, and activities, or the process by which it unfolds. This diversity means that there is a need for evaluations to be designed and implemented in a way that suits the purpose and context, instead of being standardised, which is usually proposed by existing frameworks. Most tools commonly employed in social impact measurement were not explicitly created to assess social impact (Alex et al., 2019). Instead, they are rooted in conventional economic techniques and financial accounting, reflecting a stronger connection with perspectives and requirements from the field of social finance rather than from organisations striving to enhance or monitor their activities' effectiveness. Economic-based tools are not inherently designed to capture social impact and frequently fall short of representing these impacts' full value and complexity.

In the design field, there is an increasing recognition of the importance of accurately evaluating the impact of interventions and subsequently communicating these results (European Commission, 2013; Westcott et al., 2013; Drew, 2017; Björklund et al., 2018). Evaluation has now been established as a vital component in the design process, enabling practitioners to assess the effectiveness of their interventions and make well-informed decisions for future projects. Design-led approaches have long been prominent in driving innovation, especially in addressing intricate business and societal issues (Buchanan & Margolin, 1995). Nevertheless, research is still being done regarding how to assess innovation, particularly social innovation. A design approach to measuring social impact is especially valuable owing to its emphasis on understanding human behaviour, user experience, and the needs and aspirations of the context of the study, as well as considering the contextual factors that could influence innovation processes (Foglieni & Villari, 2015; Liedtka, 2017; Foglieni et al., 2018). As a direct result, a design approach is essential in design for social innovation. These practices are not only aimed at empowering communities with effective, long-lasting, scalable, and replicable solutions but also at challenging and reshaping the public realm, stimulating the involvement of citizens and other local stakeholders, including associations, administrators, and policymakers, in the democratic discourse about the public sphere. Integrating design principles into the social innovation assessment can enhance the process, making it more user-centric and context-sensitive (Yu & Sangiorgi, 2018), leading to a deeper understanding of the impact and effectiveness of initiatives, ultimately guiding the development of more responsible and impactful strategies. Incorporating design-centric methods into the evaluation of social innovation impacts can improve our understanding of how these endeavours tackle societal issues and advance socially responsible behaviours.

In the context of public space projects, where social impact is a primary concern, the SMOTIES project addressed the evaluation of support processes for the regeneration of meaningful social settings from a methodological perspective, which examined how reflecting on impacts at an earlier stage in the project can greatly inspire creativity instead of limiting it, contrary to what is usually thought. In this article, we will explore impact and impact indicators when remote places and their social dynamics are regenerated and how designers and creativity can play a role in rethinking the very concept of impact evaluation.

Small and remote places and the social impact of cultural and creative projects

Measuring the impact of cultural and creative innovations on people, their well-being, and social cohesion is a core challenge when acknowledging the role of culture and creativity as enablers of sustainable development. Creativity and cultural expressions can contribute to well-being, participation as an active member of society, shared values, social inclusion, and the development of intercultural dialogues, as well as a free, pluralistic, and diverse media environment (European Parliament and Council of the European Union, 2021).

In SMOTIES, creativity has been the key driver for social change in 10 small and remote places in Europe. The kinds of social innovations documented throughout the project demonstrate that new approaches are needed to go beyond collecting only economic and quantitative evidence. This challenge has been common to other recent research programmes for better advocating for culture and creativity in Europe, in an effort to address the United Nations Sustainable Development Goals (SDGs) and achieve the European Green Deal and New European Bauhaus goals. In 2019, the European Commission published the Cultural and Creative Cities Monitor as a tool to support cities in shaping their policies and measuring the impact of culture (Montalto, 2019; 2023; Montalto et al., 2023). It aimed to create a methodology to show how culture plays a role in contributing to implementing the UN SDGs. Since SMOTIES focused on small towns and the impact that cultural and creative projects could have on their future development, the Cultural and Creative Cities Monitor was considered a starting point for reflecting on the type of impact that could be measured when looking at the cultural and creative performance of cities, based on UNESCO's Thematic Indicators for Culture in the 2030 Agenda.

Although it is commonly known that culture and creativity play an essential role in our changing societies, how we measure their impact is less clear. When we refer to the creation of new jobs or the establishment of cultural institutions (such as museums), a quantitative approach could work; but when our impact has to do with bringing people closer together, building a sense of community and belonging, and encouraging citizens to be active members of society, we may need to rethink our methods.

The Cultural and Creative Cities Monitor allows a better understanding of what it means to measure change in a city and evaluate how culture can make cities more attractive and thus strengthen cohesion and participatory development. In the tool, cities were divided into different scales according to their population and geographical size (L-large, M-medium, and S-small);

however, when applying this model to the small and remote places identified in SMOTIES, numbers were very low, and most indicators had a baseline of zero. Hence, there was a need to better understand how such a framework could support the project and what needed to change to be applied to an extra small, or XS, city.

Throughout the project, the impact assessment process was developed in co-design sessions in tandem with brainstorming specific creative interventions. Understanding how impact could be achieved and measured also influenced the ideation phases, creating a constant link between ideas and impact. Thus, impact was not perceived as something that needed to be measured after the project; instead, the creation of impact pathways became an integral part of the creative process. The visions and scenarios developed to frame changes in small and remote places (Auricchio et al., 2023) have been reinforced and informed by the social impacts that each SMOTIES partner defined in conversations with the relevant local community. The project scenarios were therefore interpreted based on the specific place the project was being carried out in, enhancing the design process to provide a better understanding of the impact of the situated creative intervention, which was tailored to a specific remote community.

Because of the lack of specific frameworks, during the SMOTIES project we developed a step-by-step process that allowed the partners to, first, understand what impact pathways are and, second, how to introduce and involve the local communities in their ideation processes. A final reflection on how these interventions have influenced the communities, their relationships and agency in the territory reveals how the measurement of impact is not only related to the final design of creative works in public spaces but also in the participative process itself, allowing the community to be actively involved in giving space to the future of the environment they live in.

SMOTIES: creating a methodology to define impact pathways

The remote places in which SMOTIES has operated offered different situated contexts. To identify the challenges related to measuring social impact in each remote place, semi-structured interviews involving representatives of all 10 SMOTIES partners were planned. In these interviews, partners were asked to list and explain the most significant challenges they had faced in their impact assessment work, and to answer two additional questions pertaining to each challenge: (i) to rate the challenge's significance on a scale from 1–5, with 1 representing "not significant at all" and 5 representing "extremely significant"; and (ii) to assess whether the challenge had been more significant in a small and remote place than it would have been in a node of creativity.

In total, the interviewees listed 10 challenges, two of which were mentioned by only one interviewee, while there was overlap in the other eight challenges the interviewees identified. The challenges were broken down into two clusters. Five challenges were identified as place-specific (i.e., more significant in a small remote place than they would have been in a node of creativity), while the remaining five challenges were more general (i.e., not more significant in a small remote place than they would have been in a node of creativity).

Table 1 opposite lists the five general challenges identified by the SMOTIES partners. Since many partners had limited experience in impact assessment before the project, it is not surprising that understanding impact measurement was a significant challenge. As one interviewee said, "Wherever you are and whatever you're doing, you have to know what you're doing. However, it took our team some time to understand what the impact of our project could be and how we could measure it." Another challenge was the lack of standardised metrics, which in some instances hindered partners from selecting appropriate indicators for their targeted impacts.

The open-ended nature of the participatory process adopted by SMOTIES also posed a challenge. One person explained: "We've been working very experimental and open-ended, making it hard to decide on an appropriate measurement approach. If you work with a community and take on board what they find interesting and relevant, then your project may change direction, and you may end up in a different place than you'd expected. And what you initially wanted to measure may not be relevant any more." Internal delays exacerbated this challenge for one of the partners, which impeded the roll-out of a digital tool intended to support the impact measurement process.

The most frequently cited challenge, mentioned by more than half of the SMOTIES partners, was the difficulty of measuring non-quantitative aspects. One interviewee commented: "In a place like ours, which is very small and remote, we must capture all the impact we can. But predicting when things can be assessed is challenging, as meetings

Table 1: General impact assessment challenges identified by SMOTIES partners, the number of partners affected by these challenges, and the average significance ascribed to them on a scale of 1 ("not significant at all") to 5 ("extremely significant") in a sample (i.e. 18)

General challenges	Partners affected	Average significance
Internal delays	1	3.00
Lack of standardised metrics	2	3.00
Open-ended nature of the participatory process	2	3.75
Understanding impact measurement	3	4.33
Measuring non-quantitative aspects	6	3.25

Table 2: Place-specific impact assessment challenges identified by SMOTIES partners, the number of partners affected by these challenges, and the average significance ascribed to them on a scale of 1 ("not significant at all") to 5 ("extremely significant")

Place-specific challenges	Partners affected	Average significance
Geographical remoteness	1	5.00
Limited data availability	2	4.50
Cultural differences	3	3.33
Gaining trust from the local community	4	3.13
Engaging diverse stakeholders	5	3.50

often happen organically. And even if they are planned, it can be difficult to assess things in a non-intrusive way." Another person expressed dissatisfaction with the results obtained using standard measurement tools: "We have mostly used interviews and questionnaires to gather qualitative data, but the replies are often predictable. People will say, 'Yes, things are better now, the community has a stronger identity, and we are prouder of the village. We even hosted a panel designed by designers and artists, but the results were similar.' People said, 'Yes, we know more about the valley's heritage now, and we will also travel by bike instead of by car.' But will they really? We have found that people are willing to engage with us and value projects like SMOTIES, but whether there will be any changes in their everyday lives is another matter. Maybe the long-term impact of our intervention will only become clear in five or ten years."

Several partners developed their own creative approaches to gathering qualitative data, but this could prove challenging, too. One interviewee recounted: "We decided to use postcards to assess the impact of SMOTIES events on the community. We designed beautiful postcards and asked people to write about how the village has changed. We even made a special post-box that people could put the cards in. But it didn't work. People felt intimidated. They thought, 'Who do I have to write to? And what am I supposed to write?' Many children thought they were supposed to write postcards to Santa Claus. Other children just played with the postcards; one had a chicken on it, and a girl kept playing with the chicken. There were a lot of things that went wrong, which we as a project team hadn't predicted. Often, people only tell positive stories when they hear about creative interventions. But reflecting on things that don't go well is also important."

Table 2 above lists five challenges identified by the partners as more significant in a small and remote place than they would have been in a node of creativity. Perhaps surprisingly, the geographical remoteness of the places in the SMOTIES network was not a significant challenge. It was only mentioned by one interviewee, who pointed out that the challenge was, in fact, primarily related to creating impact rather than measuring it.

A more critical challenge the partners faced was limited data availability, primarily due to the low number of local inhabitants who had contributed to the impact measurement process. Half of the interviewees reported that, with engaging diverse stakeholders being a challenge, it was difficult to collect sufficient data. As one person explained: "There are not that many people that engage with our project. And it's often the same people. We work with some associations, with schoolchildren, with the local authorities, but it's difficult to capture the voices of other village residents." This sentiment was echoed by another interviewee, who said: "We have a core group that is incredibly engaged, but out of the 600 people living in the village, there are many whom we haven't been able to reach. We have very little data on people between the ages of 18 and 35, and we have struggled to engage men over the age of 50."

Several partners believed that the issue of limited engagement was closely linked to the challenge of gaining trust from the local community. One interviewee emphasised the crucial importance of trust: "Trust is incredibly important for the kind of work we have been doing, but it takes time to build." Another person pointed out: "It's always difficult to come in as an outsider with what may be perceived as a 'saviour project'." Moreover, EU-critical views occasionally exacerbated the situation in some small remote places. As one person explained: "If you tell people you're working on an EU project, half of them will like it and the other half won't." There was disagreement on whether it was more difficult to gain trust in a small remote place than it would have been in a node of creativity. One person said that "people in small remote places sometimes have a stronger sense of ownership of the place", while another argued that there was no difference: "I don't think it's related to the remoteness of a community. It has to do with us being external. If we were working in a city, we would be working with a community anyway, and we would be from the European Union anyway."

Finally, several partners highlighted the challenge of navigating cultural differences between small and remote places and nodes of creativity. As one interviewee said: "I don't think we realised what it implies to live in a small remote place, to grow up and live in such a place, and what it means in terms of relationships with people from the city." Another person described how these cultural differences prompted the project team to reassess their entire research approach, not only concerning impact but also more generally: "We knew that working in a small remote place would be different from working in a city, but we're realising now how much these differences are changing some of our key concepts. What does it mean to innovate? What does it mean to transform? Our references for these concepts are places like New York or Milan. But we're reflecting now that places that have gone through slower evolutions don't need to follow the same trajectories as cities. Maybe we can learn from small remote places or test other ways of doing things."

The role of participatory designers in stimulating engagement in the local political discourse

The impact analysis technique was designed carefully considering the "impact pathways" or "pathway to impact" concept, as stated in the Horizon Europe application materials. These pathways represent the logical processes that led to attaining the expected project impacts over time. A pathway incorporates the project's outputs and how they will be distributed, used, and communicated. It plays a role in achieving the anticipated results within the project and, eventually, in generating broader scientific, economic, and societal implications. It is a time-sensitive representation that captures the intricate non-linear structure of research and innovation activities, incorporating quantitative and qualitative approaches and instruments. Using this linear model allowed us to link the development of long-term scenarios (Auricchio et al., 2023) – meant to drive emerging project areas and potential design trajectories – with an understanding of the complex transition. Undoubtedly, envisioning future change is a source of inspiration for any research project. However, it is crucial that any complex transition – particularly those beyond the project's scope – can initially be explained, understood, and accepted, and subsequently be observable and impactful to all relevant stakeholders to facilitate meaningful change (Spallazzo & De Rosa, 2022). During the development of the SMOTIES project, it turned out that engaging territories with untapped potential but without effective backing for regeneration projects can lead to unforeseen impacts much more quickly. The sheer existence of the project and the 'first citizen' engagement activities had a significant effect in stimulating or endorsing new ideas outside the project. The fact that co-design processes could spark debates is indeed one of the most significant outcomes that may be achieved through design for social innovation practices; we were surprised when the effects of design for social innovation went beyond the scope of the participatory activities. The research teams found that initiating a conversation about public places and economic resources led to the re-emergence of underlying debates and increased citizen agency and proactivity. Assessing the extent to which the SMOTIES actions influenced this proactivity was challenging. In this scenario, the unique bond formed between the SMOTIES teams, and the local communities played a vital role. Initially, the distance between them was seen as a barrier to building trust and a sense of ownership among the locals. However, the teams' external perspective proved beneficial by offering unbiased input to the community. This prevented individual stakeholders from manipulating the project to serve their own economic and political agendas. We contend that this did not hinder the locals from taking on the responsibility to drive the revitalisation of their communities but fostered a strong sense of active citizenship among them. The current population decrease in small and remote regions has created an opportunity to develop a new type of local leadership: innovative individuals are assuming leadership roles, collaboratively shaping their communities' future, and actively engaging in transforming the local community. This enabled remote communities to take charge of their own development, going beyond mere participation to become self-governing entities. Citizens are forming new cultural associations; existing associations are expanding their partnerships with consultancy studies to apply for regional funding for the development of projects; and initiatives are being developed with a view to greater community involvement. Designers have successfully established a secure environment where all voices may freely express themselves democratically (Puig de la Bellacasa, 2017), fostering a shared platform for a more inclusive and collaborative approach. The design process emerged as a political and placed act that contributed to the entanglements' complexity of the issues at stake and brought to the fore an agonistic perspective (Hillgren et al., 2016; Mouffe, 2013; DiSalvo, 2010) on engaging in political discourse.

As one of the partners of the project stated in the interviews mentioned above, perhaps the impacts of the SMOTIES project will be measurable only in five or ten years from now, and what we are looking at today, when some projects are being finalised, are first reflections on outputs and outcomes and how we gave shape to impact pathways, which were context-based and driven by scenario building processes. In thinking about how these remote places have allowed us to paint a picture of the future and our desired social change, we know that the social long-term impact will need time to be realised.

Working on these projects allowed us to understand how that foresight enhances impact measurement and addresses the relevant challenges. The insights that emerged when working on impacts, impact indicators and how designers and creativity play a role in rethinking the very concept of impact evaluation in remote settings, can be summarised in the following points:

- Design for social innovation should be considered as a process involving change within complex systems.
- Impact pathways should become an integral part of the creative process, as understanding how impact can be measured will influence ideation by bridging the gap between ideas and impact. Reflecting on impacts at an earlier stage of the project can greatly inspire creativity, instead of limit it.
- Design principles applied to social innovation assessment can enhance the process to be more user-centric and context-sensitive. Human behaviour and user experience perspectives on impact pathways could change how we measure a project's success; co-design processes could spark debates, which are significant outcomes achieved through design for social innovation practices.
- Empowering communities with effective, long-lasting, scalable, and replicable solutions, while challenging and reshaping public spaces, can enhance their involvement in the democratic discourse about the public sphere, so that there is no longer simply participation but self-government.

References

Akama, Y., Hagen, P., & Whaanga-Schollum, D. (2019). Problematizing replicable design to practice respectful, reciprocal, and relational co-designing with indigenous people. *Design and Culture, 11*(1), 59–84. https://doi.org/10.1080/17547075.2019.1571306

Antadze, N., & Westley, F. (2012). Impact metrics for social innovation: Barriers or bridges to radical change? *Journal of Social Entrepreneurship, 3*(2), 133–150. https://doi.org/10.1080/19420676.2012.726005

Auricchio, V., De Rosa, A., & Monna, V. (2023). SMOTIES: Scenario building for creative solutions in remote places. In C. Cipolla, C. Mont'Alvão, L. Farias, & M. Quaresma (Eds), *ServDes.2023 Entanglements & Flows Conference: Service Encounters and Meanings. Conference Proceedings* (pp. 161–183). Linkoping University Electronic Press. https://doi.org/10.3384/ecp203008

Björklund, T., Hannukainen, P., & Manninen, T. (2018). Measuring the impact of design, service design and design thinking in organizations on different maturity levels. In Service Design Proof of Concept. *Proceedings of the ServDes.2018 Conference.* Linköping: Linköping University Electronic Press.

Buchanan, R., & Margolin, V. (1995). *Discovering Design: Explorations in Design Studies.* University of Chicago Press.

DiSalvo, C. (2010). Design, democracy and agonistic pluralism. Proceedings of the Design Research Society Conference, 366–371.

DiSalvo, C. (2015). *Adversarial Design.* MIT Press.

Drew, C. (2017). An Iterative, Experience and Practice-led Approach to Measuring Impact. *Touchpoint Journal of Service Design, 9*(2), 222–225.

European Commission (2013). Implementing an Action Plan for Design-Driven Innovation. Retrieved from: http://ec.europa.eu/DocsRoom/documents/13203/attachments/1/translations/en/renditi ons/native. European Parliament and Council of the European Union (2021). Regulation of the European Parliament and of the Council establishing the Creative Europe programme (2021 to 2027) and repealing Regulation (EU) No 1295/2013

Foglieni, F., & Villari, B. (2015). Towards a service evaluation culture. A contemporary issue from social sciences to service design. Proceedings of the Cumulus Milan 2015 Conference – *The Virtuous Circle. Design Culture and Experimentation.*

Foglieni, F., Villari, B., & Maffei, S. (2018). *Designing Better Services. A Strategic Approach from Design to Evaluation.* Springer Cham. https://link.springer.com/book/10.1007/978-3-319-63179-0

Kleverbeck, M., Krlev, G., Mildenberger, G., Strambach, S., Thurmann, J.-F., Terstriep, J., & Wloka, L. (2019). Indicators for Measuring Social Innovation. In *Atlas of Social Innovation.*

Krlev, G., Bund, E., & Mildenberger, G. (2014). Measuring what matters: Indicators of social innovativeness on the national level. *Information Systems Management, 31*(3), 200–224.

Hillgren, P.-A., Seravalli, A., & Eriksen, M. A. (2016). Counter-hegemonic practices; dynamic interplay between agonism, commoning and strategic design. *Strategic Design Research Journal, 9(*2), 89–99.

Huybrechts, L., Devisch, O., & Tassinari, V. (2021). Beyond polarisation: reimagining communities through the imperfect act of ontologising. *CoDesign, 18*(1), 637–7.

Liedtka, J. (2017). Evaluating the impact of design thinking in action. *Academy of Management Proceedings, 2017*(1), 10264. https://doi.org/10.5465/AMBPP.2017.177

Manzini, E. (2015). *Design, When Everybody Designs: An Introduction to Design for Social Innovation.* MIT Press.

Montalto, V., Moura, C. J. T., Langedijk, S., & Saisana, M. (2019). Culture counts: An empirical approach to measure the cultural and creative vitality of European cities. *Cities, 89*, 1671–85.

Montalto, V. (2023). Introducing the cultural and creative cities monitor 2019. Catania, la città antica e quella del futuro: archeologia, topografia, urbanistica per la riqualificazione dello spazio urbano. *Studia archaeologica, 257*, 1011–19.

Montalto, V., Alberti, V., Panella, F., & Sacco, P. L. (2023). Are cultural cities always creative? An empirical analysis of culture-led development in 190 European cities. *Habitat International, 132*, 102739. https://doi.org/10.1016/j.habitatint.2022.102739

Mouffe, C. (2000). *The Democratic Paradox.* Verso.

Mouffe, C. (2013). *Agonistics: Thinking the World Politically.* Verso Books.

Murray, R., Caulier-Grice, J., & Mulgan, G. (2010). *The Open Book of Social Innovation.* NESTA, London.

Nicholls, A., Von Jacobi, N., Chiappero-Martinetti, E., Mildenberger, G. (2019). *The Impact of Social Innovation.* https://doi.org/10.1093/oso/9780198830511.003.0015

Puig de la Bellacasa, M. P. (2017). *Matters of Care: Speculative Ethics in More than Human Worlds.* University of Minnesota Press.

Rehfeld, D., Terstriep, J., Welschhoff, J., & Alijani, S. (2015). Comparative Report on Social Innovation Framework. Deliverable D1.1 of the Project "Boosting the Impact of SI in Europe through Economic Underpinnings" (SIMPACT), European Commission – 7th Framework Programme, Brussels: European Commission, DG Research & Innovation.

Rooke, A. (2013). Curating community? The relational and agonistic value of participatory arts in superdiverse localities.

Spallazzo, D., & De Rosa, A. (2022). The projects' outcomes: The analysis of the results in the medium-term. In F. Rizzo (Ed.), *Seven Years of Design Research at Politecnico di Milano.* Analysis of the funded research projects (pp. 103–132). FrancoAngeli Design International.

Suchman, L., & Bishop, L. (2010). Problematizing innovation as a critical project. *Technology Analysis & Strategic Management, 12*(3), 327–333.

Terstriep, J., Krlev, G., Mildenberger, G., Strambach, S., Thurmann, J.-F., and Wloka, L.-F. (2021). Measuring social innovation. In J. Howaldt, C. Kaletka, & A. Schröder (Eds), *A Research Agenda for Social Innovation* (Elgar Research Agendas). Edward Elgar Publishing. https://doi.org/10.4337/9781789909357.00024

Tsing, A. (2015). *The Mushroom at the End of the World: On the Possibility of Life in Capitalist Ruins.* Princeton University Press.

Westcott, M., Sato, S., Mrazek, D., Wallace, R., Vanka, S., Bilson, C., & Hardin, D. (2013). The DMI design value scorecard: A new design measurement and management model. *Design Management Review, 23*(4), 101–106.

Yu, E., & Sangiorgi, D. (2018). Service Design as an Approach to Implement the Value Cocreation Perspective in New Service Development. *Journal of Service Research, 21*(1), 40–58.

5. How SMOTIES Aims to Impact Remote Places. Creative Works in Public Spaces

Astrid Lelarge
Historian of urban planning,
Alternance Architecture
and Urban Planning,
and assistant professor,
Faculty of Planning
and Design, Agricultural
University of Iceland [IS]

The European Union Human Cities/SMOTIES initiative brought together 10 public institutions, design centres, national associations, creative agencies, and research centres to design a participatory project for public spaces in small remote places. This paper focuses on creative works carried out using the SMOTIES methodology and the objectives, or impacts, in remote places.

Working in remote places

The project partners selected one or more sites in a given region, which could vary in size and location, from hamlets in mountains or valleys, to villages and small towns in rural areas or in the vicinity of cities. This variety reflects how remote places are difficult to define in physical terms (Ardener, 2012). Geography identifies two components of the definition. The first dimension is relative, defining remote places as places experienced and perceived as distant in space and time. A remote place is "a distant site with reference to where the one person positing such a qualification is located", says Bocco (2016, p. 178). For Gillis (2001), remote places have become highly appealing due to space-time compression. Remote places have piqued people's interest by allowing them to travel back in time to visit "preserved" environments and have attracted a growing number of people in Europe for short and long stays in recent years. With remote working on the rise, remote places have also become potential living spaces for big city people (Barbera et al., 2019). The second geographical dimension is absolute and geometric, defining remote places as locations politically, economically, socially, and culturally remote and *marginalised*, sharing common characteristics with peripheries. According to this perspective, remote places are in a state of cultural survival and are "sparsely populated, with a limited range of economic activity, providing goods to external markets, relying on capital, finance and labor to be granted by urban centers, [...] losing particular populations, young people, retired workers to those centers" (Bocco, 2016, p. 179). European institutions use this perspective to define remote and rural regions (European Union Regional Policy, 2008 and 2011; OECD, 2020a, 2020b).

When working with and for local communities in remote places, being aware of both dimensions and perspectives is important. Because different perspectives imply different expectations. From an outsider's point of view, as is the case for SMOTIES partners, remote places may be marginalised but they are also imaginary places. And remoteness can be positive. From an internal point of view, being described as "remote" can be derogatory (Buttimer, 2015).

In order to address these challenges, a methodology was developed by Politecnico di Milano (Polimi), Alternance, and Clear Village to anchor SMOTIES projects in the local context and values, while orienting them towards the future of remote places in order to explore long-term outcomes (Auricchio et al., 2024). The methodology, which was designed for designers, involves working with local communities to study the local context from a historical and contemporary perspective and establishes five "Windows on the Future", corresponding to issues to be addressed in small and remote places: citizenship and governance, sustainable living, beyond tourism, ageing society, and distributed education. Following this methodology, project proponents and local communities designed projects in their area of expertise spanning several Windows on the Future. When drafting the projects, an impact assessment strategy was done with assistance from the Clear Village team (Van Hasselt & King, 2023) to establish goals (see table 1) and indicators to measure the extent to which objectives would be met. This approach, developed in collaboration with all partners and published in *SMOTIES Toolbox. Design tools for the creative transformation of public spaces in small and remote places* (Auricchio et al., 2024), structured SMOTIES actions.

Creative works and the Windows on the Future

Citizenship and governance

This was the most popular Window on the Future among partners and local communities. All projects were based on active citizen participation, with the main goal of promoting new forms of governance. "How people will participate in community life in the future and how they will be able to shape collective future endeavours" (Auricchio et al., 2024, p. 80) are indeed issues at the heart of the Human Cities initiative, and SMOTIES' methodology promotes public participation from an early stage.

Partners co-designed projects with local communities, specifically active members of the community, known as "local heroes", as well as with associations, public authorities, the wider community, and in some cases, visitors. The objectives of this Window, as defined by partners (Van Hasselt & King, 2023), are to empower the local community through the process of project creation, and specific interventions aiming to improve community spaces, i.e. public spaces.

All partners carried out efforts to empower the local community through projects. Events such as walks, meetings, workshops, and prototyping studios (Human Cities, 2024) were organised alongside the local context study with the objective of identifying assets and challenges in those remote places and the local community's

Table 1: Summary of the impact strategy. Each partner selected several Windows on the Future and defined one or several impacts (Van Hasselt & King, 2023)

Windows on the Future	Partners	Impacts
Citizenship and Governance	AEGEAN, Alternance, Clear Village, Cité du design, EAD, FHJ, Polimi, UIRS, UMA, Zamek Cieszyn	• Increased local engagement • Increased visibility for associations • Increased local pride • Improved local connections • Enhanced sense of community • Improved community space
Sustainable Living	AEGEAN, Cité du design, FHJ, Zamek Cieszyn	• Improved physical connections • Increased appreciation of natural environment and green spaces • Sustainable plan for recreation space • Enhanced interconnections
Beyond Tourism	Alternance, Clear Village, Cité du design, EAD, Polimi, UIRS	• Increased economic activities • Increased economy opportunities • Improved tourism economy • Increased appreciation of local culture and identity • Increased appreciation of existing landmarks • Encourage artistic activities • Improved tourism
Ageing Society	Cité du design, UMA	• Increased intergenerational connection
Distributed Education	Clear Village, Cité du design, Polimi, UIRS	• Improved knowledge exchange • New community narrative

needs and expectations regarding public spaces and public life, identifying potential places for projects, and determining and designing specific types of creative works. The participatory process undertaken by the Urban Planning Institute of the Republic of Slovenia (UIRS) is an interesting case of a bottom-up approach to public space design. In the hills of Medvode, UIRS, local heroes, and the municipality organised thematic walks with residents of three villages, and potential projects were identified following discussions on ecology, landscape, local traditions, and heritage. They revealed people's fondness for orchards, dry walls, fruit dryers, hayracks, and storage houses as part of the cultural rural landscape and heritage, which led the Institute to explore how these places and structures, seen as an integral part of the local identity, could be used for socialising. Workshops and prototyping studios involving locals followed, which gave rise to "soft interventions", particularly in the Pr' Lenart homestead in Belo where the orchard, storage house, and a dry wall were revitalised to "demonstrate the potential of such heritage as vibrant new public spaces" (UIRS, "SMOTIES Prototyping: Fruit dryers, hayracks and storage house", n.d.). Residents had initially said that there was no need to transform existing public spaces, but discussions progressively led them to change their minds, as was the case in the village of Topol pri Medvodah, where the municipality and tourism board hired an architectural office to redesign a parking lot (Niksic, 2024).

Partners brought the community together at events to create projects and/or enhance the social life in public spaces, with the aim of encouraging residents and associations to appropriate the projects, further supporting local initiatives, and increasing the sense of community by exploring how projects could unite people despite differences of opinion. By participating in projects to promote local art and culture, traditions, and history, partners also aimed to change the way people looked at their community, and thus increase local pride.

In terms of empowering the local community by carrying out specific interventions to improve community spaces, goal-oriented changes were made in public spaces, both indoor and outdoor, to enhance their attractiveness and availability to the community and promote public life and quality of life. For example, in Penmachno (Wales), Clear Village charity worked with associations and volunteers to transform what used to be a 16 m² shop and photography studio into a multifunctional community space, known as Oriel Machno or "Machno Gallery" (Clear Village, n.d.). In Joaveski (Estonia), the Estonian Association of Designers (EAD) collaborated with locals to turn an abandoned cardboard housing complex into a space for pop-up studios and art residencies, allowing locals and guests to meet and collaborate (EAD, 2024). And in Oberzeiring (Austria), students from FH Joanneum University (FHJ) designed and built installations to change the Oberzeiringer *Marktplatz*, or Oberzeiringer Market Square, a noisy, busy, dusty, and even dangerous square, which is a thoroughfare for vehicles, into a welcoming pedestrian zone that fosters a dynamic public life (FHJ, 2022, 2023, 2024).

Sustainable living

From co-designing a green recreational zone in Bobrek (Poland) and a new public space at an abandoned bus stop located in the protected natural area of Apano Meria in Syros (Greece), to promoting green mobility in Oberzeiring (Austria) and Dorlay Valley (France), SMOTIES partners and local communities established "creative solutions for sustainable living, emerging economic ecosystems, and alternative business models" (Auricchio et al., 2024, p. 87). Creative works undertaken as part of this Window focused on two objectives: improving mobility and promoting the natural environment (Van Hasselt & King, 2023).

In rural areas with less public transport and high car dependency, projects were designed to promote shared mobility and soft means of transport. A ride-sharing bench was created by design students of the FHJ and installed next to the Oberzeiring marketplace in 2023 (FHJ, 2022). A project was carried out in Dorlay Valley to use an old railway for cycling and walking, thus highlighting industrial heritage. The mapping of and signage on *La Galoche*, the abandoned railway, by the designers Costanza Matteucci and Monika Olszak (2023) resulted from the collaboration between the Mobility Group of the local association Les Ateliers du Dorlay and the design centre Cité du design. It is interesting how mobility and heritage were combined in a single project. Initially, the Mobility Group wanted to focus solely on mobility. But as the railway connected heritage sites, Cité du design supported the idea to make it a "cultural trek" (Eller, 2024).

The importance of developing quality green spaces and preserving nature is at the heart of projects conducted by the design centre Zamek Cieszyn and Department of Product and Systems Design Engineering at the University of the Aegean. These two institutions aimed to raise awareness of environmental issues among local communities and visitors. In Bobrek, where there is a lack of cultural and sports events, a recreational area designed by the architectural office Pronobis Studio was completed. In the village of San Michalis in Apano Meria, a bus stop was transformed into a place of enhanced interconnections between humans and nature (Charoupia, 2024); the design project focused on socialising and the development of flora and fauna (AEGEAN, 2024).

Beyond tourism

In this Window on the Future, partners and local communities explored ways to enhance remote places through a sustainable approach to tourism, combining cultural and economic development. Creative works focused on developing meaningful experiences to facilitate transition "from the concept of tourism (visiting a place as a visitor) to a deeper understanding and exploring the world (visiting a place to blend with the local culture and leave a mark)" (Auricchio et al., 2024, p. 93) to primarily benefit host communities.

Several projects wished to contribute to the development of the tourist activities and, therefore, the local economy. But there weren't just economic advantages. The projects focused on promoting local culture and artistic life in a way that would not simply attract visitors but benefit host communities in several ways (Van Hasselt & King, 2023) – by drawing residents' and visitors' attention to local history, heritage, traditions, art, and environmental beauty, creative works strengthened communities' identity and pride. Such was the case with the *Sögutorgin*, or "historic place", project designed by Alternance Architecture and Urban Planning in Borgarnes, which conducted comprehensive research to identify key but neglected historical public spaces and created a preliminary plan to develop three of them. The project got the municipality and residents involved and highlighted the value of local heritage primarily to locals (Alternance, 2022, 2024, n.d.).

The contribution of public space design, and design in public spaces, to the sustainable regeneration of remote places, formed the basis for the creative efforts carried out in Albugnano by Polimi's Department of Design (De Rosa & Coutsoucos, 2024). The *Citofonare Albugnano* project, meaning "ringing Albugnano's doorbell", highlighted seven strategic public spaces that were connected to each other by informational totems, displaying local history and residents' memories, and provided a place for public postering. The main projects involved transforming two public spaces into recreation areas via temporary efforts, or tactical urbanism, and semi-permanent efforts (Polimi, 2024).

Ageing society

In Sainte-Croix-en-Jarez (France) and in Estreito da Calheta (Madeira), specific projects and activities were developed to promote "the well-being of a community's wise and knowledgeable people", such as the elderly. Consistent with this Window, those projects aimed to foster intercultural and intergenerational dialogue and knowledge exchange to strengthen social cohesion, assuming that "by valuing the older generation's experiences, we enrich our collective understanding and build a foundation for a more informed future" (Auricchio et al., 2024, p. 99).

Two original creative projects, connecting villages and public spaces to memories, were designed with the objective of increasing intergenerational connections (Van Hasselt & King, 2023). To strengthen and pass on local history, the Cité du design co-created a card game known as *Le Jeu des Cartusiens* based on the history of Sainte-Croix-en-Jarez ("Mission", n.d.), and the University of Madeira's Art and Design Department produced a documentary, *Estreito é o tempo*, about the history of the residents of Estreito da Calheta, which was premiered to the public in July 2023 as one of the intergenerational activities organised in the village by the university.

Distributed education

This Window on the Future, dedicated to the development of local cultural and creative knowledge, encouraged partners and communities to explore the emancipatory potential of creative education. Activities envisaged here aimed to support the diversity of cultural expression, encourage access to "smaller and less-popular repertoires" and stimulate local creators (Auricchio et al., 2024, 105).

Initiatives were designed to enhance the creative sector and encourage knowledge exchange between individuals and groups within society, between experts or artists and the public, between experts and artists, and between locals and outsiders (Van Hasselt & King, 2023). This approach was at the heart of the Clear Village project in Penmachno, since Oriel Machno serves as an art gallery for local artists and a community space for craft workshops (Owen, 2024). In 2022, UIRS organised an exhibition in Medvode called *Majhni Kraji. Velike Ideje* (Small places. Big ideas) to raise awareness of the importance of citizen participation in enhancing public spaces, as well as a visit and a workshop for primary school children (Niksic, 2024).

Conclusion

Starting in 2020, the Human Cities/SMOTIES initiative has given rise to several projects stemming from partners' interactions with local communities. Both the external and internal perspectives were included in project creation via a participatory process. Activities connected local culture and heritage with the present and future of remote places.

Human Cities is multidisciplinary, as reflected in the diversity of its projects, from product design, and even film, to architecture and planning. But this diversity also results from the variety of public participation strategies implemented by partners, with some applying a stricter bottom-up approach to public space design, such as in choosing project sites.

This paper focused on creative works undertaken by SMOTIES partners and their objectives. Their impact strategy incorporated indicators and other tools so that partners could assess the impact of their efforts, which will be done at the end of 2024 upon completion of the Human Cities/SMOTIES initiative.

References

AEGEAN (2024). Πρόταση για μια ήπια δημιουργική παρέμβαση στο Σαν Μιχάλη. Στα πλαίσια του έργου *SMOTIES: Creative Works with Small and Remote Places.*

Alternance (2024). Borgarnes í þátíð, nútíð og framtíð. Sögutorgin. Alternance – Borgarbyggð. Reykjavik – Borgarnes.

Alternance (2022). Borgarnes í þátíð, nútíð og framtíð. Rannsókn á gamla hluta Borgarness út frá sagnfræði, borgarformfræði og umhverfissálfræði sem grunnur fyrir betri almenningsrými, gott íbúasamráð og sameiginlega framtíðarsýn. Alternance – Borgarbyggð. Reykjavík - Borgarnes.

Alternance (n.d.). Sögutorgin. https://www.sogutorgin.is/home

Ardener, E. (2012). Remote areas. Some theoretical considerations. *HAU: Journal of Ethnographic Theory, 2(*1), 519–533.

Auricchio, V. et al (2024). *SMOTIES Toolbox. Design tools for the creative transformation of public spaces in small and remote places.* Birkhäuser: Barcelona – Basel – New York.

Barbera, F., Caputo, M. L., Baglioni, S. (2019). The social and economic development, attractiveness and collective well-being of remote, rural and mountain regions closely depend on the foundational economy. In Membretti, A. et al. (Eds). *The Renaissance of Remote Places. MATILDE Manifesto.* Routledge: Oxon – New York.

Bocco, G. (2016). Remoteness and remote places. A geographic perspective. Geoforum, 77, 178–181.

Buttimer, A. (2015). Home, reach, and the sense of place. In: Buttimer, A., Seamon, D. (Eds), *The Human Experience of Space and Place.* Routledge Revivals, Abingdon. E-book.
Charoupia (2024). Personal interview, 16 May 2024.

Clear Village (n.d.). Oriel Machno. https://www.clear-village.org/oriel-machno

De Rosa, A., Coutsoucos A. (2024). Personal interview, 16 May 2024.

EAD (2024). SMOTIES WP3 EAD before and after photo descriptions.

Eller, I. (2024). Personal interview, 17 May 2024.

FHJ (2024). SMOTIES Oberzeiring; Austria. WP3 Collection of student's evaluations, 2023, Graz.

FHJ (2023). SMOTIES – WP3 Impact Strategy.

FHJ (2023). Oberzeiring. Prototyping Studio 3. Circles.

FHJ (2022). Oberzeiring. Prototyping Studio 1. Benches.

Gillis, J. R. (2001). Places remote and islanded. *Michigan Quarterly Review, 40*(1), 39–58.

Human Cities. (n.d.). *Home* [Facebook page]. Facebook. Retrieved 31 May 2024 from https://www.facebook.com/humancitiesEU

Human Cities/SMOTIES (n.d.). SMOTIES. https://humancities.eu/smoties/

Matteucci, C., Olszak, M. (2023). La mobilité douce dans la vallée du Dorlay. Février 2023–novembre 2023. Cité du design – SEM.

Mission Design Management. Action Design dans les communes 21 / 23. Fiche Projet : Collecte Mémorielle, mené par l'Association de Sauvegarde de Sainte-Croix-en-Jarez (n.d.).

Nikšič, M. (2024). Personal interview, 4 May 2024.

OECD (2020a). *OECD Regions and Cities at a Glance 2020*. OECD Publishing.

OECD (2020b). *Rural Well-being: Geography of Opportunities*. Policy highlights. OECD Rural Studies.

Olim, H. (2023). *Estreito é o tempo.* UMA.

Owen, R. (2024). Personal interview, 22 May 2024.

Polimi (2024). Integrazione di aggiornamento del progetto. Human Cities/SMOTIES: Creative Works with Small and Remote Places. 9 May 2024.

Polimi (2024). Proposta di strategia per Albugnano. Human Cities/SMOTIES: Creative Works with Small and Remote Places. 9 February 2024.

Pronobis studio (2023), Koncepcja zagospodarowania terenu rekreacyjnego osiedla Bobrek w Cieszynie. Concept. Zamek Cieszyn.

Pronobis studio (2023), Koncepcja zagospodarowania terenu rekreacyjnego osiedla Bobrek w Cieszynie. Visualisation. Zamek Cieszyn.

UIRS (n.d.). SMOTIES Prototyping: Fruit dryers, hayracks and storage house.

UIRS (n.d.). SMOTIES Prototyping: Orchards as public spaces.

Van Hasselt, F., King, J. (2023). *Impact Strategy Master.*

6. Designing Cultural and Creative Innovations in Small and Remote Places: the Role of Prototyping

Susana Gonzaga
Researcher at ID+ Research Institute for Design, Media and Culture, and assistant professor, Art & Design Department, Universidade da Madeira [PT]

Isabelle Vérilhac
Strategic designer, founder of Design With Isabelle [FR]

Alexandra Coutsoucos
Research fellow, Department of Design, Politecnico di Milan [IT]

Recognising the importance of prototyping within the framework of participatory design is grounded in a deep understanding of the evolving socio-economic landscape and the pressing need for innovative solutions. Drawing from seminal works such as Hillgren, Seravalli, and Emilson (2011), we have observed an increasing awareness of the limitations in existing models as humanity grapples with complex social, economic, and ecological challenges. The transformative impact of the industrial revolution, leading to the neglect of rural areas, is juxtaposed with recent shifts, especially post-COVID, revealing an emerging trend of re-evaluation of the relationship between people and nature, big urban centres, and small peripheral areas and communities. This dualistic dynamic, although seemingly contradictory, has spurred government institutions, exemplified by the EU, to acknowledge the imperative for a systemic transition towards more sustainable democratic models, giving rise to collaborative efforts essential for the advancement of social innovation (Domanski & Kaletka, 2017). In addition, participatory design, rooted in the socialist agenda of the 1960s, has revolutionised design practices by prioritising user involvement in design projects. This user-centric approach, coupled with stakeholders' engagement and the adoption of rapid prototyping, has proven to be a linchpin in driving social innovation (Murray et al., 2010). These design approaches and, therefore, new processes and associated skills, have transcended their traditional boundaries, becoming integral in addressing contemporary economic and social challenges. Design studios and agencies of influence like IDEO and the Nesta guide Designing for Public Service emphasise the pivotal role of design being aligned with user needs and broader social needs, advocating a prototyping approach to solutions. This global paradigm shift of design practices requires a holistic approach, urging practitioners to embrace systems thinking and focus on individual behaviour. Once confined to aesthetic considerations, such as in the 20th century, designers today have assumed a key role in unravelling the intricacies of complex social and economic problems. Co-designing practices and participatory design approaches are a new, innovative way to respond to these contemporary issues. Nevertheless, challenges abound when working directly with communities. Obstacles such as unfamiliarity with creative processes and tools, a lack of confidence to participate, and difficulty establishing emotional links pose significant barriers.

So, when approaching communities, several questions and design challenges arise immediately. Putting communities, stakeholders, and designers together at the centre of a shared concern needs guidance. Designers are the privileged facilitators who conduct and assemble all the group inputs. One of the essential tools to establish common visions is prototyping. Why prototype? See Figure 1 on the next page. In projects like SMOTIES, prototyping is a powerful tool. At its core, prototyping brings tangibility to ideas, allowing for concepts to be explored and facilitating early failure and learning. The use of prototyping tools leverages the local design capacity, fosters collaborative efforts, creates learning opportunities, and improves connectivity and engagement. These are usually inherent outcomes of an effective prototyping process because of its multifaceted role that goes beyond being a creative tool.

Existing literature underscores that prototyping is not merely a phase in the design process but a strategic endeavour for risk mitigation and a catalyst for sustainable social change. With its inherent emphasis on inclusivity, iterative development, and communication enhancement, prototyping stands at the forefront of participatory design, bridging the gap between creative ideation and meaningful community engagement. In projects where co-design is the baseline, participatory decision-making is present – thus, end users, designers, and other stakeholders work together to shape solutions that genuinely address their needs and aspirations and move from conceptualisation to tangible outcomes. By the end of the project, the prototypes represent a means to enhance the resilience of local communities, in line with the goals initially set and community desires, as we could observe in some of the outcomes achieved by SMOTIES partners.

The prototyping methodology

In the context of co-design and participatory design, particularly within the SMOTIES project, the strategic role of prototyping is a simultaneous and multifaceted endeavour. Its dual purpose involves facilitating teams in translating intangible concepts into visual forms while aiding in the iterative refinement, testing, and redesigning

Figure 1: Relevance map of prototyping in participatory design projects.
© Susana Gonzaga

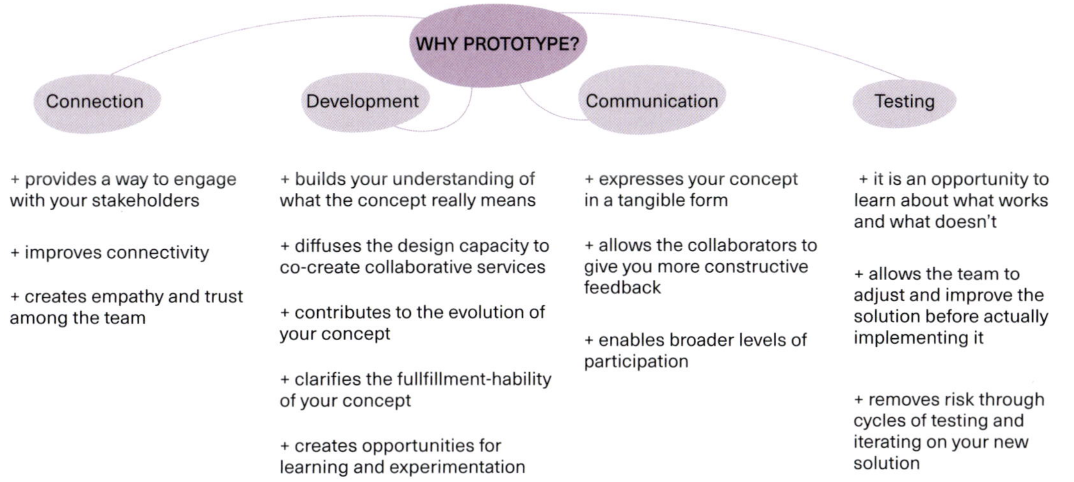

processes crucial for finalising solutions. Acting as a mediator between design practices and community desires, the prototyping strategy established within the framework of the SMOTIES project intends to help its partner organisations to better unfold local communities' wishes and aspirations into real solutions for their public spaces. Also considered an engaging tool, the prototyping strategy was designed to be divided into three major phases of the development of co-design projects: Prototyping Studios 1, 2 and 3.

- Prototyping Studio 1, or the "Visualisation" phase, entails shaping ideas to make them tangible and understanding the local community's opportunities, resources, and abilities. Locals and the research team in these participatory studios focus on materialising abstract ideas through simple visualisations such as images, collages, models, or map conceptualisations. Co-design workshops empower partners to generate these representations, fostering community trust and engagement in decision-making processes. These visual milestones help the project to go from identifying needs to proposing viable solutions, fostering collaboration among diverse stakeholders.
- Prototyping Studio 2, called the "Building and Testing" phase, builds on insights gained in the first phase, where clear guidelines are defined to inform final solutions. The idea is to have local teams collaborate on project implementation, based on the community's unique context, and test the ideas or services in community events, where the outcomes and impact of the solutions will be tested within a broader community use.
- Prototyping Studio 3, or the "Future Scenarios" phase, involves analysing feedback and envisioning future scenarios to ensure the sustainability of initiatives. This step is pivotal in sustaining the collaborative process and empowering local communities to autonomously shape their villages' future. During this phase, the researchers and local community try to create a written and visual scenario, using resources from the SMOTIES toolbox to envision future events and developments in their community.

Three SMOTIES partners were chosen to analyse the effectiveness and impact of this methodology within the SMOTIES network. One partner was responsible for designing the prototyping approach, while the other two were the first to implement it. The aim was to examine the cohesive prototyping approach across three remote locations and demonstrate its adaptability in addressing diverse challenges in different contexts. In this article, we will delve into how each phase unfolded in each remote place.

Prototyping Studio 1, Visualisation Phase, Estreito da Calheta

Estreito da Calheta is a small village founded in the second half of the 16th century on the southwest coast of Madeira Island (Portugal). When University of Madeira researchers started to engage with the local community, they were concerned about neglecting local traditions and about the lack of care for local immaterial and material heritage. Like many remote and small places in the country, Estreito da Calheta is losing its young population to urban areas and emigration, and nowadays, the village has lost its old charm, cultural activities, and opportunities to gather the community apart from its annual local religious celebrations.

It is a common misconception that prototyping techniques should only be utilised when designs are nearing completion. Visualisation is, in fact, a prime example of a prototyping technique applicable from the very early phases of a project. In the case of the parish of Estreito da Calheta, for example, the research team of the University of Madeira employed Visualisation as a means to systematically illustrate and organise the intricate challenges identified by the community, attributing to them equal importance and testing conceptual scenarios to discuss future solutions.

The research team drew up a set of scenarios using the collage technique to enable the community to identify potential concept directions that resonate with local needs early in the process. Owing to the village's geographical features, it was not possible to establish a centralised point, and bringing people together and community interaction were particularly challenging. The idea to host a gathering, where individuals could meet and engage in diverse activities, emanated from the collated visual elements and was selected by the community; a public event was held in front of the church.

Visualising issues or concept scenarios is a method of 'putting on paper', or making manifest, narratives that otherwise only exist in abstract form. This approach helps crystallise these narratives and provides an objective the community can address and elaborate on. Giving shape to ideas through visual images like drawings or collages is not only a technique for illustrating and validating but also a tool for shared decision-making in early project phases. In addition to the Prototyping Studio 1, a community engagement activity fostered participation and involvement through design-led activities. The outcome of this workshop in Estreito da Calheta was a drawing of the skyline of the iconic buildings and areas in the village on a long sheet of paper. This was used to showcase the village at a local event, engage the community, and spark a sense of local identity. Alongside the conversation corner at the event, the long-paper illustrations allowed the audience to write or draw their memories of places in the village and show the importance they have in their lives (Figure 2).

The local population's reaction to this approach was surprisingly positive. This proves how something as simple as Visualisation techniques can be used as a platform for sharing an understanding of issues that impact the territory and decision-making process, as well as bonding moments and community engagement. The first Visualisation prototypes allowed the local community to comfortably express their concerns, wishes, and desires for their village. Beyond being a tool for early project phases, Visualisation as a prototyping technique is of great value for advancing design-driven social innovation endeavours, bridging the gap between identifying needs and producing viable solutions while being a catalyst for community engagement (Figure 3).

Prototyping Studio 2, Building and Testing phase, Albugnano

Prototyping to build and test designs is the most common application of this methodology. Whether applied in engineering, scientific, or artistic pursuits, prototyping is the first attempt, after design (in the broadest sense), at translating a conceptualised object into a contextualised construct. This method aims to validate the appropriateness of material choices and assembly methods to test the object's features, functionalities, the delivery of its promise, or its realistic compatibility with its intended context.

Prototyping is typically undertaken to answer specific questions and doubts about the design. Identifying these questions before building and testing can aid in developing prototypes that focus on specific features and thus provide necessary answers without a needless waste of time and resources. This approach allows for a low-risk exploration of concepts throughout various phases of the design process and at different scales, facilitating early failure and continuous learning.

Any formally or informally design-driven discipline can benefit from building and testing prototypes when bringing an innovation effort from conception to realisation, be it physical objects, service-systems, experiences, or businesses. In the case of SMOTIES, outcomes of design and participatory practices for social innovation were prototyped to validate their appropriateness to the town and social context, and the research showed their effectiveness in satisfying needs. An example is a prototyping workshop carried out in Albugnano (Italy) as part of a series of co-design workshops conducted with local stakeholders, aimed at finding solutions to address social isolation, the conservation of local heritage and the activation of cultural expressions through the regeneration of commons, from a formal and functional perspective. In previous encounters with

Figure 2: Prototyping Studio 1, drawing the Estreito da Calheta skyline with the most iconic sites in the village. © Susana Gonzaga

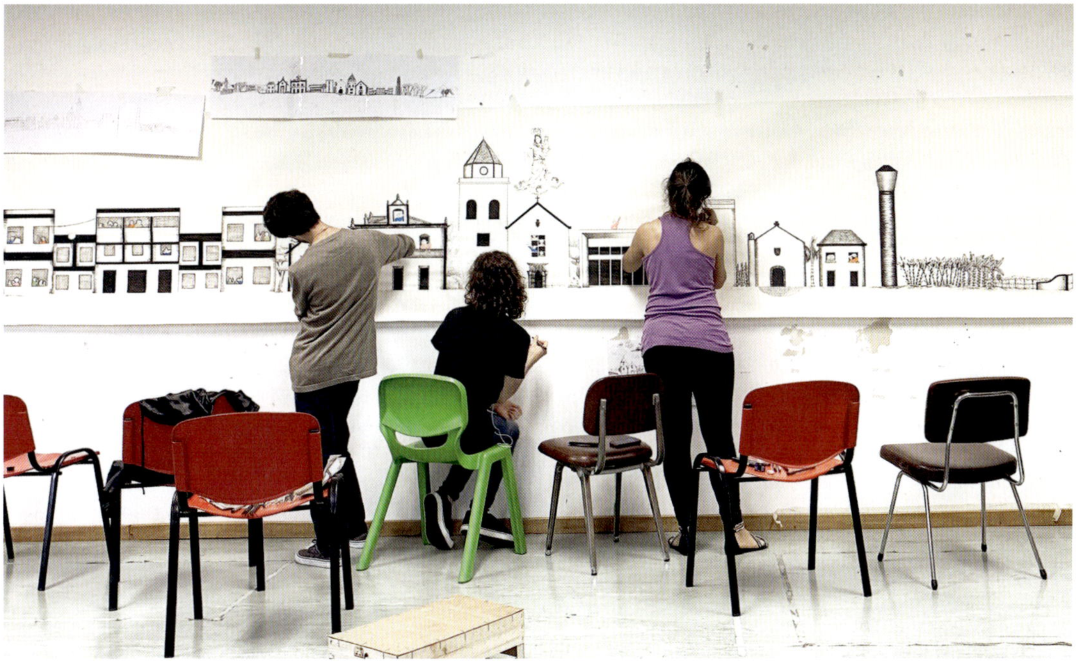

Figure 3: Testing the visualisation skyline during a public event in the parish of Estreito da Calheta in November 2022. © Susana Gonzaga

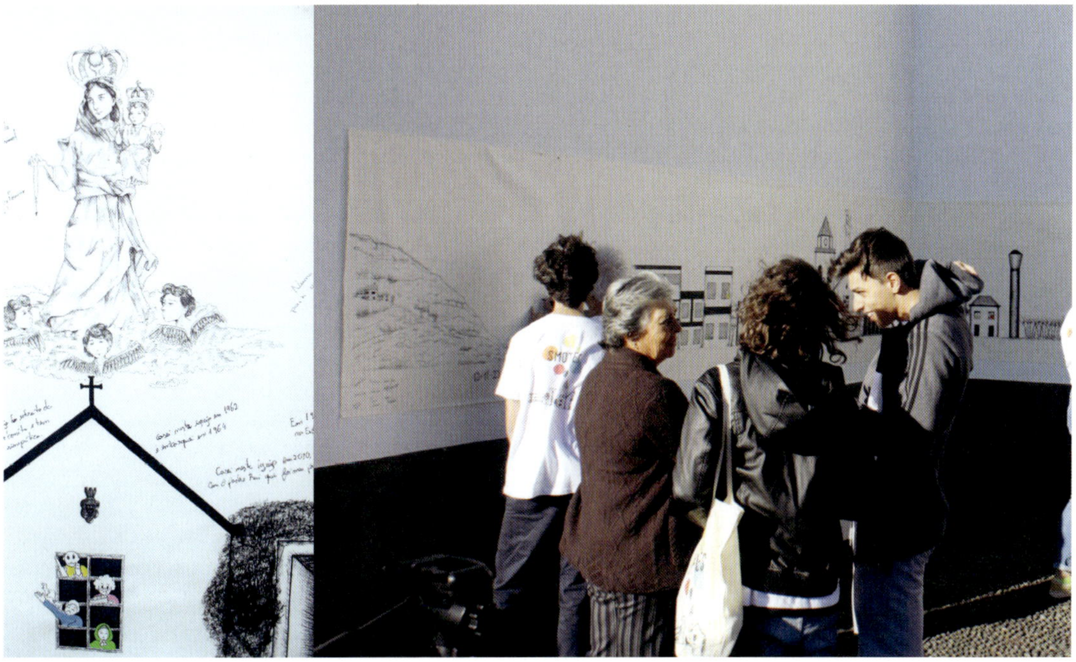

the local stakeholders, a garden in the centre was identified to resolve previously raised challenges by determining the uses of the garden and activities held there. The uses and activities ranged from the spontaneous, such as relaxing and socialising, to cultural events and performances, such as thematic lectures and theatrical plays. We used the Desktop Walkthrough tool (Auricchio et al., 2022) to explore, alongside residents, possible connections between the interactions occurring in a place and the place itself (Figure 4).

The prototyping workshop was designed to involve visitors and residents by testing two different garden layouts, which had been hypothesised in previous co-design workshops. Residents were encouraged to bring props, such as tables, chairs, benches, easels, and gazebos, to create a real-life impression of these areas and simulate their use through role-playing (Figure 5). The results of the prototyping workshop led to the expansion of the strategy to other underutilised areas in Albugnano that were already fit for hosting certain activities and functions. Testing the prototype of the garden's layout in a real-life setting and involving users allowed the research team to reuse the design, leveraging the qualities of existing places to rethink public spaces throughout the town as part of a commons system.

Prototyping helped to make ideas tangible, testing concepts and facilitating early failure and learning, while involving the community in a way that was low-risk and involved a low investment of resources. Prototyping not only provides a testing tool but also helps us to understand local opportunities, resources, and abilities, as previously said. Ultimately, prototyping is a multifaceted method that, even when carried out at a low fidelity throughout the design process, can support strategic decision-making to find solutions that are fit for purpose while involving all actors in a collective innovation effort.

Prototyping Studios 3, Future Scenarios phase, the case of the Dorlay Valley

The third phase, "Future Scenarios", involves analysing feedback and prototyping future scenarios to ensure the sustainability of the initiatives implemented. This step is pivotal in sustaining the collaborative process and empowering local communities to autonomously shape their villages' future.

In the Dorlay Valley, the dependence on cars and the lack of regular transport were crucial issues for locals. The project leveraged the famous textile heritage of the valley, especially the braid and lace industry, which was the main industrial activity in La Terrasse-sur-Dorlay in the 18th century and remains a source of pride among inhabitants. By valorising their historical know-how, the project encouraged locals to improve mobility and develop alternative ways.

In Prototyping Studio 3, the designers developed graphic materials to promote soft mobility and showcase the valley's textile heritage, including a "sensitive" map. The map was one of the main prototyping tools, aiming to provide information not typically found on conventional maps to as many of the valley's residents and occasional visitors as possible (Figure 6).

Mobility laces are made in the museum "Maison des Tresses et Lacets" at La Terrasse-sur-Dorlay, which is about traditional local know-how. Different coloured threads are used to show our current modes of transport. Other tools for identifying and promoting the alternative mobility paths have been developed as temporary signage to draw attention to heritage sites (Figure 7).

The creative experts used these tools because they fit the local context and actors well. Making shoelaces with the weaving machines in the village is symbolic and helps to promote acceptance and involvement among the residents. Moreover, all the tools have been developed through a collaborative process, involving local actors. They have been well accepted and will continue to be used after the project. However, the challenge in this type of project is maintaining the process when the creative team departs and ensuring the initiative's long-term sustainability. Fortunately, the master classes and workshops have equipped locals with collaborative skills, enabling them to continue working independently.

The tools have been tested and improved during three public events. The method involves regular exchanges between design and participative actions, which helps to achieve the goals. The *in situ* experiences with residents, students, associations, and authorities, and the participation of the wider public are all part of the collaborative approach.

Following the tests of the soft mobility path around the heritage sites of the Dorlay Valley, the residents and local associations are continuing the project by offering visits along the proposed routes that were part of the SMOTIES project. They would like to broaden the community. Based on the example set in their valley, they will become ambassadors for soft mobility: neighbouring basins are connected, cycle routes are extended, and national connections and networks are created. The challenge is in demonstrating the advantages of soft mobility over car use.

Figure 4: Plan for Albugnano (Italy): the garden's layout to be tested with temporary props using the Desktop Walkthrough tool. © Polimi DESIS Lab

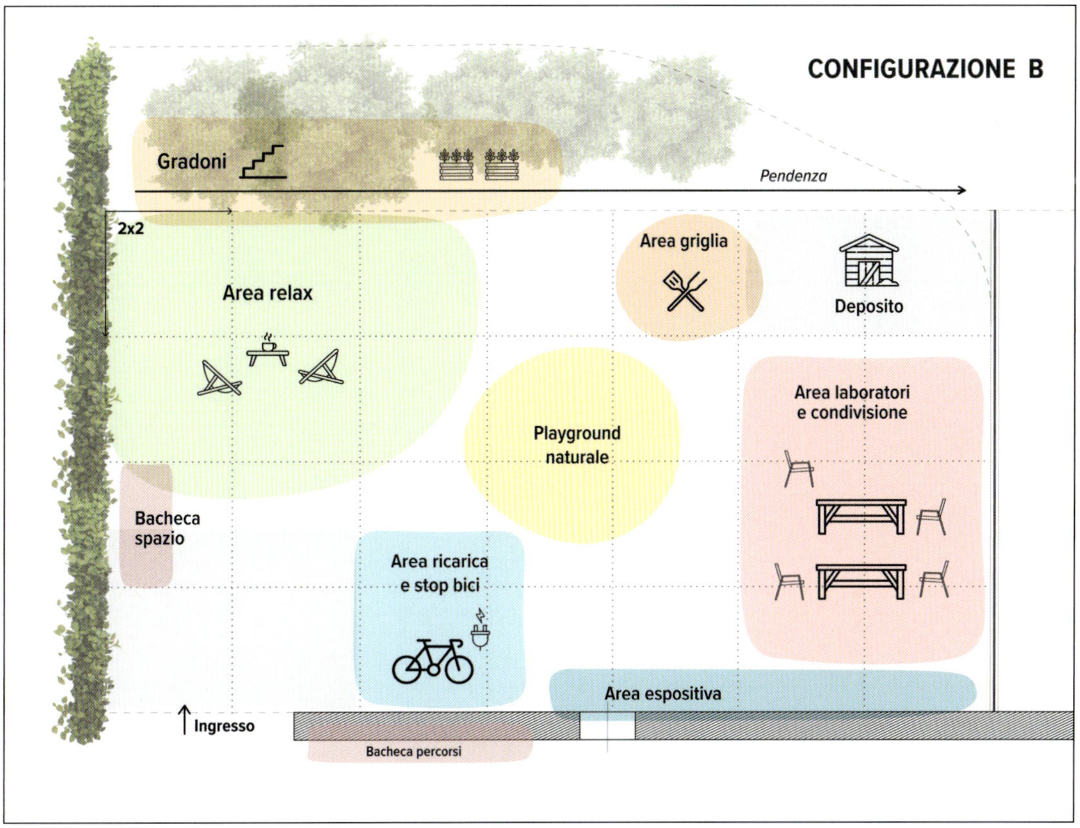

Figure 5: Albugnano's garden, lo-fi prototyping of spatial layout in July 2023. © Polimi DESIS Lab

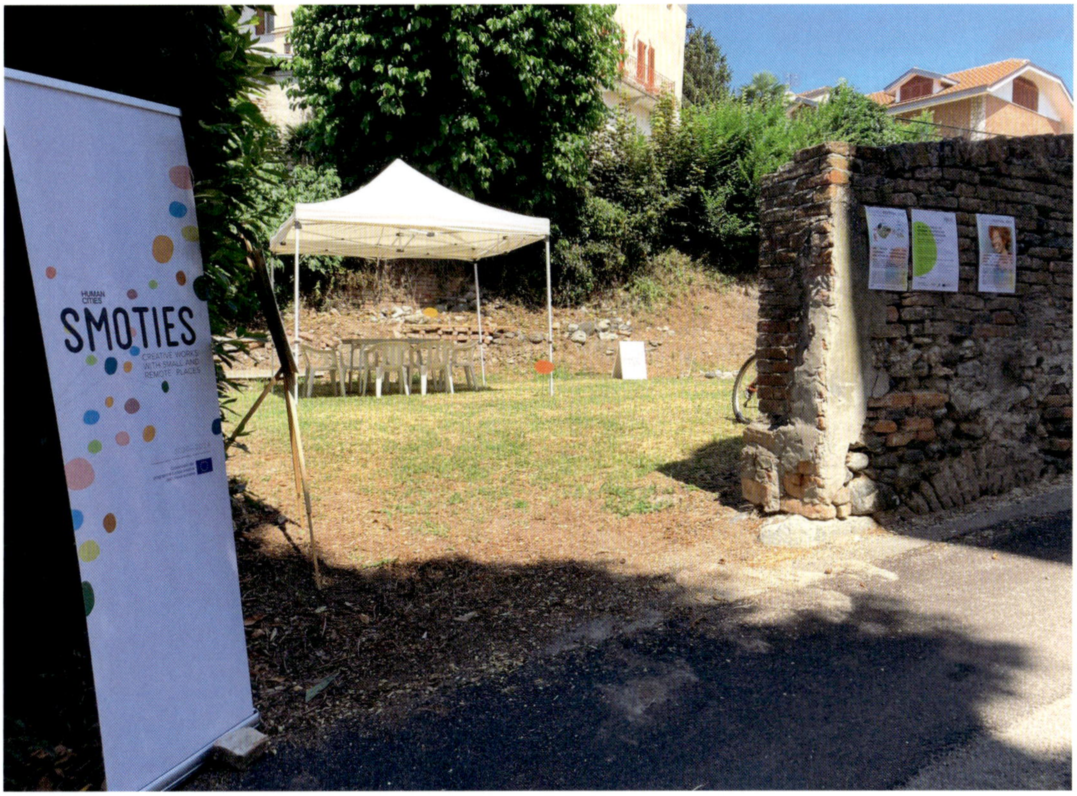

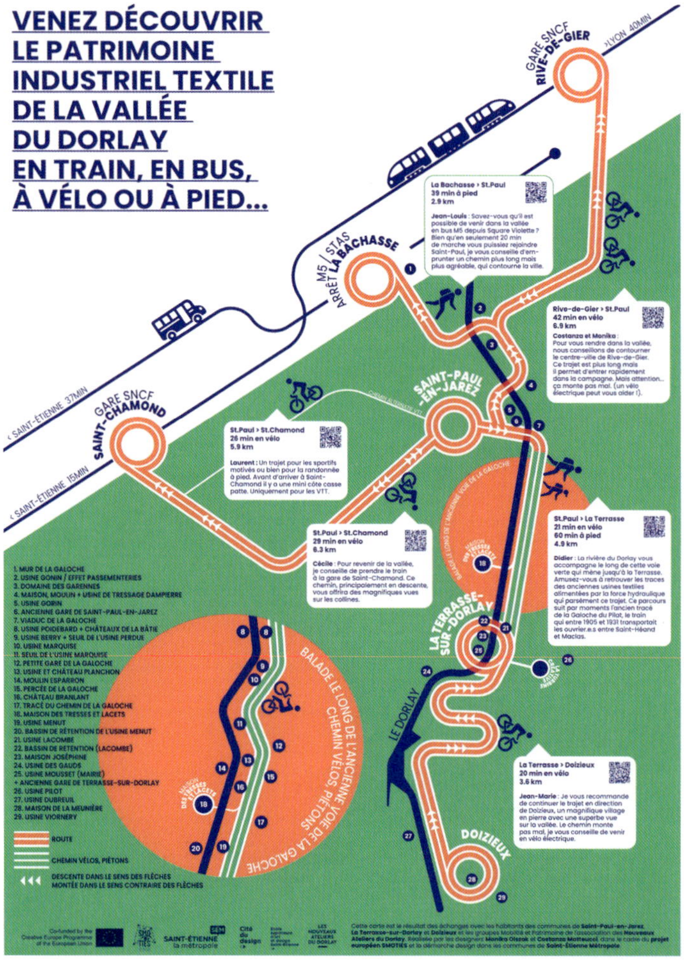

Figure 6: Dorlay Valley map. © Monika Olszak

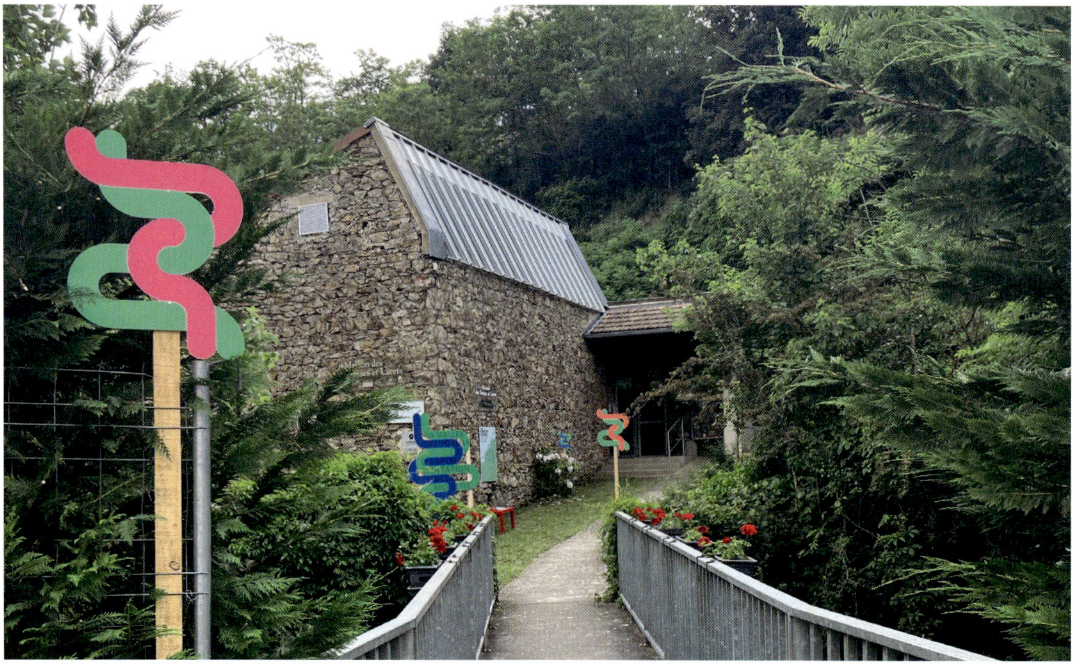

Figure 7: Temporary signage in Dorlay Valley. © Monika Olszak

Through prototyping and experimentation, Cité du design and designers, in collaboration with local stakeholders, encouraged residents and visitors to explore the possibilities of using soft modes of transport. This method links soft mobility with promoting the industrial heritage of the Dorlay Valley and anchoring innovation in the territory's tradition. The project's outcomes were exhibited during a popular European event known as *Les Journées Européennes du Patrimoine*. The Parc du Pilat took inspiration from the signage on the path in the Dorlay Valley to create permanent heritage trails. For local authorities, now is the time to invest in infrastructure to encourage and transform alternative mobility into mainstream practices.

Conclusions

The significance of prototyping tools in co-design approaches, like the one used in this article, shows the multifaceted role prototyping has in facilitating effective collaboration, promoting user engagement, and ultimately contributing to the development of innovative and user-centred solutions. The multifaceted role of prototyping boosts the resilience of local communities, even following the project. Leveraging local design capacity, fostering collaborative efforts, creating learning opportunities, and improving connectivity are inherent outcomes of effective prototyping. The prototyping methodology developed for the SMOTIES project served as a simultaneous and multifaceted endeavour involving three distinct phases: Visualisation, Building and Testing, and Prototyping Future Scenarios (Figure 8).

Applying the different phases in three partner locations allowed us to test this methodology in local communities and realise the importance of giving shape to ideas when dealing with participatory design projects. On the one hand, it allows designers to develop the projects in a more informed manner, and gives the communities the power and responsibility to care for their heritage. In the case of Estreito da Calheta, where the community grappled with identity loss and cultural stagnation, the use of collage techniques to create conceptual images demonstrated that Visualisation, as prototyping, is not exclusive to the final design stages. It systematically illustrated community challenges early in the process, providing a shared foundation of understanding for informed decision-making and community engagement.

In the Building and Testing phase, Albugnano, an Italian town, faced challenges of population decline and underutilised heritage. Here, building and testing a layout as a prototype for a new spatial configuration for one location in town and involving locals in testing its use through role-playing led to expanded considerations of various underused locations across town. In a collective effort, the Building and Testing phase brought tangibility to ideas. It demonstrated the versatility of low-fidelity prototypes to reuse concept designs in a low-risk, low-cost way.

In the Future Scenarios phase, the Dorlay Valley in France, known for its textile industry, struggles with car dependence. Future Scenario techniques played a crucial role in sustaining the collaborative process and empowering local communities to shape their villages' future independently. Through workshops and prototyping tools, residents took ownership and continued the project.

For the SMOTIES project, prototyping methods were used in all facets, exemplifying its adaptability in addressing diverse challenges in varying contexts. As a strategic and ongoing process, prototyping proves to be transformative in not only shaping sustainable solutions, but also fostering community engagement and reinforcing the importance of a strategic and holistic approach to design when working with small communities.

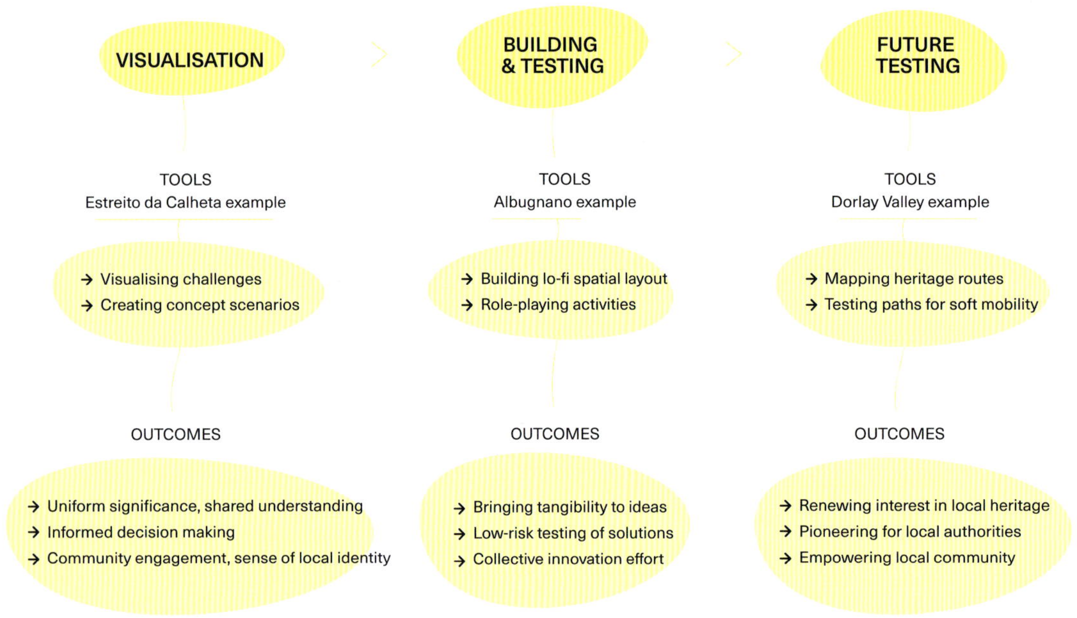

Figure 8: Tools and outcomes used in the three different phases of prototyping. © Alexandra Coutsoucos

References

Auricchio, V., De Rosa, A., & Göransdotter, M. (2022). Experiential ways of mapping: Revisiting the desktop walkthrough. In B. Camocini & A. Dominoni (Eds), *Engaging Spaces. How to Increase Social Awareness and Human Wellbeing Through Experience Design* (Vol. 6, pp. 131–158). FrancoAngeli.

Bofylatos, S. (2020). Designing resilient creative communities through biomimetic service design. *Strategic Design Research Journal,* Vol. 13, (2), 2020, 249–267.

Domanski, D., & Kaletka, C. (2017). Exploring the research landscape of social innovation. A deliverable of the project Social Innovation Community (SIC). Dortmund, Germany: Sozialforschungsstelle.

Emilson, A., Seravalli, A., & Hillgren, P.-A. (2011). Dealing with dilemmas: Participatory approaches in Design for Social Innovation. *Swedish Design Research Journal*, (1), 232–239.

IDEO (2022). *Design Kit*. Retrieved from https://www.designkit.org/methods#filter

IDEO (2016). *Designing for Public Services*. Nesta. UK

Murray, R., Caulier-Grice, J., & Mulgan, G. (2010). *The Open Book of Social Innovation* (Vol. 24). London: Nesta.

The Systems Thinker (2022). Prototyping and Cultural Change. Retrieved from https://thesystemsthinker.com/prototyping-and-cultural-change/

This is Service Design Doing (2022). *Methods*. Retrieved from https://www.thisisservicedesigndoing.com/methods

Service Design Tools (2022). Retrieved from https://servicedesigntools.org/tools

Circular Design Guide (2022). *Methods*. Retrieved from https://www.circulardesignguide.com/methods

7.

Learning and Knowing a Territory Through Walking and Exploration: Design Tools and Approaches in Dialogue with Other Sciences

Elisa Bertolotti
PhD, assistant professor of communication design, Departamento de Arte e Design, Faculdade de Artes e Humanidades, Universidade da Madeira [PT]

Noemi Satta
Independent consultant and expert in cultural innovation and strategic and participatory planning [IT]

Chiara Nifosì
PhD, assistant professor of urban planning, Department of Architecture and Urban Studies, Politecnico di Milano [IT]

Cristina Renzoni
PhD, associate professor of urban planning, Department of Architecture and Urban Studies, Politecnico di Milano [IT]

Walking is a cognitive, learning experience that amplifies all the senses, and acts on selective and interpretive skills. Choosing to cross the territory on foot means to have a physical, emotional, and aesthetic experience, which allows us to reach a new consciousness of the daily landscapes, and to overcome the prejudice towards spaces that are taken for granted, and which can then be narrated, translated, and experienced in various forms and at different times. This necessarily starts from the assumption that "every map is a project", and the mapping operations are firmly rooted in a design process.

This article focuses on the methodological research work conducted by the authors in peripheral, rural, and urban contexts of Madeira Island. Approaches, tools, and languages from adjacent disciplinary fields converge to define a research framework of methods. The starting point is therefore the description of field work in the form of various walking workshops, which focused on actively involving learning communities in processes of awareness and transformation.

1. Learning about field work in design education while walking in Estreito da Calheta

This article began with a series of experiences carried out during the spring of 2023 within the teaching activities of the Design 4 semester course of the Bachelor in Design at the University of Madeira. In collaboration with the SMOTIES project, the course was dedicated to the work of listening to, studying, and representing Estreito da Calheta, a small village some distance from Funchal, the main centre of the island of Madeira (Figures 1a, b). It was therefore considered to be a peripheral place, a periphery of a periphery, a rural context far from the city, an island within an island.[1] Although it is now easily reachable by car, many of the students of the Design 4 course (mostly from Madeira) did not know Estreito da Calheta, except for passing by in the car without ever stopping or from hearsay.

During the course we had the opportunity to host two short workshops, the first with Noemi Satta and the second with Cristina Renzoni and Chiara Nifosì.

The first workshop focused on participatory processes and especially on the first step, i.e., the research phase. Due to its cognitive character, the research phase is never neutral and asks us to design and choose paths of exploration. Making a transformation means first of all working on awareness and the ability to break out of one's own clichés, starting from the first phase of any project or process.

The second workshop was dedicated to introducing the students to field work experiences in urban planning. Unlike Urban Planning or Architecture students, Design students in this Bachelor's programme normally have fewer opportunities to look at very different scales, and their gaze often is limited to the scale of the work done with their hands or with the computer. The aim here was to stimulate the gaze towards different scales, from small to large, in order to be able to read the landscape in a more complex and articulated way and begin to see interconnections. In addition to this, we also wanted to introduce the use and design of maps as non-neutral tools produced by a work of choice, interpretation, and subsequent representation (Figures 2a, b, c; Figures 3a, b, c, d).

1. Before the construction of main roads, the life in different places of the island was pretty isolated, and to reach the main city it took hours and sometimes days of travel. See the film *Estreito é o tempo* by Hugo Olim, 2023

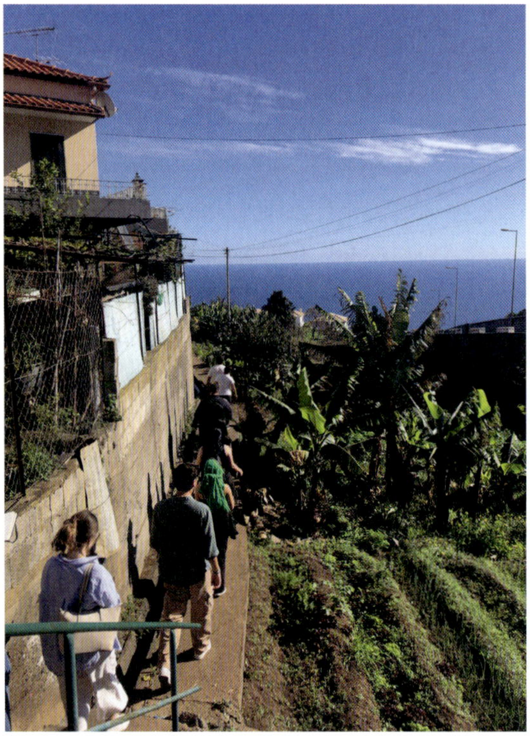

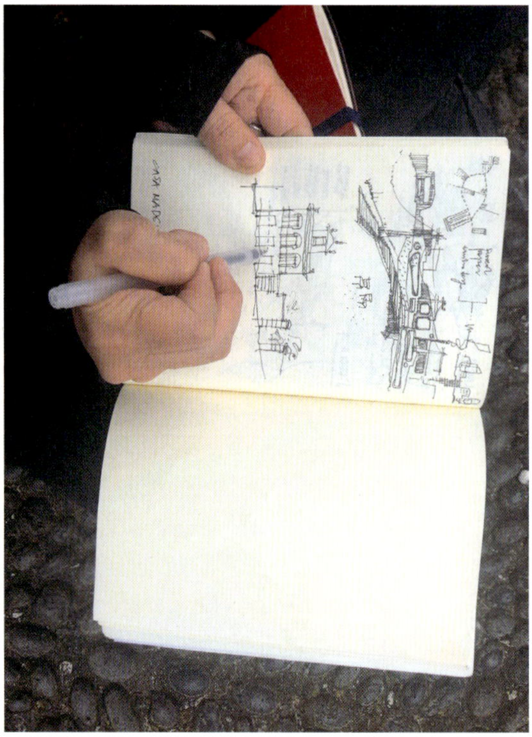

Figure 1a: First field work with Design 4 students. Estreito da Calheta, March 2024

Figure 1b: Fieldnotes – from the workshop led by Chiara Nifosì and Cristina Renzoni. Estreito da Calheta, April 2024

Figures 2a, b, c: Field work elaborations by Design 4 student José Pinho

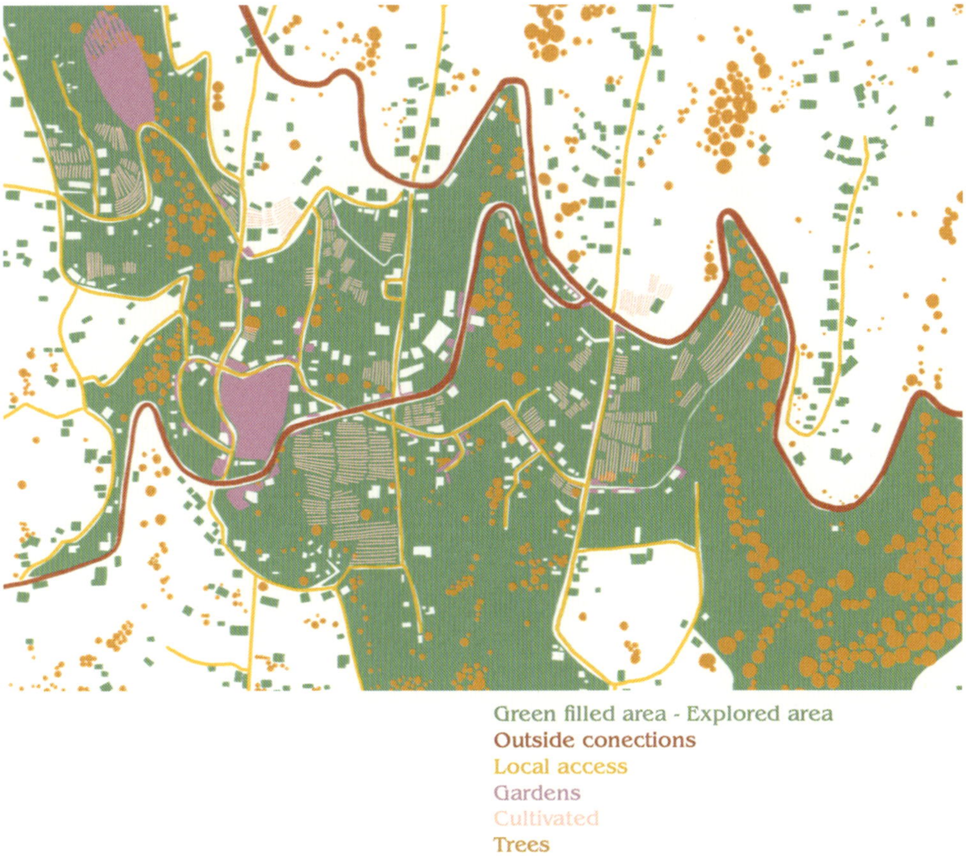

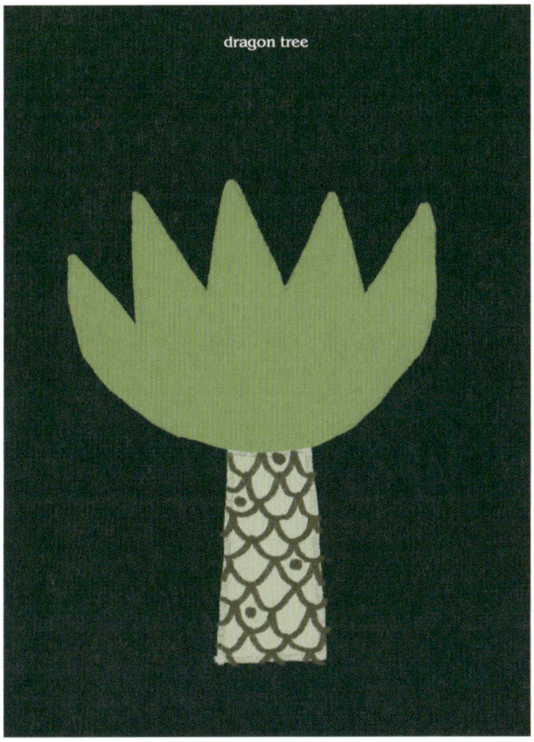

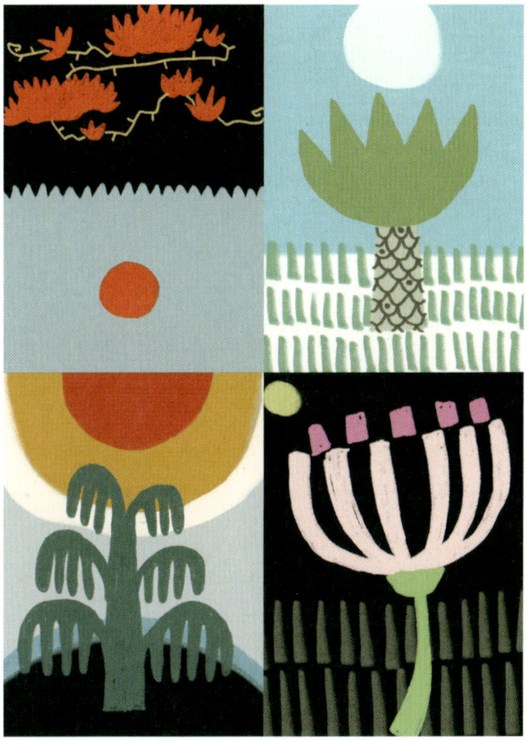

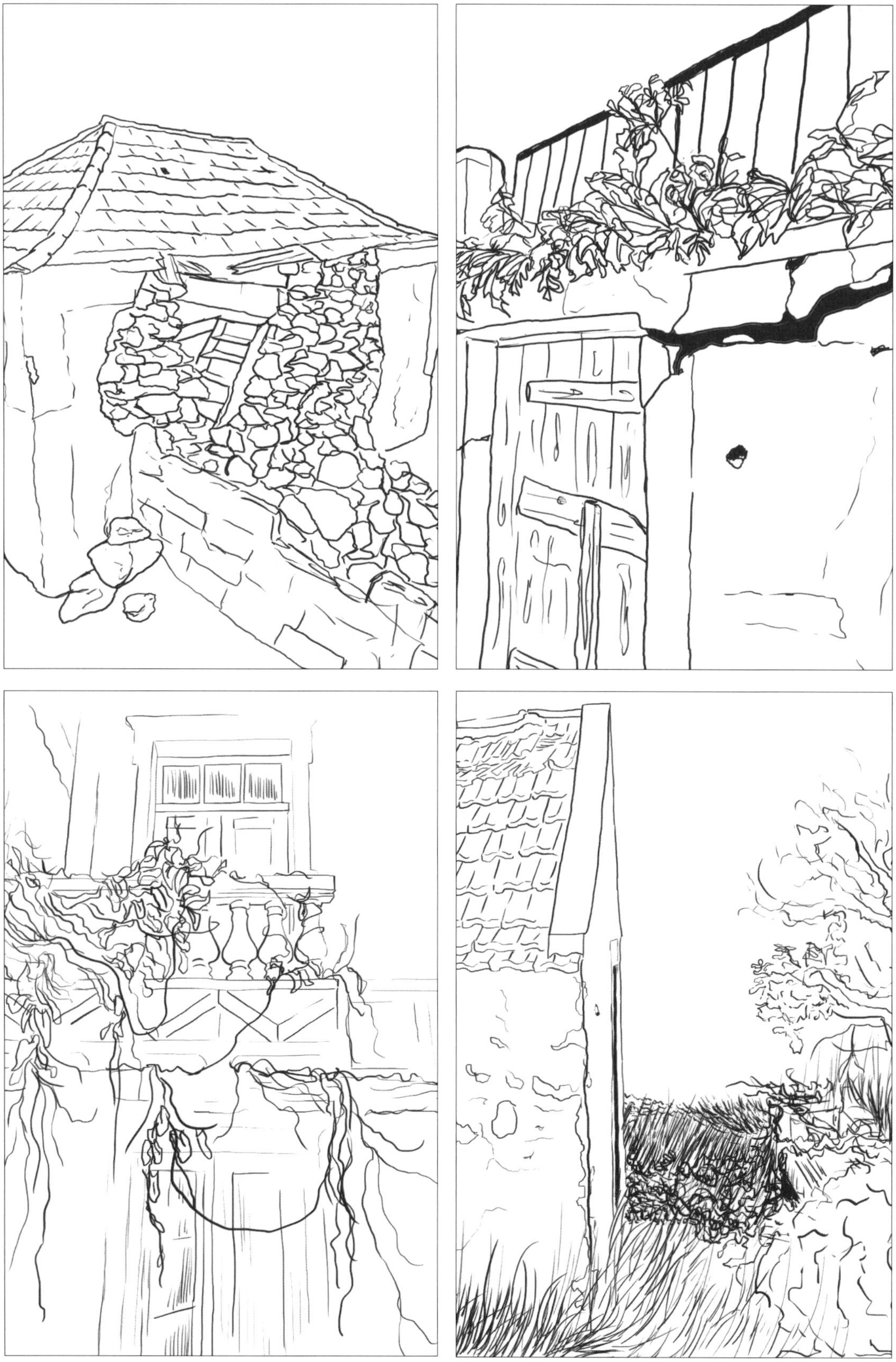

Figures 3a, b, c, d: Field work elaborations by Design 4 students Helena Câmara, Inês Rodrigues, Mariana Carvalho

But let's take a step back: why did we decide to dedicate a course to field work and to walking as a way of learning within a design curriculum? Primarily because, precisely from the perspective of imagining an educational path that makes sense in a context like that of the island of Madeira, we believe that it makes sense for research and reflection to be carried out in the context of place. Doing this means getting to know and re-know the Atlantic island, with its natural history of around six million years and its relatively recent anthropic history. This means reflecting on various issues: from the often-violent environmental impact of design; to the risk of losing a specific local cultural heritage and as well as the biodiversity developed over time in a context partially separated from the rest of the world (De Luca & Bertolotti, 2024); to the specific potential and design needs in insular contexts (Wahl, 2016); up to the question of limits, interconnections, and ecology (Borgnino, 2022).

To do this it is important to explore field work while walking in design practice as well (Bertolotti & Vezzani, 2021; De Luca & Bertolotti, 2023). Walking is in fact a practice that has always allowed us to know ourselves and the world (Solnit, 2000; Ingold & Vergunst, 2008; Kagge, 2019; Gros, 2023). It is a slow movement, which contrasts with the frenetic rhythms of contemporary life (Kagge, 2015; Gros, 2023), allowing a type of integrated learning and inviting reflexivity and slow thinking (Maffei, 2014). In placing our feet and being in contact with the ground, in breathing, in being able to give ourselves time to perceive the breath and the body, we can experience, in walking, being terrestrial (Latour, 2018) and how we are part of the landscape, where everything is interconnected and interdependent (Gros, 2023). Walking can be a practice that allows us to observe how we walk with nonhumans (Gooch, 2008) and to delve deeper into how we belong to communities that coexist in the ruins of a world in deep crisis (Tsing, 2015; Haraway, 2016; Puig de la Bellacasa, 2017).

In the following paragraphs we will delve into some of the themes that underpinned the teaching and workshop experiences mentioned above. In Paragraph 2 Noemi Satta introduces the importance of reflecting about stereotypes before beginning any field work; in Paragraph 3 Chiara Nifosì tells us how an expedition on foot can be considered an act of translation; and in Paragraph 4 Cristina Renzoni describes how maps are narratives that interpret a territory and that they are in all respects the result of a project.

2. Stereotypes and overturning of clichés: from the postcard to the territory

Participatory processes aim to involve both larger or smaller communities, on a territorial basis or on individual interests, in making decisions and effecting concrete changes with respect to specific issues in their territory or field of interest. Every initial research phase, and the territorial exploration most importantly, asks for balance between one's prior knowledge and the edge of the unknown that may turn into surprise and thus into new questions.

In the research phase, one works on power, and on voice, not only in a metaphorical sense but also in the ability to say in one's own words what the problems are, and what the solutions are. A large body of literature links critical awareness (Freire, 1998), or the use of dissent (Hirshmann, 1982), with the possibility of finding one's own autonomous capacity to represent and determine his or her own future (Appadurai, 2004), one's capacity for change. This is related to the possibility of imagining (Mulgan, 2022) politically new places, ways of living and solving fundamental issues related to democracy, the environment, health, schools, etc.

Thus, territorial exploration plays an essential role in defining if and how the desired local or social change can take place: one of the first goals is to redefine the research questions, trying to enable everyone – professionals, experts, inhabitants – to first of all recognise their own reading filters: such as the negative stigma surrounding suburbs for example, starting with the very term itself, which has now come to mean a marginalised and disadvantaged place. From the initial conception of the research we work on awareness of "automatisms" and "estrangement", that is, on the procedure that in other spheres (literary criticism, and specifically Russian formalism) serves to help to observe anew what we already know.

Automatism and estrangement, or knowing how to initiate reflection on words and images, is one of the approaches to return to "looking at things", even ordinary or familiar things, as if seeing them for the first time. This is all the more fundamental to unhinging the fatalist perception of "nothing can change": from recognising the usual definitions, labels, representations, visions, and words, to multiplying and comparing viewpoints to move towards changing the lenses of observation, which are the keys of research.

The workshop that prepares an exploration often uses 'material objects', simple and immediate devices, such as picture cards specifically structured for brain storming (Eno & Schmidt, 1975). Others from the artistic sphere (Lai, 2002) can be used to hack common concepts and clichés, or can resort to tourist postcards of a specific place to be explored. There is nothing more useful for observing clichés, partial representations of the whole ("the place only in bloom", "the island all sea"), and the main narrative characterisations.

Noble examples in this sense are those of Bruno Munari with his surreal postcards playing precisely with clichés, and Rodari to work with fantastic hypotheses (1973), to introduce the hypothetical "What if..." not only within a pedagogical pathway but in general as a trick to find, in exploration and research, new questions and new paths to work on, and also to enable change (Figures 4a, b, c).

Dealing with the capacity to renew the political and poietic imagination of a place is even more important when working in marginal areas, defined by their distance from a so-called 'centre'. What defines is therefore the other, with hetero-directed parameters that are certainly not autonomously generated.

Thus words such as: periphery, island, rural, interior, mountain, or if you extend the reasoning, young, old, women, workers, unemployed, and so on, assume fixed meanings, which tend to influence the discourse – of the citizens and the experts – meanings that can instead be overturned, rethought, renewed. We all learn together to make a lateral shift, to apply lateral thinking. Such work prepares the participants to take the floor, to tell their own stories from their own point of view: these are phases of community learning, where innovation is first and foremost linked to conceiving issues, problems, and possible solutions in new terms. The community (even a temporary community) learns to care, to look anew, to give voice and find new words, to give body to places and vocations with their exploring and walking bodies, and to create their own paths towards solutions.

3. Translating landscapes. Research by design: methodological and operative approaches

"Urban planning is done on foot", one of urbanist Bernardo Secchi's best-known lessons, reflects the experiences conducted in Madeira, which consider walking in places as a fundamental part of the design and the implementation process. A territorial transformation, today more than ever, needs to 'enter into the folds' of contexts (Fini, 2015), which, before being designed and changed, must be listened to and deeply understood.

To decodify and represent the stratification and complexity of territorial elements relationship and its coexistence capability, the proposed learning/teaching methodology explores the threshold between the walk within the territory and the translation of this experience into maps and drawings, with the awareness that this work of selection and interpretation is also a substantial part of the project.

In the words of Umberto Eco, translating means 'saying almost the same thing'. In his book *Esperienze di traduzione. Dire quasi la stessa cosa* (2013), Eco argues that translation is not about comparing two languages but is about the interpretation of a text in two different languages, thus involving a shift between cultures. Translation is one of the forms of interpretation, and interpretation should always aim to rediscover the intention of the text, what it says in relation to the language in which it is expressed and in the cultural context in which it was born. The faithful translator must choose a 'linguistic unfaithfulness' which guarantees the textual one. Urban designers undertake this same action in translating the complexity of the territory into the language of drawing, having to understand and use other disciplines, external to their field. Given a text – or a territory that Andrè Corboz compared to a palimpsest, a written and rewritten text – what must the translators/interpreters render of that text in their work of decomposition, selection, interpretation, and reassembly?

During surveys with students, we walk, decoding the space, investigating things and people, animals and plants, nature and culture, forms and materials, practices and techniques, spatial adaptations of transformation and inertia over time, looking for and building its 'vocabulary' before identifying questions and needs. From the walking experience, the urban design practice makes the 'workspace' derive. The construction of the workspace, preparatory to scenario development and transformation or adaptation, is a critical moment. It is a form of 'translation' (Figures 5a, b, c).

This methodology, which takes up the original intuition of Ian L. McHarg, in his 1969 *Design with Nature*, seeks to translate the close relationships and interdependencies between the natural and anthropised environments. This implies working in a multidisciplinary, multi-scalar and

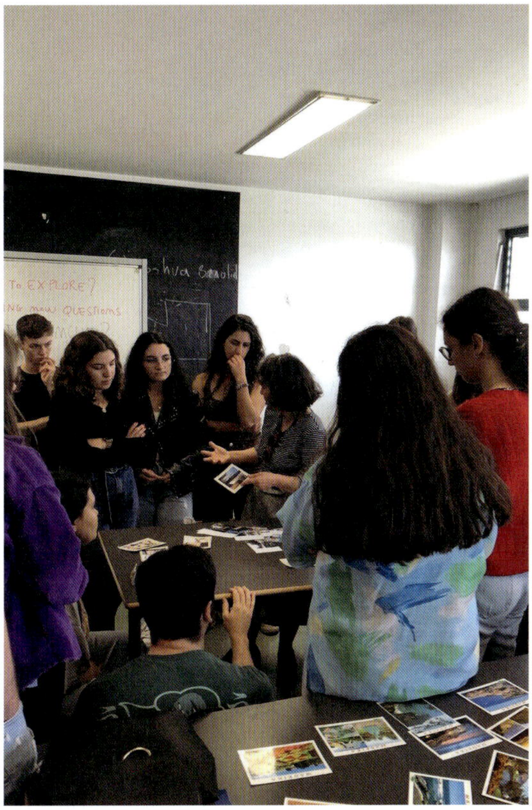

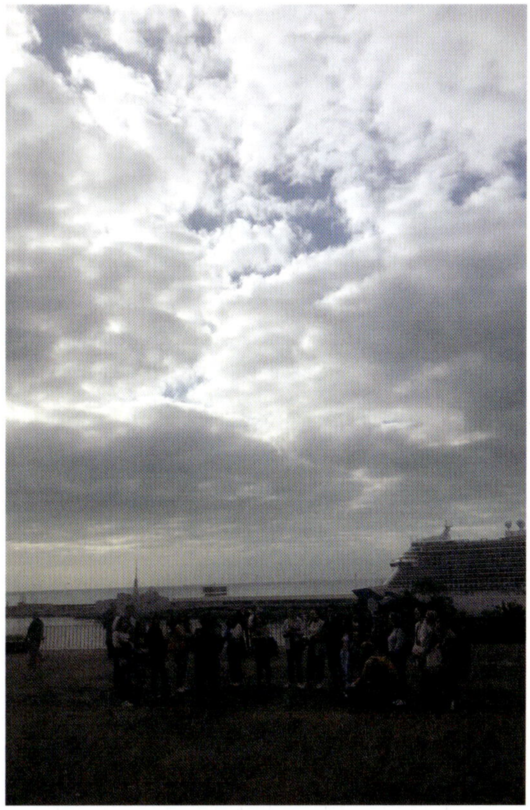

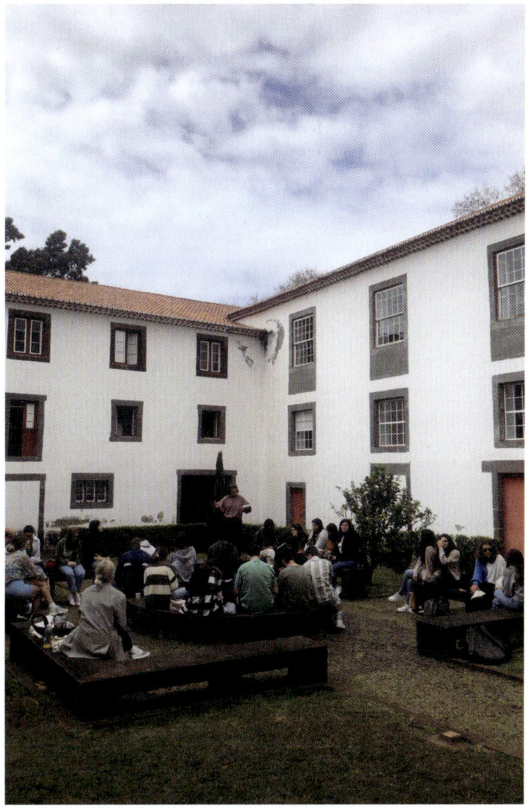

Figures 4a, b, c: Images from the workshop led by Noemi Satta. Funchal. The workshop with Noemi Satta started by the group sharing and looking at postcards of Madeira, and ended by sharing the experiences of the walks and all the new questions that emerged. Funchal, March 2024

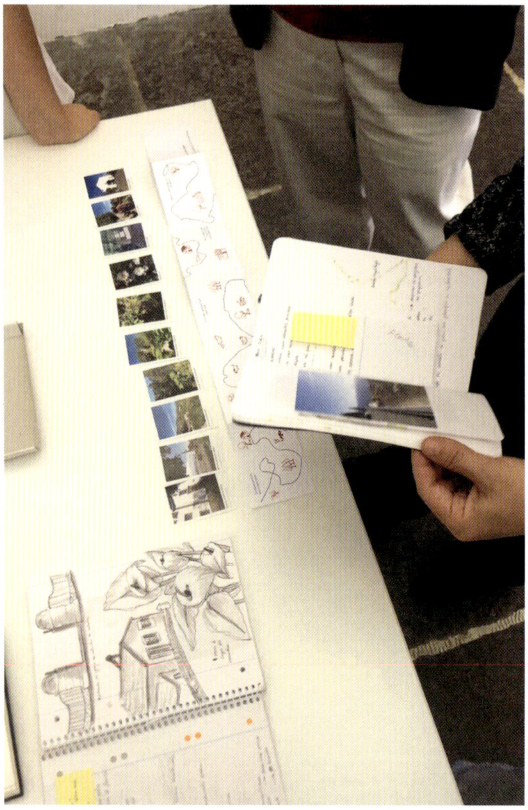

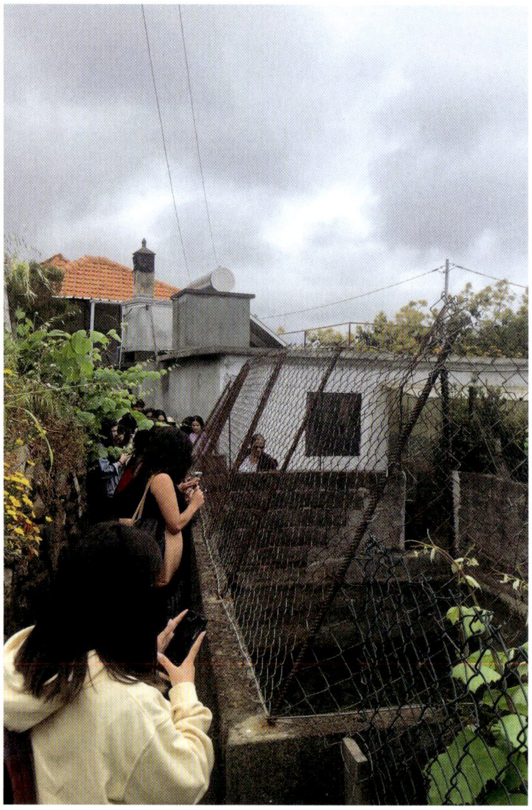

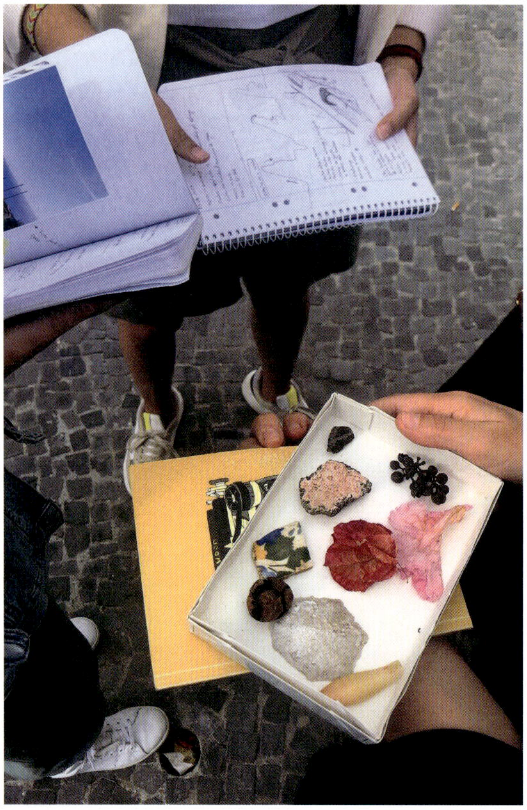

Images from the workshop led by Chiara Nifosì and Cristina Renzoni, Madeira, April 2024

Figure 5a: The day before the visit to Estreito da Calheta, students showed their initial notes and reflections made after their previous visit.

Figure 5b: Looking together at the water systems in Estreito da Calheta

Figure 5c: Observing the notes from the walk in Estreito da Calheta, April 2024

multi-temporal approach. For example, to learn from the 'raw material' of landscapes over time, we relate climate and geology – their performance, constraints and resources – to flora, fauna and human society.

A particular role within these relationships is played by the soil, a multidisciplinary strategic key to better understand climate change phenomena and to test the ecological transition integrating disciplines (biological, hydrogeological, agroforestry, etc.).

Aldo Sestini, one of the greatest geographer-geologists of the 20th century, in his drawings and texts of the Italian Touring Club's "The Landscape" in *Conosci l'Italia vol. 7* of 1963, highlights that the specificity of each landscape (of nature, of society, of activities and economies) is closely linked to its subsoil: "at the base of the landscape is [...] the earth's surface, not as a whole, but in its individual traits" (Sestini, 1963). Similarly, Bernardo Secchi later reiterates the importance of looking at the ground not as a plane but of considering it in its "thickness" (Secchi, 1986). Finally, soil is not an inert element, but a living organism. A strong image in this sense comes to us from Wes Jackson, founder of The Land Institute, who compares the soil to the elastic and resistant membrane that gives rise to many life forms, the placenta, and warns us that it is progressively losing these properties (Jackson, 1980).

The other important aspect is to understand and represent the time of the transformation processes of the places explored. In our exercise, the present condition of landscapes is often reflected, but also its evolution compared with the past and the potential projection towards the future. In a recent piece entitled "How cities will fossilise", David Farrier tells us in a very lucid way how all human actions leave a geological legacy that lasts for millennia, and how some interventions last much longer than others. Using the words of the ecologist Aldo Leopold, we must start "thinking like a mountain", and the geologist Marcia Bjornerud, speaking to us about "timefulness", underlines the need to think in a "polytemporal" way and within geological times to establish, learning from the past, our journey towards the future.

Finally, to translate phenomena such as the loss of biodiversity or climate change but also activities that are phenomena of a global scope that must however be understood and resolved locally, it is necessary to work at all scales of investigation.

An explored landscape is returned as an evolving, productive and integrated hybrid system, which responds to these multiple relationships and which combines into new environmental and architectural entities, generating new languages (Waldheim, 2016). The internal behaviour of these entities, their interaction as parts of complex systems and their potential, are assembled in multi-scalar, multi-temporal and multidisciplinary systemic static drawings (Berger, 2013) that return the multitude of information, direct and indirect data collected, and scientific knowledge, and which will support the design processes.

To conclude and return to the beginning of the chapter, urban planning done on foot in real space aims not only to get out of the classroom but also outside the walls of administrative urban planning.

In his very recent book Sentieri Metropolitani, Gianni Biondillo reminds us that we learned to walk and therefore we became intelligent, not the other way around, and that it was thanks to the intelligence of our feet that our self-awareness arose (Biondillo, 2022).

4. Narrative cartographies: the map as a project

Maps represent a powerful tool to understand, visualise, and refine interpretations of spatial and social realms. Mapping is integral to a reflexive process of sense-making, going beyond "a plastic metaphor of reality" towards elaborating interpretative keys to access the current world to a plurality of actors (Casti, 2014). Becoming critically aware of the processual nature of the map is an operation of research and theoretical and operational inquiry into the tools at our disposal for understanding and acting in space. For this reason, acquiring this awareness is a fundamental step in the learning paths of disciplines that deal from multiple perspectives with the territory and the material dimension of the relations between space and society, where a primary role is played by who is observing and from where. A map is a way we choose to interpret a certain set of information. Every map stems from the viewpoint of someone who observes a territory and intends to create a description of it. Any cartographic representation is (implicitly or explicitly) an expression of this viewpoint from the very beginning: in deciding what the centre of the map is and in determining its frame; in selecting data and sets of information to be represented or not; in highlighting some aspects rather than others. Therefore, each map results from a sequence of selection operations, and the definition and refinement of the set of arguments supporting those choices is a cornerstone of the process.

In a sort of stratigraphic exercise, the mapping process requires us to identify, recognise, and name the elemental components that articulate the field of inquiry by isolating and extrapolating from context. Such decomposition allows for simplification and captures issues often hidden by information overload and layering in search of the relationships between types of spaces, places, subjects, and uses. Critical description questions the roles and functionings of individual elements in determining the whole and seeks to grasp the rules of the game, the principles through which the system builds and changes. Each map is a selection, an interpretation that fills the blanks between observed territorial phenomena with meaning and sense, explicitly attributing weights and values. From this perspective, the conscious selection and collection of places, objects, and natures is crucial in setting up a catalogue of species of spaces (or species in spaces), measuring their morphologies and dynamics.

The narrative turn of the 1990s in the social sciences contributed to a renewed debate on the narrative potential of cartography: it paved the way for some lines of research and experimentation at the intersection of different fields of knowledge. In particular, the perspective of narrative cartography, intersecting the intertwined nature of stories and maps (Bodenhamer et al., 2015; Roth, 2021), offers insights and suggestions into the plurality of roles, forms, and messages that a mapping process can convey. Maps outline narratives while noting, highlighting, or neglecting aspects and qualities. By moving between scales and translating information and phenomena, the explorer turns into a cartographer and storyteller: maps recompose a unified narrative that unfolds the paths followed and that reconstructs the unfolding of a story. This story returns materials, sequences, temporal articulations, mutual influences, and causal links; simultaneously, it gives them a shape and a name.

The map is not the territory, but an interpretation of it. Its supposed objectivity, conveyed by the measurement of space, is mediated by a plurality of interacting factors: representations, stereotypes, investigation demands, power dynamics, sensibilities. Awareness of the processual and narrative nature of mapping allows us to confront its generative nature in more direct ways. The map as a project. The interpretative narrative of the territory is a key step in the creative process underlying the knowledge of a territory and any possible project for its future. Each map is, therefore, itself a project. All decisions made in choosing the point of view and field of relevance to extend the map, selecting the data, identifying the themes, and elaborating the narrative are the (more or less conscious) outcome of design thinking operations. From this perspective, spatial explorations driven through mapping processes represent a fruitful tool to discuss and reinvent theoretical and operative methodologies in learning processes.

5. Conclusions

Periphery

The route recounted in this chapter expresses a double deviation, one linked to the very fact of doing research and experimentation in so-called peripheral, marginal areas, where naturally the attention and presence of studies, research, and projects is less. A second deviation is expressed precisely by not stopping at the fixed meaning of some terms and instead seeking the polysemy of words, places, facts, and groups. Is "periphery" perhaps a non-central point of view? Is it even more interesting as it is lateral? Is "island" always linked to connections with the mainland (terra firma) or could it be a place to experiment with different connections and relationships? Is "map" an always dynamic reading of reality according to criteria defined from time to time by those who draw it? Whose point of view is a "postcard" telling and reflecting? What is its narrative?

The non-neutrality of research

Doing research means asking valid questions as a first step to making the research itself truly effective. Design processes are never neutral: whether they are linked to participation (with different phases ranging from desk research to the sharing of choices and decisions), to urban planning research, or to educational and training paths. The group of researchers, professionals, mediators, students, citizens, teachers, scientists, and so on, offers an almost pre-indicated research path starting from their professional grids. How can we work with a critical conscience on our own personal grids, on our own non-neutrality, or rather on our own subjectivity, sharing in a group and assuming that the group itself is a multiple and choral factor of influence on the area of analysis and research?

In the previous paragraphs we described how these questions have become opportunities to experiment with a group in training, and at the same time to exercise the critical ability of

2. The idea of taking a question for a walk is practised in the Street Wisdom project – https://www.streetwisdom.org/

being with one's own body and one's knowledge in a dynamic relationship with the territory and with what the territory expresses. We have seen how working on stereotypes or perceptive grids is the first step towards dismantling clichés and reviewing the very questions that give rise to the research. This is an aspect that calls into question the propensity of all of us to rely on reassuring narratives rather than trying to observe whether some definitions and narratives can be opened, articulated, read, and interpreted in their natural polysemy.

Doing research while walking can really help us in this sense, precisely because walking can be a way to ask yourself many questions and make them more complex: the slow pace of walking helps to focus in a different way on the tangible and intangible elements that make up and give life to a place. Walking and elaborating questions together can help in building learning communities (Hooks, 2003). And with this learning community in motion, we can take questions for walks,[2] and experience and live questions together (Wahl, 2016).

Subjectivity and interpretation

Through the *fil rouge* of walking and drawing as a method of exploration, the entire sequence of workshops (conducted by students and groups of teachers and multidisciplinary professionals) describes activities where subjectivity and interpretation are made evident.

The entire path unfolded through critical concepts and approaches. This happened in the terrain, sometimes easy and sometimes rugged, of Madeira, also bringing into play the body's ability to perceive and feel and therefore to translate another complex system of information into research questions.

All this calls for a political and poietic responsibility, of building semantic fields for the territories where we operate, research, and do education. A responsibility that begins with asking new questions and arrives with the critical awareness that the translation and representation of a landscape is a work of selecting elements, assuming many disciplinary points of view, and of interpretation. This means making bridges between contents, in a dynamic work, in a work of negotiation and of making meaning and re-signification within a shared environment (Izard, 2018).

References

Appadurai, A (2004). *The Capacity to Aspire: Culture and the Terms of Recognition*, in Culture and Public Action, Rao, V. & Walton, M., curated by Stanford, NY: Stanford University Press.

Berger, A. (2009). *Systemic Design Can Change the World*, Amsterdam: SUN Publishers.

Bertolotti, E., Vezzani, V. (2021). Walk, talk and draw: Fieldwork in nature to unpack the complexities of sustainability. In: Cruickshank, L., Galabo, R., Perez, D., Gisclard, B., Bofylatos, S., Mortati, M., Valentine, L. and Hwang, J., Safe harbours for rethinking design education? In: 14th International Conference of the European Academy of Design. [online] Lancaster: Blücher.

Biondillo, G. (2022). *Sentieri Metropolitani. Narrare il territorio con la psicogeografia*, Bollati Boringhieri.

Bjornerud, M. (2020). Ed. Italiana (trad. Lucifredi, A.), *Il tempo della Terra. Il cambiamento climatico nel contesto geologico*, Hoepli.

Bodenhamer, D., Corrigan, J., Harris, T. M. (2015). *Deep Maps and Spatial Narratives*. Bloomington, IN: Indiana University Press.

Borgnino, E. (2022). *Ecologie Native*. Milan: Elèuthera.

Brook, R., and Dunn, N. (2012). *Urban maps: Instruments of Narrative and Interpretation in the City,* Ashgate.

Careri, F. (2006). *Walkscapes. Camminare come pratica estetica*. Turin: Einaudi.

Casti, E. (2014). *Reflexive Cartography. A New Perspective on Mapping*, Philadelphia, PA: Elsevier.

Couling, N., d'Alençon, P. A., Altiok, M. (2019). Narrative cartography: capturing a holistic perspective on waterscapes, in *European Journal of Creative Practices in Cities and Landscapes*, 2(1), 11–36.

Davila, T. (2002). *Marcher, Créer. Déplacements, flâneries, dérives dans l'art de la fin du XXe siècle*. Paris: Regard.

De Luca, V., Bertolotti, E. (2024). Experiencing design fieldwork: walking interviews on madeira island. In: Martins, N., Brandão, D. (Eds), *Advances in Design and Digital Communication IV.* DIGICOM 2023. Springer Series in Design and Innovation, vol. 35. Springer, Cham. https://doi.org/10.1007/978-3-031-47281-7_5

Eco, U. (2013). Dire quasi la stessa cosa. Esperienze di traduzione, Bompiani.

Edenson, T. (2008). Walking through ruins. In Ingold T. and Vergunst J. L. (2008). *Ways of Walking. Ethnography and Practice on Foot*. Farnham: Ashgate Publishing.

Eno, B., Schmidt, P. (1975). *Oblique Strategies, Over One Hundred Worthwhile Dilemmas.*

Farrier, D. (2021). How cities will fossilise. https://www.bbc.com/future/article/20210505-how-cities-will-fossilise.

Fini, G. (ed.), (2015). *Bernardo Secchi. Il futuro si costruisce giorno per giorno*, Donzelli Editore.

Foundational Economy Collective. (2019). *Foundational Economy. The Infrastructure of Everyday Life*, Manchester University Press.

Freire, P. (1998). *Pedagogy of Freedom: Ethics, Democracy and Civic Courage*. Lanham, MD: Rowman & Littlefield Publishers.

Gooch, P. (2008). Feet following hooves. In Ingold, T. & Vergunst, J. L. (2008). *Ways of Walking. Ethnography and Practice on Foot.* Farnham: Ashgate Publishing.

Gros, F. (2023). *A Philosophy of Walking*. London & NY: Verso.

Haraway, D. (2016). *Staying With the Trouble. Making Kin in the Chthulucene*. Durham and London: Duke University Press.

Heise, U. K. (2008). *Sense of Place and Sense of Planet: The Environmental Imagination of the Global*. Oxford: Oxford University Press.

Hirshmann, A. O. (1982). *Shifting Involvements. Private Interest and Public Action*, Princeton, NJ: Princeton University Press.

Hooks, B. (2003). *Teaching Community: A Pedagogy of Hope*. New York, NY: Routledge.

Hosoe, I. (2008). *Play 40*. Milan: Corraini Editore.

Ingold, T., and Vergunst, J. L. (2008). *Ways of Walking. Ethnography and Practice on Foot*. Farnham: Ashgate Publishing.

Ingold, T. (2011). *Being Alive: Essays on Movement, Knowledge and Description.* London: New York: Routledge.

Izard, T. G. (2018). *Regenerative Empathy*, Harvard GSD. https://issuu.com/gsdharvard/docs/regenerativeempathy

Jackson, W. (1980). *New Roots for Agriculture*, Lincoln, NB: University of Nebraska Press.

Kagge, E. (2019). *Walking: One Step at a Time*. New York, NY: Knopf Doubleday.

Klinenberg, E. (2018). *Palaces for the People: How Social Infrastructure Can Help Fight Inequality, Polarization, and the Decline of Civic Life*. New York, NY: Crown.

Lai, M. (2002). *I luoghi dell'arte a portata di mano. Quattro mazzi di carte per argomentare sul fare arte leggere l'arte ridefinire l'arte*, Edizioni Arte Duchamp, Cagliari.

Latour, B. (2018). *Down To Earth: Politics in the New Climatic Regime*. Cambridge: Polity Press.

Leopold, A. (ed. 2019, trad. Roveda A.) *Pensare Come una Montagna. A Sand County Almanac.*, Ediz. Integrale, Feltrinelli.

Maffei, L. (2014). *Elogio della lentezza*. Bologna: Il Mulino.

McHarg, I. L. (1969). *Design with Nature*. New York, NY: Doubleday & Company.

Moeglin-Delcroix, A. (2016). *Ambulo Ergo Sum. Nature as Experience in Artists' Books.* Cologne: Walther König.

Moresco, A. (2022). *Il sogno del cammino*. Aboca edizioni.

Mulgan, G. (2022). *Another World Is Possible: How to Reignite Social and Political Imagination*, Hurst.

Mulgan, G. (2022). *The Imaginary Crisis – And How We Might Quicken Social and Public Imagination*, https://www.geoffmulgan.com/post/social-imagination.

Munari, B. (1992). *Saluti e baci | Esercizi di evasione*. [Love and kisses | Exercises in evasion]. Mantua: Corraini.

Psarra, S. (2009). *Architecture and Narrative: The Formation of Space and Cultural Meaning.* London: Routledge.

Puig de la Bellacasa, M. P. (2017). Matters of Care: Speculative Ethics in More than Human Worlds. University of Minnesota Press.

Rodari, G. (1973). *Grammatica della fantasia*. Turin: Einaudi.

Roth, R. E. (2021). Cartographic design as visual storytelling: Synthesis and review of map-based narratives, genres, and tropes. *The Cartographic Journal, 58*(1), 83–114.

Secchi, B. (January to February 1986). Progetto di suolo, *Casabella*, no. 520-521.

Šklovskij, V. (2003). In trs. Tzvetan Todorov, *I formalisti russi. Teoria della letteratura e metodo critico*. Turin: Einaudi.

Solnit, R. (2000). *Wanderlust*. New York, NY: Penguin.

Tsing, A. (2015). *The Mushroom at the End of the World: On the Possibility of Life in Capitalist Ruins*, Princeton University Press.

Waldheim, C. (2016). *Landscape as Urbanism: A General Theory,* New York, NY: Princeton University Press.

Wahl, D. (2016). *Design Regenerative Cultures*. Axminster: Triarchy Press.

Note
Paragraph 1 is written by Elisa Bertolotti; paragraph 2 is written by Noemi Satta; paragraph 3 is written by Chiara Nifosì; paragraph 4 is written by Cristina Renzoni. The conclusions are written by all the authors.

Acknowledgements

The partners would like to thank all organisations and individuals who contributed to the project and the writing of this book. We would also like to thank all organisations and individuals involved in the realisation of Human Cities/SMOTIES: Creative Works with Small and Remote Places, including the workshops, experiments, events, exhibitions, communication, and administration.

Human Cities/SMOTIES: Creative Works with Small and Remote Places is a European project co-funded by the Creative Europe Programme of the European Union.

Co-funded by the Creative Europe Programme of the European Union

Alternance slf, Reykjavik [IS]
Cité du design – ESADSE, Saint-Étienne [FR]
Clear Village, London [UK]
Department of Design, Politecnico di Milano, Milan [IT]
Estonian Association of Designers, Tallinn [EE]
FH Joanneum University of Applied Sciences, Graz [AT]
University of Madeira, Art and Design Department [PT]
University of the Aegean, Department of Product and Systems Design Engineering, Ermoupoli [GR]
Urban Planning Institute of the Republic of Slovenia, Ljubljana [SI]
Zamek Cieszyn [PL]

Editors

Cité du design – ESADSE, Saint-Étienne [FR]
Inge Eller

Department of Design, Politecnico di Milano, Milan [IT]
Annalinda De Rosa, Davide Fassi

Michael Dumiak

Authors

Michael Dumiak
Independent reporter and editor

Valentina Auricchio
PhD, associate professor, Department of Design, Politecnico di Milano

Elisa Bertolotti
PhD, assistant professor of Communication Design, Art and Design Department, Faculty of Arts and Humanities, University of Madeira

Beatriz Bonilla Berrocal
PhD candidate, Department of Design, Politecnico di Milano

Helen Charoupia
Researcher, Department of Product and Systems Design Engineering within Complex Systems and Service Design Lab, University of the Aegean

Alexandra Coutsoucos
Research fellow, Department of Design, Politecnico di Milano

Annalinda De Rosa
PhD, researcher, Department of Design, Politecnico di Milano

Inge Eller
European and international programmes manager, Cité du design – ESADSE

Davide Fassi
PhD, full professor, Department of Design, Politecnico di Milano

Susana Gonzaga
PhD, assistant professor, Art and Design Department, Faculty of Arts and Humanities, University of Madeira

Nina Goršič
Architect and researcher, urban renewal, cultural heritage and accessibility, Urban Planning Institute of the Republic of Slovenia

Frank van Hasselt
Chief executive, Clear Village

Astrid Lelarge
Historian of urban planning, Alternance Architecture and Urban Planning, assistant professor, Faculty of Planning and Design, Agricultural University of Iceland

Vanessa Monna
Post-doc research fellow, Department of Design, Politecnico di Milano

Chiara Nifosì
PhD, assistant professor of Urban Planning, Department of Architecture and Urban Studies, Politecnico di Milano

Matej Nikšič
Architect, urban planner, lecturer in urban design, Urban Planning Institute of the Republic of Slovenia

Cristina Renzoni
PhD, associate professor of Urban Planning, Department of Architecture and Urban Studies, Politecnico di Milano

Anwar Samara
Student of Urban Planning, Faculty of Architecture, University of Ljubljana

Noemi Satta
Independent consultant and expert in cultural innovation and strategic and participatory planning

Isabelle Vérilhac
Strategic designer, founder of Design With Isabelle

Coordinator

Department of Design, Politecnico di Milano, Milan [IT]
Davide Fassi
Full professor and scientific coordinator of the SMOTIES project

Annalinda De Rosa
Full professor and scientific co-coordinator of the SMOTIES project

Paola Russo
Research fellow and project assistant of the SMOTIES project

Valentina Auricchio
Associate professor

Alexandra Coutsoucos
Research fellow and project assistant of the SMOTIES project

Vanessa Monna
Post-doc research fellow

Nadia Pirovano
Research fellow

Marco Finardi
Collaborator

Alternance slf, Reykjavik [IS]
Birgir Þröstur Jóhannsson
Architect

Astrid Lelarge
Historian of urban planning

Páll Jakob Líndal
Environmental psychologist

Sigríður Kristjánsdóttir
Geographer and planner

Cité du design – ESADSE, Saint-Étienne [FR]
Inge Eller
European and international programmes manager, Cité du design – ESADSE

Nathalie Arnould
Design manager, Saint-Étienne municipality and Saint-Étienne metropolitan government

Isabelle Vérilhac
Head of innovation and international affairs, Cité du design – ESADSE

Josyane Franc
Former head of international affairs, Cité du design – ESADSE

Clear Village, London [UK]
Frank van Hasselt
Josie King
Kristin Luke

Estonian Association of Designers, Tallinn [EE]
Ilona Gurjanova
Communication designer and curator, president, Estonian Association of Designers; main organiser of Tallinn Design Night Festival

Kirke Tatar
Communication and marketing manager, Estonian Association of Designers and Tallinn Design Night Festival

Kevin Loigu
Communications manager and photographer

FH Joanneum University of Applied Sciences, Graz [AT]
Anke Strittmatter
Architect, urbanist and associate professor, urban planning and exhibition design

Bettina Gjecaj
Lecturer, strategic communication management

Lucia Jarošová
Research assistant, graphic designer, exhibition design, and communication

Sigrid Bürstmayr
Senior lecturer, exhibition design and communication

Anika Kronberger
Researcher and senior lecturer, interaction design

Christoph Neuhold
Lecturer, communication, media, sound and interaction design

Professor Erika Thümmel
Exhibition design

Universidade da Madeira, Art & Design Department, Madeira [PT]
Susana Gonzaga
PhD, assistant professor, Art and Design Department, Faculty of Arts and Humanities, University of Madeira

Elisa Bertolotti
PhD, assistant professor of Communication Design in Art and Design Department, Faculty of Arts and Humanities, University of Madeira

Pau Galbis, PhD, assistant professor in Art and Design Department, Faculty of Arts and Humanities, University of Madeira

Luisa Santos Freitas
Junior researcher

Sara Patrícia Abreu
Junior researcher

University of the Aegean, Department of Product and Systems Design Engineering, Ermoupoli [GR]
Argyris Arnellos
Principal investigator

Helen Charoupia
Researcher

Kypriani Bartzoka
Researcher

Paris Xyntarianos Tsiropinas
Researcher

Urban Planning Institute of the Republic of Slovenia (UIRS) [SI]
Matej Nikšič
Architect and researcher, urban planner, lecturer in urban design

Nina Goršič
Architect and researcher, urban renewal, cultural heritage and accessibility

Nada Hozjan
International cooperation and project office

Mojca Sfiligoj
Cultural manager, Pr' Lenart, Belo

Zvonka Simčič
Artist, Hiša na hribu/House on the Hill, Žlebe

Mojca Senegačnik
Artist, Hiša na hribu/House on the Hill, Celje

Zamek Cieszyn, Cieszyn [PL]
Magdalena Chorąży-Suchy
Director, lawyer, interpreter

Anna Sowińska
Sociologist

Agnieszka Niczyporuk
Interior designer, lawyer, painter

Imprint

Book Project Management
Victoria Calligaro
Inge Eller

Acquisitions Editor
David Marold
Birkhäuser Verlag,
A-Vienna

Project Editor
Regina Herr
Birkhäuser Verlag,
CH-Basel

Production Editor
Angelika Gaal
Birkhäuser Verlag,
A-Vienna

Graphic Design
Audrey Templier

Printing
Holzhausen Druck
GmbH, A-Wolkersdorf
Austria

Cover photo: Showcase of the updates in Joaveski as part of the "Joaveski REstart" event in October 2022. © Kevin Loigu

Part III was subjected to a double-blind peer review process conducted under the responsibility of the Book Editors and by scholars and researchers external to the SMOTIES partnership and appointed explicitly by them.

Library of Congress Control Number: 2024912921

Bibliographic information published by the German National Library

The German National Library lists this publication in the Deutsche Nationalbibliografie; detailed bibliographic data are available on the Internet at http://dnb.dnb.de.

ISBN 978-3-0356-2907-1
e-ISBN (PDF) 978-3-0356-2913-2
DOI: https://doi.org/10.1515/9783035629132

P.O. Box 44, 4009 Basel, Switzerland
Part of Walter de Gruyter GmbH, Berlin/Boston
The book is published with open access at www.degruyter.com.
9 8 7 6 5 4 3 2 1

www.birkhauser.com